FOOD
AND
WINE
PAIRING
A SENSORY EXPERIENCE

FOOD
AND
WINE
PAIRING
A SENSORY EXPERIENCE

ROBERT J. HARRINGTON

WILEY

JOHN WILEY & SONS, INC.

Chapter-opening photo credits:

p. 3: Courtesy of Carroll Falcon
p. 65: Courtesy of Chef John Folse & Company
p. 101: Courtesy of Nicholls State University
p. 129: Courtesy of Carroll Falcon
p. 167: Courtesy of Nicholls State University
p. 187: Courtesy of Nicholls State University
p. 287: Courtesy of Nicholls State University

This book is printed on acid-free paper. ∞

Published by John Wiley & Sons, Inc., Hoboken, New Jersey

Published simultaneously in Canada

For general information on our other products and services or for technical support, please contact our Customer Care Department within the United States at (800) 762-2974, outside the United States at (317) 572-3993 or fax (317) 572-4002.

Wiley also publishes its books in a variety of electronic formats. Some content that appears in print may not be available in electronic books. For more information about Wiley products, visit our web site at www.wiley.com.

Library of Congress Cataloging-in-Publication Data:
Harrington, Robert J., 1958–
    Food & wine pairing: a sensory experience / by Robert J. Harrington.
        p. cm.
    ISBN: 978-0-471-79407-3
  1. Cookery. 2. Wine and wine making. I. Title. II. Title: Food and wine
pairing.
    TX714.H36527 2007
    641.5--dc22
                                                            2006034744
Printed in the United States of America

SKY10034521_052522

CONTENTS

PREFACE   XI

ACKNOWLEDGMENTS   XIII

PART A: MASTERING THE ART AND SCIENCE OF FOOD AND WINE PAIRING   1

CHAPTER 1:   THE WINE AND FOOD PYRAMID: A HIERARCHY OF TASTE   3

Introduction   4
Objectives of Food and Wine Pairing   4
Aperitif: The Italian Wine and Food Perspective   5
Food-and-Wine Pairing Mechanics: Matching Traditions   8
Overview of Book Methods   11
Key Elements of Wine and Food: A Hierarchical Perspective   11
Summary: Where Do We Go from Here?   13
Classic Italian Wine and Food Examples   14

CHAPTER 2:   TASTE BASICS AND THE BASICS OF WINE EVALUATION   19

Introduction   20
Aperitif: Elements of Wine Service   20
Sensory Evaluation   22
Basics of Wine Evaluation   23
Setting Up a Tasting Session   27
The Art and Science of Wine Evaluation   28
Palate Mapping   31
Tasting Instructions   31
Summary   32
Exercises   33

CHAPTER 3:   GASTRONOMIC IDENTITY: THE EFFECT OF THE ENVIRONMENT AND CULTURE ON PREVAILING COMPONENTS, TEXTURE, AND FLAVORS IN WINE AND FOOD   45

Introduction   46
Aperitif: How Should Menus and Wine Lists Be Organized?   47
The Environment   50
Wine: The Impact of Geography and Climate   50
Culture   56
History and Ethnic Diversity   56
Trial and Error, Innovations, and Capabilities   57
Gastronomic Identity   58
Old World and New World   58
Summary   61
Optional Exercises   62

CHAPTER 4:   GASTRONOMIC IDENTITY II: FOOD AND CUISINE: THE EFFECT OF THE ENVIRONMENT AND CULTURE ON GASTRONOMY, WINE AND FOOD MARRIAGES, AND TOURISM   65

Introduction   66
Aperitif: Chef John Folse & Company   67
The Environment   78
Food: The Impact of Geography and Climate   79
Culture   80
History and Ethnic Diversity   81
Trial and Error, Innovations, and Capabilities   81
Gastronomic Identity   82
Old World and New World Wine and Food Marriages   83
Wine, Food, and Tourism   85
Summary   86
Exercises   87

PART B: THE FOUNDATION: WINE AND FOOD TASTE COMPONENTS   97

CHAPTER 5:   THE IMPACT OF SWEETNESS AND ACIDITY LEVELS IN WINE AND FOOD   101

Introduction   102
Aperitif: Which to Choose First, Wine or Food?   102
The Impact of Sweetness Levels in Wine and Food   103
Sweetness Levels in Wine   103
Sweetness Levels in Food   104
Types of Sweeteners   105
Perceived Sweetness Levels   105
Interaction Between Wine and Food Sweetness   106
Acidity: From Flat to Tart (and Beyond)   107
Acidity Levels in Wine   107
Acidity Level Descriptions   108
Acidity Levels in Food   108
Interaction Between Wine and Food Acidity   109

Summary   111
Exercises   112

CHAPTER 6:   SALT, BITTERNESS, AND BUBBLES   129

Introduction   130
Aperitif: Peller Estates Winery   130
Saltiness   131
Bitterness   132
Sparkling Wine and Pairing   133
Effervescence: The Great Equalizer?   136
Summary   137
Exercises   138

PART C: WINE AND FOOD TEXTURE
CHARACTERISTICS   145

CHAPTER 7:   WINE TEXTURE CHARACTERISTICS:
TANNIN, OAK, AND BODY   149

Introduction   150
Aperitif: The Exemplary Nature of a Symbiosis Between Food Dishes and Cognacs   151
Texture in Wine   154
Tannin   155
Mouthfeel Wheel   155
Alcohol Level   156
The Impact of Oak   157
Overall Wine Body   157
Maturity, Micro-oxygenation, and Other Factors   159
Summary   160
Exercises   161

CHAPTER 8:   FOOD TEXTURE CHARACTERISTICS: FATTINESS,
COOKING METHOD, PROTEIN, AND BODY   167

Introduction   168
Aperitif: Canoe Restaurant and Bar   168
Fattiness in Food   169
Cooking Method and Protein Interactions   170
Overall Food Body   171
Interaction of Wine and Food Textures   172
Summary   172
Exercises   173

PART D: FLAVORS: ARCHITECTURAL ELEMENTS IN
THE WINE AND FOOD PAIRING PROCESS   187

CHAPTER 9:   THE IMPACT OF SPICE   189

Introduction   190

Aperitif: Bayou La Seine—An American Restaurant in Paris   190
Wine Varietals and Styles   193
Food Types and Styles   194
How Spice Is Assessed: Identifying Hot, Savory, or Sweet   195
Impact on Pairing Possibilities   198
Summary   200
Exercises   201

CHAPTER 10:   FLAVOR INTENSITY AND FLAVOR PERSISTENCY   207

Introduction   208
Aperitif: Release Weekend Wine and Food Menu from On the Twenty   209
Identifying Flavor Types in Wine and Food   211
Food Flavor Categories   212
Wine Flavor Categories   213
Assessing Flavor Intensity   214
The Interaction of Wine and Food Flavor Intensity   215
Assessing Flavor Persistency   216
The Interaction of Wine and Food Flavor Persistency   217
Summary   218
Exercises   219

PART E: THE WHOLE ENCHILADA: PUTTING IT ALL TOGETHER   229

CHAPTER 11:   MENU PLANNING: HORIZONTAL AND VERTICAL PAIRING DECISIONS   233

Introduction   234
Aperitif: Food and Wine of the Pacific Northwest   234
General Menu Planning Suggestions   237
Basic Wine Sequencing Recommendations   237
Pacific Northwest Menu   240
Wine and Food Pairing Instrument   249
Wine and Food Match Decision Tree   253
A Profiling Approach to Match Level Assessment   253
Summary   263
Exercises   264

CHAPTER 12:   WINE AND CHEESE: A NATURAL AFFINITY?   269

Introduction   270
Aperitif: Cheese, an Inspiration and an Education   270
Wine and Cheese Pairing   271
Cheese Categories   273
Summary   280
Exercises   280

CHAPTER 13:   THE GRAND FINALE: DESSERT AND DESSERT WINES   287

Introduction   288
Aperitif: Niagara's Wine Region   288
Dessert Wine Categories   289
Dessert Selection and Wine Pairing   295
Dessert Categories   295
Summary   302
Exercises   303

CHAPTER 14:   THE CUSTOMER EXPERIENCE: PRODUCT, SERVICE, AND TRAINING ISSUES   307

Introduction   308
Aperitif: Product-Service Considerations for a Food and Wine Program   308
The Total Experience: Creating Distinctive Food and Wine Capabilities   309
Wine and Food Training Process   310
Summary   311
Exercises   312

GLOSSARY   313
INDEX   317

PREFACE

My goal in writing this book is to present a practical approach to the process of food and wine pairing. **Food and Wine Pairing: A Sensory Experience** provides students with a clear understanding of the direct and interacting effects of food and wine elements on the perception of match. The target audience for this book is undergraduate students (hospitality, culinary arts, and tourism), graduate students with an interest in gastronomy, industry professionals, and other individuals who have an interest in wine and food.

While this book covers many fundamental concepts of wine evaluation and service, my goal in writing the book was to integrate my background in the culinary arts, business, and sensory analysis to present a contemporary, hands-on approach to this topic area. In other words, my approach looks at the process of food and wine pairing from a culinary perspective first and assumes wine provides an additional opportunity for layering of components, texture, and flavor as part of the dining experience.

This book provides comprehensive coverage of the key food and wine pairing concepts in a concise and reader-friendly manner. It is organized into five parts, with each section building on the preceding ones.

PART A: Mastering the Art and Science of Food and Wine Pairing

The first section discusses the hierarchy of taste concept, the basics of wine evaluation, and the notion of gastronomic identity.

PART B: The Foundation: Wine and Food Taste Components

These chapters provide information on the foundation tastes of sweet, sour, salt, and bitter in food and the qualities of dryness, acidity, and effervescence in wine.

PART C: Wine and Food Texture Characteristics

This section addresses wine texture (the impact of tannin, oak, and body), food texture (the impact of fattiness, cooking method, protein type, and body), and the interaction between wine and food texture elements.

PART D: Flavors: Architectural Elements in the Wine and Food Pairing Process

The chapters in this section discuss the implications of spice, flavor type, flavor intensity, and flavor persistency for wine and food matching.

PART E: The Whole Enchilada: Putting It All Together

This section summarizes the food and wine interactions developed in the first four sections and provides a systematic process for predicting match levels using sequential and mixed tasting methods. In addition, it provides guidance on pairing wine with cheese, wine and dessert combinations, and service issues such as training and menu/wine list development.

PEDAGOGICAL FEATURES THAT HELP STUDENTS

I have also included the following features within each chapter to enhance the students' learning experience:

- **Aperitifs** are introductory discussions intended to whet the appetite before the main material in each chapter. Many feature various practitioners in the industry. Others cover specific issues and provide additional insight related to the topic at hand.

- **Outlines** correspond to the organization of the chapter and highlight the key sections and ideas to help students succeed in learning the material.

- **Key terms** are given at the beginning of each chapter, discussed within each chapter, and defined in the glossary at the end of the text.

- **End-of-chapter summaries** provide an overview of the main points covered in each chapter to help reinforce the material.

- **Discussion questions** help to reinforce comprehension of the key concepts covered in each chapter.

- **Exercises** provide students with meaningful experiences that highlight the direct impacts of food and wine components, texture, and flavor on the perception of match. Each exercise builds on earlier ones to create a systematic process to develop skill in and understanding of the pairing process. The exercises include objectives, procedures, materials needed, and evaluation sections that increase reflection on food and wine relationships.

- **Recipes** are provided for many of the exercises as well as additional recipes with wine selections to reinforce the concepts and provide opportunities for additional experimentation.

RESOURCES FOR INSTRUCTORS

- **Exercise material:** All of the chapters (except Chapter 1) have exercises that have been tested in real student settings. Each exercise concisely lays out the exercise objectives, things to do before the exercise, materials needed, the exercise strategy, and any tasting instructions. The layout is intended both to provide a framework for instructors who are novices at teaching this topic and to provide added value for veteran instructors. Each chapter includes evaluation sheets, glassware placemats, wine suggestions, and applicable recipes that are easily copied for use in the classroom.

- **Instructor's manual (ISBN 978-0-470-04513-8):** Includes lecture outlines, sample syllabi, suggested answers to discussion questions, and a test bank.

- **Companion Web site:** Includes electronic files for the Instructor's Manual with test questions and PowerPoint slides containing lecture outlines for every chapter. Please visit www.wiley.com/college to access these files.

I believe that knowledge and experience in food and wine pairing provides an opportunity for rewarding dining experiences, whether your aim is to become a more knowledgeable industry professional or to be a more knowledgeable consumer. My hope is that this course material will assist in demystifying the food and wine pairing process so that wine consumption with food enhances our daily lives, regardless of our backgrounds.

ACKNOWLEDGMENTS

I would like to acknowledge and express my appreciation to all those who assisted in the development of this work. Specifically, I want to recognize Cindy Rhoads, developmental editor at John Wiley & Sons, Inc., for her efforts and guidance throughout this process. Also, I want to express sincere appreciation to the reviewers, Jeffery Stewart of Niagara College, Ontario, and John Eliassen and Ray Colvin of Western Culinary Institute, whose input substantially improved the final version of this book. I wish to give a special thanks to research assistants Rhonda Hammond and Rachelle Kelly, who assisted me in development of the material and exercises in this text. Finally, I wish to thank the following list of contributors who made this book possible.

Enrico Bazonni, director of U.S. programs for the Italian Culinary Institute for Foreign Professionals (ICIF)

Frederic and Judith Bluysen, owners of the store and catering company Thanksgiving and the restaurant Bayou La Seine

Tony DiDio and Lauber Imports

Ruben Elmer and the staff at Canoe Restaurant & Bar, Toronto

John Eliassen, winemaker and professor at Western Culinary Institute

John Folse, CEC, AAC, executive chef/CEO of Chef John Folse and Company

Rhonda Hammond, School of Hospitality and Tourism, Purdue University

Rachelle Kelly, School of Hospitality and Tourism Management, University of Guelph

Kevin Maniaci of the restaurant On the Twenty

Leonard Pennachetti of Cave Spring Cellars and the restaurant On the Twenty

Andrea Pollock of Peller Estates and Julie Flecknell of Andes Wines

Karen Stassi of Chef John Folse and Company

Theresa Suraci and Bruce McAdams of Oliver Bonacini restaurants

Jeffery Stewart, professor and coordinator of the tourism programs in the School of Hospitality and Tourism at Niagara College

Eléonore Vial, Philippe Rispal, Yvelise Dentzer, Paul James Kirrage, and Etienne Boissy of the Institut Paul Bocuse, Lyon, France.

Michaela York, director of communications for Chef John Folse and Company

Faculty, staff, and students of the Chef John Folse Culinary Institute at Nicholls State University

Faculty, staff, and students of the School of Hospitality and Tourism Management at the University of Guelph

Finally (and most importantly), I would like to acknowledge and thank my wife, Teresa Harrington, for her assistance and support during this process.

MASTERING THE ART AND SCIENCE OF FOOD AND WINE PAIRING

My interest in food and wine has spanned more than three decades, and in the past several years, this interest has taken center stage. This text was developed as a response to the need to create an experiential methodology to demystify the food-and-wine pairing process. The main focus of this process is on taste characteristics of food and wine from both culinary and sensory perspectives.

The discussions and exercises in this text are designed to provide you with an increased depth of experience in food and wine pairing and knowledge of how food and wine elements interact and transform one another. The first section of this text focuses on the basics of wine evaluation, an understanding of the gastronomic identity, and its relationship with wine and food marriages.

Chapter 1 introduces the concepts and methodology used throughout this text. The food-and-wine pairing process combines techniques derived from the general sensory literature, the wine evaluation literature, and the culinary arts literature. The heart of the process relies on a systematic approach used to induce, quantify, analyze, and assess the responses to food and wine products based on what is perceived through the senses of sight, smell, taste, touch, and hearing.

Chapter 2 provides an overview of the sensory process as applied to wine evaluation. Wine evaluation encompasses a visual examination, olfactory examination, and taste examination. The exercises in this chapter will arm you with tools to clearly identify the primary taste characteristics in wine and food (sweet, sour, bitter, and salty) as well as to differentiate bitterness from astringency. The wine evaluation exercises will allow you to reinforce previous experiences in wine tasting and provide a clear differentiation of the most common wine varietals based on color, smell, body, and taste.

Chapters 3 and 4 focus on the concept of gastronomic identity. A region's gastronomic identity is determined by the environment and cultural elements that impact prevailing components, textures, and flavors in wine and food. The dominant elements in the environment determining wine characteristics include geography and climate. Culture elements include religion, history, level of ethnic diversity, innovations, capabilities, traditions, beliefs, and values. Historical events have had a substantial impact on the wine industry throughout the world. Old World and New World wine regions have differing histories, traditions, and geography. The boundaries between the Old and New Worlds are blurring with the sharing of new technologies and viticulture practices. Old World traditions are being adopted by New World producers as they take a closer look at the relationship between the land and the grape. Just like all cuisine, the wine industry is in constant evolution created by a fusion of unique and identifiable products and traditions that change over time. The food and wine industries are constantly evolving and provide a myriad of opportunities for professionals of all ages to take part.

The pairing of food and wine is an interesting topic and even more interesting when experiential tastings are involved. The upcoming exercises will provide you with a tool kit of ideas, concepts, and knowledge to enable you to quickly identify key wine and food elements so that you will be able to pair wine and food with confidence.

I hope that you enjoy reading the material in this book as well as doing the end-of-chapter exercises. The material and experiences presented in this text just scratch the surface of the possibilities and variety available in the market today. The background and experience you develop throughout the readings and exercises will bolster your confidence in wine, food, and combining the two. I hope this process piques your curiosity and that you will continue this exciting lifelong journey of learning and experimentation.

CHAPTER 1

THE WINE AND FOOD PYRAMID: A HIERARCHY OF TASTE

CHAPTER OUTLINE:

Introduction

Objectives of Food and Wine Pairing

Aperitif: The Italian Wine and Food Perspective

Food and Wine Pairing Mechanics: Matching Traditions

Overview of Book Methods

Key Elements of Wine and Food: A Hierarchical Perspective

Summary: Where Do We Go from Here?

Classic Italian Wine and Food Examples

KEY CONCEPTS:

- Motivations of wine and food pairing
- Food and wine sensory pyramid
- Primary components
- Texture elements
- Flavor intensity, persistency, and spiciness

INTRODUCTION

While we all have a lifetime's worth of experiences and knowledge relating to food tastes and characteristics, most people do not enjoy wine with meals on a daily basis. As a result, the general population lacks a fully developed ability to instinctively match appropriate wines with particular foods. Selections of appropriate wine and food pairings provide restaurant operators with opportunities to increase business profitability through their wine sales and to increase customer satisfaction with the overall dining experience.[1] However, it is quite challenging for foodservice industry professionals as well as the general dining public to come up with synergistic wine and food matches, and both restaurant operation and the culinary arts would be greatly enhanced by the demystification of food and wine pairing.

While I was researching and developing the methods presented in this text, it became apparent that the books currently on the market provide discussions of wine and food item selections but provide little depth of information concerning direct relationships and reactions between food and wine components, flavors, and textures.[2] In testing the methods presented in this text, it also became apparent that most people have difficulty understanding wine terminology, indicating a need for more user-friendly definitions for the terms most frequently used. In other words, while a need for a greater understanding of wine and food pairing exists, readily available methods and techniques are lacking. This text addresses these concerns by providing more accessible methods and processes to educate and train individuals in food and wine pairing and evaluation.

To Pair or Not to Pair? Typical food-and-wine pairing advice focuses on suggestions such as "noisettes of venison with Cumberland sauce are best served with a 2000 Robert Mondavi Zinfandel." This type of advice is meaningless for the purposes of increasing our understanding of the food-and-wine pairing process. In fact, it limits our ability to develop an instinctive capability to match food and wine. On a day-to-day basis, most of us would rather know things such as "If I am preparing chicken for my next meal, does it matter whether it is baked, grilled, or fried when I'm deciding what wine to serve with it?" In reality, there are very few wine choices that will ruin a meal, but good choices can raise the experience of a meal from enjoyable to memorable. The method used in this text provides principles that can be useful when selecting wines for either a meal you are preparing, a meal you have while dining at your favorite restaurant, or a dinner party you attend as a guest.

If you are a restaurateur by profession, an increased understanding of basic pairing objectives will increase your confidence when you provide wine and food pairing selections to your customers. From a business perspective, your staff's ability to recommend the wine that will best complement the foods served can significantly increase the average check and thus bottom-line profits. It will also enhance customers' perception of professionalism of service and make their dining experience more satisfying, resulting in more return business and positive word-of-mouth advertising.

OBJECTIVES OF FOOD AND WINE PAIRING

The primary objective of the food and wine pairing method used in this text is to develop skills in identifying the key elements in food and wine that will directly impact pairing them, whether the pairing is based on contrasts or similarities. An example of basic food contrast would be a peanut butter and jelly sandwich. The contrast of the savory saltiness of the peanut butter with the sweet, fruity jelly is great. An example of a food item with similarities is s'mores, in which all of the major components are sweet: graham cracker, marshmallow, and milk chocolate. However, there is a contrast in terms of texture—crispy graham cracker with gooey marshmallow and chocolate. Such contrasts and similarities serve as the basic considerations for wine and food pairing.

As you develop your knowledge of the key issues related to food and wine pairing (components, flavors, and textures; contrast or similarity; and a rudimentary understanding of flavor/component differences in wines of the world), your ability to predict exceptional food and wine pairings will greatly improve. You will determine the ultimate food and wine parings through practice, practice, and more practice. Each food and wine practice session, in and of itself, can be a delightful, life-changing experience.

Using music as an analogy, elements of food and wine can be thought of as "notes" that can be arranged in a variety of ways and at a variety of levels. Just as a musician merges groups of notes into chords and arranges them into a pleasant melody, the chef or winemaker combines food or wine "notes" on a range of scales into chords of taste, texture, and flavor. The finished dish or wine becomes a pleasant melody in its own right. A food and wine "composer" then combines the appropriate dishes and wines into a potential multicourse "concerto" of taste that appeals to all of the senses and heightens the gastronomic experience beyond the possibilities of drinking the wine or eating the dish separately. Food and wine can serve as equal partners in this arrangement, or a particular food item or wine may take on a supporting role, as a particular situation dictates.

How to select the ideal wine for a particular food dish? That is the question!

In the following Aperitif, Enrico Bazzoni, director of U.S. Programs for the Italian Culinary Institute for Foreign Professionals, carries this musical analogy forward and shares the past and present Italian perspective on wine and food pairing, highlighting the desire to achieve balance and harmony in food and wine, as in business and the rest of life. At the end of this chapter, Enrico also provides some classic Italian recipes and pairing examples.

Aperitif | The Italian Wine and Food Perspective

One of the most famous pieces of music ever written is Antonio Vivaldi's *The Four Seasons*. It is used as a theme in movies, in TV commercials, and on the radio. More than four hundred years after its first performance, it is still one of the best-sellers in the music business. Every violinist in the world has played it over and over, interpreted it, modified its cadence, its structure, its tempo, trying to express the "real" way Vivaldi must have heard it in his head through variations. No matter how many changes occur through various interpretations, *The Four Seasons* manages to retain its mercurial qualities, with some of the most exuberant and yet haunting melodies of any piece of music ever written.

Vivaldi also called the piece *Il cimento dell'armonia e dell'invenzione*, which literally translates to "the contest of harmony and invention." This alternative title suggests that, after having written the piece, the composer realized that this was indeed the ultimate example of the eternal search and the constant struggle for balance between divine harmony and human invention in music.

This is a struggle with which we are faced every day of our lives. Because we usually spend our days on a less intellectual plane, we don't recognize the fact that we are always trying to build bridges between opposites, like earth and heaven. Sometimes we pray, maybe we meditate a little; we may even think about the afterlife and so on, but soon we have to come back to our routines, to our everyday lives.

Nevertheless, although we may not realize it, this struggle never leaves us. It's always there, even in the most minute and seemingly unimportant events of our daily lives. It may sound far-fetched to compare an exalted work of art with the minutiae of our lives, but it is clear that in our professions we seek to achieve a balance between the demands of our jobs and the demands of our lives. We seek balance within our families and within ourselves. We also seek balance between spirituality and material goods.

In the culinary arts, we seek balance regarding the satisfaction of our physical senses. A person who consistently eats too much is called a glutton and is ridiculed and shunned by society, as are the drunkard, the miser, and all those other unsavory, immoderate types of people who fill the wells of Dante's Inferno. *In medium stat virtus* is what our Latin forebears used to say—virtue is found in the middle.

Perhaps this concept of seeking balance is best expressed in the words of Gianfranco Lercara, Italy's gold-medal-winning sommelier, who teaches wine studies at the Italian Culinary Institute for Foreign Professionals in Costigliole d'Asti, near Turin, Italy: "In the Italian eno-gastronomic experience," he says, "wine accompanies food, and food is always constantly searching for the best wine. One must understand the term 'to accompany' as the perfect marriage of both elements, where there may not be prevalence of one over the other, but where there is the best possible expression of both."[3]

It has not been very easy for the Italian culinary-enological culture to reach this position. Historically, wines from one region were traditionally paired with the foods of that region. In areas where red wine was more popular or plentiful, it was not uncommon to see it served with fish or seafood, without too much thought being given to the character of the wine or the food. Each was appreciated and savored on its own; there was no search for "synergy," as we strive for nowadays.

It's important to note that the concept of wine and food pairing is not a totally new idea in Italy. In fact, the importance of wine and food pairing has been a part of Italian life since Roman times. The famous food connoisseur Archestratus, founder of the first culinary school in the Western world, wrote that "a fat eel [the Romans were particularly fond of eels, which they farmed in pools] is particularly good when accompanied by a good Phalernum," referring to a wine still produced in the region of Naples. In many cases, traditional pairings work perfectly, as in the choice of a Lambrusco wine to accompany the traditional zampone (a local specialty consisting of a pig's foot stuffed with forcemeat, bacon, truffles, and seasoning) in Modena or Bologna, or the choice of Tocai del Collio (a native white grape variety from northeastern Italy) with prosciutto di San Daniele in the Friuli–Venezia Giulia region.[4]

In these cases, the interaction between these regional items creates a natural match. In other cases, however, each time a morsel of food is tasted, followed by a sip of wine, the palate has to adjust and adapt to the often sharp contrasts resulting from the interaction of the wine and food. Prior to the 1960s, food and wine pairing in Italy was a concept relegated to a very small number of connoisseurs, the affluent, and the nobility, who in most instances would choose a French wine rather than an Italian one to accompany their meals.

Although Italy has always produced some excellent wines, and a substantial number of good wines, the majority of the wine production has always been of the bulk commercial variety. For some vintages, production reached 1.8 billion gallons,[5] and "good" Italian wines were considered the exception rather than the rule. Then, in 1963, the Italian government issued the DOC (*denominazione di origine controllata*) laws, regulating all the phases of wine production, including territory, vines, yields, alcohol content, sugar levels, names of wine, and labels used. In an attempt to control and maintain the product in as natural a state as possible (and to avoid adulteration), Italian DOC laws strictly prohibited addition of sugar to the must. In a spectacular leap forward, Italy's wine production jumped from a process focusing on quantity to one that focuses on quality.

Many changes have occurred since 1963, and some well-known vintners have even chosen to innovate outside of the restrictive DOC structure and produce local or regional "boutique wines" of high quality that fetch astronomical prices. This is possible precisely because of the introduction of the DOC laws, which established the basic patterns of quality production and stimulated research in the field: the use of several dozen autochthonous vines, the cultivation of imported varieties, and innovation in vinification processes (temperature control, barrels, and barriques of different sizes and woods). In a relatively short time, the Italian (and the world's) consumer no longer had to resort to French wines in order to drink a good wine with a meal—wines of consistently high quality, and eventually of prestige, were now produced at home in Italy. The centuries-old tradition of consumers drinking ordinary wine with meals shifted to making a conscious act of choice and culture. The quasi-mechanical process of drinking a specific wine with a certain meal because "that's the way it has always been done" has now become a more intellectual process, with a search for interaction, compatibility of flavors, nuance, and balance. With this has come a new set of rules. These rules serve as general guidelines to help the wine and food amateur as much as the professional. They should be not restrictive but indicative; they should not interfere with the expansion of knowledge but help to stimulate its growth.

Following the older French and English schools of thought, Italian wine connoisseurs adopted the same general set of rules regarding the use of specific wines with certain foods, such as "white wines with fish and red wines with meat," "whites should be chilled and reds should be kept at room temperature," and some other generalizations, used to avoid making the grossest mistakes. Eventually (and inevitably), more sophisticated guidelines came into play. Sometimes these guidelines were heavily influenced by scientific information, such as from chemical analysis, or by other, more esoteric notions. Many of these ideas make it difficult for the beginner or even for the expert to understand, let alone to be on par with, the current ideology in wine and food pairing.

The Italian Culinary Institute for Foreigners in Castello di Costigliole d'Asti, overlooking the village of Costigliole d'Asti, Italy (courtesy of the Italian Culinary Institute for Foreigners).

It is therefore most important to remember that while this intellectual process is common and universal today, the experience in itself is always an individual and personal one. Rules have been established for those (especially beginners) who may prefer to use somebody else's experience and advice in order to acquire a well-grounded knowledge of the subject in the shortest amount of time. These people will never eat a raw artichoke while drinking red wine because "it is a well-known fact" (predicated by somebody else) that a substance in the artichoke, cyanin, will clash with the tannins in the red wine, thus making your mouth a battlefield of contrasting sensations. (The best thing to drink with a raw or cooked artichoke is a nice fresh glass of water.) On the other end of the spectrum, for those who prefer to take the road less traveled, there is the empirical method, which calls for eating a raw artichoke while drinking red wine, in order to experience firsthand what the clashing of sensations in your mouth feels like. The empiricist takes the long way around, disregards the rules, makes "mistakes" on purpose, and does not listen to the guru of the day. The empiricist uses an abundance of wines with the proverbial cornucopia of foods. Most importantly, he or she makes use of this process in the company of good friends and family and enjoys every step of this exercise, which should never be intimidating and is always void of prejudice. Fortunately, there is an ample supply of quality wines and even more foods in the Italian repertoire to satisfy the most demanding research, which makes this process a most rewarding experience.

The basic evaluation process for the Italian wine and food empiricist is as follows: all foods and wines are evaluated, and each evaluation is collected and recorded on a simple form. Each wine is evaluated for:

1. Visual observation: color, clarity, hue, density
2. Olfactory qualities: nose (aroma, bouquet)
3. Taste qualities: sweetness, fruitiness, acidity, bitterness, tannins, thinness, heaviness, finish, etc.
4. Overall impressions: general qualities, balance

Although some people maintain that the visual observation is not important in the pairing of food and wine, I think that it is silly to disregard such an important factor, especially today, when so much weight is put on food presentation, colors of ingredients, and so on. The color of the wine should also be considered as an important factor in the process of pairing. We say, "We eat with our eyes first"; we should say, "We eat *and drink* with our eyes first."

For each category, there are many more points of evaluation, especially in the areas of olfactory and taste sensations. Many individuals sense different impressions based upon their experiences with their noses and palates. It is very interesting to catalogue these impressions and attempt to determine a general theory across a group of evaluators.

The same evaluation form is used for each food tasted, with each dish evaluated for:

1. Eye appeal and color combination
2. Aromatic character
3. Sweetness, saltiness, acidity, leanness, fatness, and texture
4. Overall impressions

Lastly, both sets of evaluations are paired and given a final grade. This task can become overwhelming if you want to analyze many wines with many dishes. There could be thousands of combinations. A suggested method to simplify things is to cook a specific dish with a particular wine in mind to pair with it. This method can be very gratifying, especially for those who have acquired a strong level of cooking knowledge and are not constrained by the written recipe. In the equation of wine and food pairing (great match = wine elements + food elements), the wine tends to remain unchangeable while the food has more inherent flexibility. For instance, it is easier to change the character of a dish than the personality of a 2004 vintage Sangiovese. For this reason, many meals, ordinary or extravagant, are now designed around the wines offered, rather than vice versa.

After a certain amount of experimentation (and inevitable mistakes—none too unpleasant and all forgivable), certain patterns begin to emerge that may or may not follow the rules and guidelines of old. From there, it is possible to move on to a second tier of evaluations and perfect the process by adopting a scale for each category, let's say from 1 to 10. Each wine characteristic should then be evaluated based on degrees of color, clarity, hue, bouquet, and so on, rated on this 1 to 10 scale. The same can be done for the food items. When using this method, we will obtain an *intensity scale*, which will help us to decide which wine can optimally be paired with which food.

At the end of this chapter, there are two examples of wine and food pairings, derived from my own experience. Enjoy!

FOOD AND WINE PAIRING MECHANICS: MATCHING TRADITIONS

As pointed out by Enrico Bazzoni, "red wine with meat and white wine with fish" is a basic premise of food and wine pairing. In some cases, it may be a person's entire food-and-wine pairing repertoire. Differing cultures have developed different perspectives on the food-and-wine pairing process and its importance. For example, the traditional French system of pairing dictates a series of rigid rules to follow. The general American attitude seems to be "if it feels good, drink it," leading to the American restaurateur's attitude of "they'll order

Currently residing in New York, Enrico Bazzoni is originally from Genoa, Italy. He is a chef and expert in Italian food and wine. He is the director of U.S. programs for the Italian Culinary Institute for Foreign Professionals (ICIF). Additional information regarding ICIF is available at www.icif.com.

what they like." As discussed in this chapter's Aperitif, the Italian pairing method appears to be based on an understanding of complementary and contrasting elements in food and wine.

All of these pairing systems have merit based on the respective cultural perspectives, tradition, and business models. Each of these systems is based on often conflicting truisms regarding food and wine pairing and the individual differences between restaurant customers. A perfect food and wine combination does not guarantee a happy customer, and there are no perfect food and wine pairings that everyone will love. For instance, a marriage of fine French Sancerre and salty raw oysters will not matter if the person doesn't care for oysters. In pairing for individual guests, there is a significant amount of personal preference involved—servers should select and recommend a range of choices, in terms of both wine type and price. Remember, whether we are talking about weight (as in the case of red wine with red meat) or other food and wine elements, food and wine combinations can be complementary or contrasting. The crisp acidity of a dry Sauvignon Blanc can provide a contrast to a piece of grilled fish much as the juice of a fresh lemon does. A complementary example may be the echo of raspberry in a young Pinot Noir matched with a raspberry reduction sauce. Classic contrasting examples include Sauternes and foie gras or California Cabernet and bittersweet chocolate. Sweet wines and savory foods don't always complement each other but can be magical in some cases.

There are several food and wine combinations that most experts recommend. Some examples are champagne and caviar (the effervescence of the champagne cuts through the salty brine of the caviar), Port and Stilton cheese (appeals to our contrasting senses much like chocolate candy and salty popcorn at the movies), California Chardonnay and lobster (big buttery wine with big buttery lobster), Cabernet Sauvignon and beef or lamb (the classic mellowing effect of rich and fatty meat on full-bodied reds with tannin), and Fumé Blanc and grilled fish or seafood (think fresh-squeezed lemon).

While it is helpful to memorize these basic combinations and general dos and don'ts regarding food and wine pairing, these ideas provide little help in clearly defining the reasons why these are important rules or superior matches. The following chapters provide a set of general principles for understanding the direct and interacting effects of food and wine elements. Unlike rules, they provide guidance in determining the best matching choices for food and wine by considering dominant components, textures, and flavors.[6] Further, each chapter provides exercises that arm interested students with cost-effective and eye-opening experiences that can serve as a basis for future evaluations.

Food and wine matching may be approached from several perspectives depending on your confidence in selecting wines, your state of mind at the moment, or the objective of the gathering where the food and wine will be served. There are several levels of match: no match, refreshment, neutral, good, or synergistic. All of these matching objectives are useful, and the decision to use one or the other is determined by the situation. The objective of the method in this text is to provide you with a tool kit that allows you to confidently achieve any of these pairing objectives.

No Match The interaction of wine and food when tasted together has a negative impact on the senses. This is common when the food item is high in acidity, salt, bitterness, or spiciness. An example of a no-match situation would be a custard-type dessert such as ice cream, bread pudding, or crème brûlée with a dry, high-acid wine such as Sancerre (Sauvignon Blanc). Clearly, the sweetness of the food and dryness of the wine clash, and this will accentuate the high acidity in the wine, creating a sense that the wine is excessively sour and bitter. A second example is Chinese hot-and-sour soup with a young, tannic Australian Cabernet Sauvignon. The soup is spicy and sour; the wine is astringent, has high alcohol, and is bold. The spiciness and sourness in the soup will create a sharp, astringent, and bitter taste in the wine. The high alcohol in the wine will emphasize the spicy character of the soup.

Refreshment Many times wine serves simply as a satisfying refreshment to accompany a certain food choice. In this instance, wine plays a supporting role in the food-and-wine relationship, serving as a pleasant, refreshing beverage that accompanies the food choice. The refreshment match may be appropriate when the food choice has characteristics that severely limit any synergistic wine choice. In this case, some of the basic elements of the wine match the food item, but the body and flavors of the food or wine do not match. This is not always a bad thing. For example, highly seasoned or spicy foods may need a refreshing wine to cool and cleanse the palate for the next bite. Or you may be in the mood for a refreshing and relaxing wine to accompany the meal. You do not always need or want to create a concerto of taste transformation for each daily meal. An example of a refreshment match is a spicy dish such as Panang curry. Panang curry is a popular item at many Thai restaurants. It can be prepared with beef, chicken, or pork and includes intensely flavored items such as curry paste, fish sauce, and coconut milk. This spicy and intense dish could be served with a German Kabinett (Riesling) or a Riesling from the Alsace region of France to create a refreshing backdrop.

Neutral Many of the large-production wines on the retail shelf are designed to minimize any poor pairing "damage" and eliminate poor matching situations. These pairing situations are average and pleasant but are missing an element of individuality and thus cannot provide a superior gastronomic experience.[7] Also, in many cases, you may be hosting or attending a gathering that has a wide variety of food choices (such as a potluck dinner); neutral pairing may be desirable in these situations so that the wines selected will go reasonably well with a wide range of food styles and cuisines. A neutral match could be created by serving a large-production, unoaked Chardonnay such as Almaden, Taylor California, or Turning Leaf with your Thanksgiving feast. The wine in this case serves as a neutral partner to avoid clashing with a diverse collection of food items that can be sweet, sour, bitter, and salty.

Good Match In this situation, you have found a wine that matches the food item's basic components (sweet, sour, bitter, salty) and overall body. The difference between a good match and a synergistic one is that in the good match, the flavors (flavor intensities, spiciness, and flavor styles) do not match entirely. An example of this relationship level is a German Riesling Spätlese Halbtrocken served with baked or sautéed trout. This wine is very food-friendly—fruity, moderately sweet, and well-balanced. Served with the trout, it creates a good or even very good match. To move this combination to the next level, the addition of herbs (such as thyme or basil) or serving the fish lightly smoked and with a bit of horseradish would add a greater balance in persistence and intensity. These additions would also add some great contrasts in flavors—fruity versus herbal, fruity and sweet versus smoky and a little spice.

Synergistic Match The word *synergy*, derived from the Greek *synergos*, means the combined effect of the whole is superior to the sum of the individual parts. In terms of food-and-wine pairing choice, many times synergy is the ultimate objective—the wine and food combine to create a totally new and superior gastronomic effect. This situation is analogous to the musical concerto created by the composer tying together a variety of chords, melodies, and movements into a heightened combined effect on the senses.[8] The combination of foie gras and French Sauternes, German Eiswein, or Canadian ice wine comes to mind when I think of classic synergistic relationships.

OVERVIEW OF BOOK METHODS

Wine and food experts agree that no one person can be an authority with complete knowledge in wine and food pairing.[9] There are just too many wines in the world and too many variations in cuisine style, ingredients, and preparation methods for one person to be knowledgeable about all of them. Even so, understanding the basics of wine and food pairing can provide both professionals and the dining public with the keys to properly marry food and wine elements. A central tenet of the method in this text is the concept of a hierarchy of tastes that can assist us when making pairing decisions. The approach used in this food-and-wine pairing process is based on a synthesis of research and literature on the subject and both culinary and sensory perspectives.

Steak and lobster, a traditional combination. Which pairing rule should you follow—red wine with meat, or buttery lobster with a buttery Chardonnay?

KEY ELEMENTS OF WINE AND FOOD: A HIERARCHICAL PERSPECTIVE

Pairing experts do not agree on what is most important in making choices about what wine and food to serve together. Is it the texture or body of the food and wine? Is it the flavors? Or is it primary sensory components (sweetness, saltiness, acidity, bitterness)? Some pairing experts base their choices on a combination of flavors and primary sensory components. For example, they identify six key food flavors (salty, sour/sharp, savory, spicy, smoky, and sweet)[10] and assess food and wine in terms of aromas, flavors, and their intensity.[11] In another approach, food flavors are described using a variety of adjectives: *fruity, nutty, smoky, herbal, spicy, cheesy, earthy,* and *meaty*.[12] Primary wine "flavor" descriptors are *dry, crisp, oaky,* and *tannic,* with secondary terms such as *buttery, herbal/grassy, spicy,* and *floral*.[13] But these arrays of elements to consider when paring wine with food illustrate the difficulty in determining the one key driver behind particular matching choices. For instance, acid in food may be an important consideration, but only when it is above or below average levels. Similarly, flavors may have a significant impact on wine and food pairing only when the length of flavor persistence or the flavor intensity is above the norm.

Based on the established direct effects of the food and wine elements, it is useful to separate these elements into three general categories: main taste components, texture elements, and flavor elements. While these three categories are not mutually exclusive, keeping them separate provides a greater ability to distinguish the key drivers of possible food and wine matches. Designating three categories of elements also allow the evaluator to distinguish between these categories in a hierarchical fashion. The Food and Wine Taste Pyramid (Figure 1.1) illustrates that an evaluation of food and wine elements can be thought of as a hierarchy of tastes, starting with main taste components, then moving to texture and on to flavor.

Flavors

Texture

Components

Figure 1.1
Food and Wine Sensory Pyramid—A Hierarchy of Taste

Components   Components can be defined as "very basic elements that correspond to basic sense perception on the tongue."[14] Food and wine components are the foundation for elements that impact the pleasant feeling brought about by the complementary or contrasting characteristics of a positive gastronomic experience. The components most typically perceived are described as sweetness, saltiness, bitterness, and sourness.

Texture   A second key category is the texture inherent in the wine and the prepared dish to be paired. Texture relates to body,[15] power,[16] weight,[17] and structure.[18] The texture of both the food and the wine, whether similar or contrasting, becomes the "glue" or "cement" that holds the structure of the food-and-wine pairing selection together.

Texture is the characteristic in food or wine that creates a specific mouthfeel or tactile sensation in every corner of the mouth rather than a perceptible flavor or taste component identifiable in specific parts of the tongue. Unlike components, textures are relatively easy to identify, and like components and flavors, they can be used to provide similarity or contrasts in matching.

Texture can be described in a variety of ways. In wine, it can be described as thin, velvety, medium-bodied, or viscous. In food, it may be described as grainy, loose, dry, oily, or rough. Temperature can also serve as a texture contrast. Warm or hot foods served with cold wine can provide a refreshing and satisfying contrast. The most common representation of texture is a basic continuum from light to rich. The combinations of food and wine can be similar or contrasting. Pairing food and wine with similar light or rich textures is a safer bet, but contrasts can be effective if the rich wine or food doesn't overpower the lighter pairing item.

Flavors   A third category of elements in food and wine is flavors. Flavors and components are sometimes confused, but while components are tied to basic sensory perceptions of the tongue, flavors are closely tied to our perceptions of specific characters inherent in the food or wine based on aroma and taste sensations. Flavors are a result of a retronasal process that occurs when aromas are picked up through the back of the mouth and then flow into the nasal cavity.[19]

Flavors act as "architectural elements" of food-and-wine pairing selections. As with a building, architectural elements or flavors add interest and complexity to the overall structure of the food and wine paired. For this reason, flavor elements are placed at the top of the sensory hierarchy. While they are not necessarily the most important element for consideration when determining an optimal pair, they represent a final consideration once the foundation (components) and glue (texture) are determined.

The most common flavor descriptors include *fruity, nutty, smoky, herbal, spicy, cheesy, earthy,* and *meaty.* In terms of pairing importance, the length of persistence and intensity of a specific flavor can have an effect on either the food or the wine. These flavor characteristics can be used to describe either similar or contrasting flavors when referring to a food and wine pair. The food and wine flavor categories used in the evaluation system presented later in this text include dominant flavor(s), flavor intensity, and spicy flavors.

As you progress through the readings and exercises in this text, you will become familiar with key elements of both food and wine as well as how they interact with each other to create a "chord" of gastronomic excitement. Later chapters provide further detail on evaluation methods and help students understand the process of tying the complex elements of a particular dish to the complexity of a certain wine.

A sensory hierarchy is presented throughout this text, providing important information about both wine and food elements. The objective throughout the text is to make the array of terms for these elements as concise as possible and focus on only the key elements of food and wine that are perceptible to the majority of knowledgeable evaluators. This sensory perspective is based on substantial research in this area. The objectives of the process used in this text are to (1) demystify wine terminology and create a method to train palates to identify the primary flavor characteristics of wine and food, (2) provide a method to clearly understand the cause-and-effect relationship of food and wine, (3) establish rating scales of components, textures, and flavors so that individuals will be able to effectively understand, communicate, and rank the levels of these elements over time, and (4) provide a wine and food pairing tool that creates accurate predictions of match levels.

Wine Sensory Pyramid   The Wine Sensory Pyramid (Figure 1.2) illustrates that wine has three main categories of elements: components, texture, and flavors. Wine also has three primary sensory components that form the foundation for a match with the primary sensory components in a particular food: level of sweetness, presence and level of effervescence, and level of crispness or acidity. There are several things to consider when determining the texture of wine, including tannin level, alcohol content, presence and level of oak, and an overall feeling of body. It should be noted that while oak aging may impact the color, body, flavor, and aroma of wine, its effect on the body of the wine is likely to be a key factor when matching according to the body or power of the food item.[20] Primary considerations when determining the flavors of wine include identifiable flavor descriptor(s) or type(s), the persistence of flavor, the intensity of flavor, and any spicy characteristics.

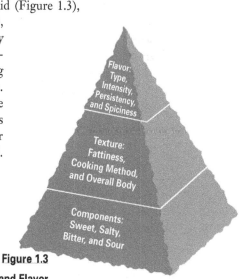

Figure 1.2

Wine Sensory Pyramid—Components, Texture, and Flavor

Food Sensory Pyramid   As shown in the Food Sensory Pyramid (Figure 1.3), primary food components include the levels of sweetness (natural or added), saltiness, bitterness, and sourness of a finished food dish or product. Primary texture considerations include fat level in the protein or additional plate elements (natural or added), the cooking method used, and the overall feeling of body or texture across all of the food items included in the particular dish.

As with wine flavors, primary food considerations include identifiable flavor type(s), the persistence of flavor, and intensity of flavor. Spicy flavors in food and wine can be particularly important for matching purposes, for when the spice level in food goes up, your wine choices become more limited.

Figure 1.3

Food Sensory Pyramid—Components, Texture, and Flavor

SUMMARY: WHERE DO WE GO FROM HERE?

The discussions and exercises in this text are designed to provide you with (1) a depth of experience in tasting and evaluating food and wine combinations, (2) the basics of wine evaluation and differences between varietals' characteristics, (3) an understanding of gastronomic identity—that is, the impact of history and culture on food and wine choices—and its relationship to wine and food marriages, and (4) knowledge of how food and wine elements interact and transform each other.

The methods used throughout this text will provide you with a tool kit of ideas, concepts, and knowledge to enable you to quickly identify key wine and food elements so that you will be able to properly pair wine and food with confidence. The experimentation method used in the exercises within each chapter presents both traditional and unconventional wine choices/combinations for your consideration. Does a particular wine choice match the food or not? Does this particular pairing choice open your eyes to a surprising new partnership?

Chapter 2 provides an overview of wine evaluation in general and exercises to help reinforce the wine evaluation concepts presented. Chapters 3 and 4 introduce and explore the idea of gastronomic identity. The remaining chapters provide further discussion of the food and wine matching process and exercises to help illustrate how wine and food matches can be predicted and to demonstrate the interactive and synergistic effects of food and wine elements.

DISCUSSION QUESTIONS

1. What are the key motivations for an interest in food and wine pairing?

2. Describe some traditional food and wine marriages.

3. What are the key elements associated with wine and food pairing?

4. Describe the primary wine components, texture, and flavor elements.

5. Describe the primary food components, texture, and flavor elements.

CLASSIC ITALIAN WINE AND FOOD EXAMPLES

The following recipes and wine-and-food pairing examples are derived from Enrico Bazzoni's experience and use the basics of the Italian pairing process. Keep in mind that these pairings are suggestions, and like all pairings, they are impacted by personal preferences. As Enrico points out, "I am very partial to tones of color, for example, and my grades in the examples below are highly subjective. Factors influencing my judgment (and everybody else's) are, among others, experiences, memories, and personal preferences. Readers should remember that they are ultimately the best judges in these matters."

This process gives an overview of similar things to come in this text as you take the road less traveled in wine and food. Enjoy this overview and the classic Italian recipes provided by Chef Bazzoni.

EXAMPLE 1

For this first wine and food pairing example, I have selected a classic wine and dish from the Chianti region. The wine is a Chianti Classico whose origin is within a subregion of the Chianti Classico DOCG in an area between Siena and Florence. The primary grape used in Chianti and Chianti Classico is Sangiovese. The dish (Egg Pappardelle alla Lepre) is a very traditional dish from the Chianti region and is made with wide egg noodles and hare sauce.

Wine: Badia di Coltibuono, Chianti Classico 2003

Organic, hand-picked grapes: Sangiovese 90 percent, Canaiolo 10 percent.

Vintage notes: extremely hot and dry weather.

Table 1.1   2003 Badia di Coltibuono Chianti Classico Profile

Examination	Description	Score out of 10 points
Color	Brilliant. Ruby-red, intense.	9
Nose	Deep, penetrating, alcoholic. Floral bouquet, berries.	9
Taste	Concentrated flavors. Woody, moderate acidity, round and well-balanced. Alcohol level 14%	10
Overall impression	An excellent Chianti Classico with moderate tannins, soft body.	10
Total		38 out of 40 points

Food Item: Egg Pappardelle alla Lepre (Wide Fresh Egg Fettuccine with Hare Sauce)

Yield: 6 servings

Ingredients

5 oz (150 ml) extra-virgin olive oil
¼ bunch parsley, chopped
1 large onion, chopped
2 stalks celery, chopped
2 carrots, chopped
1 hare, cut up into 6 pieces, reserving the
    head, lungs, liver, and blood
8 oz (240 ml) Chianti
4 oz (120 ml) milk
Salt and pepper
1 lb (454 g) pappardelle (wide fresh egg
    fettuccine)
½ c (112 g) grated pecorino cheese
½ c (112 g) grated parmesan cheese

Preparation

In a large pot combine the oil and the chopped vegetables. Cook vegetables over medium heat until beginning to brown. Add hare parts, including head, lungs, and heart. Reserve liver. Cook until all the liquid from the meat evaporates. Add wine and let cook until it evaporates. Add hare's blood, diluted with a bit of warm water to avoid coagulation. A few minutes later, add milk. Stir well, cover, and let cook until hare is tender. Remove meat, let cool, and bone. Cut meat into bite-size pieces and return to the pot. Add liver, cut up into bite-size pieces. Cook 5 to 7 minutes longer. Add salt and pepper to taste. While hare is finishing, drop pappardelle into a pot of hot boiling salted water and cook for 3 minutes. Drain, dress with sauce, and serve with grated cheeses.

Table 1.2   Egg Pappardelle alla Lepre Profile

Examination	Description	Score out of 10 points
Visual	Deep brown, brilliant hue, with vivid contrast between the noodles and the sauce.	7
Aromatic character	Moderate aromatic character. Deep liver perfume. No spices.	7
Taste:	Deep blend of sweetness from carrots and liver. Lean. Pungent.	9
Overall impression	Rich, satisfying fall flavors. Exotic. Well balanced by noodles and enriched by cheeses, accented with salt (pecorino cheese).	10
Total		33 out of 40 points

The Badia di Coltibuono pairs with this dish perfectly. The moderate acidity of this Chianti Classico balances well with the lean character of the sauce. The wine works well with the hare in the sauce and the natural sweetness of the liver finish. The alcohol content abates the aggressive quality of the hare. Even the colors balance each other: the brilliant ruby of the wine serves as a counterpoint to the deep brown of the sauce.

EXAMPLE 2

This example utilizes a white wine from the northeast region of Alto Adige. The Pinot Bianco grape is used, which produces wines that are light, refreshing, and dry. It is paired with marinated asparagus wrapped in prosciutto. Asparagus, artichokes, and other vegetables in the thistle family such as cardoons are thought by many to be wine killers and can create a bad taste reaction if poor wine selections are made. The Pinot Bianco seems to stand up to the asparagus, debunking this wine "truth."

Wine: Alois Lageder Pinot Bianco—Alto Adige

Grapes: Pinot Bianco

Vintage notes: territory subject to great temperature differences between day and night. Fermentation takes place over four months in temperature-controlled stainless-steel vats.

Table 1.3 Alois Lageder, Pinot Bianco Profile

Examination	Description	Score out of 10 points
Color	Light yellow, brilliant with hint of green reflections.	10
Nose	Fresh and flowery with delicate notes of apple and peach.	9
Taste	Full body flavor, elegant. Moderate finish, lively. Alcohol 12.5%. Acidity medium-low.	7
Overall impression	Very well-rounded wine; excellent balance between body and fresh flavor.	9
Total		35 out of 40 points

Food Item: Marinated Asparagus with Prosciutto di Langhirano

Yield: 3 servings

Ingredients

12 spears (about 1 lb [454 g]) fresh
    asparagus, trimmed
1 tbsp (15 ml) extra-virgin olive oil
1 tbsp (15 ml) balsamic vinegar
3 tbsp (45 ml) red wine vinegar
12 thin slices prosciutto

Preparation

Place the asparagus into a pot of boiling water. Cook for 1 minute, then immediately place them into a pot of lightly salted chilled water with ice cubes in it. Allow the asparagus to cool. Mix the oil and vinegars well to form an emulsion. Drain the asparagus and toss them into the oil and vinegar mixture, making sure they are well coated. Drain excess sauce. Trim the fat from the prosciutto slices. Wrap each asparagus spear with a slice of prosciutto and serve.

Table 1.4 Marinated Asparagus with Prosciutto di Langhirano Profile

Examination	Description	Score out of 10 points
Visual	Brilliant green and red, shiny, translucent. Very appealing.	9
Aromatic character	Very subdued grassy perfume.	6
Taste	Excellent contrast of flavors: fresh grassy asparagus, soft, sweet prosciutto, light salt, balanced by sweet-and-sour quality of sauce.	10
Overall impression	Simple dish delivers an extraordinary charge of flavors in the mouth. Surprising.	10
Total		35 out of 40 points

The Pinot Bianco tames the asparagus' deep grassy flavor and the strong flavor of the dressing. In fact, the wine seems to form an alliance with the soft, salty sweetness of the Prosciutto di Langhirano. The wine and food elements balance each other perfectly.

NOTES

1. J. M. Van Westering, "Gastronomy, the Importance of Combining Tastes," in J. S. A. Edwards (ed.), *Culinary Arts and Sciences; Global and National Perspectives* (Bournemouth, UK: Computational Mechanics Publications, 1996), 15–24.

2. F. Beckett, *How to Match Food and Wine* (London: Octopus Publishing Group, 2002); Andrea Immer, *Great Tastes Made Simple: Extraordinary Food and Wine Pairing for Every Palate* (New York: Broadway Books, 2002); L. Johnson-Bell, *Pairing Wine and Food* (Short Hills, NJ: Burford Books, 1999); J. Simon, *Wine with Food* (New York: Simon and Schuster, 1996).

3. G. Lercara, *Tecnica dell'Abbinamento Cibo—Vino* (Costigliole d'Asti, Italy: Italian Culinary Institute for Foreigners, 2006), 111.

4. Ibid., 113.

5. B. Roncarati, *Viva Vino* (London: Wine and Spirit Publications, 1987).

6. D. Rosengarten and J. Wesson, *Red Wine with Fish: The New Art of Matching Wine with Food* (New York: Simon and Schuster, 1989).

7. Johnson-Bell, *Pairing Wine and Food.*

8. See Rosengarten and Wesson, *Red Wine with Fish.*

9. Johnson-Bell, *Pairing Wine and Food;* Rosengarten and Wesson, *Red Wine with Fish.*

10. Beckett, *How to Match Food and Wine.*

11. Simon, *Wine with Food.*

12. Rosengarten and Wesson, *Red Wine with Fish.*

13. Andrea Immer, *Great Wine Made Simple: Straight Talk from a Master Sommelier* (New York: Broadway Books, 2000).

14. Rosengarten and Wesson, *Red Wine with Fish,* 67.

15. Immer, *Great Tastes Made Simple.*

16. S. Kolpan, B. H. Smith, and M. A. Weiss, *Exploring Wine,* 2nd ed. (New York: John Wiley and Sons, 2002).

17. Simon, *Wine with Food.*

18. Rosengarten and Wesson, *Red Wine with Fish.*

19. M. W. Baldy, *The University Wine Course,* 3rd ed. (San Francisco: Wine Appreciation Guild, 2003).

20. Immer, *Great Tastes Made Simple.*

Enrico Bazzoni wishes to provide a special thanks to Tony DiDio and Lauber Imports for the Italian wine suggestions.

CHAPTER 2

TASTE BASICS AND THE BASICS OF WINE EVALUATION

CHAPTER OUTLINE:

Introduction

Aperitif: Elements of Wine Service

Sensory Evaluation

Basics of Wine Evaluation

Setting Up a Tasting Session

The Art and Science of Wine Evaluation

Palate Mapping

Tasting Instructions

Summary

Exercises

KEY CONCEPTS:

- Sensory testing approaches
- The 6 S's of wine evaluation
- Wine serving temperature
- Identifying sweetness, saltiness, acidity, bitterness, and tannin
- Differences between varietals in terms of primary wine components, textures, and flavors

INTRODUCTION

We begin the journey of food and wine pairing with an overview of the sensory process, how primary components are recognized on the tongue, and how tactile sensations such as tannin are determined. A substantial amount of this chapter focuses on the basics of wine evaluation and tasting procedures, to provide a strong grounding in the basics for those who are new to wine tasting and to reinforce previously acquired skills if you have substantial tasting experience.

Aperitif | Elements of Wine Service

Many elements of wine service are steeped in tradition and ritual. The sensory experiences involved in opening and pouring wine can delight guests and help make the wine a highlight of the meal—or, if approached the wrong way, intimidate guests and make this an awkward moment. Whether your restaurant is casual, fine dining, or anywhere in between, presenting, opening, and pouring a bottle of wine in a way that makes your guests feel comfortable and special should be at the heart of basic wine and food service. A stereotypical view of wine service may evoke snooty sommeliers, a snobby atmosphere, and uneasy guests, but in fact today's sommeliers and masters of wine are trained to be less intimidating and provide valuable education and friendly service for all guests.

The proper method of opening and pouring wine is an important ritual of wine service.

OPENING BOTTLES THAT HAVE A CORK

1. If serving wine to guests in a restaurant setting, present the bottle with the label facing the host prior to opening to ensure that it is the bottle she or he expected.

2. Place the bottle on the table and remove wine capsule.

3. Insert the corkscrew and remove the cork. There are a number of different styles of corkscrews on the market, but many professionals consider the style known as the waiter's friend to be the most useable. To use the waiter's friend, place the tip of the corkscrew (a metal helix) in the center of the cork and screw the helix in about halfway down its shaft. Rest the spur of the corkscrew arm on the lip of the bottle and pull the cork about halfway out. Next, screw the remainder of the helix into the cork and pull the cork the rest of the way out of the bottle; you should hear a soft pop. This two-step process reduces the possibility of breaking the cork if it is extra long, dry, or crumbly. It has the added benefit of minimizing the likelihood that pieces of cork will break off and end up floating in the bottle.

4. If you are opening the bottle for the purchasing host, tradition requires that the host be shown the cork. Just place it on the table next to the host's wineglass. The tradition was begun to ensure that the wine in the bottle is from the producer shown on the label: most wine corks have the producer's name on the side, and an unmarked cork or a cork with a different name might mean that a less desirable wine has been placed in the bottle. Nowadays, the host will be looking to see if the cork is crumbling; if so, it may deserve a smell to see if there are musty or mildewy odors. If such odors are present, the host should pay particular attention when tasting the wine. It is estimated that between 3 and 5 percent of all wines are "corked," which means that the seal has been broken due to a defective cork and the wine may have an off taste.

5. To finish preparing the bottle for service, wipe off the lip of the bottle with a clean and professionally folded cloth napkin.

OPENING BOTTLES THAT HAVE A SCREW CAP

If you are opening a screw cap bottle, simply twist it open. (Screw caps are airtight, keeping the wine's aroma and flavor fresh. But, of course, the soft pop of the cork and the showmanship of removing the cork are missing from the experience. This would be a good time to discuss the move by many top-quality wine producers to screw caps because they are at least as effective as corks for storing wine. This discussion will minimize any issues or misconceptions guests may have about the relationship between wine quality and type of closure.) To finish preparing the bottle for service, wipe off the lip of the bottle with a clean and professionally folded cloth napkin.

POURING ETIQUETTE

If you are the host, it is your responsibility to check the wine for faults. In a restaurant setting, this is the responsibility of the person who ordered the wine. The basic procedure for pouring wine is:

1. Stand behind the person you are serving, to her or his right. Grasp the wine bottle at its center so that the label is facing the guest as you pour. Thus, the bottle label should be facing to your left.

2. With the wineglass upright on the table, hold the lip of the wine bottle just above the rim and slightly off center. Gently tilt the bottle to pour a stream of wine into the glass. If presenting the wine to the host, pour about an ounce in her or his glass.

3. Finish the pouring process by giving the bottle a slight twist toward you before taking it away from over the glass; this will help minimize drips.

4. The host will taste the wine and either approve it or disapprove it. Generally, the host will approve the wine unless there are faults present.

5. Once the wine has been approved, you will pour a glass for each of the other guests before finishing with the host's glass. The guest that is served first is the most senior woman at the table; then the other women are served, followed by the men, and finally the host (or yourself if you are the host and pouring wine).

6. The wineglasses should not be filled more than one-third to one-half full for two reasons. First, of course, it is to allow the guests to be able to swirl and sniff effectively. The second reason is to maintain a constant temperature in each glass. Wine warms up very rapidly in such a small container, and part of the wine server's job is to make sure the guests have enough wine to drink (without pressuring them) as well as to top off wineglasses to maintain proper drinking temperature.

To further ensure proper wine service, review the suggested serving temperatures in Table 2.1.

SENSORY EVALUATION

Sensory evaluation is defined as a systematic approach used to induce, quantify, analyze, and assess the responses to products based on what is perceived through the senses of sight, smell, taste, touch, and hearing. Our senses are remarkable tools for analyzing the many environmental stimuli we come into contact with on a daily basis. These senses also provide analytical tools for evaluating food and wine.

Categories of Testing
Two main categories of testing are used in the basic sensory evaluation process. Affective testing is used to determine general consumer reactions related to product quality and potential consumer acceptance of a product. For findings to be valid, this type of testing requires a relatively large number of individuals (seventy-five or more) who are representative of the target population segment. The affective testing process requires little or no preliminary training of the individuals involved. There are three common types of affective testing: paired comparison (e.g., comparing Pepsi and Coke), ranking (rank in order of preference), and rating (on a scale from "like extremely" to "dislike extremely").

A second type of testing approach is analytical testing. This sensory testing approach is used to discover detectable differences between or among samples. It can also be used to learn the nature of any differences. Analytical testing requires a smaller group (usually twelve to twenty individuals), and each participant must have a substantial level of training. The trained panelists assess differences in color, odor, taste, texture, and other aspects of quality.

Using Your Senses as an Analytic Tool
Our senses have a keen ability to detect differences in a variety of stimuli in the environment. To focus our senses for wine and food evaluation, we need to (re)learn to smell and taste. The basics of wine evaluation provide tools to assist in this learning or relearning process. The basics of the wine evaluation process, tasting session considerations, sample evaluation sheets, and general tasting instructions are discussed in the following sections. The exercises at the end of the chapter assist in this learning process through palate mapping and tasting the major wine varietals.

BASICS OF WINE EVALUATION

Wine tasting is "the interpretation of the sum of sensations perceived either simultaneously or successively."[1] While the aim of an analytical evaluation of wine is to determine and distinguish the key elements of the product, these elements or sensations form a whole that impact our sense of pleasure and quality. This whole can be described as a bundling of unique attributes to form what is, ideally, a balanced and cohesive final product. As with any product, the attributes of wine are based not only on taste but also on sight, smell, sound, and touch.

While the emphasis in this text is primarily on taste, the visual and aromatic characteristics of wine provide us with clues about the potential match of the wine with particular food dishes as well as the quality of the wine itself. The next step is to briefly go over the basics of wine evaluation: a visual examination, an olfactory examination and, finally, an examination of the taste. This basic process has been described as the six S's of wine tasting: seeing, swirling, smelling, sipping, spitting (or swallowing), and savoring.[2]

The Look of Wine: Visual Examination

The first step in assessing wine is to take a look at it. Visual inspection of the bottle and of an individual glass of wine provides us with a substantial amount of information about the style of the wine, aging or fermentation method, level of alcohol, and other clues.

To begin the task of the visual examination, you need to create an environment that allows an inspection of its color and clarity. Most restaurant dining rooms are much too dark to evaluate the color of wine. To effectively assess wine color, you must have sufficient incandescent or natural light (not fluorescent, which can create a false and unpleasant color impression). Next, hold the glass against a white background such as a tablecloth or white paper. Tilt the glass away from you at a 45 degree angle, then look at the color and clarity of the wine from the rim inward.

◆ **Color.** The color of wine can vary substantially and provides us with clues on varietals, growing region and climate, all of which can help us make educated guesses about the ultimate taste of the wine. The depth of color is not necessarily an indicator of wine quality but provides clues to the wine's structure, weight, and length of finish.[3]

While color varies by the varietal of the grape used, reds can vary from opaque to almost black. Light-colored reds may be a sign of cool climate, and darker colors in reds (as in whites) tend to indicate warmer regions. Unlike in whites, richness of color can be evidence of youth in a red wine.

White wines can be as clear as water or a deep yellow. A pale color indicates a young white that was bottled early without any aging in wood; the wine should taste fresh, young, and well-balanced. Aged whites or those left in oak will tend to be darker in color. Rosé can range from a pale salmon pink to a dark pink.

When the objective is to compare the color across two or more wines, it is recommended that you use identical glasses, fill the glasses to the same level (one-third full), and have a white background, preferably with direct light.

◆ **Clarity.** After inspecting the color of wine, the next step in the visual examination is to assess the clarity or transparency. The clarity provides an indication of the quality of winemaking technique and whether or not the bottle has been properly handled. Level of clarity can be judged as cloudy, about clear, clear, crystal clear, or brilliant.

◆ **Swirling.** The process of swirling wine provides a look at the consistency in wine and opens up its aromas. The need to swirl without spilling is one reason not to overfill wineglasses. With the glass sitting on the table, grip the bottom of the stem, lift the glass slightly, and swirl in a counterclockwise motion (if you are right-handed). An easier method for those who are less experienced is to swirl the glass by the stem but keep it on the table rather than above it.

An experienced wine taster never grips a wineglass by its bowl unless the wine is served too cool; then, cupping the bowl with your hands can be used to warm the wine. This warming effect assists in releasing tastes and flavors.

✦ **Consistency.** The consistency in wine refers to how fluid or viscous a wine is; normal viscosity varies by type of wine. The consistency is generally assessed by looking at the "legs" or "tears" that form on the inside of the glass. Tears are droplets that form on the inside of the glass when the wine is swirled, then run down back into the wine.

Sometimes tears are taken as a sign of quality, but it is generally agreed that tears are a sign of high alcohol. While tears are primarily formed due to the relative evaporation rates of water and alcohol, some experts suggest they may be impacted not only by the alcohol level but also by residual sugar, glycerin, pectin, and other elements responsible for aroma.[4] As an example, the higher residual sugar, glycerin, and alcohol found in Sauternes or ice wine will result in more substantial tears than seen with Sauvignon Blanc or Sémillon. Dry, light white wines are normally lower in alcohol and will by definition have less prominent tears than higher-alcohol red or white wines such as Cabernet Sauvignon or Chardonnay.

✦ **Effervescence.** The next step is to inspect the wine for carbonation. Generally, this examination is needed only for champagne and other sparkling wines. Some wines have a slight carbonation that may or may not be intentional. Examples of moderately carbonated wines include Fendant (a refreshing white wine common to Switzerland) and Moscato (a sweet and fruity white wine from the Piedmonte region of Italy).

Three characteristics of carbonation are important for determining quality. First is an inspection of bubble size. Bubbles can range in size from rough or large down to fine. Fine bubbles are an indication of a higher-quality fermentation and carbonation process. Second, the wine should be inspected to determine if the number of bubbles is appropriate for the type of carbonated wine; the quantity can be ranked from insufficient to numerous. Finally, the persistence of the bubbles, from short-lived to long-persistent, provides an indication of quality. Certainly if you are paying for a good bottle of sparking wine or champagne, you want one in which the bubbles have a long persistency.

The Smell of Wine: Olfactory Examination

Much of what is perceived as taste or flavor stems from our ability to smell. While humans have a substantial ability to smell, we also have the ability to tune out smells that are constantly present, so that we're not overwhelmed by all of the odors in the environment. As a result, over time we may become unable to identify some smells without a visual cue (such as the presence of the food generating the smell). This tendency can make it difficult for some people to identify specific smells in wine.

✦ **Nosing Steps.** To maximize your ability to identify aromas and bouquet in wine, you need to follow a simple process. First, fill the glass one-third full. This will allow you to properly swirl the wine and fully release aromas. Next, swirl the glass gently in a circular motion to release the aromatic compounds. Tilt the glass toward you and place your nose inside the bowl. Take one deep sniff, or three or four short sniffs, then remove your nose from the glass to consider the aroma. This is what is considered the "first nose" of the wine and is your first impression of the aroma. After swirling the wine a second time and allowing the aromas to open up more fully, you will follow the same smelling procedure. Did you notice a change in the aroma in this "second nose" of the wine compared to the first? Many times the aroma will be quite different the second time after the wine has had more time to breathe and be exposed to the air.

The aroma of a wine is often the subject of elaborate descriptions of wine that many times are included in the winemaker's notes on the bottle label or espoused by many wine enthusiasts—but can come across to many of us as pompous. The aroma wheel developed by Ann C. Noble can be very useful in determining categories of flavors and specific descriptions for each. For more information on the aroma wheel and to purchase plastic-laminated copies, you can go to Ann C. Noble's Web site at www.winearomawheel.com.

Other flavor considerations are the aroma's intensity, quality, and persistency. Intensity of aroma can range from weak to very aromatic. Quality of aroma can be described using six descriptors (which are not ranked): *elegant, ordinary, agreeable, disagreeable, complex,* and *simple*. Persistency of the aroma deals with how long the aroma sticks with you: after you smell the wine, does the aroma quickly fade from your senses or does it linger for some time?

◆ **Bouquet.** The terms *bouquet* and *aroma* are often used interchangeably. Strictly speaking, these mean two different things. *Aroma* refers to the smell of a young wine; it is also used generically when discussing the smell of wine. Aromas are developed either naturally based on the varietal or created due to the winemaking techniques used. *Bouquet* refers to the smell that develops once the wine is bottled. This can be a function of the aging process, and thus bouquet represents the smell of a mature wine. Basically, the concept of bouquet embraces any physical and chemical changes that impact the wine's smell once the wine is put into the bottle.[5]

◆ **Sipping, Swallowing, Spitting.** The act of tasting is fairly easy to describe in general terms, but in practice the specific technique varies from one taster to the next. Basically, wine is drawn into the mouth and brought into contact with different parts of the mouth and tongue. The liquid may be kept in contact with parts of the palate for a short period or a longer time. Tasters may make tongue and cheek movements as well as suck in a little or a lot of air to further aerate the wine. Then, some or the entire wine sample can be swallowed or spat out depending on the purpose of the tasting. For amateur or social events that involve wine tasting, there is generally little reason to spit out the wine during the tasting process. For tastings involving a specific sensory evaluation purpose and involving more than just a few wines, spitting is a necessary part of the process. In any tasting situation, the palate can quickly become fatigued. When the tasting involves alcohol, the ability to use our senses as an analytic tool quickly deteriorates. Sommeliers and other wine professionals may need to taste a couple of hundred wines each week. Swallowing all of that wine would have detrimental effects on their evaluation abilities as well as their health.

The Taste of Wine: Taste Examination In general, the primary taste components in wine include sweetness, acidity, and the balance between the two (and to a much lesser extent levels of saltiness and bitterness). There are also several tactile elements that provide important areas of differentiation, particularly in the wine and food matching process. These elements create a feeling of texture and body in wine and include tannin, alcohol level, and an assessment of overall body. The assessment of overall body is derived from tannin and alcohol but also the amount of extract and oak. Extract is the particles of fruit that remains in the finished wine and can create a more intense mouthfeel. Oak may be used in the process of aging wine and has an impact on a wine's body, color and flavor. Oak can be thought of as a winemaker's "marinade."[6] Depending on wine traditions in the region and preferences of the winemaker, wine can have no oak aging or substantial aging in oak. The amount of color, flavor, and body oak imparts to the finished wine is impacted by several variables: the length of time the wine is left in oak, the type of oak (typically American or French), the age of the barrels (how many times they have been used), the barrel size, and how dark the inside of the barrel has been "toasted."

Wine can also be evaluated on its flavor. Several factors are important to consider here. The first consideration is identifying the type or types of flavors present. This process is partially completed during the smell portion of the process but also during actual tasting process. Flavors can be identified as odors prior to taking any wine into the mouth. Flavors can also be identified in what is called a retronasal process.[7] As the wine enters the back of your mouth, you will be able to pick up flavors that are entering your nasal cavity from the interior of your mouth (recall your lack of ability to taste when you have a head cold).

◆ **Savoring.** Two other elements of flavor are needed during wine evaluation and in determining good wine and food matches: flavor intensity (that is, how weak or powerful the flavor elements are) and flavor persistence. It is important to consider flavor intensity in both wine and food so that both take center stage in the pairing process rather than one becoming a supporting partner. As with flavor intensity, a match of flavor persistency is important for the wine and food pairing process, but flavor persistency is also a primary indicator of wine quality. This is often called the length or finish of a wine. Basically, you are receiving a bigger bang for your buck when a good wine leaves a pleasant lingering flavor in your mouth. The assessment of flavor persistency is determined by the number of seconds that the pleasant taste and aroma lasts. Usually, this persistence will last somewhere between three and fifteen seconds.[8]

Other indicators of quality include a balanced flavor and texture, complexity level, and clean taste with no obvious faults.[9]

Psychological and Physiological Factors
A number of psychological factors can influence the perception of wine quality and taste characteristics: the taster's personality, external elements, and biases based on preconceived notions of a particular winemaker, type of wine, or region.

The methods used in sensory analysis are strictly controlled to maintain proper temperature, lighting, and minimize off odors. Techniques such as colored glassware and red lights can be used to eliminate psychological preferences for specific colors in wines and other food items. Visible textures in food and wine influence our perception of taste and flavor—for example, ice cream prepared in the same batch but presented both frozen and thawed will create differing perceptions of taste and flavor prior to actual tasting. Similarly, because tears in wine are perceived by many as a sign of quality, this visual indicator of texture may give tasters a preconceived notion of quality in the wine sample.

The Italian wine and food evaluation room at the Italian Culinary Institute for Foreign Professionals, Costigliole d'Asti, Italy (courtesy of the Italian Culinary Institute for Foreigners).

Marketing of wine—including bottle, cork (or other closure), and label—is a way of signaling to the customer that the product provides a certain level of value and meets a range of possible customer needs. These human needs are very complex and can range from social needs for fun and belonging, or esteem needs for prestige, to name a few. All of these psychological "hot buttons" can be pushed when tasting wine and viewing the wine bottle, label, and closure type. As astute observers, we need to minimize these effects by being aware of potential bias and neutralizing it as much as possible. This can be done by blind-tasting wines for quality and minimizing any discussion about the wines until everyone is finished evaluating them.

When all else fails, concentration and awareness of potential biases are key elements to minimize potential psychological issues. While you taste wine, you should do your best to ignore what is going on around you, the label, and the bottle. Instead, you should concentrate on creating a clear impression of the wine based on the developing sensations conveyed in the wine. It may be helpful to close your eyes and focus by using your nose, tongue, and palate to "see" the attributes contained in the wine. These attributes can easily be clouded by comments from "experts" surrounding you, the appearance of the wine bottle, or the closure used (that is, a screw cap as compared to a natural cork). A properly organized tasting session does everything possible to minimize the impact of these psychological factors.

There are a number of physiological pitfalls inherent in the tasting or sensory process. The first is the impact of adaptation. As discussed previously, our senses adapt to filter out continuous stimuli so that we can focus on what is changing in the environment. The same thing happens with taste, where the adaptation process is often called palate fatigue, and it is an important consideration when planning food or wine sensory exercises. Because of this, most experts suggest that no more than six to eight wines be evaluated in one session unless the tasting panel is highly skilled in sensory techniques.

A second factor is that differences occur between tasters in their thresholds of taste and smell. Substantial individual differences between perceived levels of sweetness, bitterness, and odor identification thresholds have been found. Another potential pitfall is odor blindness—where a person loses the ability to smell all odors or certain odors.

Other physiological factors that inhibit our ability to taste and smell include taste modifiers (such as orange juice, mouthwash, or toothpaste), serving temperature (colder temperatures decrease our perceptions of sweetness and body, mask odors, and increase our perception of acidity), and smoking.

SETTING UP A TASTING SESSION

The following tasting session set-up suggestions can assist in minimizing many of the issues identified as potential pitfalls.

The time of day has an impact on our ability to analyze wine elements. Generally, the late morning is when our senses are most acute. The physical setting also has a substantial impact. Having sufficient lighting (preferably natural) is a necessity. Bright colors in the room should be avoided, along with harsh lighting and shiny surfaces. In addition to appropriate lighting, a white background should be provided to allow true color depth and hues to be identified.

Glasses should be plain and unadorned, made from good-quality and relatively thin glass or crystal. The INAO (Institut National des Appellation d'Origine) wine-tasting glass is recognized as the standard. It has an egg-shaped bowl designed to enhance the concentration of aroma and allow the wine to be swirled without spilling. It is relatively inexpensive and can be purchased online or at local wine stores. The typical wine-tasting glass is about 6 to 7 inches tall (15–18 cm) and holds about 7 to 10 ounces of wine (20–30 cl).

Depending on the nature of the tasting, the room may be set up in what would normally be an office, classroom, or dining area. However, more professional organizations will install specially designed tasting rooms that allow tasters to sit down. In this situation, each taster has a separate booth with partitions at the side and front. To the left of the booth is a spittoon with running water to rinse the spittoon and for rinsing glasses. Most have a shelf to the front of the taster that allows for glasses and other equipment to be placed. The colors of the booth are usually neutral with a white background area in the center and some sort of small spotlight for inspecting color and clarity.

The sequence in which wines are served can have an impact on wine evaluation. For a consistent evaluation process, I recommend organizing the wine tasting much as you would the ordering of wines for an elegant wine and food dinner. In general, you should taste lighter wines before more full-bodied wines, lower-alcohol wines before higher-alcohol ones, whites before reds, lighter aromatic wines before powerful ones, and dryer wines before sweeter wines.

Temperature, of both the tasting room and the wine, is an important consideration in wine tasting. Temperature has a substantial influence on our senses. The thermal sensitivity of our mouth is primarily found above the thicker parts of our lips and on the tip of our tongue. These are the areas that typically come in first contact with things that we eat or drink and serve as a natural warning device. Most wine is tasted within the 50–68°F (10–20°C) range. When setting up a tasting, it is important to ensure that wines being compared are tasted at the same temperature, for temperature has a significant impact on the way that wine smells and tastes. It is also important to ensure that a consistent temperature is maintained throughout the evaluation process. Studies have shown that a variation of only 3–4°F can explain discrepancies in the amount of tannin indicated by tasters of red wine.[10] A more consistent temperature can be maintained by filling glasses no more than one-third full and topping them off as the tasting progresses. Wine in a bottle will warm up to room temperature more slowly than the wine in individual glasses. Wine poured in a glass that has an initial temperature at or below 50°F (10°C) will warm up about two degrees every four minutes. Wine poured at an initial temperature of 60°F (15°C) will warm up two degrees about every eight minutes.[11]

Many of the substances in wine that create odors are volatile in nature and evaporate quickly at higher temperatures. These substances fill the air space in the glass above wine and are why a wine's aroma and bouquet appears to be more enhanced at 60°F than at 50°F. Aroma and bouquet will be practically nonexistent at 45°F or below (about 8°C). Conversely, because of alcohol's evaporation process, any appeal in the bouquet is destroyed in wines that are tasted above 68°F. Perceivable wine faults also have a tendency to increase at higher temperatures and become minimized when tasted cold.

The best temperature for drinking wine may not be the same as the best temperature for tasting it. Professional tasting is generally completed with all wines between 59 and 68°F (15–20°C). This is quite different from the standard serving temperatures, shown in Table 2.1.

Any distraction caused by foreign odors can be a problem when trying to assess fleeting aromas in wine. The desired surroundings should be free from kitchen smells, tobacco smoke, and other odors. In social settings, this can be difficult to achieve. But tasters should do everything in their power to heighten their sensory abilities, including refraining from smoking a least an hour before a tasting (and certainly not during), washing your hands prior to tasting to remove possible odors, not wearing perfume or cologne, and allowing a sufficient amount of time after brushing your teeth, using mouthwash, or eating mint candies.

Most tasting occurs in some sort of group setting. Group tasting creates several potential problems when attempting a serious evaluation. Others' opinions can be valuable, but they also may give rise to errors if based on the wrong information. Studies have shown that members of a group are easily swayed to concur with other group members when that member is perceived to be knowledgeable.[12] Wine tasting is not an opinion survey, and discussion on tasting opinions should not be entered into until all members have been able to thoroughly evaluate each sample and reflect on their feelings. Thus, maintaining quiet during a wine tasting is essential (though it can be difficult if in a nonprofessional setting).

Each tasting sequence may have a number of different themes that address particular problems or areas of interest. These may include comparisons of two or more wines for preferences, to evaluate the impact of changes in winemaking techniques, to assess the impact of particular additives or the taste of a particular blend, and so on. In any case, all tasting situations pose either implicit or explicit questions, whether you taste for pleasure or for professional reasons.

These questions must be addressed prior to setting up any tasting exercise. For instance, the point of a pleasure tasting event may simply be to give a pleasurable experience to the consumer that appeals to people's sensual, cultural, and intellectual interests. On the other hand, professional tasting can be done to judge the influence of different root stocks on the final product, come to a decision about whether to grant or refuse the right to use an appellation of origin on a wine's label, award medals at competitions, and help a company make decisions about whether or not to sell a given product to the consumer.

THE ART AND SCIENCE OF WINE EVALUATION

The evaluation of wine and food is both an art and a science. The science portion of the evaluation process provides us with specific technique for improving the consistency of the process. It also provides a clear measurement of wine and food elements and the levels present or absent from a product. The art portion comes into play because most wine and food quality measures are based on a sense of balance and the interplay between character-

Table 2.1 Recommended Temperatures for Serving Wines with Food or Drinking

Wine Type	Temperature
Tannic red wines: Australian Shiraz, Cabernet Sauvignon, Rhône wines, vintage Port, Bordeaux, Châteauneuf-du-Pape	63–65°F/17–18°C
Medium-bodied red wines: southern French reds, southern Italian reds, Rioja, Toro, Pinot Noir, Valpolicella, young Chianti	58–61°F/14–16°C
Red wines with light tannin: young Beaujolais, red Sancerre, Bardolino, young Spanish and Portuguese reds	54–55°F/12–13°C
Fuller-bodied and aromatic white wines, sweet wines, rosés, Sherry and white Port: Chardonnay, Sauternes, Tokaji, white Rioja	48–50°F/9–10°C
Light, crisp and sparkling white wines: Alsace, Chablis, Riesling, good Champagne and sparkling wine, Sancerre, Sauvignon Blanc	45–46°F/7–8°C
Cheap sparkling wines	36–39°F/2–4°C

istics. The approach throughout this book is one of combining the art and science of wine and food evaluation.

The wine literature is littered with a wide variety of evaluation sheets and processes based on profiles, mathematical formulas, ranking systems, and descriptions. One attempt at a universal classification of wine types is based on the work of Pierre Coste.[13] Coste suggested four general categories of wine, based on the purpose of drinking as observed in his home country of France. The first category is what he termed the "French national drink." This style of drinking is where no real tasting takes place—wine is drunk as a matter of habit, used solely to moisten food and to quench one's thirst. The wines in this category are the simplest and most common in taste—generic table wines. The second category he terms "false fine wine." Drinkers in this category follow a blind faith in tradition and are considered "label drinkers"—the wine they consume has a significant history of origin but the current quality is illusory. The third category up the ladder is termed "good wines," and wines in this group are well balanced, attractive, and easy to drink. Generally, these wines are drunk young with a taste of fruit (in reds) and floral (in whites). The drinkers regard the enjoyment of wine as a real and uncomplicated pleasure. The top-level category is termed "fine wines," which can be thought of as works of art—unique and flawless. The drinking of these wines becomes almost a religious ritual event, and the process is reserved for the informed amateur and privileged gourmet.

While Coste's classification system provides an interesting point of differentiation for wines and those who drink them, his explanations have a ring of elitism to them. A more down-to-earth approach might be Zraly's classification of wines as either everyday wines, once-a-week wines, once-a-month wines, or once-a-year or special-occasion wines.[14] In this case, it acknowledges that those who drink wine may drink it for different purposes at different times. Therefore, low-cost wines of good relative quality and higher-cost wines at the higher end of the quality spectrum both have their place in our daily lives and routines. In my view, good values in wine should not be looked down upon but instead provide nice "lubrication" for daily enjoyment (in moderation, of course).

Evaluation Sheets The wine evaluation process and systems that are used to evaluate wines vary from relatively simple to complex. I have provided two examples of wine evaluation sheets at the end of this chapter. One is based on the Italian process (Figure 2.3,

Optional Wine Sensory Analysis Sheet) and one is a simpler evaluation sheet that allows you to assess a flight of three glasses of wine on one evaluation sheet (Figure 2.2, Wine Evaluation Sheet). In reviewing these two analysis sheets, you will find many similarities and some differences. The first similarity is that wine evaluation is a serious process. Much time and effort has been expended to create valid and reliable instruments to assess wine quality. Second, both include visual, olfactory, and taste evaluations, as well as an overall evaluation of harmony or balance.

There are also some distinct differences. The Figure 2.3 evaluation sheet is much more thorough and includes temperature considerations of both the wine and the room in which the tasting takes place. Based on our discussion earlier on the importance of proper organization of a tasting session, this would appear to be important information when assessing the outcomes of the tasting. The Figure 2.2 evaluation sheet is much more condensed and streamlined. The streamlined version allows for better evaluation across a group of wines, whereas the longer version increases the need for space in the tasting room to accomplish the same task.

The point is that a variety of tools exist for evaluating wine quality. All use similar language and analyze core areas of the wine. The choice of whether to use a more thorough version or a streamlined one depends on the purpose of the tasting and the experience of the evaluators. Feel free to use these and other tools at your next wine tasting or when enjoying a glass of wine. Which one seems to work best? Why?

Descriptions To review and reinforce the basics of wine evaluation, an end-of-chapter exercise (Exercise 2.2) focuses on distinct and identifiable differences of wine components, texture, and flavors. Table 2.2 provides a list of what are considered the classic wine grapes. These wines all come from vinifera varieties of grapes and make up the majority of quality wine sold across the globe.[15] While there are more than 5,000 grape varieties to choose from, there are about 150 that are commercially grown in significant amounts. There are a number of quality grape varietals, such as Zinfandel, Nebbiolo, Sangiovese, Petite Syrah, Vidal, Malbec, Pinot Grigio, Viognier, and so on, that may be personal favorites, but the nine listed below have stood the test of time as classics in vinifera wine production.

Exercise 2.2 features six varietals—three white and three red—that have been described as the "big six" wine grapes and make up the majority of varietal wines sold in North America.[16] These varietals include Riesling, Sauvignon Blanc, Chardonnay, Pinot Noir, Merlot, and Cabernet Sauvignon. While in North America, quality wines are named after the varietal (if containing at least 75 percent of that grape type in the United States), they can also be given a regional name or a brand name. Naming wines after the region is a typical practice of France, Italy, and Spain. Names such as Bordeaux, Champagne, and Chablis indicate wine-producing regions in France, and the AOC (*appellation d'origine contrôlée*) designates growing practices as well as grape varietals that are allowed to be used in the final product. Italian wines may be named after the region or in combination with the varietal

Table 2.2   Classic Varietals

White Wine Grapes	Red Wine Grapes
Chardonnay	Cabernet Sauvignon
Chenin Blanc	Merlot
Riesling	Pinot Noir
Sauvignon Blanc	Syrah (Shiraz)
Sémillon	

name (e.g., Moscato d'Asti or Nebbiolo d'Alba). Wines can also receive a brand name. The brand-name wines can be at the higher end of the price spectrum, such as Opus One or Dom Pérignon, or at the more moderate end, such as Blue Nun or Mateus. Brand names are generally blends of grape varieties but can also be blends of vintages (as is the case for the majority of Champagnes, which are nonvintage).

PALATE MAPPING

Since 1914, the primary taste components have been described as sweet, sour, bitter, and salty.[17] While recent research suggests that this is an oversimplification of the nature of taste, sensory researchers utilize these elements as primary tastes when evaluating edible products. Recent research suggests that taste elements may actually form a taste continuum rather than four separate and distinct elements, much like how we perceive color across a continuum or spectrum of color variations. Future research may delineate secondary taste components just as we are able to distinguish secondary and primary colors.[18] Some physiologists suggest other elements may exist in wine, such as oiliness, alkalinity, and fattiness.[19]

Researchers in Japan proposed a fifth element, umami (ooh-MOM-me). This element is not as dominant in Western cultures as it is in Eastern ones. The typical example of umami is the taste of soy sauce, but other examples include tomatoes, edamame, and monosodium glutamate. While very few question the existence of umami, most wine evaluators find little value in using it as an indicator for food and wine pairing or wine evaluation in general.[20]

While other elements may exist, the four-element model of primary taste components provides a useful framework to utilize in evaluating wine and food products. While individuals vary significantly in their sensitivities to these elements, it is rare for an individual to be unable to recognize these elements when they occur at above-normal levels.

The elements of sweet, sour, salty, and bitter are sensed in roughly the same locations on most people's tongues. Hence, it is important to evaluate how and where these taste elements are perceived in the mouth to enhance your ability to differentiate between acidity, bitterness, and astringency when these elements are combined in a wine or food item.

TASTING INSTRUCTIONS

Recent research indicates that the entire mouth experiences taste sensations. The taste within our mouth is thought to evolve as it goes from a stage of attack through evolution and finally to a final impression. The attack phase in wine usually lasts about two to three seconds and is generally dominated by any sweet tastes present. The evolution phase lasts an additional five to twelve seconds, with a progression from the dominant sweet character to the sensations of acidity and then bitterness. The final impression is dominated by any lasting effects of acidity and bitterness, which can last for anywhere from five seconds to over two minutes.[21] For this discussion and the exercises that follow, the focus is on tasting sweetness, saltiness, acidity, bitterness, and tannin (astringency).

Sweetness balances acidity in food and wine. It is generally the first component we perceive as it hits the tip of our tongue. A sweet sensation in wine can be derived from the presence of residual sugars or from the presence of alcohol or glycerin. One method to test your sensitivity to sweetness and to evaluate where you perceive it is to place some sugar crystals on your tongue and experience where it impacts your tongue and inside your mouth in general.

Saltiness is one of the primary taste components. Salt is vitally important in the seasoning of food items but, with few exceptions, it is present in wine at undetectable levels. Because salt is a taste enhancer, you will come to learn its effectiveness in enhancing wine and food pairings.

Acidity is present in food and wine. The right balance between sweetness and acidity is vital to white wines, as is the correct balance of sweetness, acidity, and tannins to red wines.[22] Your tongue reacts most strongly to acidity. Acidity creates a feeling of crispness in wine when present in sufficient levels. The absence or lack of acidity in wine creates a flat or "flabby" feeling in the mouth.

Bitterness is often confused with astringency. Astringency is created in wine through the presence of tannin. Astringency is defined by the tactile sensation of dryness and roughness throughout the mouth, while bitterness is associated with a bitter sensation on the back of one's tongue. When tasting bitter foods or solutions, you will notice how it affects your tongue and mouth. Like saltiness, bitterness is much less important to wine tasters and is usually present in high levels only in wines that have had substantial problems during processing or handling or in which the grapes were affected by a bacterial disease. However, bitter tastes in food can complement or contrast with characteristics in wine. Bitter beverages include products such as Campari or Angostura bitters. Bitter foods include radicchio and the white pithy parts of citrus peels.

In daily eating and drinking, tea provides a great example of tannin. The next time you drink a cup of tea, notice how it creates a slight puckery feeling in your mouth and inside your cheeks. Then allow the tea to become cold and taste it again. Did the puckery feelings increase? Now add some milk to the tea. Did the puckery feeling decrease? This lessening effect illustrates the interaction between tannin and fattiness in food that features in the classic relationship between young red wines and dishes made from beef or lamb.

Research suggests that the astringent characteristics in tannins increase with colder temperatures. This could be one reason why red wines, which generally have more tannin than white wines, are served at warmer temperatures than their white wine counterparts. The astringent effects of tannin in wine can range from nonexistent to very high.

SUMMARY

The food-and-wine pairing process combines techniques derived from the general sensory literature, the wine evaluation literature, and the culinary arts literature. The heart of the process relies on sensory evaluation techniques, defined as a systematic approach used to induce, quantify, analyze and assess responses to food and wine products based on what is perceived through the senses of sight, smell, taste, touch, and hearing. This chapter provides an overview of this process as applied to wine evaluation. Wine evaluation encompasses a visual examination, olfactory examination and taste examination.

When setting up a sensory tasting of wine or food, it is important to consider both physiological and psychological factors that may impact the outcome. Some of these factors include temperature, room lighting, extraneous odors, talking during the process, and time of day.

The exercises at the end of this chapter will arm you with tools to clearly identify the primary taste characteristics in wine and food (sweet, sour, bitter, and salty) as well as to differentiate bitterness from astringency. The wine evaluation exercise will allow you to reinforce previous experiences in wine tasting and provide a clear differentiation of the most common wine varietals based on color, smell, body, and taste.

DISCUSSION QUESTIONS

1. Define sensory analysis.

2. What are the six S's of wine evaluation?

3. What are the proper serving temperatures of various red and white wines? Why?

4. Where on the tongue do you perceive the tastes of sweet, sour, bitter, and salty? Does everyone perceive them in the same location on the tongue?

EXERCISE 2.1

TASTING SWEETNESS, SOURNESS, BITTERNESS, SALTINESS, AND TANNIN

Recent research indicates that the entire mouth experiences taste sensations. Take this opportunity to individually map your own palate according to where you taste the basic four components of sweetness, saltiness, acidity, and bitterness. Additionally, the tannin evaluation portion of this exercise will allow you to identify the difference between the taste sensation of bitterness and the tactile all-over-the-mouth sensation of tannin.

Sweetness is generally the first component you perceive as it hits the tip of your tongue. The sweetness in wine can be derived from the presence of residual sugars or from the presence of alcohol or glycerin. Saltiness is one of the primary taste components in food. Salt is vitally important in the seasoning of food items but, with few exceptions, is present in wine at undetectable levels. Salt is a taste enhancer, and you will come to learn its positive and sometimes negative impact on wine and food pairings. Acidity is present in food and wine. Acidity creates a feeling of crispness or tartness in wine when present in sufficient levels. Often it is described as a refreshing or "electric" feeling on the sides of the tongue.

Bitterness is often confused with astringency. Astringency is a tactile sensation of puckeriness throughout the mouth, while bitterness is a sensation at the back of the tongue. When tasting bitter foods or solutions, you will notice how it affects your tongue and mouth. Tannin is present in most red wines and to a much lesser extent in white wines that have been aged in oak. To evaluate the level of tannin, you will assess the amount of drying and rough feeling in your mouth and inside your cheeks.

OBJECTIVES

The main goal of this exercise is to provide an introduction to the identification of the basic four sensory components: sweetness, saltiness, sourness, and bitterness. After completing it, you will be introduced to tannin and understand the difference between tannin (astringency) and bitterness. The exercise allows you to locate where you sense the four basic taste sensations of sweetness, acidity, saltiness, and bitterness on your palate. While tasting for acidity, you will be introduced to four different types of acid, including tartaric acid, malic acid, citric acid, and acetic acid.

Mise en Place: Things to Do Before the Exercise Review the sections of this chapter describing the primary taste components. Assemble the following ingredients and materials.

MATERIALS NEEDED

Table 2.3   Materials Needed for Exercise 2.1

Sweetness: ¼ tsp (1 g) sugar granules per student Solution of 1 c (225 g) sugar to 1 qt (.95 l) water	Saltiness: ¼ tsp (1 g) table salt per student Solution of 1 c (225 g) salt to 1 qt (.95 l) water
Acidity: 4 T (60 g) cream of tartar to 3 c (710 ml) of water (tartaric) ¼ tsp (1.25 ml) distilled white vinegar per student (acetic) 1 qt (.95 l) apple juice (malic) 1 lemon slice per student Solution of lemon juice to 1 qt (.95 ml) water (citric)	Bitterness: ¼ tsp (1 gram) ground coffee or instant coffee granules per student 1 c (240 ml) water/100 drops of bitters Solution of 1 c (240 ml) coffee diluted in 1 qt (.95 l) water Tannin: 1 qt (.95 l) strong unsweetened tea
1 paper plate per student 9 sample cups per student	15 stalks of celery (to cleanse the palate), cut into pieces
1 tasting instruction sheet with tongue diagram	1 spit cup per student

Source: Adapted from J. Robinson, *How to Taste: A Guide to Enjoying Wine* (New York: Simon and Schuster, 2000), 17–26; D. H. Cook, "The Tongue . . . A Sense of Taste" (2000), www.iit.edu/~smile/bi9105.html (accessed August 15, 2004).

STEPS

1. Make sure the cups of solution samples are distributed to each member of the tasting group and provide each member with a paper plate divided into five sections. On the plate place the salt granules, a lemon wedge, the sugar, the coffee, and bite-sized pieces of celery.

2. Have each person taste each of the first four items and identify each item as being salty, sour, sweet, or bitter by writing it on the paper plate.

3. The celery (you could substitute bread or crackers) should be chewed between the samples to thoroughly cleanse the palate.

4. Distribute the palate tasting sheet with tongue diagram (Figure 2.1, Palate Mapping Exercise: Tongue Diagram).

5. Taste each of the solution samples, cleansing the palate between each sample. Hold the sample in your mouth, exposing all areas of the mouth, including the top of the palate and under the tongue. You may swallow the sample or spit it out.

6. Indicate on the tongue diagram where you experience each taste sensation the most in your mouth. Also, record any further observations in the area provided.

   a. *Sweetness.* Taste the sample. Using the tongue diagram, mark where you sense sweetness the most. Use additional space to record observations of any other area in your mouth that you perceive sweetness.

   b. *Bitterness.* It is important to know where you will experience bitterness on your palate. Taste the bitter solution and indicate on the diagram and in your notes where you experience the bitter flavor the most on your palate.

   c. *Saltiness.* Taste the saline solution. As before, concentrate on your palate to figure out where you experience the sensation of saltiness the most and indicate the location on the diagram. Use the space provided to record where you observe the taste of salt elsewhere on your palate.

   d. *Acidity.* Taste each of the samples and discern where you sense them the most on your palate. Diagram where you taste the different types of acidity on the tongue. By familiarizing yourself with these acid types, you'll be better prepared to discern them in wines. Record your observations in your notes and compare the difference between this and bitterness.

   e. *Tannins.* Now taste the tannic solution. Notice the puckery or drying feeling in your mouth and inside your cheeks. Record your observations in your notes and compare the difference between this and your notes on acidity and bitterness.

Now that you've mapped your palate, the next time you taste for a specific component in a dish or wine, you'll want to recall your experience. In order to detect and validate the taste components, be sure to expose the part of your palate that is most sensitive to the specific component while tasting.

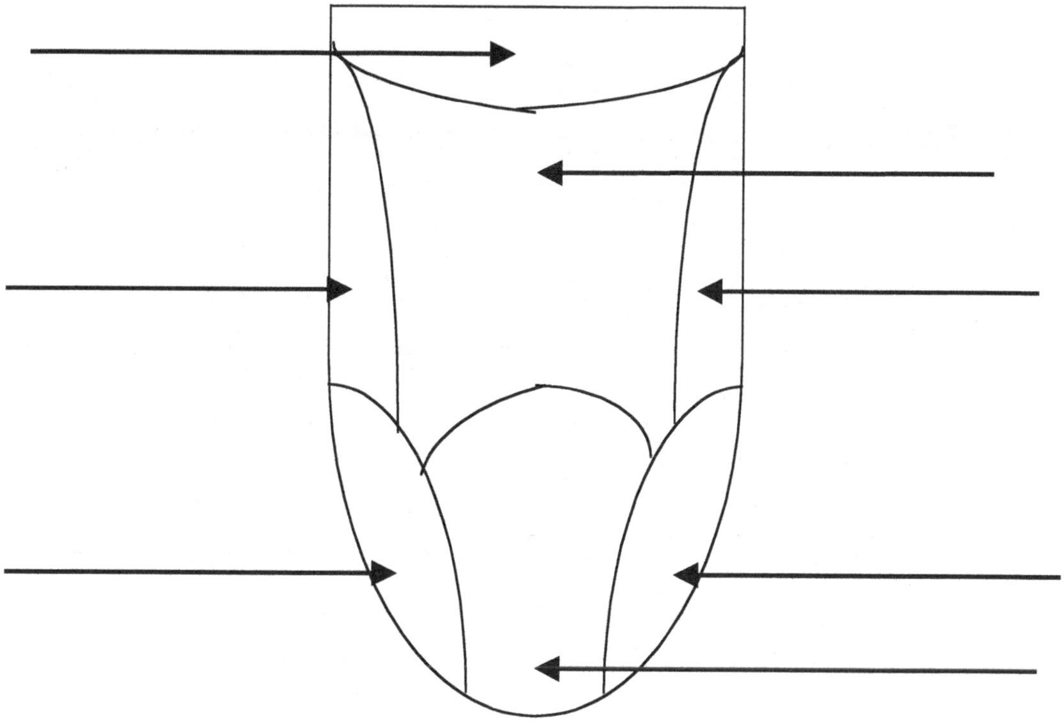

Figure 2.1

Palate Mapping Exercise—Tongue Diagram

Observations:

EXERCISE 2.2

TASTING THE MAJOR VARIETALS: BASICS OF WINE EVALUATION AND DIFFERENTIATION IN WINE COMPONENTS, TEXTURES, AND FLAVORS

Wine selection can be a daunting task without a clear understanding of varietals' typical characteristics.

While some sixty types of vinifera grapes exist, the most common wine grapes from vinifera vines are Chardonnay, Chenin Blanc, Riesling, Sauvignon Blanc, Sémillon, Cabernet Sauvignon, Merlot, Pinot Noir, and Syrah (Shiraz). These varietals can be further narrowed in the North American market to what some call the "big six."[23] These six varietals make up the vast majority of quality wines sold in North America and provide a great example of the spectrum of wine styles from light-bodied and fruity to full-bodied and intense. The six wines evaluated in this exercise are Riesling, Sauvignon Blanc, Chardonnay, Pinot Noir, Merlot, and Cabernet Sauvignon.

OBJECTIVES

1. To introduce the distinctive characteristics of the individual grape samples that constitute 80 percent of the quality wines sold in the United States, including three whites (Riesling, Sauvignon Blanc, and Chardonnay) and three reds (Pinot Noir, Merlot, and Cabernet Sauvignon).

2. To introduce and understand the importance of body. How to identify body visually and by tasting wine.

3. To allow students to identify their initial favorites from this group of wine varietals.

4. To instill a deeper knowledge of the typical elements of the six major varietals. This knowledge will provide greater immediate knowledge when shopping for wine and selecting wine on a wine list.

Mise en Place: Things to Do Before the Exercise Review the sections of this chapter describing wine evaluation (the six S's—seeing, swirling, smelling, sipping, spitting or swallowing, and savoring). Assemble the following ingredients and materials. Before evaluating the wines, wash your hands to remove any distracting odors. Review the section on setting up a tasting session. Follow these general guidelines to ensure the room is properly prepared for a tasting session.

MATERIALS NEEDED

Select wine samples for each of the varietals listed below:

Table 2.4 Materials for Exercise 2.2

Body Style	White	(Wine choice)	Red	(Wine Choice)
Light	Riesling		Pinot Noir	
Medium	Sauvignon Blanc		Merlot	
Full	Chardonnay		Cabernet Sauvignon	
1 white paper placemat per student with numbered circles to place wineglasses			Crackers to cleanse the palate	
1 spit cup per student			Napkins	
Corkscrew			Drinking water for each student	
1 copy of the Aroma Wheel per student			6 wineglasses per student	
1 glossary of wine terms per student			1 tasting instruction sheet for each student	

STEPS

1. Buy the wines.

2. Set up the glasses using the placemats (Figures 2.4a, b) in the following order:

3. Open the wines and pour about one-ounce servings in number order. To maintain a proper temperature in whites, you may want to pour each wine individually or group them by whites and then reds for initial evaluation.

4. Following the wine evaluation sheet outline (Figure 2.2 or Figure 2.3), complete the information for each wine: wine type/category, wine producer, vintage, date, and temperature.

5. Taste the wines in number order. Make sure all tasters are working quietly on each wine sample.

6. Using the tasting instructions, aroma wheel, and glossary at the end of the text, take notes about your personal observations in order to train yourself to recognize the wine's characteristics.

TASTING INSTRUCTIONS

WHITE WINES

Riesling (Number 1)

- *Sight.* Visually inspect the wine. What is the color and clarity? The typical color of Riesling is pale yellow-green.

- *Swirl and smell.* Inspect the viscosity and smell the aroma (follow the nosing instructions). What aromas can you identify? Close your eyes and smell the sample; write down any descriptive associations that you pick up. These may be typical

Table 2.5 Six Wine Varietals in Ascending Order

1	2	3	4	5	6
Riesling	Sauvignon Blanc	Chardonnay	Pinot Noir	Merlot	Cabernet Sauvignon

associations, such as tree fruits (apples, pears, etc.), or less traditional ones, such as lychee fruits or Jolly Rancher watermelon candy. After you have determined the impression of the aroma identity, see if you can match it to those on the aroma wheel.

- *Sip and spit/swallow.* What stands out as dominant elements in this wine?
- *Savor.* How intense is the wine? How long is its finish? Does it have any spicy characteristics?

    Make notes about your observations. Pay particular attention to sweetness level, acidity level, lack of tannins, body, flavor intensity, finish, and dominant flavors.

    Riesling is light-bodied and, generally, loaded with fruity aromas and flavors. Can you identify the fruit aromas and flavors? Riesling is best grown in cooler climates, providing a balance between residual sugar and acidity.

Sauvignon Blanc (Number 2)

- *Sight.* Visually inspect the wine. What is the color and clarity? The typical color is straw yellow. Does this sample match this description? Is it lighter or darker in color than the Riesling?
- *Swirl and smell.* Inspect the viscosity and smell the aroma. What aromas can you identify? Close your eyes and smell the sample; write down any descriptive associations. This varietal is typically powerful and distinctive. Typical associations in Sauvignon Blanc can be grassy, pungent, and herbaceous. More specific descriptions such as canned asparagus, green pepper, or hay are also common. After you have identified the aroma, see if you can match it to those on the aroma wheel.
- *Smell the Riesling again.* Is the contrast subtle or unmistakable?
- *Sip and spit/swallow.* What stands out as dominant elements in this wine? Is it fuller-bodied than the Riesling? It should feel a bit heavier and richer in your mouth. Record your observations. The distinctive, pungent taste of Sauvignon Blanc should be easily recorded in your sensory memory bank.
- *Savor.* How intense is the wine? How long is its finish? Does it have any spicy characteristics?

    Make notes about your observations. Pay particular attention to sweetness, acidity, lack of tannins, body, flavor intensity, finish, and dominant flavors.

Chardonnay (Number 3)

- *Sight.* Visually inspect the wine. What is the color and clarity? The color should be more of a yellow-gold and darker than the other two white wines.
- *Swirl and smell.* Inspect the viscosity and smell the aroma. The viscosity will be heavier than the previous two wines. What aromas can you identify? Close your eyes and smell the sample; write down any descriptive associations. From the aroma, you will sense that the Chardonnay is fuller-bodied than the Sauvignon Blanc or Riesling. Do you smell oak, smoke, vanilla, or butter? What fruit aromas can you identify?
- *Sip and spit/swallow.* What stands out as dominant elements in this wine? Taste and feel the difference in body. The Chardonnay is richer and heavier than the Riesling or Sauvignon Blanc.
- *Savor.* How intense is the wine? How long is its finish? Does it have any spicy characteristics?

    Make notes about your observations. Pay particular attention to sweetness, acidity, lack of tannins, body, flavor intensity, finish, and dominant flavors.

RED WINES

Pinot Noir (Number 4)

- *Sight.* Visually inspect the wine. What is the color and clarity? Tilt the glass against the white placemat. The wine should be relatively translucent. It is lighter-colored than the Merlot and Cabernet Sauvignon samples. This is a typical characteristic of Pinot Noir wines.
- *Swirl and smell.* Inspect the viscosity and smell the aroma. Is the viscosity heavier or lighter than the previous wines? What aromas can you identify? Close your eyes and smell the sample; write down any descriptive associations.
- *Sip and spit/swallow.* What stands out as dominant elements in this wine? Taste and feel the difference in body and tannin compared to the white wines.
- *Savor.* How intense is the wine? How long is its finish? Does it have any spicy characteristics?

    Make notes about your observations. Pay particular attention to sweetness, acidity, lack of tannins, body, flavor intensity, finish, and dominant flavors. Pinot Noir should have a silky texture; many tasters describe Pinot Noir as having a red wine flavor with a white wine texture. Pinot Noir is the lightest-bodied of the red grapes in this grouping.

Merlot (Number 5)

- *Sight.* Visually inspect the wine. What is the color and clarity? Tilt the glass against the white placemat. The deeper color indicates a fuller-bodied wine than the previous examples. What else does the darker color indicate?
- *Swirl and smell.* Inspect the viscosity and smell the aroma. What aromas can you identify? Close your eyes and smell the sample; write down any descriptive associations. Notice the aroma is more intense than the Pinot Noir's—an indication of a fuller-style wine.
- *Sip and spit/swallow.* What stands out as dominant elements in this wine? Taste and feel the difference in body. Do you notice a more puckery sensation? How would you describe its intensity? The Merlot is obviously richer and heavier than the Pinot Noir.
- *Savor.* How intense is the wine? How long is its finish? Does it have any spicy characteristics?

     Make notes about your observations. Pay particular attention to a lack of acidity, tannins, alcohol level, body, flavor intensity, finish, and dominant flavors.

Cabernet Sauvignon (Number 6)

- *Sight.* Visually inspect the wine. What is the color and clarity? Is it darker than the previous wines? Some Cabernet is almost inky in color. Cabernet is naturally dark and full-bodied.
- *Swirl and smell.* Inspect the viscosity and smell the aroma. What aromas can you identify? Close your eyes and smell the sample; write down any descriptive associations. Is it stronger and more intense than you expected?
- *Sip and spit/swallow.* What stands out as dominant elements in this wine? Taste and feel the difference in body. Is the puckery sensation greater than that of the Merlot?
- *Savor.* How would you describe its intensity?

     Record your observations of its intensity and lingering effect on your mouth.

RANKING THE MAJOR VARIETALS

     Once you have evaluated the six wines, go back and rank-order them in terms of components, texture, and flavors.

1. *Dry to sweet.* Rank the wines from driest to sweetest. This is not always as straightforward as it might seem. The interaction of acidity and residual sugar can balance and lessen our initial impression of sweetness. Recall the palate mapping exercise. Where did you identify the sweet sensation on your tongue? Alcohol can also be perceived as sweetness on the tip of the tongue. Evaluate the warm sensation to sort out residual sugar from alcohol.
Driest = 1. _____ 2. _____ 3. _____
         4. _____ 5. _____ 6. _____ = Sweetest

2. *Acidity (crispness).* Rank the wines from least tart to most tart (acidic). Be sure to try to separate acidity from bitterness and astringency. Here again recall the location of acidity, bitterness, and astringency sensation from the palate-mapping exercise.
Least tart = 1. _____ 2. _____ 3. _____
         4. _____ 5. _____ 6. _____ = Most tart

3. *Tannin.* Rank the wines from no tannin to high tannin. Focus on the puckery sensation throughout your mouth. Can you determine differing levels of astringency in these wine samples?
No tannin = 1. _____ 2. _____ 3._____
         4. _____ 5. _____ 6. _____ = Highest tannin

4. *Body.* Rank the wines from lightest body to heaviest body. Inspect the viscosity and color for clues. How heavy does the body feel in your mouth? Think of dairy products—is the mouthfeel similar to skim milk, 2 percent milk, whole milk, half and half, or heavy cream?
Lightest body = 1. _____ 2. _____ 3. _____
         4. _____ 5. _____ 6. _____ = Heaviest body

5. *Flavor intensity.* Rank the wines from least intense to most intense flavor. Would you describe the flavor intensity as having no flavor, having weak flavor, moderate intensity, intense, or powerful?
Weakest flavor = 1. _____ 2. _____ 3. _____
         4. _____ 5. _____ 6. _____ = Most intense

6. *Flavor persistence.* Rank the wines for length of finish from least persistent to most persistent flavor. After swallowing or spitting out each wine sample, see how long you can identify the dominant flavor(s) in your mouth: 3 seconds or less, 4–6 seconds, 7–9 seconds, 10–12 seconds, or 13 seconds or more.
Least persistent = 1. _____ 2. _____ 3. _____
         4. _____ 5. _____ 6. _____ = Most persistent

7. *Dominant flavor(s)*. Taste each wine sample and identify the dominant flavor and category below.

Riesling dominant flavor(s) _____

Mark with an X all flavor categories that apply to the Riesling:
Fruity ___ Nutty ___ Smoky ___ Buttery ___ Herbal ___ Floral ___ Earthy ___ Other ___

Sauvignon Blanc dominant flavor(s) _____

Mark with an X all flavor categories that apply to the Sauvignon Blanc:
Fruity ___ Nutty ___ Smoky ___ Buttery ___ Herbal ___ Floral ___ Earthy ___ Other ___

Chardonnay dominant flavor(s) _____

Mark with an X all flavor categories that apply to the Chardonnay:
Fruity ___ Nutty ___ Smoky ___ Buttery ___ Herbal ___ Floral ___ Earthy ___ Other ___

Pinot Noir dominant flavor(s) _____

Mark with an X all flavor categories that apply to the Pinot Noir:
Fruity ___ Nutty ___ Smoky ___ Buttery ___ Herbal ___ Floral ___ Earthy ___ Other ___

Merlot dominant flavor(s) _____

Mark with an X all flavor categories that apply to the Merlot:
Fruity ___ Nutty ___ Smoky ___ Buttery ___ Herbal ___ Floral ___ Earthy ___ Other ___

Cabernet Sauvignon dominant flavor(s) _____

Mark with an X all flavor categories that apply to the Cabernet:
Fruity ___ Nutty ___ Smoky ___ Buttery ___ Herbal ___ Floral ___ Earthy ___ Other ___

8. Write any other comments, thoughts and observations that you identified during this evaluation process:

_____

_____

_____

_____

_____

_____

Sample #_____

Wine_____ Producer_____ Year_____

Visual   **Clarity:**   Cloudy--------About Clear--------Clear--------Crystal Clear---------Brilliant

                Color: *White:* Colorless---Green-tinge---Straw-Yell----Yell-Gold----Deep Gold----Amber/Brn

                           Red: Purple------Ruby Red----Deep Red---Red/Brn----Mahogany-----Brown

Aroma _____

Taste   **Sweetness:**   Bone Dry-------Dry-------Medium Dry-------Sweet------Very Sweet
                Acidity: Cloying-------Flabby (Flat)-----Crisp---------Tart (Green)------Acidic

                Oak: No Oak---------Slight Oak-----------Moderate Oak------------High Oak

Tactile Sensations   **Tannin:**   Lacking-------Some----------Enough--------Strong-------Astringent

                Alcohol: Light-------Little Warmth------Enough-------Warm-------High Alcohol

                Body: Thin---------Light---------Medium-------Full Bodied---------Heavy

Flavor and Other Observations:

Sample #_____

Wine_____ Producer_____ Year_____

Visual   **Clarity:**   Cloudy--------About Clear--------Clear--------Crystal Clear---------Brilliant

                Color: *White:* Colorless---Green-tinge---Straw-Yell----Yell-Gold----Deep Gold----Amber/Brn

                           Red: Purple------Ruby Red----Deep Red---Red/Brn----Mahogany-----Brown

Aroma _____

Taste   **Sweetness:**   Bone Dry-------Dry-------Medium Dry-------Sweet------Very Sweet
                Acidity: Cloying   Flabby (Flat)   Crisp---------Tart (Green)------Acidic

                Oak: No Oak---------Slight Oak-----------Moderate Oak------------High Oak

Tactile Sensations   **Tannin:**   Lacking-------Some----------Enough--------Strong-------Astringent

                Alcohol: Light-------Little Warmth------Enough-------Warm-------High Alcohol

                Body: Thin---------Light---------Medium-------Full Bodied---------Heavy

Flavor and Other Observations:

Sample #_____

Wine_____ Producer_____ Year_____

Visual   **Clarity:**   Cloudy--------About Clear--------Clear--------Crystal Clear---------Brilliant

                Color: *White:* Colorless---Green-tinge---Straw-Yell----Yell-Gold----Deep Gold----Amber/Brn

                           Red: Purple------Ruby Red----Deep Red---Red/Brn----Mahogany-----Brown

Aroma _____

Taste   **Sweetness:**   Bone Dry-------Dry-------Medium Dry-------Sweet------Very Sweet
                Acidity: Cloying-------Flabby (Flat)-----Crisp---------Tart (Green)------Acidic

                Oak: No Oak---------Slight Oak-----------Moderate Oak------------High Oak

Tactile Sensations   **Tannin:**   Lacking-------Some----------Enough--------Strong-------Astringent

                Alcohol: Light-------Little Warmth------Enough-------Warm-------High Alcohol

                Body: Thin---------Light---------Medium-------Full Bodied---------Heavy

Flavor and Other Observations:

Figure 2.2

Wine Evaluation Sheet

Participant_____   Wine Temperature _____
Wine Category_____ Number ____   Ambient Temperature _____
Wine Denomination _____   Date_____ Hour_____
_____ Vintage_____ Location_____

Visual

Clarity: Cloudy--------About Clear--------Clear--------Crystal Clear---------Brilliant

Color: *White:* Colorless---Green-tinge---Straw-Yell----Yell-Gold----Deep Gold----Amber/Brn

Red: Purple------Ruby Red----Deep Red---Red/Brn----Mahogany-----Brown

Consistency: Fluid----Some Consistency---Enough Consistency---Strong Consistency---Viscous

Effervescence: *Bubble size:* Rough/Large-------Fine Enough-------Fine

# of Bubbles: Insufficient----------Enough----------Numerous

Persistence: Short-lived-----Persistent Enough-----Long Persistency

Observations_____

Olfactory

Intensity: Devoid-------Little-------Enough--------Intense-------High Intensity

Persistence: Devoid-------Little-------Enough------Persistency-----High Persistency

Quality: Common------Fair---------Pleasant-------Fine----------Excellent

Aroma Description_____

Observations_____

Taste

Sweetness: Bone Dry-------Dry-------Medium Dry-------Sweet------Very Sweet

Acidity: Cloying-------Flabby (Flat)-----Crisp---------Tart (Green)------Acidic

Alcohol: Light-------Little Warmth------Enough-------Warm-------High Alcohol

Tannin: Lacking--------Some-----------Enough--------Strong------Astringent

Softness: Rigid----------Little----------Enough----------Soft----------Past Soft

Salty/Mineral: Devoid--------Some----------Enough---------Strong--------Very Salty

General Structure: Lean---------Weak---------Sufficient--------Sturdy---------Heavy

Balance: Little------------Enough------------Equilibrium

Intensity: Devoid------Little-----Enough------Intense------Very Intense

Persistence: Short------Little------Enough-----Persistent-----Highly Persistent

Quality: Common-----Fair-------Pleasant-------Fine---------Excellent

Flavor

Final Considerations

Harmony: Little---------Enough----------Complete

Evolutionary State: Immature----Young----Ready----Mature----Old

Approach to Typology_____

Observations:

Figure 2.3

Optional Wine Sensory Analysis Sheet

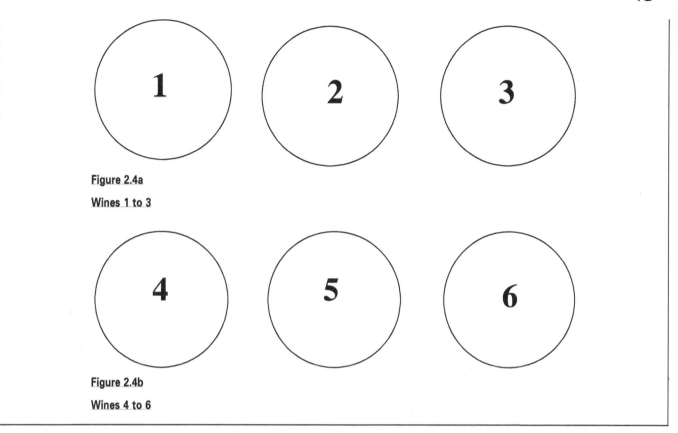

Figure 2.4a

Wines 1 to 3

Figure 2.4b

Wines 4 to 6

NOTES

1. E. Peynaud, *The Taste of Wine: The Art and Science of Wine Appreciation*, 2nd ed. (New York: John Wiley and Sons, 1996), 19.
2. W. A. Schmid, *The Hospitality Manager's Guide to Wine, Beers, and Spirits* (Upper Saddle River, NJ: Prentice-Hall, 2004).
3. Peynaud, *The Taste of Wine*.
4. A. Lichine, *Alexis Lichine's New Encyclopedia of Wines & Spirits* (New York: Alfred A. Knopf, 1987).
5. M. A. Amerine and E. B. Roessler, *Wines: Their Sensory Evaluation* (San Francisco: W. H. Freeman and Company, 1976); M. W. Baldy, *The University Wine Course*, 3rd ed. (San Francisco: Wine Appreciation Guild, 2003).
6. Andrea Immer, *Great Wine Made Simple: Straight Talk from a Master Sommelier* (New York: Broadway Books, 2000).
7. Baldy, *The University Wine Course*; Peynaud, *The Taste of Wine*.
8. Peynaud, *The Taste of Wine*.
9. Peynaud, *The Taste of Wine*; J. Robinson, *How to Taste: A Guide to Enjoying Wine* (New York: Simon & Schuster, 2000).
10. Peynaud, *The Taste of Wine*.
11. Ibid.
12. Ibid.
13. Ibid.
14. K. Zraly, *Windows on the World Complete Wine Course* (New York: Sterling Publishing Company, 2003).
15. K. MacNeil, *The Wine Bible* (New York: Workman Publishing Company. 2001).
16. Immer, *Great Wine Made Simple*.
17. Peynaud, *The Taste of Wine*.
18. Ibid.
19. Robinson, *How to Taste*.
20. Andrea Immer, *Great Tastes Made Simple: Extraordinary Food and Wine Pairing for Every Palate* (New York: Broadway Books, 2002); Peynaud, *The Taste of Wine*.
21. Peynaud, *The Taste of Wine*.
22. Ibid.
23. Immer, *Great Wine Made Simple*.

CHAPTER 3

GASTRONOMIC IDENTITY: THE EFFECT OF THE ENVIRONMENT AND CULTURE ON PREVAILING COMPONENTS, TEXTURE, AND FLAVORS IN WINE AND FOOD

CHAPTER OUTLINE:

Introduction

Aperitif: How Should Menus and Wine Lists Be Organized?

The Environment

Wine: The Impact of Geography and Climate

Culture

History and Ethnic Diversity

Trial and Error, Innovations, and Capabilities

Gastronomic Identity

Old World and New World

Summary

Exercises

KEY CONCEPTS:

- Heat summation units
- Climate zones
- Flavor profiles
- Macroclimates, mesoclimates, and microclimates
- Appellations
- American Viticultural Areas
- Prohibition
- Terroir
- Classic wine and food marriages

45

INTRODUCTION

G*astronomy* has been defined in a variety of ways, including guidance on proper food and drink, a historical topic, and a reflection of a society's culture.[1] For our purposes, *gastronomy* is defined as relating to historical, cultural, and environmental impacts on the "how, where, when and why of eating and drinking."[2]

The how, where, when, and why of eating and drinking is important to society and all participants in the foodservice industry. Knowledge of appropriate combinations of food and drink is important to those experiencing the combinations as well as those designing and preparing them. While many of the Old World cultures have a history of identifying and defining their gastronomy, North America has just begun to do so. Only in the last twenty-five years has the idea of culinary identity been promoted in locations across this large continent. While culinary identity stresses the use of local ingredients and identifies the impact of a variety of cultures on food, it does not provide for a discussion of the additional layering possibilities of taste, texture, and flavors provided by the "copilot" in this equation—drink.

The concept of gastronomic identity illustrates the influences of the environment (geography and climate) and culture (history and ethnic influences) on prevailing taste components, textures, and flavors in food and drink. The objective of this chapter is to begin to flesh out the idea of gastronomic identity, show its value, and provide a jumping-off point for further discussion.

Why is this discussion important? Gastronomic identity has significant consequences for successful wine tourism, culinary tourism, and the introduction of history as a value-added feature of these tourism products. Further, as a point of discussion, it allows us to more clearly articulate the "product" that is provided by firms in the wine and culinary industries.

Danhi suggested that six main elements are critical in determining a country's "culinary identity": geography, history, ethnic diversity, culinary etiquette, prevailing flavors, and recipes.[3] Geography is a defining factor in gastronomic identity, as it is critical in determining the definitive pantry of a specific region—the wine grapes that can be grown, indigenous food products, and staple agricultural products that are readily available. Historical events have a significant impact on identifiable characteristics through the introduction of ad-

ditional ingredients, cooking techniques, traditional methods of viticulture, and winemaking methods to a region. The ethnic diversity in a particular location has a profound impact on the traditional foods prepared and the fusion of cuisines that creates unique and identifiable products over time. Ethnic diversity also impacts viticulture and winemaking techniques brought into the area from home countries. This diversity changes over time and creates a continuous evolution of wine and food products based on a fusion of perspectives and cultures. Danhi refers to culinary etiquette as another identifier of a regional cuisine, defining it by how and what a particular culture eats. The four basic taste characteristics of sweet, sour, bitter, and salty (and what is the fifth to some people, umami) provide a range of prevailing flavor profiles to identify gastronomic characteristics and preferences in wine and food items. Finally, the recipes in a locale or region provide defining elements through the use of available ingredients, techniques, and presentations.

Recipes can also be thought of as a winemaking concept. Winemakers need to consider the proper blend of grapes both by varietal and selection as well as the preparation techniques during fermentation and aging. This is the same basic thought process considered in food recipes—but it may be more closely akin to baking or pastry production, given its more scientific nature.

The culinary identity concept has been utilized successfully in all segments of the foodservice industry, providing many firms with a "barrier to imitation" from competitors—a competitive hurdle that is difficult for rivals to duplicate.[4] For example, U.S. firms have been successful at utilizing a Louisiana heritage perspective in restaurants ranging from quick service (Popeye's Chicken and Biscuits) to fine dining (Chef John Folse's Bittersweet Plantation, Commander's Palace). This identity perspective has not generally been applied to wine. Wine is commonly defined by country of origin, climate zones, or whether the wine's characteristics are derived from Old World or New World traditions.[5]

While a number of factors influence agri-food systems in societies,[6] this chapter focuses on a gastronomic identity perspective to describe the wine characteristics of a region. Figure 3.1 provides a framework of the gastronomic identity perspective. To begin the task of sorting out this concept, the impact of the environmental elements and cultural elements on prevailing components, textures, and flavors in wine are discussed. This chapter concludes with a discussion of how the environment and culture of a region impacts flavor profiles and wine production. Flavor profile refers to differences in flavor attributes and the intensity of flavor attributes in food and wine. Preferences for flavor profiles differ from one region to the next. The next chapter continues this discussion but addresses regional food influences, classic wine and food marriages, and traditional and nontraditional styles of wine and food.

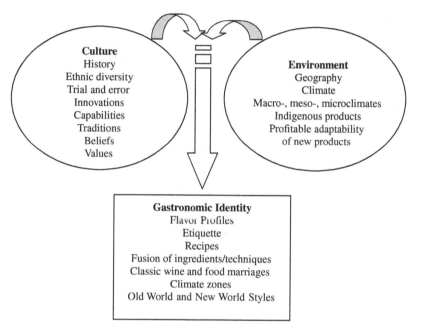

Figure 3.1

Gastronomic Identity: The Impact of the Environment and Culture on Prevailing Components, Texture, and Flavors in Wine and Food

Aperitif | How Should Menus and Wine Lists Be Organized?

Presentation in a restaurant setting involves a number of elements including the layout and design of the menu and wine list. The physical menu and wine list are some of the most important marketing tools related to a food and beverage operation. When considering the overall menu and wine list, you should evaluate five main components: presentation, pattern, structure, pricing, and other general requirements. Are these considerations related to gastronomic identity? Absolutely! An important consideration in menu organization involves questions of whether or not wine and food is organized by region or more traditional methods of classification. This consideration has implications for differentiating a restaurant's products, training, and sales potential.

In a general sense, menu and wine list presentation considerations include style of font, font size, the size of the physical menu or wine list, the style (formal, casual, traditional, etc.), the color of menu or wine list, layout (number of pages, front & back, tri-fold, etc.), and descriptions (wording, titles, and terminology). The menu and wine list pattern includes decisions about the outline of item categories, location of items, special presentations styles, menu or wine list types (static, cycle, single-use, a la carte, prix fixe), and the degree of choice of items (both the variety and number of items). A menu or wine list's structure is concerned with decisions regarding the regional appeal of the menu, the variety in price range levels, and meal periods in which the items will be served. Menu and wine list pricing are important considerations and decisions include the pricing methodology (mark-up method, prime cost, contribution margins, and cost percentages), and pricing psychology issues (odd number, below zero, zero, other than zero). Other general requirements include aesthetic factors (food and wine variations in flavor, texture, color, shape, and methods of preparation), the ability to produce and replicate the type of service needed and price elasticity of items consistently. Ultimately, the final menu and wine list should reflect the needs of both internal (servers, kitchen staff, stewarding, purchasing, and management) and external customers (guests and suppliers).

While the design of both the menu and wine list are of equal importance, the wine list design may create additional psychological concerns for the guest. Wine lists can range from an extensive "book" in an expensive leather binding to a one-time use word processed copy, or a verbal rendition of available house wines and wines by the glass. The decision on the type of wine list has important cultural connotations in and of itself.

For many guests, the wine list can be very intimidating. How can I select a wine from the myriad of choices? What price should I choose? Will I appear cheap if I select a lower priced bottle or pretentious if I select a higher priced one? What if I mispronounce the name of the wine, winemaker, or village name?

Obviously, the restaurateur's job is to minimize the intimidation issue and create an environment of customer engagement, potential value-added education, and create a sense of curiosity rather than intimidation for the guest. This is not to say that the traditional large wine list is not appropriate in many situations, but it may not be the best vehicle to sell wine in all situations, and knowing your clientele is an important element to consider when deciding the style of wine list to create.

There are a number of ways a wine list can be structured. Most are categorized by country of origin, by wine type (whites, reds, sparkling, and fortified), or varietals. While this is not a bad way to structure a wine list, it doesn't do a great job of providing an immediately identifiable relationship between the wine styles and food styles. A second method of structuring a wine list is to organize the wines by climate zone: cool, moderate, and warm. Within each category, the wines can be organized from the lightest to the most powerful. This can be done either by creating the climate zone categories or arranging the wines in an ascending order from lightest to most powerful within the traditional structure of country or region. This method of categorization is used when creating a progressive wine list. If maintaining a varietal framework, you would start off with a group of Rieslings organized from lightest to fullest, then Sauvignon Blancs, and so on. For wines which do not fall within the neat and traditional wine varietal categories, you may need to create a special category such as worldly wines, unique offerings, international favorites, or some other terminology.

Part of the structure has to do with the length of the wine list. How long should it be? Well, that depends on several variables. What are your competitors doing? How much storage space and financial resources are you willing to commit? And, how much variety is sufficient for the menu and clientele? The length factor will be closely tied to decisions regarding wine storage. Will you create an elaborate wine cellar? At its most basic level, this decision is based on whether or not you have proper storage space available. For a storage area to be adequate, it must maintain a constant temperature of 50–55 degrees F (10–13 degrees C), be away from direct sunlight, and free from vibration. A wine cellar also has substantial financial implications as you could have large sums of capital tied up in inventory for many years. Although these considerations are beyond the scope of this text, issues relating to the time-value of money, such as the investment potential of laying down quality wines for several years and the wine cellar investment and maintenance are all important considerations. Most restaurants plan on short-term wine investments with the vast majority of wines sold within 30 to 60 days.

For a 100-seat restaurant, a minimum number of wines should be about 60 or so. This number is divided among sparkling, whites, reds, and desserts. Sixty different bottles may seem like a lot, but when it is divided into these basic categories it is a sufficient number of bottles to provide a satisfactory level of taste variety.

A second consideration is whether or not to include a wine item or bin number on the wine list. This can be advantageous for several reasons. First, it lessens the chance of confusion about which bottle is being ordered by the guest. Second, if you happen to run out of a particular wine or want to promote sales of another one, it may be easier to note and remember specific numbers rather than a list of names. It is also easier to track for inventory purposes and reordering. Finally, guests and servers may be apprehensive to order (or suggest) a foreign bottle of wine for fear of mispronouncing the name of the wine, producer, or village. It is safer to simply give the bin number to the guest, wine server, or sommelier.

Other issues to consider when creating a wine list include the region in which you are located. Does the wine list feature regional wines? How much balance (or lack of balance) should you include among regional wines, other domestic wines, and foreign wines? There is no easy answer here. My personal preference is to always feature local and regional foods and wines. But, many people have specific favorites or may want to try wines that are not something they can get locally, or they may be influenced by the current wines that are in fashion. Therefore, knowing your customer base is an important deciding factor. On average, U.S. consumers drink about 80 percent domestic wines and 20 percent imported wines. Imported wines that currently top the list are those from Australia and Italy followed by France, Spain, Chile, and New Zealand. It is also true that red wines currently outsell white wines at a rate of 60 percent (red) to 40 percent (white).

Price is an important factor. This issue is tied to your mark-up strategy as well as decisions you make concerning the range of wine prices on the menu. The range of prices that you provide on the wine list has huge implications on your total wine sales. About 60 percent of the wines on any wine list should be in the moderately priced category as these will be the largest sellers. Typically, mid-priced wines sell for between $25–40 per bottle on a wine list. About 20 percent of sales will be wines priced at less than $25 and about 20 percent will be priced at $40 or more.

As a manager of this process, it is important for you to track wine sales, particularly at a new establishment, to determine if you have the correct inventory levels, mix of wine types, and an accurately priced wine list. Specific items to track include the number of bottles sold per customer, the percentage of white wine to red wine sold, the average price of a bottle of wine sold, and the ten most popular wines on your wine list. It is also valuable to have staff report any diner's requests for wines that are not currently on your wine list.[3]

A successful wine-by-the-glass program integrates food-and-wine recommendations with an attractive pricing structure.

The price of an item is determined, in part, by the competitive analysis and customer information gathered during the strategic business planning process. This process is not stagnant but will continually adapt to changes in the environment. Many operators use a cost percentage method to determine menu prices and wine prices. Others use a set mark-up per bottle that can range from 100 percent to 300 percent of the cost of the bottle of wine. Some operators have had great success marking up all bottles by a set amount. For instance, an operation could add a set cost of $15 to each bottle of wine based on the estimated cost of storage, service, and an acceptable profit. When a bottle costs the operator $5, the customer pays $20 for the bottle in the restaurant. For a bottle that costs the operator $35, the customer would pay $50, which represents a good value for the guest. Compare this to a 200 percent markup method. In this case, the $5 bottle would be sold to the guest for $15 and the $50 bottle would be sold for $150. The former method provides a good value for the customer at both wine price levels and encourages more wine sales with food. And, it may be argued that the variable costs of serving the bottle of wine are the same (excluding the capital costs of holding the more expensive wine in inventory). The latter mark-up method seems to discourage sales of the wines in the mid-priced and higher end ranges of the wine list. Overall, prices are evaluated by the consumer based on the uniqueness of the item, the level of service provided, product quantity, and overall quality. So, all of these considerations will need to be reconciled before creating a final pricing strategy for the overall wine list.

One of the main sources used to promote a wine and food program are the menu and wine list themselves. Many successful restaurants have distinctly separate wine lists and menus. But, others are creating a closer connection between wine and food by including tasting notes on wine lists and menus, integrating the wine list with the food menu, and creating menus with specific pairing suggestions. Some wine-by-the-glass programs include daily wine recommendations that are sold by the glass to accompany specific menu items to encourage wine with meals. Wine-by-the-glass programs can feature one to 30 wines. To begin a wine-by-the-glass program, it is important to begin with a manageable number, probably no more than 5 or 6 different wines unless you make an initial investment in a preservation system. In order for a program work without a preservation system, the wines will need to be refrigerated at night and held for no longer than 48 hours. You will get about five five-ounce glasses per bottle. Pricing of wines by the glass varies and is usually based on a targeted beverage cost percentage (usually anywhere from 20–30 percent). A good rule-of-thumb is to sell a glass of wine in this program for what the bottle costs the operator. You will notice that this method creates a beverage cost of about 20 percent and your cost is covered when you sell your first glass.

While the connection between the creation of a wine list and the following discussion of gastronomic identity may not be readily apparent, the culture of the environment a restaurant operates in has a huge impact on internal business decisions – one example being the organization of a menu and wine list.

THE ENVIRONMENT

The impact of the external environment has been a prominent area of concern in a variety of areas related to wine, food, and the restaurant business: wine production, food production, management, and product innovations.[7] As shown in Figure 3.1, prominent environmental factors in defining gastronomic identity include geography, climate, indigenous products, and the integration of new wine or food products over time.

While the issue of environment for this discussion primarily relates to the impact on wine components, texture, and flavor, related environmental concerns in the wine field such as organic production techniques, pesticide-free farming, sustainability, and other "green" techniques merit acknowledgment. A growing number of grape growers and winemakers are embracing practices that promote sustainable agriculture and healthier wine choices. Many realize the benefits of nonpolluting viticulture practices for both their local soil and vineyards and the planet as a whole. Winery owners such as John Williams of Frog's Leap (Rutherford, California) and Catherine Castling of Domaine de Clovallon (Bédarieux in the Languedoc region of France) use organic tools and techniques to maintain and resuscitate vineyard soil.[8] The Niagara Peninsula winery Stratus created the first building in Canada to achieve Leadership in Energy and Environmental Design (LEED) certification from the Canada Green Building Council. As of 2006, Stratus was the only winery worldwide to fully achieve this designation with its buildings. Additional information on what it means to be LEED certified can be gathered at the U.S. Green Building Council Web site, www.usgbc.org.

WINE: THE IMPACT OF GEOGRAPHY AND CLIMATE

Geography and climate impact the wines that an area is capable of producing, whether or not a winemaking venture will be profitable, and whether the product will achieve an acceptable level of quality. The geography and climate impacts ripeness of wine grapes as well as flavors and type of fruit aromas in red and white wines. For the purposes of wine and food pairing, geography and climate can have a substantial impact on ripeness and quality. The ripeness of the grape impacts sweetness levels, acidity levels, and alcohol levels. These issues can greatly influence wine and food selections for proper matching.

While grapevines are adaptable to most well-drained soils, a number of factors impact the ultimate wine characteristics and wine quality. The amount and timing of moisture is an important factor, and the effects of wind and excessive sun can also be severe. Quality wine grapes cannot be grown everywhere; generally they are grown between 30° and 50° latitude either above or below the equator. Latitudes nearer the poles would provide a too-limited growing season coupled with severe winter cold that would kill even dormant vines. Near the equator, it never becomes cold enough for the vines to have the dormant period that is needed for successful grape growing, and the high humidity can induce fungal diseases.

Other limitations to grape growing include the local geography, pest prevalence, and the weather. In many cases, grape growing can be extended outside the normal range using a variety of techniques.[9] In Quebec, Canada, the harsh winters can freeze the dormant vines, so an approach known as "hilling" is used, in which earth is banked over the roots of the grapevine to protect them during the winter. This technique is also used in Russia and parts of China.[10]

Climate is an important consideration in wine and food pairing. Climatic factors impact fruit ripeness, acidity level, alcohol level, tannin, and flavors. One method used to organize wine categories is to indicate whether a wine is from a cool, moderate, or warm zone. White wines from cool growing regions can typically be described as having flavors of apples and pears (cool-climate tree fruits). Red wines from cool climate zones have aromas and flavors that can be described as like those of cranberries, red currants, or red cherries. In moderate climate growing regions, the resulting flavors include citrus, peaches, apricots, nectarines, or melons for white wines and black cherries, black currants, plums, or blueberries for red wines. A warm climate area produces white wines with tropical fruit flavors such as mangos, pineapple, papayas, guavas, or bananas. Warm-zone red wines can take on flavors of dried and heavier fruits such as raisins, figs, or prunes.[11]

The winemaker's notes may provide hints to a wine's climate and style characteristics. These notes are often provided on the back of the wine label and may include a description of aromas, flavor characteristics, body, whether or not it has been aged in oak, and food pairing suggestions. A description of black fruits in the wine's aroma or flavor indicates that the wine was produced in a moderate climate zone; mention of red fruits indicates a cool zone. The cooler region's fruit flavors may also suggest higher acidity and lower alcohol levels driven by less ripe fruits. Thus, all else being equal, wines from cool zones will have a slightly tarter and lighter style than those from a warmer zone.

In terms of overall quality, cooler climates are generally preferred to hot climates. Cool growing climates allow grapes to stay on the vines for a longer period while retaining desirable levels of acidity. Cool climates also allow wine grapes to develop needed complexity, which is further enhanced by aging the wines *sur lies*. The term *sur lies* is French for "on the lees," which refers to the gooey deposit of dead yeast at the bottom of the fermentation vessel. Aging new wine on the lees is thought to increase mouthfeel, texture, and complexity in the finished product.

Warm-climate grapes have more definitive fruit flavors and are bolder in nature. The weakness of warmer-climate grapes is that they develop more quickly. This situation creates wines with less complexity and lower acidity.[12]

The heat-summation method of classifying vineyard regions is a useful tool for comparing climate zones across different wine areas of the world. It is calculated on the basis of the total number of days when the average temperature (based on ten-year data) is greater than 50°F. If a region's average daily temperature was 70°F, for instance, this would provide 20 heat summation units (also called degree days) per day during the growing season (70 − 50 = 20). The coldest regions that generally grow wine grapes have about 1,700 degree days, and the warmest have 5,200 degree days.[13]

The concept of climate zones based on heat summation units can be a defining characteristic of wine styles. When professional wine tasters evaluate wines as part of a blind tasting, one of the first ways that they try to identify and differentiate the wines is according to whether the flavors and style are characteristic of cool climates or warm climates. For instance, Chardonnay is a very adaptable grape variety that grows well in a wide range of climates. So if a clear separation is identifiable on the basis of climate factors, it can become easier to identify the characteristics of a wine and, in the case of wine and food pairing, predict better wine and food matches.

The climate map concept is also a valuable tool for restaurant servers, allowing them to quickly determine the general style of a wine by looking at the label or wine list description and identifying its geographic location. A good way to assist in this determination is to organize wines on the wine list by climatic characteristics rather than by country or by domestic/foreign categories.

There are a few caveats with this approach to characterizing wines. Within a country, region, and even subregion, it can be difficult to generalize completely. Many grape-growing regions are very broad with respect to climate zone. The Okanagan Valley region of British Columbia in Canada ranges from moderately warm in the southern portion to cool in the north. The Napa Valley appellation is such a large area that at least three of the five climate regions are contained in it, ranging from very cool (Carneros) to moderately warm (northern Napa Valley).

Macroclimate, Mesoclimate, and Microclimate Another reason for a possible discrepancy is the impact of macroclimates, mesoclimates, and microclimates. *Macroclimate* refers to the climate of an overall region. *Mesoclimate* represents the local climate of a whole vineyard, and *microclimate* is the climate specific to an individual plot within a vineyard. Some go as far as to include the climate between the soil and grapevine canopy as part of the microclimate definition.

Many wine-growing areas have local climates that create cool and hot spots. California exemplifies a macroclimate region with many mesoclimates that range from very cool to very warm. Many of the cooler coastal valleys of California have much in common with the wine-growing regions of Germany, Burgundy and Bordeaux. The warmer areas of California have much in common with the areas of southern France, Spain, and Algeria.

Many times mesoclimates and microclimates are near bodies of water (ocean, lakes, or rivers) that reflect the sun's light and heat in cool zones, creating hot spots in cooler areas (such as in Germany) or cooling effects in otherwise warmer growing areas (such as the California coast). Higher altitudes explain some of the cool spots, such as the Río Negro region in Argentina. Lower areas in high-altitude regions (i.e., valleys) may provide protection from severe cold or substantial winds, such as the Niagara Escarpment protecting the Niagara Peninsula in Canada.

The region known as Côte d'Or in France is an important part of the Burgundy appellation and provides an example of the impact of slope and altitude on macro-, meso-, and microclimates. There are several theories about the meaning of the name Côte d'Or, which means "hillsides of gold." Some claim that the name refers to the golden color of the slopes in autumn, while others suggest the name stems from the revenue generated.[14] Still others believe the name refers to the mesoclimate of the region's vineyards, which face east to maximize the sunshine and heat. A French word meaning "east" is *orient*, suggesting that Côte d'Or may be a contraction for Côte d'Orient.[15]

Table 3.1 lists five climate zones, ranging from very cool (2,500 or fewer degree days) to very warm (4,001 or more degree days), based on Winkler and Amerine's definitions. In spite of the caveats pointed out above, this table provides a valuable tool for wine and food pairing. It provides a general sense of the climatic influence that can be expected in these regions across North America, other parts of the New World, and several locations in the Old World. These ranges can provide guidance in determining the acidity levels, tannin, alcohol levels, and flavor characteristics likely to be found in wines from various locations.

Table 3.1   Approximate Climate Zones Based on Heat Summation Units*

Climate Zone	Heat Summation Units	Locations
Region 1	< 2,500 F (< 1,390 C)	**New World—North America** *California:* Anderson Valley, Carneros, Edna Valley, Marin, Mendocino, Monterey, Napa (near the city), Russian River Valley, Santa Clara, Santa Cruz mountains, and parts of Sonoma *Canada:* northern Okanagan Valley *Idaho:* panhandle region, parts of Snake River Valley *Oregon:* Willamette Valley, parts of Umpqua Valley *Washington:* Puget Sound **New World—Other** *Australia:* Tasmania, Coonawarra, Piccadilly Valley *Chile:* East Rapel Valley, West Aconcagua, Casablanca Valley *New Zealand:* Hawk's Bay, Canterbury, Marlborough, Cloudy Bay **Old World** *France:* Chablis, Loire, Côte d'Or, Champagne, Alsace *Germany:* Mosel-Saar-Ruwer, Baden, Rheinhessen, Rheingau, Platz *Switzerland:* Valais, Geneva
Region 2	2,501 to 3,000 F (1,391 to 1,670 C)	**New World—North America** *California:* Alexander Valley, Anderson Valley, Chalk Hill, Edna Valley, Mendocino, Monterey, Napa Valley, Potter Valley, Russian River Valley, Santa Clara, and parts of Sonoma *Canada:* Niagara Peninsula, southern Okanagan Valley *Idaho:* parts of Snake River Valley *New York:* Finger Lakes, Lake Erie, Long Island, Hudson Valley *Oregon:* Western Umpqua Valley, Rogue Valley *Washington:* Columbia Valley, Walla Walla Valley, Yakima Valley **New World—Other** *Argentina:* Rio Negro Valley *Australia:* Adelaide Hills, Barossa Valley, Pemberton, Victoria *Chile:* Maipo Valley, Curicó Valley, West Rapel, East Aconcagua *South Africa:* Stellenbosch, Walker Bay **Old World** *France:* Médoc, Hermitage *Hungary:* Great Plain region *Italy:* Piedmont, Tre Venezie *Spain:* Penedès, Galicia

Table 3.1 (*Continued*)

Climate Zone	Heat Summation Units	Locations
Region 3	3,001 to 3,500 F (1,671 to 1,940 C)	**New World—North America** *California:* Alameda, Alexander Valley, Contra Costa, El Dorado, Knights Valley, Lake, McDowell Valley, Mendocino, Monterey, northern Napa, Paso Robles, Placer, Redwood Valley, Riverside, San Benito, Santa Clara, and parts of Sonoma *Washington:* parts of Columbia Valley, Rattlesnake Hills, Red Mountain **New World—Other** *Argentina:* Mendoza Region *Australia:* Margaret River, parts of New South Wales, Queensland, McLaren Vale, Swan District *South Africa:* Paarl **Old World** *France:* Rhône region, Languedoc-Roussillon *Italy:* Tuscany, southern Veneto
Region 4	3,501 to 4,000 F (1,941 to 2,220 C)	**New World—North American** *California:* Amador, Calaveras, El Dorado, Fresno, Merced, Riverside, Sacramento, San Diego, San Joaquin, Yolo *Italy:* Sicily **New World—Other** *Argentina:* Calchaquí Valley *Australia:* Hunter Valley (New South Wales) **Old World** *Greece* *Spain:* Central regions – Rioja, Ribera Del Duero
Region 5	4,001 or more F (2,221 or more C)	**New World—North America** *California:* Amador, Calveras, Fresno, Kern, Madera, Merced, Sacramento, San Bernardino, San Diego, San Joaquin, Stanislaus, Tulare *Texas:* South Plains **New World—Other** *Argentina:* Famatina Valley *North Africa* *Australia northern areas of Western Australia and Northern Territory* **Old World** *Italy:* Calabria *Southern Spain:* Sherry (Jerez)

Source: Adapted from M. A. Amerine and V. L. Singleton, *Wine: An Introduction,* 2nd ed. (Berkeley: University of California Press, 1977); J. Arkell, *New World Wines: The Complete Guide* (New York: Sterling, 1999); D. Jackson and D. Schuster, *Grape Growing and Wine Making* (Orinda, CA: Altarinda Books, 1981).

*As should be apparent from the discussion in this chapter, climate varies due to a number of factors. Placement of a particular locale within one region or another will vary due to mesoclimate and microclimate as well as how the boundaries were drawn in creating each viticultural area.

Also, these climate guidelines provide clues to the quality of varietals produced in these areas.

It is easy to see that a wide range of wine styles can be produced based on the variety of climate characteristics. These climate zones impact the grapes grown in each area, the level of grape ripeness, level of acidity, and fruit flavors identified in the finished wine.

Appellations

Appellations An appellation, found on the wine bottle label, refers to the location where the grapes and other agricultural products are grown. Many appellations are sanctioned by a government or trade association that has authority to define and regulate procedures in order to guarantee quality and genuineness. A wine appellation may be very broad (Washington State), moderately specific (Columbia Valley), or very specific (Horse Heaven Hills, a specific area within the Columbia Valley designation); it may even refer to a single vineyard. The more specific the location, the more confidence you can have in the wine's climate-influenced characteristics.

Until the 1970s, France was the only country with wine laws based on the geography of the entire country. The official French system of *appellation d'origine contrôlée* (AOC) has grown to become the model for the world. The majority of well-known French wines are AOC wines. Over the past thirty years, the United States, Canada, Chile, Australia, New Zealand, Italy, Spain, Germany, Austria, South Africa, Portugal, Greece, Argentina, and Bulgaria have begun mapping their respective appellations.

European systems identify and regulate wine-growing regions. These regulations can include place name (region, district, village, or single vineyard), type of grapes grown, minimum alcohol levels, maximum yield, certain viticulture practices, and final taste. Besides France, appellation systems are well developed in Italy (*denominazione di origine controllata e garantita* [DOGC], *denominazione di origine controllata* [DOC], and *indicazione geografica* [IGT]), Germany (*Qualitätswein mit Prädikat* [QmP] and *Qualitätswein bestimmter Anbaugebiete* [QbA]), Spain (*denominación de origen calificada* [DOCa], *denominación de origen* [DOC], and Portugal (*denominação de origem controlada* [DOC]).

Programs for New World countries continue to evolve. Most wine-growing countries have an official agency that approves and defines appellations within its political boundaries. Australia and New Zealand are struggling with the appellation idea and whether to create appellations by trade agreement or through government regulation. In the United States, more than 175 appellations have been approved by the agency responsible for regulating appellation geographic boundaries, the U.S. Alcohol and Tobacco Tax and Trade Bureau (TTB).

California has seen an expanding number of American Viticultural Area (AVA) designations, with more than ninety-two approved. California as a whole can be divided into at least thirteen definable wine-growing regions: Mendocino County, Lake County, Sonoma County, Napa County, Alameda County, Santa Clara County, Monterey County, San Benito County, San Luis Obispo County, Santa Barbara County, South Coast, Central Valley, and the Sierra Foothills. Each of these areas may have multiple AVA appellations and subappellations.

The county that has carved out a lasting reputation for creating highly prized and classic-styled wines is Napa. Within the Napa Valley, more than eighteen subappellations have been created to reflect the complex geography, differing climates, and localized terroirs of the region. The southern end of the valley (near the town of Napa) is considerably cooler than the northern end. Further, differences in taste can occur depending on whether the grapevines are grown on the valley floor or on mountain slopes that maximize the exposure to sun and are above the fog line.[16]

The idea of terroir is uniquely French in origin and a relatively new concept for wine makers in the New World growing areas. It generally reflects the unique interaction of natural factors (climate, soil, water, wind, etc.) and human skills that create definable characteristics in a specific wine-growing location. Napa Valley's most famous terroir is the Rutherford Bench. Others include the Oakville Bench and the Stags Leap District. The concept is intertwined with history and culture. (Further implications of terroir are discussed later, in the history section.)

AVAs are constantly evolving, and approval is based on an explanation of why and how the region is a separate and identifiable growing area, based on history, climate, soil, water, and so on. In contrast to appellations developed in European traditions (which regulate varietals and viticulture methods as well as geographic boundaries), American growers can plant any grape varietals of their choice, with harvests as large as the vines will sustain or as small as their quality concerns command. From a wine and food pairing perspective, this freedom limits the usefulness of U.S. appellations as guides to wine characteristics without additional knowledge about the grower, producer, and location. The French, German, Italian, and Spanish systems provide greater confidence in using appellations as a guide to wine quality and characteristics. A limitation in this is that vintage plays a much larger role in these Old World locations because of greater reliance on the weather (water, sun, wind) and less on planned factors (such as irrigation).

CULTURE

Cultural studies of food by sociologists and anthropologists have become much more common over the past century. Researchers have described food habits as a sort of customary behavior that underpins the rituals of a stable society. These authors suggest that norms in eating patterns both reflect broader structures of the society and indicate that "taste is culturally shaped and socially controlled."[17] In relation to the concept of gastronomic identity, it can be surmised that food and wine habits derive from a variety of cultural norms and events over time. These include the history of the region, the food systems employed, the amount and location of trade, traditions, beliefs, and capabilities development. Capabilities development refers to learned abilities in a location such as farming techniques, wine making techniques, innovative behaviors and so on. The following sections discuss these factors in relation to their impact on wine.

HISTORY AND ETHNIC DIVERSITY

The history of wine and food in any region has developed over time with many twists and turns.[18] Historical events and governmental policies have a substantial impact on wine and food products. Taxation structures, inheritance customs, and land tenure systems all affect how much food or wine grapes a farmer might keep for consumption or to sell at the market and how much would be diverted to the ruling body.[19] In Italy, grapes are grown virtually everywhere to produce wine. This creates possible problems for the government in terms of proper taxation of the value of the grapes, the wines produced, and the distillation of grappa (a beverage made from the must of grapes left after the pressing process). The Italian government estimates the amount of grapes grown based on the acreage of vineyards and keeps track of the amount of wine produced and the weight of the grapes after pressing to determine more exact figures.

The history of wine grape growing and winemaking in North America explains much of practices used throughout its industry. Canada's wine history dates back more than four hundred years, with much of the early traditions of wine culture brought by immigrants from Germany and Italy; these later became the basis for early commercial wine production. In 1525, the governor of Mexico (Hernando Cortés) ordered the planting of grapes. Fearing the colony would become self-sufficient in producing its own wine, the king of Spain outlawed further new plantings in Mexico in 1595. This moratorium was enforced for 150 years, effectively eliminating the growth of commercial wine production in Mexico. The Franciscan missionary Junípero Serra planted the first California vineyard in 1769 at Mission San Diego, and Serra continued to plant vineyards until his death in 1784. The first European vines in California were planted in 1833 near Los Angeles by a Hungarian immigrant, Agoston Haraszthy. Haraszthy provided much optimism and enthusiasm for the potential of wine production in California and is considered the founder of the California wine industry.

One historical event, Prohibition, greatly impacted wine production and wine grape growing across both the United States and Canada. Prohibition was intended to reduce drinking by abolishing businesses that manufactured, distributed, and sold alcoholic beverages. In the United States, the movement grew out of concern for increasing alcohol consumption and its negative effects on society. This concern was partially driven by the growing numbers of immigrants from Europe and the fear that a culture of drink among some sectors of the population was spreading.

The dry movement began in 1816 and persisted explicitly for more than a hundred years—banning the sale of alcohol on Sunday, removing the mention of wine from school and college texts, creating dry counties (and provinces), and finally becoming a national movement in the United States and Canada.

The U.S. prohibition movement continued to pick up steam in the late nineteenth century, and prohibition was enacted into U.S. law in 1920 with the Eighteenth Amendment to the U.S. Constitution. Two organizations were the main lobbying forces behind this amendment: the Anti-Saloon League and the Woman's Christian Temperance Union. While the movement had much support prior to the U.S. entry into World War I, it gained significant support during the war mobilization. The dry movement was billed as a sacrifice to support the armed forces, family, and the American way, and it exploited the patriotic emotions surrounding the war effort to initiate this constitutional amendment. Prohibition was repealed in 1933 with the Nineteenth Amendment to the U.S. Constitution.[20]

The Canadian prohibition movement followed a similar path, with Prince Edward Island being the first province to enact alcohol prohibition in 1901. Quebec was the last province to do so, in 1919, and the first to repeal it, in 1920. The majority of Canadian provinces repealed prohibition during the 1920s, with Prince Edward Island being last to repeal it, in 1948.

During Prohibition, alcohol consumption dropped to 30 percent of pre-Prohibition levels. From 1919 to 1925, wine production dropped 94 percent. Wineries that survived made wines for medicinal and sacramental uses. Alcohol consumption did not return to pre-Prohibition levels until four decades after its repeal.[21]

What was the impact of Prohibition on the wine industry? Even after repeal, the "drys" have influenced alcohol use, with many states and provinces creating monopoly liquor stores to restrict consumption. Dry forces are not dead—they continue to pursue obstructionist legislation encumbering direct wine sales to consumers and preventing the inclusion of information on wine labels about the potential health benefits of wine.

The above examples are but a few of the influences culture and history have had on how, where, when, and why we drink what we do. The impact of history and ethnic diversity is distinctly apparent in wine production. In the wine-producing regions of California, Canada, and other parts of the New World, the influence of French, Hungarian, Italian, and German wine makers is evident. The unique history and cultural diversity of a locality affect the local winemaking industry and create a distinct identity and differences in finished wine styles that differentiate one wine region from another.

TRIAL AND ERROR, INNOVATIONS, AND CAPABILITIES

Trial and error is at the heart of innovations and lasting traditions in wine production. Innovations can have a lasting impact, such as the techniques furthering the evolution of

Champagne by Dom Pérignon and others during the seventeenth century.[22] Another example is the more recent innovation of temperature-controlled stainless-steel tanks for wine storage and fermentation. These relatively new tanks minimize the negative impact of oxidation (contact with air) and maintain a constant cool temperature during the fermentation process, which is particularly important for the production of white wines.[23]

Trial and error in viticulture and winemaking have left a lasting impression on both Old World and New World products. Europeans had more than eleven hundred years of winemaking experience prior to settling the New World. Despite stutters over the last three hundred years, the absence of rules, regulations, and traditions has allowed the New World regions to pioneer new technologies, experiment with different varietals, and rebound into a thriving industry over the past century.

While the Old World methods were used as original models for New World wine production, it can be argued that the series of failures and renaissances in the New World provided an opportunity to continuously update viticulture practices, as well as pioneer and harness new winemaking technology. This process of adaptation and trial and error may be the most significant factor in developing the forward-thinking New World wine industry.

What does all this mean for wine and food pairing decisions? First, gastronomic identity is also determined by the capabilities of those in the region and local area. Do local producers have the capability to produce quality wine and food products? Do they have the innovative capacity to differentiate themselves (or the region) from the competition? Capabilities of this sort can be limited to a firm, can be locally based, or may become regional. Locally based capabilities allow the development of new innovations that ultimately impact identifiable gastronomic products and services.

GASTRONOMIC IDENTITY

From the above discussion, it should be apparent that a variety of factors affect the wine, food, and gastronomic identity of a region. While this identity is constantly evolving, the identification of characteristics can provide the knowledgeable observer with tools to estimate the impact of these factors on general trends in prevailing flavors, textures, and component characteristics. Food trends are derived through a continuous interaction and evolution of fashion, traditions, culture, and climate, and wine trends are derived in a similar fashion. Gastronomic traditions are created through a fusion of ingredients and techniques as a result of the marrying of diverse cultures, ethnic influences, and history. Gastronomic traditions are restricted through limitations on product availability, know-how, trade, and climate. To tie the idea of gastronomic identity to regional grape growing and wine production, the following sections provide a brief overview of the impact of Old World and New World traditions and climate zones on classic (and not-so-classic) marriages in wine and food.

OLD WORLD AND NEW WORLD

While the cool/moderate/warm climate zone concept forms a continuum of wine style range, the Old World/New World perspective suggests a dichotomy between the two generalized regions of the wine and food world. The Old World includes the traditional wine-growing regions of Europe: France, Italy, Spain, Germany, Greece, Hungary, Austria, Bulgaria and Switzerland. The New World includes the United States, Australia, Argentina, Canada, Chile, New Zealand, and South Africa. As a broad brushstroke, Old World wines are described as subtler in style, more refined, and understated. New World wines are described as having a bolder style and being more intense, lush, and opulent. There are a number of reasons why these generalizations may hold, including differences in growing conditions, differences in tradition, and taste preferences.

Old World traditions include classical music, refined fashion, stone castles, and stately manor houses. In fine wine, there is a "bottled tradition" resulting from generations' worth of trial and error. The wines produced here are more commonly made under appellations that control the style of wine to a certain extent (permitted grapes, boundaries of growing area, maximum vineyard yield, minimum alcohol content [minimum ripeness levels]), viticulture practices (irrigation), and vinification (aging requirements).[24] New World grape growers and wine producers have a freer rein in decisions on viticulture issues and production techniques, though this is becoming less evident as wine industry professionals determine the best terroir to grow particular grapes of the highest quality and focus on wine styles that are particular to a region and location. Ontario wine producers' adherence to Vintners Quality Assurance Ontario (VQA) requirements and the institutionalization of Ontario ice wine are evidence of how wine products become a regional tradition.

As noted earlier, the idea of terroir is uniquely French in origin. There is no direct translation into English, but Fanet provides a good definition: "an umbrella term for a subtle interaction of natural factors and human skills that define the characteristics of each wine-growing area."[25] The concept of terroir is applied to both food and wine in France. The basic idea was established through the *appellations d'origine contrôlée* (AOC) in response to a portion of the population that was diametrically opposed to standardized farming and intensive methods of production (a "homogenization" of agricultural production). The system is based on limiting production to specific areas (terroirs) and the regulation of production techniques used. The rationale for this idea is to enhance the natural environment through the use of sustainable farming and production methods. This leads to distinct products with characteristics that cannot be duplicated elsewhere.

In terms of wine, the concept of terroir is important in the Old World tradition of a perceived close connection between the people and the land and soil.[26] The final Old World wine product has, in many cases, earthy characteristics. The earthiness in wine pairs well with many of the traditional food items that have a substantial amount of earthy (and sometimes funky) character, such as potatoes, truffles, cheeses, mushrooms, and the like. The Old World wines are more likely to be made from grapes grown in poor, rocky soil (i.e., Bordeaux, Douro [Port], and Mosel), and many aspects of life in the Old World regions often seem to revolve around food. In many parts of the Old World, wine with food is as common as having salt and pepper on the table is to us in North America. The wines in these regions are styled to share the stage and complement the food. Traditional foods and wines that accompany them have, in many cases, developed over many years of refinement to meet local tastes, utilize local products, and create an additional taste and flavor "layering" between the food and wine. Food flavors are, generally, deep and rich but not bold.

The New World concept suggests a more recent perspective based on a fusion of ethnic and cultural influences. North American and other New World traditions have a much different history of music, fashion, and architecture. In contrast to European traditions, U.S. traditions of music, fashion, and architecture have brought us rock 'n' roll, rhythm and blues, T-shirts and caps, and imposing skyscrapers in steel and glass. New World wines are generally described as fruit-driven or fruit-forward—bold, lush, opulent fruit rather than subtle notes of earthiness and floral, spicy, or herbaceous flavors.[27]

Table 3.2 provides an incorporation of the wine climate zone concept, the Old World/ New World descriptions of wine, and Old World/New World classic wine and food matches

In the current global marketplace, traditional boundaries between the Old World and New World are becoming increasingly blurred.

Table 3.2   Climate Zones and Old/New World Traditions

Climate Zone	Regions 1 to 2 = Cool	Regions 2 to 3 = Moderate	Regions 3 to 5 = Warm
Old World examples of wine and food matches	Red Burgundy with Boeuf Bourguignon (Burgundy region of France) Sancerre and goat cheese (Sancerre, France) Alsace Riesling and Choucroute (Alsace, France)	Red Bordeaux and lamb (Bordeaux region of France) Beaujolais and Salade Lyonnaise (Lyon, France) Barolo and tagliatelle (Piedmont region, Italy)	Nero d'Avola and spaghetti with meat sauce (Sicily, Italy)
New World examples of wine and food matches	Oregon Pinot Noir and wild salmon (Willamette Valley, Oregon) New Zealand Sauvignon Blanc and a fusion of influences	Buttery Chardonnay with Dungeness crab (California) Zinfandel with grilled anything, barbecue, or pizza (California)	Sauvignon Blanc with chicken breast or chips served with salsa Shiraz with grilled pepper steak (Australia) Malbec with Beef Empanadas (Argentina)
Typical styles based on climate zone	A cool and less sunny growing season. Lean and unripe fruit with apple and pear flavors in whites and red fruits (cranberries, red currants, and cherries) in reds. Wines are usually more subtle and elegant in style.	A temperate and moderately sunny growing season. Ripe and juicy fruit styles with citrus, peach, apricot, nectarine, and melon flavors in whites. Reds have flavors of dark fruits such as black cherries, black currants, plums, blueberries, and blackberries. Resulting wines are of a medium intensity.	A warm and very sunny growing season. Overripe and lush fruits styles in these bolder and more intense wines. Whites have fruit flavors of mangos, pineapples, papayas, guavas, and bananas. Red wines have overripe and sometimes dried fruit flavors such as figs, raisins, and prunes.

Source: Lower section adapted from Andrea Immer, *Great Wine Made Simple: Straight Talk from a Master Sommelier* (New York: Broadway Books, 2000).

based on climate zone. Brief descriptions of the growing season, wine fruit style, white and red wine fruit flavors, and overall wine style are provided along with Old World examples of wine and food matches and New World examples of wine and food matches.

The Old World countries provide many classic marriages in food and wine. These examples create matches between many of the components, textures, and flavors inherent in the wine and foods. It seems most wine books and books discussing fine cuisine have a focus on French traditions of wine and food. Why? Are the French the largest wine producers? No, Italy ranks first among wine-producing countries worldwide.[28] Does France produce the best wine? Not necessarily, as many other countries around the globe rival France in wine quality. But the viticultural history of France is still the template used for premium wine production techniques, and the formulation of the AOC system was the first of its kind. Therefore, the focus on French wines in many wine books is based on its historical preeminence and foundation of quality control. The same can be said regarding the books on fine cuisine. French cuisine has a long history of codification of classical sauces, recipes, and professional techniques. The French tradition is also important for classic marriages in food and wine.

New and Old World Confusion
An important event more than thirty years ago opened a crack in this Old World/New World dichotomy. In 1976 British wine writer Steven Spurrier arranged a blind tasting of five Napa Cabernets and five Napa Chardonnays to be pitted against five red Bordeaux from the Mêdoc and Graves districts and five white Burgundies from the Côte de Beaune district. A condition of this tasting was that all of the

tasting panel members would be French judges. During the tasting, the judges consistently mistook French wines for California, and California wines for French. In the end, the French judges selected a Napa Valley Cabernet as the top red and a Napa Valley Chardonnay as the best white. This event was a defining moment for California wines, with the best of California beating France's best. This also brings into question the validity of the separation between Old World and New World styles in wine.

Over the past few years, traveling winemakers and roving viticulturists have blurred the traditional lines between the Old and New World wine industries. The industry is seeing more and more joint ventures between the New World and Old. Joint wine production ventures in California, Chile, Australia, and elsewhere point to a continued sharing of wine industry know-how. Cross-fertilization of viticulture ideas and winemaking technology have facilitated this process. Many of the Old World winemakers are working "out of the box," using nontraditional varietals, viticulture methods, and labeling techniques.

Another reason for the blurring of boundaries is the development of a greater number of cool-climate regions within the New World. These locations are likely to deliver quality wines with more finesse and European style. Also, Old World producers continue to embrace and utilize New World technology. New World winemakers are creating new traditions incorporating the ideas of terroir and appellations to the industry. Where are we headed in the future? More blurred lines? Or reestablishment of unique regional characteristics as an area of competitive differentiation?

A neighborhood wine store in Paris, France—evidence of the significance in the French terroir concept.

SUMMARY

A region's gastronomic identity is determined by the environment and cultural elements that impact prevailing components, textures, and flavors in wine and food. The dominant elements in the environment determining wine characteristics include geography and climate. Cool, moderate, and warm climate zones can have a substantial impact of fruit ripeness, acidity, tannin, alcohol, and flavors. All of these elements have an impact of on food pairing decisions. Macro-, meso-, and microclimates also impact final wine characteristics. Climate and geography influence the type of grapes that can be grown and whether a region will be able to profitably adapt wine grapes to the region.

Cultural elements include religion, history, level of ethnic diversity, innovations, capabilities, traditions, beliefs, and values. These events have a significant impact on identifiable characteristics through the introduction of new winemaking technologies, viticulture practices, and the development of a quality wine-growing region. Pro-

hibition had a substantial impact on the wine industry throughout North America. Appellations have a long tradition in France and other parts of the Old World. The use of appellations in the New World is increasing in importance and has important consequences related to microclimates and terroir.

Old World and New World wine regions have differing histories, traditions, and geography. But the boundaries between the two are becoming blurred with the sharing of new technologies and viticulture practices. Old World traditions are being adopted as New World producers take a closer look at the relationship between land and grape. Just like all cuisine, the wine industry is in constant evolution thanks to the constantly changing interaction of unique and identifiable products, traditions, and etiquette. The "New World" concept of the near future may end up referring to new frontiers in international winemaking rather than a dichotomy based on geographic and traditional boundaries.

DISCUSSION QUESTIONS

1. What are the key elements of the gastronomic identity concept?

2. What is the impact of climate zones on wine characteristics?

3. What are macroclimates, mesoclimates, and microclimates?

4. Will the reds grown in regions that are very cool or very warm be of the same quality as those in the more moderate zones? Why or why not?

5. In terms of whites, which varietals are preferable from cool, moderate, or warm zones?

6. If desiring higher acidity to create a match with the food you are serving, which wine styles are a safer bet for matching purposes?

7. What regions are considered New World? Old World?

8. What is the role of appellations?

OPTIONAL EXERCISES

To identify some of the subtle differences between Old World and New World wines, try some of the comparisons listed below. The exercises at the end of Chapter 4 incorporate Old and New World comparisons with foods to demonstrate the impact of these subtle differences on matching decisions. For the optional comparisons listed below, focus on identifying differences due to climate zones, fermentation, aging techniques, and whether the wines have a general sense of terroir to them.

Table 3.3   Old World Versus New World Wine Tasting Comparisons

A Loire Valley Savennières or Vouvray versus a Chenin Blanc from Washington, California, Ontario or the Okanagan Valley

A Riesling from Mosel (Germany) or Alsace (France) versus a Riesling from New York State, Washington, Ontario, Oregon, or California

A Sancerre or Pouilly-Fumé versus a Sauvignon Blanc or Fumé Blanc from New Zealand, Washington, California, or Canada

A Chablis, Pouilly-Fuissé, or any white from the Burgundy region versus a Chardonnay from Australia, California, Chile, or Washington

A red Burgundy versus a Pinot Noir from Oregon, Washington, California, or Okanagan Valley

Chianti, Chianti Classico, or Chianti versus a Sangiovese from California, Washington, or Australia

A Côtes du Rhône or Côte Rôtie versus a Syrah/Shiraz from Washington, California, Australia, or South Africa

A red Bordeaux from the "right bank" (the towns of St. Emilion, Pomerol) versus a Merlot from Washington, California, Chile, Australia, South Africa, or the Okanagan Valley

A red Bordeaux from the "left bank" (the towns of Margaux, St-Julien, St-Estèphe, Pauillac, or the district of Médoc) versus a Cabernet Sauvignon or Meritage from Washington, California, Chile, Australia, South Africa, or the Okanagan Valley

NOTES

1. B. Santich, "The Study of Gastronomy and Its Relevance to Hospitality Education and Training," *International Journal of Hospitality Management* 23 (2004): 15–24.

2. Ibid., 17.

3. R. Danhi, "What Is Your Country's Culinary Identity?" *Culinology Currents,* winter 2003, 4–5.

4. R. J. Harrington, "Part I: The Culinary Innovation Process, A Barrier to Imitation," *Journal of Foodservice Business Research* 7, 3 (2004): 35–57.

5. M. A. Amerine and V. L. Singleton, *Wine: An Introduction,* 2nd ed. (Berkeley: University of California Press, 1977); Andrea Immer, *Great Wine Made Simple: Straight Talk from a Master Sommelier* (New York: Broadway Books, 2000).

6. P. Atkins and I. Bowler, *Food in Society: Economy, Culture, Geography* (New York: Oxford University Press, 2001).

7. K. Albala, *Food in Early Modern Europe* (Westport, CT: Greenwood Press, 2003); Amerine and Singleton, *Wine: An Introduction;* M. Farjoun. "Towards an Organic Perspective on Strategy." *Strategic Management Journal* 23 (2002): 561–94; Harrington, "Part I."

8. S. Kolpan, B. H. Smith, and M. A. Weiss, *Exploring Wine,* 2nd ed. (New York: John Wiley and Sons, 2002); C. Castling, personal communication, December 17, 2004.

9. Amerine and Singleton, *Wine: An Introduction.*

10. T. Aspler, *Vintage Canada: A Tasteful Companion to Canadian Wines* (Whitby, ON: McGraw-Hill Ryerson, 1993), 136.

11. Immer, *Great Wine Made Simple.*

12. Bruce Zoechlein, *A Review of Méthode Champenoise Production* (Virginia Cooperative Extension: Publication 463–017W, 2002).

13. Amerine and Singleton, *Wine: An Introduction;* A. J. Winkler, *General Viticulture* (Berkeley: University of California Press, 1974).

14. A. Lichine, *Alexis Lichine's New Encyclopedia of Wines & Spirits* (New York: Alfred A. Knopf, 1987).

15. K. MacNeil, *The Wine Bible* (New York: Workman, 2001).

16. J. Arkell, *New World Wines: The Complete Guide* (New York: Sterling, 1999).

17. Atkins and Bowler, *Food in Society,* 5.

18. M. McWilliams and H. Heller, *Food Around the World: A Cultural Perspective* (Upper Saddle River, NJ: Prentice-Hall, 2003): 5.

19. Albala, *Food in Early Modern Europe,* 7.

20. Ohio State University, "Why Prohibition?" http://prohibition.osu.edu/whyprohibition.htm (accessed December 30, 2005).

21. Ohio State University, "U.S. Consumption of Beverage Alcohol," http://prohibition.osu.edu/consumption.htm (accessed December 30, 2005).

22. MacNeil, *The Wine Bible.*

23. Arkell, *New World Wines.*

24. Ibid., 31; Immer, *Great Wine Made Simple.*

25. J. Fanet, *Great Wine Terroirs* (Berkeley: University of California Press, 2001), 10.

26. J. B. Nadeau and J. Barlow, *What Makes the French So French: Sixty Million Frenchmen Can't Be Wrong* (London: Robson Books, 2005).

27. Immer, *Great Wine Made Simple.*

28. MacNeil, *The Wine Bible.*

CHAPTER 4

GASTRONOMIC IDENTITY II: FOOD AND CUISINE: THE EFFECT OF THE ENVIRONMENT AND CULTURE ON GASTRONOMY, WINE AND FOOD MARRIAGES, AND TOURISM

CHAPTER OUTLINE:

Introduction

Aperitif: Chef John Folse & Company

The Environment

Food: The Impact of Geography and Climate

Culture

History and Ethnic Diversity

Trial and Error, Innovations, and Capabilities

Gastronomic Identity

Old World and New World Wine and Food Marriages

Wine, Food, and Tourism

Summary

Exercises

KEY CONCEPTS:

- Implementation of a gastronomic identity business model
- Culinary identity movement
- "Homogenization" of agricultural products
- Food appellations
- Physiological factors
- Layers of taste components, texture, and flavors

INTRODUCTION

Whether tourists are described as "visitors in their own region" or by the more traditional concept of someone traveling to a new area for business or leisure, local cuisine is frequently as an important factor for tourists, especially those interested in wine or culinary tourism. A growing industry trend over the past two or three decades has been an interest in regional foods, cultural diversity, culinary tourism, and the idea of gastronomic identity. The Aperitif featuring Chef John Folse demonstrates how this interest is being capitalized on in the business world. In the foodservice industry, whether the identity is based on the firm location or the overriding theme of a restaurant concept, a determination and definition of the gastronomic identity of the location of interest provides an important area of differentiation for the firm or unit.

This general trend appears to be in part a continuation of the "identity movement" of the 1960s and 1970s that fostered nouvelle cuisine and other social movements.[1] General research indicates that identity movements can have an evolutionary and lasting impact on professions, professional identity, and ultimately consumers' expectations. Rao and colleagues described the French nouvelle cuisine movement of the 1970s as a social reaction that followed similar movements in the theater, film, and art communities of the time. Institutional logics and role identities in the culinary community were refined from classical French traditions to nouvelle exploration. Rao and colleagues described five dimensions that changed during this process: culinary rhetoric, the rules of cooking, archetypal ingredients, the role of the chef, and the organization of the menu.[2]

The main defining characteristic of culinary rhetoric is a change in the name of dishes from the classical methods to the nouvelle. The culinary rhetoric of the classic period utilized names based on places or on names of nobles and larger-than-life patrons of famous restaurants. Nouvelle cuisine focused on the use of poetry, imagination, and innovation in menu language based on a theory of "exceptions, nuances, [and] refinements."[3] The rules of cooking during the classical period focused on conformity to the principles of Escoffier. The rules of cooking in the nouvelle cuisine movement featured new ingredients and new cooking techniques and presented old ingredients/techniques in new ways. Archetypal ingredients of classical cuisine include "high game, shellfish, cream, poultry, [and] river fish,"[4] while nouvelle cuisine features "fruits, vegetables, potatoes, aromatic herbs, exotic ingredients, [and] sea fish."[5] The nouvelle movement moved the chef to the center of operations, removing flambéing and other tableside preparations from the role of the front of the house. Finally, the organization of the menu became very narrow (even going so far as the elimination of the menu) and focused on the cuisine of the market or season to maximize the emphasis on freshness.

To me, the nouvelle cuisine identity movement demonstrates that a cuisine, dining habits, recipes, and etiquette are entrenched in tradition. Changes in what, how, when, where, and why a society eats and drinks can be evolutionary or revolutionary (as was the case for nouvelle cuisine).

Danhi as well as Rao and colleagues identify many important factors for defining a cuisine and a culinary identity movement. While a number of factors influence agri-food systems in societies,[6] the restaurant profession, and the logic of institutional foodservice, this chapter focuses on a gastronomic identity perspective in describing food characteristics of a region. This chapter uses the framework presented in Chapter 3 (see Figure 3.2) to contemplate relationships and their impact on the what, how, where, when, and why of local eating, using both Old World and New World examples. This framework can be a useful model for gastronomic tourism strategic planning as well as restaurant concepts centered on regional and local cuisine.

Aperitif | Chef John Folse & Company: Cajun/Creole Cuisine

In terms of gastronomy, the Cajun and Creole culture is, arguably, the most interesting in North America. Cajun and Creole cuisine has some of the most identifiable regional dishes in the world, and Louisiana has a unique climate, geography, history, and tradition. Most importantly, the Cajun and Creole cultures are closely connected to food, which is of central importance in the region's social structure.

While there are a number of famous (and infamous) restaurateurs, entrepreneurs, culinarians, and food manufacturers from Louisiana, there is perhaps only one person that embodies all of these attributes—Chef John Folse. John was born in St. James Parish, Louisiana, in 1946. Like many Cajuns, Folse learned early the secrets of Cajun cooking and Louisiana's unique ingredients. Part of the fabric of life in south Louisiana is a close connection to the definitive pantry of the swamplands. This cultural bond with the land and food not only represents a source of survival but also embodies an important social connection to religion, class, family, and so on.

Well known throughout the culinary world, John Folse emerged onto the culinary scene in 1978 with the opening of his landmark restaurant, Lafitte's Landing Restaurant in Donaldsonville, Louisiana. From the beginning, he set out to market "a taste of Louisiana" to the region and worldwide. During the 1980s, Chef Folse became known as "Louisiana's culinary ambassador to the world." He introduced Louisiana's indigenous products and cooking techniques to Japan in 1985, Beijing in 1986, and Hong Kong and Paris in 1987. During the 1988 presidential summit between Ronald Reagan and Mikhail Gorbachev in Moscow, he made international headlines with the opening of Lafitte's Landing East in Russia, the first American restaurant there. In 1989, John became the first non-Italian chef to create the Vatican state dinner in Rome. And during the 1990s he opened promotional restaurants in London, Bogotá, Taipei, and Seoul.

In part due to his international success, Chef John Folse has created a thriving company that leverages the food and history of Louisiana, providing a unique brand based on the man himself and his unique surroundings. His cornerstone business—Lafitte's Landing Restaurant—spawned the creation of a number of related endeavors, including a catering and events management division that serves clients both regionally and nationally (White Oak Plantation); a publishing division producing cookbooks as well as works by other authors; an international television series called *A Taste of Louisiana*; a food manufacturing division, Chef John Folse & Company Manufacturing, that produces custom manufactured foods for the retail and foodservice industry; the naming of the Chef John Folse Culinary Institute at Nicholls State University in his honor; a radio cooking show called *Stirring It Up*; an artisan baking and pastry division; a bed-and-breakfast and fine dining restaurant in his former Donaldsonville home, Bittersweet Plantation; and a dairy division, Bittersweet Plantation Dairy, offering a full line of top-quality fresh and aged cheeses.

Chef John Folse and his company demonstrate the contribution an entrepreneur and restaurateur can make toward ensuring the continuation and recognition of a locale's gastronomic identity. He has done this by serving as a storyteller, historian, innovator, and authentic Louisiana personality. His efforts provide an example of how commercial operators can influence and shape our culinary taste while preserving the historical integrity of the what, how, when, and why of eating and drinking. His success and accompanying recognition can be attributed, at least in part, to the successful implementation of a gastronomic identity business model. Chef Folse's business methods add value to the customer experience and at the same time enlighten the customer. He has had continued success with this basic business model utilizing all types of media (restaurants, catering, publishing, television, radio, and manufacturing). A good example of this is his publications. John Folse has written numerous cookbooks that chronicle the gastronomic identity concept as it applies to Louisiana. Unlike most cookbooks, he adds varying degrees of gastronomic identity elements to each publication. His most recent work, *The Encyclopedia of Cajun and Creole Cuisine*, goes beyond any cookbook in this regard. In nearly 850 pages, he covers Louisiana's history, ethnic diversity, food, culture, recipes, and noteworthy contributors to the current food scene.

Why has his company been such a success? And why did he decide to focus on this particular business model? There is no single answer to these questions, but as with any successful entrepreneurial endeavor, the value of timing, tenacity, vision, and engagement is evident.

Chef Folse emerged on the culinary scene during a period of renewed interest across North America in regional cuisine and the emergence of the celebrity chef. The concept of place of origin was becoming an important dining factor, in terms not just of ingredients but also of history and culture. While other regional cuisines in the United States are of interest to those in the profession, customers, and tourists, Cajun and Creole cuisine is perhaps the most clearly identifiable in regard to recipes, ingredients, preparation, culinary terms, and dining etiquette. John is one of many celebrity chefs propelled into the limelight over the past several decades—but he seems to have taken a route in close connection with many professional associations such as the American Culinary Federation (ACF), Distinguished Restaurants of North America (DiRoNA), and the Research Chefs Association (RCA) rather than solely on the basis of popular media exposure. This path seems to have given him greater sustainability than the flash-in-the-pan type of celebrity chef. I think of him first and foremost as a professional chefs' celebrity chef rather than a pop culture celebrity chef.

As with all successful entrepreneurs, it is obvious that John has an innate sense of purpose to his work that is larger than any individual person or company. Folse's family has nearly three hundred years of history in south Louisiana. Chef Folse views his quest to preserve the cultural heritage of Louisiana as a result of both birth and obligation. This sense of obligation is apparent in his relentless motivation, tenacity, and commitment to cultural preservation.

Chef John Folse's White Oak Plantation, Baton Rouge, Louisiana—a successful catering business that follows a gastronomic identity business model (courtesy of Chef John Folse & Company).

Also, it cannot be denied that much of his success stems from his willingness to engage with not just local but also national and international communities. Having been associated with him in Louisiana, I have never known him to be unwilling to volunteer his time to charitable organizations, be a guest speaker for professional and educational organizations, or serve as an officer in a variety of industry organizations. This service has earned him numerous accolades, including ACF National Chef of the Year, Louisiana Restaurateur of the Year, membership in the Fine Dining Hall of Fame, induction into the DiRoNA Hall of Fame, RCA Pioneer in Culinology, and two honorary doctorates (from Johnson and Wales in 1992 and from Baltimore International Culinary College in 1995).

With more than twenty-five years of success as one of the world's top culinary-based entrepreneurs, Chef Folse continues to share his culinary talents and expertise with students and the public, relentlessly promoting Cajun and Creole cuisine worldwide. His integration of a gastronomic identity business model across a diverse group of business endeavors has been a groundbreaking development in North America, and he would not want it any other way.

The next section highlights one of Chef John Folse & Company's divisions, White Oak Plantation. The Plantation is headquarters for the national catering division, and the physical space is designed to provide guests with a sense of Louisiana's history in architecture, gardens, cuisine, dining etiquette, and service. For additional information on Chef John Folse, his company, products, or Cajun and Creole recipes, visit his company's Web site at www.jfolse.com.

THE WHITE OAK EXPERIENCE

White Oak Plantation sits on thirteen majestic acres in the heart of Baton Rouge. The design of the main house was inspired by Oak Alley Plantation, a well-known historic landmark in the region. It is surrounded by sixteen magnificent Doric columns and sixteen-inch-thick solid masonry walls, giving the traditional "old fortress" appearance that was so popular in the architecture of the 1800s in Louisiana. Just as travelers did in the 1800s, guests take a step back into the past and enjoy the experience of the old Deep South as they arrive on the property. Inside the home, a grand stairway and the main parlor with its twenty-six-foot ceiling, three-tiered antique crystal chandelier, gorgeous period paintings, and antique furnishings will impress and give you a sensation of being in another time period of history. The grand French ballroom features a black and white simulated marble floor and LeBaron crystal chandeliers. The kitchen is a replica of a New Orleans French Quarter landmark, Jean Lafitte's Blacksmith Shop and Gallery. The patios and courtyard areas were designed with the old French Quarter flavor and styles in mind. The main patio area features an open hearth for cochon de laits (fire-roasted suckling pig—a Cajun tradition), along with a large fountain fashioned after the one found at the Court of Two Sisters restaurant in the French Quarter.

The Plantation employs three full-time horticulturists to keep the grounds and gardens trimmed and in bloom year round. Featuring a variety of flowers, fruits, and vegetables amidst species of Louisiana trees, the gardens reflect the evolution of cuisine and culture of Louisiana's Cajun and Creoles, with many of these items utilized in the Plantation's events and dinners. Guests are encouraged to visit the grounds, which feature a lake, Persimmon Hill, and Cathedral Lane. A man-made meandering creek bordered in stone and a wooden bridge add to the ambiance. Each June, the Plantation is host to the Tomato and Herb Fest. The festival features a cooking competition, seminars, and, of course, tasting of Louisiana's heirloom tomatoes and herbs.

White Oak Plantation caters a variety of events, from company picnics and crawfish boils to family reunions, weddings, corporate seminars, relaxed parties, and elegant seated dinners. A consistent element in all of the events is an obvious commitment to the gastronomic identity of South Louisiana. From the time you walk onto the property until the time you leave, you get a sense of history, innovation, and a commitment to details that bring it all to life.

To give a sense of how Chef Folse integrates gastronomic identity into his culinary operations, a menu for Mardi Gras from White Oak Plantation is provided. What should be obvious from the Mardi Gras menu is the impact of cultural heritage, ethnic influences, regional preparation methods, history, indigenous foods, ritual, and local names. The recipes that follow highlight all these influences.

One thing to consider when looking through this menu is the question of what wine to serve with each course. A misconception about Cajun cuisine is that it is all hot and spicy. If it were the case, there would be a very limited number of wines that would be appropriate to serve with Cajun food, and those that were would be mainly a refreshment. But as you will notice from these recipes, the dishes are well seasoned but not necessarily hot and spicy. For the most part when dining in Louisiana, Louisiana hot sauce is served as a condiment, so if you like it hot you can adjust the dish to your liking.

As you look at these recipes (or, better yet, prepare them—these are some great dishes), try to think about the wines you might serve with them and why. As you progress through the upcoming chapters, it will become easier to make wine recommendations. Your taste combination preferences will provide additional guidance. I have provided some of my wine suggestions with each recipe.

Mardi Gras at White Oak Plantation
~Appetizer~
Oysters Marie Laveau
~Soup~
Chicken & Sausage Gumbo
~Salad~
Fiesta Macque Choux
~Vegetable~
Voodoo Greens
~Seafood~
Crab Cakes Rex
~Poultry~
Sweet & Spicy Chicken Etouffe
~Meat~
Soul Pork Roast
~Dessert~
Cajun Pralines
Mardi Gras King Cake

Figure 4.1

Mardi Gras at White Oak Plantation (courtesy of Chef John Folse & Company)

Food Item: Oysters Marie Laveau (courtesy Chef John Folse)

Yield: 6 servings

Marie Laveau was the voodoo queen of Bourbon Street. Legend has it that the pirate Jean Lafitte often met Marie at the Old Absinthe House late in the evening where they enjoyed oysters on the half shell while trading secrets of Barataria Bay.

Ingredients for Oysters

3 dozen select oysters (reserve liquid)
3 tbsp (42 g) butter
1 tsp (5 g) minced garlic
1 tsp (5 g) chopped parsley
½ oz (15 ml) Pernod or Herbsaint

Preparation for Oysters

In a heavy-bottomed sauté pan, melt butter over medium-high heat. Stir in garlic and parsley and sauté 2 minutes. Add oysters and cook until edges begin to curl, but do not overcook. Deglaze with Pernod and cook 1 minute. Remove oysters, reduce liquid by half, and reserve for sauce.

Ingredients for Sauce

¼ lb (113 g) butter
½ c (113 g) diced onions
¼ c (57 g) diced celery
2 tbsp (28 g) minced garlic
¼ c (57 g) sliced green onions
½ c (113 g) white crabmeat or ½ c (113 g) chopped cooked shrimp
2½ tbsp (36 g) flour
3 c (720 ml) heavy whipping cream
1 oz (30 ml) dry white wine
Reserved cooked liquid from oysters
Reserved raw liquid from oysters
⅛ tsp (0.5 g) nutmeg
¼ c (57 g) diced red bell pepper
¼ c (57 g) diced yellow bell pepper
Salt
Cracked black pepper
Parmesan cheese

Preparation for Sauce

Preheat oven to 375°F. In a one-quart heavy-bottomed saucepan, melt butter over medium-high heat. Add onions, celery, garlic and green onions and sauté 3 minutes. Stirring constantly, add crabmeat or shrimp and sauté 1 minute. Whisk in flour until a white roux is achieved, then whisk in cream and wine. Bring to a low boil, stirring constantly as mixture thickens. Pour in cooked liquid from oysters and reserved oyster liquid. Reduce heat to simmer and cook 10–15 minutes, adding hot water if sauce becomes too thick. Add nutmeg and bell pepper, then season with salt and pepper. Place 6 oysters in each au gratin dish, top with a generous serving of sauce, and bake until bubbly. If desired, sprinkle Parmesan cheese on top prior to baking. Serve with garlic croutons.

This recipe is particularly wine-friendly. The classic wine matches with oysters are Champagne, Sancerre (Sauvignon Blanc), or cool-climate Chardonnay. This recipe utilizes baked oysters, the earthy goodness of garlic and onions, and a sauce of cream, oyster liquor, crab, and anise flavor. Of course, a sparkling wine or Champagne would be wonderful with this dish. Because this dish is a more decadent preparation, a New World Chardonnay from the United States, Australia, or Chile would make a great match on the basis of the buttery flavor and the flavor intensity.

Food Item: Chicken and Sausage Gumbo (courtesy Chef John Folse)

Yield: 8–10 servings

Chicken and sausage are the most popular gumbo ingredients in Louisiana. The ingredients were readily available since most Cajun families raised chickens and made a variety of sausages. Oysters were often added to this everyday dish for a special Sunday or holiday version.

Ingredients

One 5-lb (2.25 kg) stewing hen
1 lb (500 g) smoked sausage or andouille
1 c (240 ml) oil
1½ c (340 g) flour
2 c (450 g) diced onions
2 c (450 g) diced celery
1 c (225 g) diced bell peppers
¼ c (57 g) minced garlic
3 qt (2.8 l) chicken stock
24 button mushrooms
2 c (450 g) sliced green onions
1 bay leaf
Sprig of thyme
1 tbsp (14 g) chopped basil
Salt
Cracked black pepper
Louisiana hot sauce
½ c (113 g) chopped parsley
Cooked white rice

Preparation

Using a sharp boning knife, cut hen into 8–10 serving pieces. Remove as much fat as possible. Cut smoked sausage or andouille into ½-inch slices and set aside. In a two-gallon stockpot, heat oil over medium-high heat. Whisk in flour, stirring constantly until golden brown roux is achieved. Stir in onions, celery, bell peppers, and garlic. Sauté 3–5 minutes or until vegetables are wilted. Blend chicken and sausage into vegetable mixture and sauté approximately 15 minutes. Add chicken stock one ladleful at a time, stirring constantly. Bring to a rolling boil, reduce to a simmer, and cook approximately 1 hour. Skim any fat or oil that rises to top of pot. Stir in mushrooms, green onions, bay leaf, thyme, and basil. Season to taste using salt, pepper, and hot sauce. Cook an additional 1–2 hours, if necessary, until chicken is tender and falling apart. Stir in parsley and adjust seasonings. Serve over hot white rice.

Note: You may wish to boil chicken 1–2 hours before beginning gumbo. Reserve stock, bone chicken, and use meat and stock in gumbo.

Of course, this Chicken and Sausage Gumbo is great accompanied by a cold beer, but there are also a number of wine possibilities. The New World Chardonnay from the oyster course could be continued here but the gumbo lends itself to a number of wine opportunities (as long as the gumbo is not too spicy). The rich and smoky flavors of the gumbo could be matched by similarity or contrast with Riesling, Gewürztraminer, Pinot Grigio, Sauvignon Blanc, Chardonnay, and Pinot Noir.

Food Item: Fiesta Macque Choux Salad (courtesy Chef John Folse)

Yield: 6 servings

Macque Choux is an early Louisiana dish that borrows its name from the Creole word for corn, *maque*, and the French word for cabbage, *choux*. Although cabbage doesn't appear in the dish today, it is believed to have been in the original vegetable casserole. Today, macque choux is a baked corn and shrimp dish enjoyed by the Cajuns of River Road. This fiesta salad gives the two-hundred-year-old recipe a Mexican twist.

Ingredients for Vinaigrette

1¼ c (300 ml) olive oil
½ c (120 ml) white wine vinegar
¼ c (60 ml) lime juice
¼ c (57 g) cilantro leaves
1 avocado, diced

Preparation

Combine olive oil, vinegar, lime juice, and cilantro in a food processor. Pulse for 1 minute. Add avocado and pulse again until blended. Do not overblend. Pour vinaigrette into a bowl and chill.

Ingredients for Salad

2 dozen (16–20 count) shrimp, peeled and deveined
½ c (120 ml) lime juice
¼ c (60 ml) lemon juice
½ c (120 ml) tequila
2 tbsp (30 ml) triple sec
1 tbsp (14 g) chopped basil
1 tbsp (14 g) chopped thyme
Salt
Cayenne pepper
1–2 red bell peppers
1–2 yellow bell peppers
1 c (225 g) whole-kernel corn
1 c (225 g) diced Creole tomatoes
½ c (113 g) diced zucchini
½ c (113 g) canned black beans, rinsed
½ c (113 g) diced Bermuda onions
1 tbsp (14 g) minced jalapeños
¼ c (57 g) chopped cilantro
2 tbsp (30 ml) olive oil

Method

In a large mixing bowl, combine shrimp, lime juice, lemon juice, tequila, triple sec, basil, and thyme. Season with salt and cayenne pepper. Toss and marinate shrimp in refrigerator for approximately 30 minutes. While shrimp are marinating, roast red and yellow bell peppers directly over an open flame or under the broiler, turning frequently, until skin blisters and blackens. Place hot peppers in a brown paper bag and let sit for 10–15 minutes. Peel blistered skin from peppers under cold running water. Seed and dice peppers. In a large bowl, toss peppers, corn, tomatoes, zucchini, black beans, onions, jalapeños, and cilantro. Set aside. Remove shrimp from marinade. Discard marinade. In a heavy-bottomed sauté pan, heat olive oil over medium-high heat. Sauté shrimp 2–3 minutes or until pink and curled. Remove from pan. Toss shrimp and roasted pepper salad with ½ cup of avocado vinaigrette. Garnish the rim of a large margarita glass by dipping it in lime juice and minced cilantro. Fill glass with salad. Garnish with lime slice. Serve with tortilla chips.

Matching wine with salad is always a tricky issue. The keys to matching wine with a salad involve two characteristics: tartness and richness. In the preparation of a salad, the chef should ensure the acidity is not so high that wine pairing will become impossible. In this case, a relatively safe bet is a crisp white such as a New Zealand Sauvignon Blanc.

Food Item: Voodoo Greens (courtesy Chef John Folse)

Yield: 8–10 servings

Voodoo is a religion brought to Louisiana by slaves that blends elements of Roman Catholicism, African traditional religion, and magic. Just as a voodoo sorceress can wield mysterious power over her intended prey with a supernatural potion, this dish can hold you under its spell with a vast array of herbs, greens, sausages, and meats. Partake of voodoo greens if you dare!

Ingredients

1 bunch mustard greens
1 bunch collard greens
1 bunch turnip greens
1 bunch watercress
1 bunch beet tops
1 bunch carrot tops
1 bunch spinach
3 c (680 g) diced onions
1/4 c (57 g) minced garlic
3 qt (2.8 l) chicken stock or water
1 lb (454 g) smoked sausage, sliced
1 lb (454 g) smoked ham, diced
1 lb (454 g) hot sausage, sliced
1/2 lb (227 g) smoked ham hocks
1 tsp (5 g) thyme
1 tbsp (14 g) filé powder
Salt
Cayenne pepper
Louisiana hot sauce

Preparation

Rinse greens 2–3 times under cold running water to remove all soil and grit. Pick out bad leaves, remove large center stem, and chop greens coarsely. In a 12-quart pot, combine greens, onions, garlic, stock, and meats. Bring mixture to a rolling boil, reduce to a simmer, and cook 1–1 1/2 hours, stirring occasionally. Remove ham hocks from pot and cut away skin. Remove meat from bone, chop coarsely and return to pot. Add thyme and filé powder, then season with salt, cayenne, and hot sauce to taste. Continue to cook until vegetables are extremely tender. Serve as a vegetable side dish or stuffing for chicken and fish.

The Voodoo Greens are probably the most difficult dish to match on this menu. Greens are naturally bitter and can have a metallic taste when served with wine. But, not unlike the German classic marriage of sauerkraut, pork, and Riesling, an off-dry Riesling could be paired successfully with this mixture of herbs, greens, sausage, and meat.

Food Item: Crab Cakes Rex (courtesy Chef John Folse)

Yield: 8 servings

The crab cakes of bayou country are usually dense in texture due to the abundance of bread crumbs in the recipe. For a more appetizing texture, this recipe has fewer bread crumbs and more crabmeat.

Ingredients	Preparation
1 lb (454 g) lump crabmeat, picked over	In a sauté pan, melt butter over medium-high heat. Add onions, celery, bell peppers, and garlic. Sauté 3–5 minutes or until vegetables are wilted. Remove and cool slightly. In a large mixing bowl, combine sautéed vegetables and all remaining ingredients except crabmeat, ½ cup bread crumbs, and oil. Use hands to gently fold in crabmeat, continually checking for shell or cartilage. Adjust seasonings if necessary. Gently form crab mixture into 1-by-2½-inch patties. Dust lightly with bread crumbs, then place on a cookie sheet. Chill in refrigerator at least 1 hour. In a sauté pan, heat vegetable oil over medium-high heat. Sauté crab cakes 2–3 minutes on each side, turning each cake over gently to avoid breaking. Place crab cake in center of dinner plate and top with White or Red Rémoulade Sauce.
3 tbsp (43 g) butter	
½ c (113 g) diced onions	
½ c (113 g) diced celery	
½ c (113 g) diced red bell peppers	
¼ c (57 g) minced garlic	
1 c (227 g) Italian bread crumbs	
¼ c (57 g) thinly sliced green onions	
¼ c (60 ml) mayonnaise	
1 egg	
2 tbsp (29 g) minced parsley	
2 tsp (10 ml) Worcestershire sauce	
2 tsp (10 ml) lemon juice	
2 tbsp (28 g) Old Bay seasoning	
1 tsp (5 ml) Creole mustard	
Salt	
Cracked black pepper	
Louisiana hot sauce	
½ c (113 g) Italian bread crumbs	
¼ c (60 ml) vegetable oil	

This recipe has many wine-friendly ingredients, like the oyster recipe: garlic, peppers, onions, and crab. The rémoulade sauce accompanying it creates a bit more heat, but a wine choice of Champagne or New World Chardonnay from the United States, Australia, or Chile would be appropriate here as well.

Food Item: Sweet and Spicy Chicken Étouffée (courtesy Chef John Folse)

Yield: 6 servings

In many cultures, sweet and spicy go hand in hand, like sweet and sour. In south Louisiana, where sugar and cayenne pepper are found together in so many recipes, it is obvious how this dish evolved.

Ingredients

One 3-lb (1.5 kg) fryer, cut into 8 serving
    pieces
1/4 c (60 ml) Worcestershire sauce
4 tsp (19 g) salt
3 tsp (14 g) cayenne pepper
1/4 tsp (1 g) black pepper
1 tbsp (14 g) granulated garlic
3/4 c (170 g) flour
1/2 c (120 ml) vegetable oil
3 c (680 g) sliced Bermuda onions
1 c (225 g) diced celery
1 c (225 g) sliced red bell peppers
1 c (225 g) sliced yellow bell peppers
2 c (470 ml) chicken stock
1/4 c (57 g) brown sugar

Preparation

In a mixing bowl, combine chicken with Worcestershire, salt, cayenne, black pepper and garlic. Marinate chicken in seasonings 1 hour at room temperature. (It is acceptable to leave chicken at room temperature for this length of time, but it must be cooked immediately following marinating.) Place chicken on a large cookie sheet and reserve marinating liquid. Dust meat with flour and set aside. In a cast-iron Dutch oven, heat oil on medium-high. Carefully brown chicken without scorching. Remove and set aside. Sauté onions, celery, and bell peppers 2–3 minutes or until vegetables are wilted. Add chicken stock, reserved marinade, and brown sugar. Bring to a rolling boil, then return chicken to pot. Reduce heat to simmer, cover, and cook 45 minutes or until chicken is tender. Adjust seasonings if necessary. Serve over steamed white rice.

Sweet and spicy foods can be more difficult to match with wine. An off-dry white or fruit-forward red are probably your best bets. Off-dry white possibilities include Moscato d'Asti, Riesling, or Gewürztraminer. Red wine possibilities include Syrah (Shiraz), Côtes du Rhône, Spanish Rioja, or Zinfandel.

Food Item: Soul Pork Roast (courtesy Chef John Folse)

Yield: 6 servings

The word *soul* is used to describe the music and the cooking style created in the slave quarters and cotton fields of the South. Lesser cuts of meat, trimmings, and leftover vegetables were often thrown into an iron pot in a slave cabin to create a dish that far surpassed an entrée in the "main house." It takes a lot of soul to create something out of nothing.

Ingredients for Roast and Stuffing

One 5-lb (2.25 kg) Boston butt roast
1/4 c (57 g) minced garlic
1/4 c (57 g) sliced green onions
1 tsp (5 g) thyme
1 tsp (5 g) basil
2 jalapeño or cayenne peppers, diced
4 tbsp (57 g) salt
4 tbsp (57 g) cracked black pepper
Louisiana hot sauce

Preparation

In a small mixing bowl, combine garlic, green onions, thyme, basil, peppers, salt, and pepper. Using a paring knife, pierce approximately ten 1-inch holes in roast and season each pocket with an equal amount of mixture. Season outside of roast completely with additional salt, additional black pepper, and hot sauce to taste.

Ingredients for Roasting

1/4 c (60 ml) vegetable oil
2 c (450 g) diced onions
1 c (225 g) diced celery
1 c (225 g) diced bell peppers
6 garlic cloves, chopped
6 carrots, sliced 1 inch thick
1 quart (.95 l) beef or chicken stock
1 c (225 g) sliced green onions
1/2 c (113 g) chopped parsley
Louisiana hot sauce

Preparation

In a heavy-bottomed Dutch oven, heat oil over medium-high heat. Place roast in pot and sear 3–5 minutes on all sides. Surround roast with onions, celery, bell peppers, garlic and carrots. Pour in stock, bring to a rolling boil, and reduce to a simmer. Cover and place in oven. Cook 2–2 1/2 hours or until roast is tender. Add green onions, parsley and a dash of hot sauce. Remove roast and place on a serving platter. Allow to rest 15 minutes before slicing. Serve over steamed white rice with a generous portion of pan drippings and a slice of corn bread.

This pork dish has a lot of flavor with a touch of piquancy. Serve it with medium- to full-bodied reds such as Syrah (Shiraz), Rioja, Chianti Classico, or Zinfandel. Or you could serve it with a full-bodied white such as a toasty New World Chardonnay.

Food Item: Cajun Pralines (courtesy Chef John Folse)

Yield: 50 pralines

The Ursuline nuns brought knowledge of great pastry making to Louisiana when they arrived in the 1700s. Their most important contribution was the gift of praline candy to the city of New Orleans. Although this candy was originally made with hazelnuts, bayou country recipes used pecans because of regional abundance. If desired, pecans may be toasted before being added to the pralines. To toast, bake pecans on a sheet pan at 275°F for 20–25 minutes or until slightly browned.

Ingredients	Preparation
1½ c (340 g) sugar ¾ c (170 g) light brown sugar, packed ½ c (120 ml) milk 1 tsp (5 ml) pure vanilla extract ¾ stick (85 g) butter 1½ c (340 g) pecans	Combine all ingredients over heat and stir constantly until mixture reaches soft-ball stage (234–240°F). Remove from heat and stir until thickened. Praline mixture should become creamy and cloudy, and pecans should stay in suspension. Drop spoonfuls onto buttered wax paper, foil, or parchment paper. *Note:* When using wax paper, be sure to buffer with newspaper underneath, as hot wax will transfer to whatever is beneath.

The Cajun Pralines and Mardi Gras King Cake are very sweet indeed. To diminish some of this sweetness, the higher alcohol in a fortified wine such as tawny Port would provide a nice backdrop for these decadent desserts.

Food Item: Mardi Gras King Cake (courtesy Chef John Folse)

Yield: 10 servings

The king cake is the traditional dessert of the Carnival season and was originally served on the Feast of the Epiphany. To make the dessert fun and unique, a bean was pressed into the dough prior to cooking. Whoever got the slice containing the bean had to host a party for all guests in attendance. Today the bean has been replaced with a plastic baby to signify the New Year.

Ingredients for Dough

1/2 oz (14 g) instant yeast
1 1/2 c (360 ml) warm water
1/2 c (113 g) sugar
5 c (1.13 kg) flour
1/2 c (113 g) dry milk powder
2 tsp (10 g) salt
2 eggs, beaten
1 c (240 ml) melted butter

Preparation

In a measuring cup, combine yeast and 1/2 cup water. Set aside. In a large mixing bowl, sift together all dry ingredients. Using a dough hook on an electric mixer, blend dry ingredients 2–3 minutes on low speed. In a separate mixing bowl, combine eggs, 3/4 cup butter, and remaining water. Slowly pour egg mixture and bloomed yeast into mixing bowl with flour, gradually increasing speed. Mix 8–10 minutes or until dough separates from bowl. An additional 1/2 cup of flour may be sprinkled into bowl if dough is too wet. Brush a large stainless-steel bowl with melted butter until coated, then place dough inside. Brush dough with remaining butter and cover tightly with plastic wrap. Allow dough to proof in a warm place 1 hour or until double in size.

Ingredients for Glaze

2 lb (907 g) powdered sugar
1 pinch salt
1 tbsp (15 ml) almond extract
3/4 c (180 ml) water
3 tbsp (43 g) cinnamon

Preparation

In an electric mixer, combine sugar and salt. Mix on low speed while slowly pouring in almond extract and water. Add cinnamon and continue to blend until glaze is smooth. Set aside.

Ingredients for Assembly

1/4 c (60 ml) melted butter
1/2 c (113 g) sugar
1 tbsp (14 g) cinnamon
Egg wash (1/2 c [120 ml] milk plus 2 eggs, beaten)
Purple, green, and gold sugars (available at pastry and cake decorating outlets)

Preparation

Preheat oven to 350°F. After dough has proofed, roll out onto a well-floured surface into an 18–by-12-inch rectangle. In a small bowl, combine sugar and cinnamon. Brush top of dough with melted butter, then sprinkle with sugar and cinnamon mixture. Cut cake vertically into 3 even sections. Pinch together end of each strip. Starting from the joined end, form into a basic three-strand braid. Shape braid into a circle and pinch together to hold form. Brush entire cake with egg wash and proof in a warm place until it doubles in size. Bake 20–25 minutes or until golden brown. Drizzle glaze over entire cake and sprinkle with colored sugars.

THE ENVIRONMENT

There are many factors in the external environment that impact food, food production, traditions, the fusion of styles, and product offerings. In the following sections, the focus is on the impact of geography and climate on indigenous food products and the integration of new food products over time. Many of the same issues presented in Chapter 3 for wine apply equally to food.

FOOD: THE IMPACT OF GEOGRAPHY AND CLIMATE

How have geography and climate affected food and the culinary world? Geography and climate impact the agricultural products that are produced, which in turn impact our food habits. The items available in our environment affect flavor preferences, eating habits, recipes, and dining etiquette.

For most of human history, food has been consumed near where it was produced. If a society had good access to freshwater fishing, for example, fish was a prominent part of dietary patterns. Early societies and settlers in an area obtained food from the local environment, and regions that provided an adequate food supply provided a basis for the development of new settlements and more advanced civilizations. In Europe, regional variations in soil type, rainfall, temperature, and altitude constrained what could be grown successfully, and so food products vary significantly across Europe. Cereal production tended to be limited to low-lying and irrigated plains, while mountainous areas were generally utilized for livestock grazing and pasture. Southern European climates supported citrus fruits, olives, and Mediterranean vegetables. Populations in coastal areas were dependent on fish and other seafood as a large part of their diet.[7]

While eating is essential for life, the enjoyment of eating good food is dependent on cultural preferences for specific flavor profiles. As indicated in Chapter 2, all of us can identify the dominant taste sensations of sweet, salty, sour, and bitter. Our preference or tolerance for specific levels of these sensations is based in part on our country of origin, eating habits, and the climate in which we live. This reflects learned preferences for specific flavor profiles based on readily available products. For example, chestnuts are a common food in certain parts of Europe, including the mountainous Cévennes region in France as well as numerous locations in northern Italy and Spain.[8] But you would not find chestnuts eaten with any frequency in the southern United States or other areas where they are not indigenous.

Another reason for focusing on regionally produced food products is closely tied to food quality. Generally, locally produced items are perceived as being of good quality—particularly perishable products such as fruits and vegetables. Most of us can relate to childhood memories of locally grown products consumed during the peak of the season, such as Louisiana crawfish, Maine lobster, vine-ripened tomatoes, or fresh asparagus.

The idea of terroir can be applied to food items as well as to wine, as is often done in France. As noted in the chapter on wine, the terroir concept is closely tied to both history and nature. It is diametrically opposed to intensive farming practices that treat the soil as "an inert substrate that could be 'laced' with synthetic fertilizers and water to improve productivity."[9] While intensive farming has led to agricultural surpluses and the ability to consistently feed Western populations, consumers have become increasingly concerned about food safety, traceability, and sustainability. After more than fifty years of increasingly standardized foods, many segments of the population desire a more varied diet.

During this same period, the AOC (*appellations d'origine contrôlée*) concept was steadily winning converts. The basic principle was to enhance the soil and climate while creating distinctive food products that have characteristics closely linked to the place of origin. This continues as a trend with movements such as Slow Food (initially started in Torino, Italy) and others that recognize the value of local foods and the potential problems associated with intensive methods of production.

There are two main forces at work in this relationship between a region and its food: nature and people. Nature provides the unique soil and climate characteristics. Soil types can vary substantially from heavy and fertile to light and sandy or dry and stony, to name a few examples. The effect of climate differences (shown for wine in Chapter 3) apply to food products as well.

People provide know-how and capabilities to ensure the proper seed stock is sown in the correct type of soil at the right time and that the food product is properly cared for, harvested at the appropriate time, stored properly, handled correctly, and fabricated as tradition dictates if it is to become a value-added food item such as cheese, cured meats, pastries, and so on.

Faced with global demand and intensive farming methods, producers can choose to keep their costs and prices down, following a low-cost producer strategy. Or they may choose to identify with a specific location and differentiate their product through working with nature and utilizing specific methods of production, leading to distinctive products with characteristics that cannot be duplicated elsewhere.[10] This is the heart of the terroir concept and has been applied to, among other products, Bresse chicken and Dijon mustard from France, Parmigiano Reggiano from Italy, Neufchâtel cheese from Switzerland, Walla Walla sweet onions from Washington state, and Creole tomatoes from Louisiana. As with wine production, the AOC idea enhances the natural environment through the use of sustainable farming and production methods while providing a market niche for producers.

Geography and climate impact not only the food products that are readily available at a particular location but also interact with human physiological characteristics to impact eating habits. For example, while wheat and ancient relatives of wheat (spelt, farro, and einkorn) were available at a variety of climatic regions, staple food products based on wheat varied from region to region not only because of cultural or religious differences but also because of the relationship among climate, physiology, and cooking method. For example, societies that are known for artisan breads and other baked goods, which are cooked for a relatively long time in ovens that generate a lot of heat, are generally located in the more northern, cooler climates such as France, Germany, and northern Italy. In warmer climates, people may not have wanted to increase their physical discomfort by generating additional heat by using ovens, and so they adapted the use of wheat for food products that do not require such extended cooking, such as pasta (well known throughout Italy) and flat breads of various types prepared in southern Europe and North Africa. Additionally, the decision whether or not to utilize an oven may be connected to the cost of the fuel to heat it—poorer regions may not have had the means to do this.

Capsicum peppers are another example of how diet can interact with physiological properties as well as climate. While peppers have been part of the European diet since the 1600s, their use in dishes are associated with warmer climate zones across the globe. The spread of chiles throughout the world over the past five hundred years has been truly remarkable, but their use in traditional foods has remained limited to warmer climatic zones. Few northern Europeans adopted widespread use of peppers—they were hard to grow in that climate, and the populations there did not need the cooling achieved when pepper ingestion results in sweating. Originating in North America (and discovered for Europeans by Columbus on a Caribbean island), the capsicum pepper is used frequently in places such as South America, Thailand, India, Mexico, and many of the U.S. southern and southwestern states, including Louisiana, Texas, and New Mexico.[11]

CULTURE

Food and wine habits are strongly affected by a variety of cultural norms and events, including the history of the region, the food systems employed, the amount and location of trade, traditions, beliefs, and local capabilities. Regional cuisine never stands still, either—it is constantly evolving in response to changes in environment, tradition, flavor preferences, product availability, and current fashion.

The Business Perspective From an operator's perspective, aspects of the environment that affect foodservice operations and product and service innovations include suppliers of food and beverage, competitors' actions and anticipated reactions to the introduction of new products, customer preferences and demand analysis, financial or capital markets, labor markets, growing consumer and regulatory concerns in the areas of food safety and nutrition, and technological developments.[12] From a business perspective, all of these areas will influence gastronomic identity over time. Innovations in foodservice operations (wine, food, services, or a combination) can quickly take advantage of emerging trends and seasonal ingredients to satisfy consumers' increasing desire for variety.[13] The continuing profitability and popularity of specific agricultural products, foodservice products, and service are impacted by both the business environment and the environment characteristics driven by geography and climate. Seasonality of products can drive business decisions as well—in most cases, seasonal ingredients have the advantage of maximizing food quality while minimizing cost for the operator.

HISTORY AND ETHNIC DIVERSITY

Historical events and governmental policies have a substantial impact on agricultural products.[14] Population growth, agricultural innovation, and increased global trade have continually changed the face of regional cuisine since the sixteenth century. Trade and immigration have had a substantial impact on cuisine, food products, flavor profiles, and dining etiquette over the course of several centuries.

As trade relations develop between countries, so does the bartering and commercial trading of food products. This situation is particularly exemplified by the spice trade during the fifteenth through seventeenth centuries. The modern concept of the globalization of food masks the complex and heterogeneous nature of food production, allocation, and use characteristics within the global economy.[15]

Gastronomic traditions are impacted by adventurers' contact with other people and regional gastronomy, both in the past and today. Many times trade brings new and exotic foods and beverages from distant places to be combined with local ingredients and preparation methods, which evolve into a fusion cuisine or specific local traditions in wine production. Trade brings new ingredients, preparation methods, and dining etiquette to faraway places. A prime example of the fusion concept is the local food of Louisiana. These local traditions have evolved into a unique regional cuisine influenced by seven cultures over the course of several hundred years: those of Spain, France, Germany, Italy, Britain, Native Americans, and Africa.[16]

Immigration patterns, population diversity, and historical events have impacted dietary patterns throughout North America. For instance, the impact of Asian cultures on the West Coast of the United States is obvious. Restaurants featuring national cuisines of Japan, Thailand, Korea, and Vietnam abound. The fusion of these cultures' ingredients and cooking methods are the norm in many "American" restaurants from Seattle, Washington to Los Angeles, California.

TRIAL AND ERROR, INNOVATIONS, AND CAPABILITIES

Trial and error is at the heart of both innovations and lasting traditions in food production. Gastronomic identity is also determined by the capabilities of those in the region and local area. The Aperitif featuring Chef John Folse & Company at the beginning of this chapter provides an example of a firm that has established gastronomic identity capabilities in a variety of venues. These capabilities can be developed over time, based on trial and error, and the process can create wine, food, or pairing innovations to outfox the competition. Capabilities of this sort may be limited to a firm, locally based, or regional, as is true of wine. Locally based capabilities allow the creation of new innovations that ultimately impact identifiable gastronomic products and services.

External to any particular firm are the factors that drive the agricultural production and distribution system in any given region. Factors of production—capital, credit and financial services, labor markets, information, and training, as well as supplies of seeds, chemicals, and equipment—are required to provide an appropriate infrastructure for farmers, wholesalers, and retailers. There must be people who have an interest in producing food and the ability to do so, along with business that serve agricultural producers. Further, capabilities must also be available in the form of intermediaries (wholesalers, import/export, storage, and transportation), food industries (processing, manufacturing, catering, and retailing), and regulation (health and nutrition policies, quality and safety monitoring, and security measures). Finally, for an agricultural system of any kind to operate, the final products have to be valued by and accessible to the consuming public, which must have the means (purchasing power) and desire (food habits and culture) to acquire them.[17]

GASTRONOMIC IDENTITY

What does all of this mean in regard to gastronomic identity? To recap, regional flavor profiles, dining etiquette, and regional recipes are predominantly derived through a continuous interaction and evolution of fashion, traditions, culture, and climate. All cuisines and gastronomic traditions are created through a fusion of ingredients and techniques as a result of the marrying of diverse cultures, ethnic influences, and history. These gastronomic traditions are tempered or restricted by limitations in product availability and know-how.

The Development of Regional Gastronomic Identity in Italy

Prior to the widespread development of global distribution channels, there was really no such thing as a truly national cuisine in Europe or elsewhere. The political entity currently known as Italy did not come into being until 1860. The five major regions that make up present-day Italy provide an example of vastly differing culinary traditions. Milan and the surrounding region have a rich tradition of dairy farming as well as a history of a wide variety of agricultural production of fruits and vegetables; rice is an important food item, and the traditional dish risotto alla Milanese features butter (rather than olive oil) as the cooking medium for sautéing the regional short-grain rice, which is then finished with stock, saffron, and cheese. Venice provides an example of the influence of its lucrative trade with Asia and the incorporation of spices such as nutmeg and cinnamon; not surprisingly, given its position on the sea, Venice places seafood in a prominent role in its cuisine. The region of Tuscany is renowned for its production of olive oil and a fondness for beans (the local population is often called *mangia fagioli*—bean eaters), the latter due to the Tuscans being impoverished throughout the early modern period and the scarcity of available meat products.[18] The cuisine of Rome and the surrounding area was based on young meats such as lamb, veal, and kid. The cuisine of Naples ranged along a spectrum from lavish to frugal; many of the foods identified in North America as "Italian" come from Naples, such as tomato sauce, mozzarella, pizza, and spaghetti.[19]

Italian regional cuisine provides an example of how differing indigenous products are incorporated into the local cuisine as well as how new products are adapted into the diet based on fashion and the profitability of importing or producing food items that were previously foreign or exotic. As is apparent throughout the discussion of the impact of the environment on wine and food, geography and climate provide many answers to the gastronomic identity but are only part of the story. Culture, history, trade, and ethnic diversity have a comparable impact on components, texture, and flavor profiles in both wine and food.

OLD WORLD AND NEW WORLD WINE AND FOOD MATCHES

Repertoires of traditional foods and wines that accompany them have, in many cases, developed over many years of refinement to meet local tastes and utilize local products. Such associations create an additional taste and flavor layering between the food and wine. In such matches, food flavors are generally deep and rich but not bold.

Table 4.1 provides a number of classic regional wine and food matches. This table outlines some of the classic matches from Old World countries such as France, Italy, and Spain. Additionally, New World wine and food combinations are provided from California, Washington, Australia, New Zealand, and South America. The first column lists the country of origin, the second column includes the wine and food description, and the third column contains a brief description of interacting wine and food elements. These examples provide a sense of the classic marriages (old and new) deeply rooted in the gastronomic identity of each country and regions within countries.

General Wine and Food Relationships Demonstrated There are several consistent food and wine element relationships in these classic marriages. First, there are several examples of matching food texture to wine texture. In Bordeaux, fattiness in lamb is matched with the tannins in these predominately Cabernet Sauvignon wines. The richness of foie gras works with the richness of Sauternes due to the palate-cleansing qualities inherent in this crisp, sweet wine.

Similar to the red Bordeaux and lamb match, the Tuscan combination Bistecca alla Fiorentina and Chianti matches food fattiness to tannin as well as body to body based on the cooking method employed for the food (grilling).

Second, there are several examples of food and wine matches that use a flavor match: the earthy flavors in Coq au Vin with those of a red Burgundy, the earthy/intense flavors of dishes made with white truffle paired with intense wines using Nebbiolo grapes, and the buttery flavors in California Chardonnay matched with similar flavors of butter-dipped Dungeness crabmeat.

The impact of wine acidity is highlighted in a number of situations. Tangy foods paired with crisp white wines are an acid-to-acid match in marriages such as Sancerre with goat cheese. And the acidity of German or Alsatian Riesling is a contrast to the fattiness in pork and other meat dishes.

The classic Old World combination of oysters and Chablis.

Port wine matched with Stilton cheese provides a classic example of a contrasting match, with the sweetness of the Port standing out against the salty character of the cheese.

All in all, these marriages indicate that there are substantial differences in the type of matches in different locales, whether Old World or New World. But there appear to be some consistent relationships in the perception of match among components, texture, and

Table 4.1   Classic Regional Wine and Food Matches

Region	Wine and Food Match	Description
France—Bordeaux	Red Bordeaux and lamb	The rich fattiness of young lamb matches with the wine tannins to create a smooth characteristic in the mouth. The strong texture and flavor of lamb matches the substantial body of this Cabernet/Merlot blend.
	Sauternes and foie gras	The richness of Sauternes matches with the richness of foie gras. The acidity in the Sauternes cuts through the fattiness of the foie gras.
France—Burgundy	Coq au Vin and red Burgundy	The earthiness of the onions, naturally raised bird, and mushrooms pair with the earthy character of the Old World Burgundy. The bridging technique of including the wine during the cooking process assists in the marriage. The cooking method and bridging technique creates a body match with the Pinot Noir–based wine.
France—Beaujolais	Poached pork sausages with warm potatoes bathed in olive oil and shallots and Beaujolais wine	The Beaujolais is bursting with fruitiness. Relatively low in tannin, this humble wine works great with humble and down-to earth foods.
Southern France	Lamb and the Rhône wines made from Syrah, Grenache, and Mourvèdre	Rich, gamy, wild flavors of lamb marry with the rich wines.
France—Loire	Sancerre or Pouilly-Fumé and Crottin de Chavignol (a small disk of goat cheese made in Chavignol)	A small disk of goat cheese made in Chavignol and high-acid wines made with Sauvignon Blanc provide perfect tangy counterpoints.
	Tarte Tartin and Quarts de Chaume	A sweet, lightly honeyed dessert wine from Chenin Blanc grapes paired with caramelized tart apples on a light crust.
France—Alsace	Pork and game with hearty vegetables, potatoes, cabbages, and onions served with Alsace Riesling	Perfect cold-weather foods pair wonderfully with this region's Riesling. The acidity of the Riesling provides a nice contrast to cut through the fattiness of the pork and game as well as to provide an additional layer of taste sensation with the other food items.
Italy—Piedmont	White truffle dishes with Barbaresco and Barolo	Earthy and intense flavors of dishes made with white truffle paired with intense wines using Nebbiolo grapes.
Italy—Tuscany	Bistecca alla Fiorentina and Chianti	A large slab of grilled beef served with wine made from Sangiovese grapes—fatty, full-bodied food with tannic reds.
Spain—Rioja	Wild mushrooms in garlicky olive oil served with red Rioja	The earthy character of wild mushrooms, extra-virgin olive oil, and garlic paired with the Old World earthiness in Spanish Rioja.
Spain—Jerez	Garlic shrimp with Manzanilla	Shrimp sautéed in olive oil, dried red pepper, and lots of garlic paired with the salty, briny olive-scented characteristics of Manzanilla.
Spain—Penedès	Pan con tomate served with Cava	Thick slices of warm grilled country bread rubbed on both sides with the cut side of a juicy ripe tomato, drizzled with extra-virgin olive oil, and sprinkled with salt. Served as summer night fare with Spanish **méthode champenoise** sparkling wine. The wine-friendliness of garden-fresh tomatoes combines with food-friendly, refreshingly acidic Cava.
Portugal	Port and roasted nuts or cheese	Blue cheeses (Stilton, Gorgonzola, etc.) with Port are a classic contrasting match. The saltiness of the blue cheese (or nuts) contrasts with the sweetness of Port (think of popcorn and candy at the movies).

Table 4.1 (*Continued*)

Region	Wine and Food Match	Description
Germany	High-acid Rieslings and every meat dish imaginable	No oak and varying levels of sweetness make them the most versatile white wine with food. The acidity and complexity of German Riesling makes it very food-friendly—it can be paired with a wide range of foods including grilled sausages and pork roast.
United States— California	Dungeness crab dipped in butter with Chardonnay	The butter-dipped crab matches with the buttery Chardonnay (malolactic fermentation) when the wine is not overly oaky. The sweetness of the crab contrasts with the light acidity of the Chardonnay.
	Zinfandel with grilled anything; Petite Sirah with grilled steak	The sweet charred flavor and crusty texture makes any food more red-wine-friendly. The wine's simple jammy and fruit-forward character makes it a match with everything from grilled veggies to chicken to steak.
United States— New York	Hudson Valley foie gras and New York ice wine	The richness of ice wine matches with the richness of Foie Gras. The acidity in the wine cuts through the fattiness of the foie gras.
Washington	Pacific Northwest oysters with Riesling, Sémillon, or Sauvignon Blanc	The oysters are briny and minerally. The higher acidity in Washington white wines complements the oysters much like a squeeze of fresh lemon.
Oregon	Pinot Noir and wild Pacific salmon	The higher acidity and lower tannin in these cool-climate Pinots match well with the fattiness and texture of salmon cooked over an open fire.
Canada	Ice wines and desserts	The intensely sweet and yet refreshingly acidic ice wines match with less sweet desserts such as poached fruit, fruit tarts, crème brulée, and sugar cookies.
Australia	Grilled pepper steak and Shiraz	The peppery characteristics of Australian Shiraz match with the body and spice of grilled pepper steak and is also great with lamb, duck, or venison.
New Zealand	New Zealand fusion cuisine with Sauvignon Blanc	The fusion of European traditions combined with indigenous products and tropical techniques creates a cuisine that includes chiles, lime, and many tropical fruits. These ingredients pair nicely with the high acidity, slight sweetness, and pungent character of Sauvignon Blanc.
South Africa	Barbecued meat with Pinotage and Shiraz	Grilled antelope, deer, lamb, sausages, and beef cooked without any seasoning match the body of South African reds; the meat fattiness mellows the tannic nature of the wines.
Argentina	Malbec and beef	Malbec is Argentina's most interesting wine. Its exotic nature allows it to be paired with beef prepared as empanadas, roasted, or barbecued.

flavors that crosses cultural boundaries. The upcoming sections and exercises investigate many of these traditional relationships.

WINE, FOOD, AND TOURISM

Does gastronomic identity have implications for wine or food tourism? The interest in food as a travel motivation has been clearly documented as a type of special-interest tourism. In gastronomic tourism, visitors travel to go to a specific restaurant, market area, or winery, with nearly all of the trip's activities related to food and other gastronomic endeavors.

As shown by the earlier discussion of Chef John Folse, the ability to leverage a gastronomic identity in a business model can be used to attract customers with a variety of interests. In this example, part of the value added is the education of the consumer—tying together history, culture, and food products to create a unique bundle of activities.

Old World wine and food marriages provide additional examples where consumers are taught about terroir and its contribution to the sense of place inherent in the attractiveness of a tourist destination. *Place* has been suggested as an encompassing term to describe the unique combination of "physical, cultural and natural environment [that] gives each region its distinctive touristic appeal."[20] This concept overlaps with terroir and distinctive local food and wine products. All of these elements create a bundle of activities described as "touristic terroir."

SUMMARY

The gastronomic identity of a region or locale is greatly influenced by the location's climate, geography, culture, history, and traditions. This concept is what makes traveling to new places so special. Intensive farming and production techniques have lowered the cost of many products and made more items universally available worldwide—but what has been the cost to gastronomic experiences?

Many firms, such as Chef John Folse & Company, have found making use of a gastronomic perspective a rewarding and profitable opportunity. This opportunity provides unique experiences for locals and visitors alike while preserving (and in many cases exposing) a part of history. Many regions have incorporated this idea into their strategic plan. The Canadian Tourism Commission, for example, has set forth an ambitious plan that embraces the idea of gastronomic tourism to promote Canadian food and drink (check out their Web site at www.canadatourism.com/ctx/app). And a number of museums have started using authentic food and cooking techniques to create an interactive atmosphere that brings history to life.

The intent of Chapters 3 and 4 has been to provide some "meat" to the notion of gastronomic identity and its relationship to tourism, menus, and pairing opportunities. The following exercises will further reinforce and clarify the interactive differences in wine styles and food styles based on the environment and culture. As you go through these exercises and identify taste, texture, and flavor differences, make it a point to determine the nature of the differences. Are they climate-driven? Historical? Or due to other factors?

DISCUSSION QUESTIONS

1. What is an "identity movement"?
2. What were the main characteristics of the French nouvelle cuisine movement?
3. How has trade impacted gastronomic identity?
4. How would you define the term *terroir*?
5. Define the gastronomic identity where you reside based on the geography, climate, fusion of cultures, etc.

a. What is a product or recipe specific to your locale?
b. What climate zone do you believe your locale is in?
c. Are there typical food-and-drink combinations from the region?

EXERCISE 4.1

Harvest-fresh vegetables combined with the earthiness inherent in root vegetables creates an undeniably wine-friendly combination and hints at the way terroir links food and wine. Many vegetables create a more wine-friendly atmosphere when added to cooked dishes (remember the combination in Oysters Marie Laveau). Root vegetables such as onions, garlic, and shallots often require cooking to bring out the natural sweetness and accentuate their earthy character. Beans and potatoes are other sweet and earthy examples, and when they are accented with onions or garlic, the combination creates a rustic but magical taste. Other earthy vegetables include beets, cauliflower, cabbage, turnips, parsnips, and even greens.

The three traditional dishes in the following exercise provide a glimpse of the wine affinity of the onion family. The featured wines exemplify differences based on climate zone characteristics. This exercise points out the classic characteristics of climate zones that provide great clues for food and wine pairing. In analyzing the match potential with the food items, be sure to consider the body of the particular dish (light or full-bodied), the cooking method (light, such as steamed or poached, or heavy, such as broiled or braised), and the style of the dish (rustic, homey, or upscale and luxurious).

OBJECTIVES

The objectives of this exercise are to reinforce your understanding of climate zone differences and to expose you to the compatibility factors between earthy-sweet root vegetables and wine. Tasting wines from different climate zones side by side will allow you to clearly differentiate the acid, fruit, and body characteristics of wines from cooler and warmer climates. When tasting these wines with food items to determine the best match, this exercise reinforces the relationships of earthy flavors, natural sweetness, cooking method, texture, and body with the acid, sweetness, fruit, tannin, and body of wine.

Mise en Place: Things to Do Before the Exercise

Be sure that the production of the food recipes (at the end of this chapter) and their timing is well planned out and clearly understood. The mise en place for the recipes should be done in advance and plans for transporting the item samples to each taster and the cleanup process should be determined ahead of time.

MATERIALS NEEDED

Table 4.2   Materials Needed for Exercise 4.1

1 white paper placemat per student with numbered or labeled circles to place wineglasses (Figure 4.2)	Crackers to cleanse the palate
1 spit cup per student	Napkins
Corkscrew	Drinking water for each student
Utensils for tasting food	4 wineglasses per student
Prepared dishes: Onion Rings, Roasted Garlic, Onion Soup	Paper plates and bowls to serve dishes

STEPS

1. Choose four wines from the list below.

Table 4.3 Suggested Wines for Exercise 4.1

Cool Zone		Moderate Zone	
Riesling from Germany or Canada (Niagara)		Riesling from Alsace (France), Australia, or California	
Sauvignon Blanc from the Loire Valley, Sancerre, or New Zealand		Sauvignon Blanc from California, Bordeaux (France), or Chile	
Optional List (if the tasting group has substantial exposure to climate zone tastings, you might chose wines from this list).			
Alsace Pinot Blanc or Alsace Riesling	Italian white (from southern regions)	Beaujolais	Côtes du Rhône

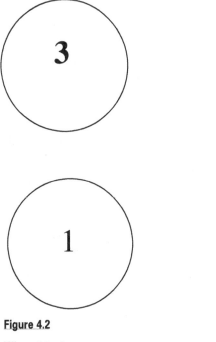

Figure 4.2

Wines 1 to 4

2. Chill the wines.

3. Distribute the placemats (Figure 4.2) and set up the glasses.

4. Open the wines and pour them.

5. Taste the wines and evaluate them. Focus on identifying the differences between the cool-climate and moderate-climate examples. Do the cool-climate and moderate-climate fruit styles, aromas, and flavors match those suggested in Chapter 3 (Table 3.2)?

   a. *Sight.* Are the cool-climate wines lighter in color than the moderate-climate samples?

   b. *Swirl and smell.* What are the differences in the aromas between the cool-climate and moderate-climate wines? Are there differences between the Rieslings' floral characters? What are the differences between the Sauvignon Blancs? Fruit character? Herbaceous characteristics?

   c. *Sip, spit, and savor.* What are the taste differences? Does one have more acidity, body, alcohol, or intensity?

6. Distribute the dishes.

7. Taste the foods and evaluate them.

8. *Onion Rings.* Based on your analysis of each wine and the Onion Rings, select the wine that you believe will be the best match with this dish. Why did you select this wine? Taste that wine with the onion rings. Did the match meet your expectations? Next, taste each of the other wines with the Onion Rings. Rank the wines by level of match with the food, from least match to best match. Record any other observations.

Least match = 1. _____ 2. _____ 3. _____ 4. _____ = Best match

Observations: _____

9. *Roasted Garlic.* Select the wine that you believe will be the best match with the Roasted Garlic. Why? Did you perceive similar components, body, or flavors? Taste that wine with the dish. Did the match meet your expectations? Now taste each of the other wines with the garlic. Rank the wines by level of match, from least match to best match. Record any other observations.

Least match = 1. _____ 2. _____ 3. _____ 4. _____ = Best match

Observations: _____

10. *Onion Soup.* Select the wine that you believe will be the best match with the soup. Why did you select that wine? Did you perceive similar components, body, or flavors? Now taste that wine with the soup. Did the match meet your expectations? Next, taste each of the other wines with the soup. Rank the wines by level of match with the soup, from least match to best match. Record any other observations.

Least match = 1. _____ 2. _____ 3. _____ 4. _____ = Best match

Observations: _____

11. Discuss and analyze the results. Did any one wine match all or the majority of the dishes relatively well? Did a particular wine do a poor job of matching overall? What do you believe was the primary determining factor of a match between the wines and food? If you did the optional tasting and tasted both reds and whites, which do a better job? Was a particular varietal more food-friendly? Why or why not?

EXERCISE 4.2

TERROIR, TAKE 2: THE EARTHY GOODNESS OF MUSHROOMS, TRUFFLES, AND WINE

This exercise is intended to show the wine-friendly character of some classic earthy foods. It is also designed to reinforce the understanding of differences between Old World and New World wines by tasting them side by side with some earthy food dishes.

Mushrooms and truffles are two foods with a clearly identifiable earthy character to them. The recipes that follow feature mushroom duxelles, black truffles and potatoes (two earthy ingredients), white truffles and risotto, and portobellos. There are many examples of earthy foods, including beets, frogs' legs, brown rice, lentils, rainbow trout, and crawfish, to name a few. The duxelles recipe is included because it is a staple of the French kitchen (I fondly recall making frequent batches of duxelles as a young chef to top fish, stuff poultry, as an hors d'oeuvre topping, a key ingredient in Beef Wellington, and so on). It is easy to prepare and provides a relatively light dish filled with earthy goodness.

The black truffle and mashed potato recipe combines the earthy taste and scent of black truffles with the earthy texture of potato. When visiting the south of France with a group of students, I had the good fortune to visit a *marché aux truffes* (a traditional truffle market) and visiting the largest black truffle house in the region, located in Cahors. While there I had one of my most memorable meals: black truffle omelets, good bread, and local red wine in a thirteenth-century building. We ate them off paper plates, standing up in a not-yet-completed catering kitchen, with our wine in plastic cups. It was marvelous!

The white truffle and risotto recipe features two items that are definitely Old World and earthy. The white truffle comes from the Piedmont region in northwest Italy, near the town of Alba. Whereas black truffles are generally served as part of a cooked dish, white truffles have a distinct aroma, texture, and flavor and should not be served in cooked. White truffles are served sliced thinly atop everything from pasta, to salads and carpaccio. In this case, it is added as a garnish at the end of the risotto preparation. White truffles are one of the most heavenly foods in the world—and are priced accordingly. Late fall white truffles are superior to summer truffles, and I find the Italian white truffles to be superior to the New World ones that are currently available. However, Oregon white truffles make a reasonable substitute at a much lower cost.

The Grilled Portobello Mushrooms provide an earthy and meaty example for wine pairing. The portobello is a big brown mushroom—an overgrown crimini. Portobellos have become a popular "vegetarian meat" across the United States.

There are several wine styles that can be investigated from both the Old World and New World with these items.

While performing this tasting exercise, you should assess the impact of a food's earthiness on the wine and food relationship. Does it enhance the relationship across the board? Or is the match dependent on the wine? How does the richness of the food item interact with the light or rich body of the wine? What impact did cooking technique have on this body relationship? What part does wine sweetness and acidity play in this relationship? Could you differentiate Old World from New World wines of the same varietal?

OBJECTIVES

The primary objectives of this exercise are to compare the distinct differences between Old World and New World wine styles as well as to expose you to the compatibility of earthy food and wine flavors with a body match. It also will ex-

pose you to how cooking techniques affect the relationship between matching food and wine levels. This exercise ties in with the discussion of gastronomic identity, Old World and New World characteristics of wine and food, and climate differences in varietal characteristics.

Mise en Place: Things to Do Before the Exercise First, review the discussion of how the differences between the Old World and New World manifest in food. Also, make sure that the production of the foods is well planned out to ensure that hot food will be served at the right temperature. Mise en place for the recipes should be done in advance and plans for transporting the item samples to each taster and the cleanup process should be determined ahead of time.

MATERIALS NEEDED

Table 4.4 Materials Needed for Exercise 4.2

1 white paper placemat per student with numbered circles to place wineglasses (Figure 4.2)	Crackers to cleanse the palate
1 spit cup per student	Napkins
Corkscrew	Drinking water for each student
Utensils for tasting food	4 wineglasses per student
Prepared dishes: Duxelles, Black Truffle Mashed Potatoes. White Truffle Risotto, Grilled Portobellos	Plates and bowls to serve dishes
White Wines	**Red Wines**
Old World Chardonnay (white Burgundy)—select a wine from Mâcon, Pouilly-Fumé, Chablis, Meursault, or Chassagne-Montrachet	Old World Pinot Noir (red Burgundy)—select a wine from Mercurey, Santenay, Bourgogne, Savigny-les-Beaune, or Nuits St. Georges
New World—select a Chardonnay from Australia, California, Chile, or Argentina	New World—select a Pinot Noir from Oregon, cool regions of California or New Zealand

Optional wine suggestions for additional comparisons include Italian Barolo or Barbaresco (from the Nebbiolo grape) and/or Spanish Fino, Manzanilla, or Oloroso Sherries.

Students should bring the following to the tasting exercise: a copy of the Aroma Wheel, and the glossary (at the end of this book).

STEPS

1. Buy the wines.

2. Chill the white wines.

3. Distribute the placemats (Figure 4.2) and set up the glasses.

4. Open the wines and pour them.

5. Taste the wines and evaluate them. Focus on identifying the differences in style between the Old World and New World examples. Is the Old World example more subtle, elegant, and earthy? Is the New World wine bolder, lush, and fruit-forward?

   a. *Sight.* Is the Old World wine lighter in color than the New World sample?

   b. *Swirl and smell.* What are the differences in the aromas between the Old and New World wines?

   c. *Sip, spit, and savor.* What are the taste differences? Does one have more acidity, body, alcohol, or intensity?

6. Distribute the dishes.

7. Taste the foods, evaluate them, and note observations.

8. *Duxelles.* In this exercise there are two Pinots (1 Old World and 1 New World) and two Chardonnays (1 Old World and 1 New World). Based on your analysis of each wine and each dish, select the wine that you believe will be the best match with the Duxelles. Why did you select that wine? Did you perceive similar components, body, or flavors? Now taste that wine with the Duxelles. Did the match meet your expectations? Next, taste each of the other wines with the Duxelles. Rank the wines by level of match with the food from least match to best match. Record any other observations.

   Least match = 1. _____ 2. _____ 3. _____ 4. _____ = Best match
   Observations: _____

9. *Grilled Portobello Mushrooms.* Select the wine that you believe will be the best match with the portobellos. Why did you select that wine? Did you perceive similar components, body, or flavors? Now taste that wine with the portobellos. Did the match meet your expectations? Next taste each of the other wines with the portobellos. Rank the wines by level of match with the portobellos from least match to best match. Record any other observations.

   Least match = 1. _____ 2. _____ 3. _____ 4. _____ = Best match
   Observations: _____

10. *Black Truffle Potatoes.* Select the wine that you believe will be the best match with the potatoes. Why did you select that wine? Did you perceive similar components, body, or flavors? Now taste that wine with the potatoes. Did the match meet your expectations? Next, taste each of the other wines with the potatoes. Rank the wines by level of match with the potatoes from least match to best match. Record any other observations.

   Least match = 1. _____ 2. _____ 3. _____ 4. _____ = Best match
   Observations: _____

11. *White Truffle Risotto.* Select the wine that you believe will be the best match with the risotto. Why did you select that wine? Did you perceive similar components, body, or flavors? Now taste that wine with the risotto. Did the match meet your expectations? Next, taste each of the other wines with the potatoes. Rank the wines by level of match with the risotto from least match to best match. Record any other observations.

   Least match = 1. _____ 2. _____ 3. _____ 4. _____ = Best match
   Observations: _____

12. Discuss and analyze the results. Did any one wine match all or the majority of the dishes relatively well? Did a particular wine do a poor job of matching overall? What do you believe was the primary determining factor of a match between the wines and food? Did reds or whites do a better job? Old World or New World wines?

TASTING EXERCISE RECIPES

Food Item: Onion Rings

Onions Rings seem simple enough but can come out greasy or quickly become limp. I prefer floured rings that are well seasoned to battered ones. The addition of cornstarch to this recipe helps to retain their crispy texture. Add your favorite seasoning salt or herbs as desired.

Yield: 6–8 servings (enough for 20–25 tastings)

Ingredients

3 large white onions, peeled and thinly sliced
Frying oil
2 eggs, beaten
1/2 c (120 ml) water or milk
2 c (450 g) flour
1/2 c (113 g) cornstarch
1 tbsp (14 g) salt
1/2 tbsp (7 g) black pepper
1 tbsp (14 g) finely chopped parsley

Preparation

Heat the frying oil to 375°F. Combine the beaten eggs and water in a small bowl. Combine the flour, cornstarch, salt, pepper, and parsley in a shallow pan. Dredge the onion rings in the flour mixture. Shake off the excess flour and dip in the egg wash. Shake off the excess egg wash and dredge one more time in the flour mixture. Fry in the hot oil until golden. Serve immediately.

Food Item: Roasted Garlic

Yield: enough for 20–25 tastings

Ingredients

8 heads garlic
3 tbsp (45 ml) extra-virgin olive oil

Preparation

Preheat the oven to 375°F. Lay the garlic heads on their side and cut a small part of the top off to expose the tips of each garlic clove. Drizzle the exposed garlic tops with olive oil. Place garlic heads (tops facing up) in a baking pan and bake for 30 minutes to 1 hour, until garlic cloves feel soft when pressed. Squeeze the roasted cloves from their jackets. Roasted garlic can be eaten as is, spread over crostini by itself or with other ingredients, or incorporated into a batch of hummus.

Food Item: French Onion Soup (courtesy Chef John Folse)

Yield: 6 servings (enough for 20–25 tastings)

Ingredients

¼ c (57 g) butter
2 tbsp (30 ml) olive oil
4 large onions, finely sliced
2 tbsp (28 g) minced garlic
1½ tbsp flour (optional)
½ c (240 ml) Pinot Noir
4 c (.95 l) beef broth
2 large bay leaves
Salt
Pepper
6 thick slices French bread
¾ c (170 g) grated Swiss cheese

Preparation

In a large cast-iron Dutch oven, heat butter and oil together. Once oil is hot, add onions and garlic and cook over medium heat for approximately 30 to 45 minutes, stirring occasionally, until caramelized but not burned. For a slightly thicker soup, sprinkle in the flour and blend well. Deglaze with Pinot Noir. Add broth, bay leaves, and salt and pepper to taste and bring to a rolling boil. Reduce to a simmer, cover, and cook for 30 minutes. Remove bay leaves and adjust seasonings if necessary. Preheat broiler. Place 6 soup cups on a cookie sheet and fill three-quarters full. Place a slice of French bread on top of each portion of soup and cover evenly with Swiss cheese. Place under broiler until bread is toasted and cheese is fully melted. Serve immediately.

Says Chef John Folse, "This classic soup was traditionally the hangover remedy sold in all-night cafés in Paris. It was thought that the rich beef broth flavored with sautéed onions and topped with a hearty crouton would revive revelers in the early hours of the morning following a night of indulgence."[21]

Food Item: Duxelles

Yield: 8 servings (enough for 20–25 tastings)

Ingredients

3 oz (85 g) unsalted butter
1 c (225 g) finely minced onion
4 c (907 g) finely chopped fresh mushrooms
2 cloves garlic, minced
1½ c (360 ml) white wine
Salt
Pepper to taste

Preparation

Melt butter over medium heat and sauté onion until transparent. Add the mushrooms and garlic and cook for 3–5 minutes. Add white wine to the mixture and cook over medium-high heat until the liquid has evaporated. Season to taste with salt and pepper. The mixture can be used immediately or prepared in advance and stored in the refrigerator until ready for use.

Duxelles are great as a stuffing for chicken, as a topping for beef, fish, or veal, in omelets, or served on crostini as an appetizer.

Food Item: Grilled Portobello Mushrooms

Yield: 6–8 servings (enough for 20–25 tastings)

Ingredients

12 large portobello mushrooms
3 tbsp (43 g) butter
3 tbsp (45 ml) olive oil
1 tbsp (15 ml) lemon juice or balsamic
      vinegar
3 cloves garlic, minced
1 tbsp (14 g) chopped herbs such as basil,
      thyme, oregano, tarragon, or chives
      (optional)
Salt
Black pepper

Preparation

Brush or wash the mushrooms, remove and discard stems, scrape out the dark gills if desired, slice the caps into 3/4-inch strips, and set the mushrooms aside. Melt the butter and combine it with the olive oil, lemon juice, garlic, and herbs. Brush the mushrooms with the butter mixture. Grill or broil the mushrooms for approximately 4–5 minutes on each side. Brush the grilled mushrooms with additional butter mixture if desired and season with salt and black pepper.

The grilled mushrooms are tasty on their own, as a sandwich (try them with sliced tomato and goat cheese on a baguette), or atop steak, chicken, or pork.

Food Item: Black Truffle Potatoes

Yield: 6–8 servings (enough for 20–25 tastings)

Ingredients

2 lb (907 g) russet potatoes, peeled and cut
      into 1-inch pieces
1 c (120 ml) half and half
1/2 c (113 g) unsalted butter, at room
      temperature
Salt
Black pepper
2 tbsp (10 g) black truffles, chopped

Preparation

Place the potatoes in a pot of boiling salted water and cook uncovered until tender (about 20 to 30 minutes). Remove from heat and drain. Mash the potatoes with a potato masher or ricer until lumps are removed. Stir in the butter and half and half. Add the chopped truffles and season to taste with salt and pepper. Transfer to a serving bowl and serve.

Black truffles with mashed potatoes make a luxurious yet earthy side dish. Truffle oil can be added or used as a substitute if black truffles are unavailable.

Food Item: White Truffle Risotto

Yield: 6–8 servings (enough for 20–25 tastings)

Ingredients

3 c (680 g) Arborio rice
2/3 c (150 g) unsalted butter
1/2 c (113 g) minced onion
9 c (2 l) fresh chicken stock
1 c (225 g) freshly grated Parmigiano
      Reggiano or Grana Padano
2 oz (60 ml) white truffle oil
3 oz (85 g) fresh white truffles, brushed clean
Salt
White pepper

Preparation

Sauté the onion in 1/3 cup butter until it begins to turn golden. Add the rice, stir, and cook over medium heat for 1–2 minutes. Add 2 cups of the chicken stock and stir constantly until nearly all the liquid is absorbed. Add additional stock 1 cup at a time, stirring constantly and allowing each to become almost fully absorbed before adding more, until the rice is tender but firm. This should take about 20 minutes. Remove from heat and add the remaining butter and grated cheese. Add the truffle oil and season with salt and pepper to taste. Slice truffles thinly (use a truffle slicer). Divide the risotto into individual servings and garnish with sliced truffle. Serve immediately.

Risotto can be served as a first course or as a side dish for poultry, game, fish, or meat.

NOTES

1. H. Rao, P. Monin, and R. Durand, "Institutional Change in Toque Ville: Nouvelle Cuisine as an Identity Movement in French Gastronomy." *American Journal of Sociology* 108, 4 (2003): 795–843.

2. Ibid.

3. Ibid., 806.

4. Ibid., 801.

5. Ibid., 807.

6. P. Atkins and I. Bowler, *Food in Society: Economy, Culture, Geography* (New York: Oxford University Press, 2001).

7. K. Albala, *Food in Early Modern Europe* (Westport, CT: Greenwood Press, 2003).

8. Ibid.

9. J. Fanet, *Great Wine Terroir* (Berkeley: University of California Press, 2003), 10.

10. Ibid.

11. W. H. Eshbaugh, "History and Exploitation of a Serendipitous New Crop Discovery," in J. Janick and J. E. Simon (eds.), *New Crops* (New York: John Wiley & Sons, 2003), 132–39.

12. M. D. Olsen, B. Murthy, and R. Teare, "CEO Perspectives on Scanning the Global Hotel Business Environment," *International Journal of Contemporary Hospitality Management* 6, 4 (1994): 3–9; R. J. Harrington, "Part I: The Culinary Innovation Process, A Barrier to Imitation," *Journal of Foodservice Business Research* 7, 3 (2004): 35–57.

13. H. Moskowitz, "Creating New Product Concepts for Foodservice—The Role of Conjoint Measurement to Identify Promising Product Features," *Food Service Technology* 1 (2001): 35–52.

14. Albala, *Food in Early Modern Europe*.

15. A. Immer, *Great Tastes Made Simple: Extraordinary Food and Wine Pairing for Every Palate* (New York: Broadway Books, 2002).

16. J. D. Folse, *The Encyclopedia of Cajun & Creole Cuisine* (Gonzales, LA: Chef John Folse & Co., 2004).

17. Atkins and Bowler, *Food in Society*.

18. Albala, *Food in Early Modern Europe*, 119.

19. Ibid., 121.

20. C. M. Hall, R. Mitchell, and L. Sharples, "Consuming Places: The Role of Food, Wine and Tourism in Regional Development." in C. M. Hall, L. Sharples, R. Mitchell, N. Macionis, and B. Cambourne (eds.), *Food Tourism Around the World* (Oxford: Elsevier Butterworth-Heinemann, 2003), 25–59.

21. Folse, *Encyclopedia of Cajun & Creole Cuisine*, 274.

THE FOUNDATION: FOOD AND WINE TASTE COMPONENTS

The Food-and-Wine Taste Pyramid presented in Chapter 1 illustrates that food-and-wine elements can be thought of in terms of a hierarchy of taste, from components to texture to flavors. A synthesis of the literature and my own research indicate that the primary sensory components (sweetness, saltiness, sourness, and bitterness) will have a big impact on food-and-wine relationships.

To begin the task of developing skills in identifying the key element(s) in food or wine that will directly impact matching, whether based on contrasts or similarities, Part B focuses on the primary taste components of wine and food. The following two sections of this book (Parts C and D) address the other two categories of food-and-wine elements: texture and flavor. This step-by-step format allows you to study each of the direct effects of components, texture, and flavor in a hierarchical fashion.

This process will provide you with a foundation of knowledge that can be used to sort out the direct effects of elements from their interaction with other elements of a food or wine. After completing the next two chapters, you should be able to identify the direct impact of wine acidity and the interaction of acidity, sweetness, and bitterness in wine. For food-and-wine pairing, you will be able to predict the interaction of wine sweetness, acidity, and effervescence with food sweetness, acidity, bitterness, and saltiness. This type of knowledge will greatly improve your ability to predict exceptional food-and-wine pairings.

Primary Taste Components

Primary taste components are defined as basic elements that correspond to the tongue's basic sensory ability. Food-and-wine components are foundational elements that have a strong influence on the pleasant feeling of complementary or contrasting characteristics that a positive gastronomic experience provides.

Wine has three primary sensory components: sweetness, acidity (sometimes called crispness), and effervescence. These form the foundation of a match with the primary sensory components in food: sweetness, sourness, saltiness, and bitterness.

This book includes two sensory anchor scales, one for wine and one for food. They use a 0-to-10 scale and include sample wines and foods for component and texture and descriptions for flavor elements.

The Food Sensory Anchor Scale (Figure B.1) is divided into three main sections (components, texture, and flavor) with a total of nine elements (sweetness, acidity, saltiness, bitterness, fattiness, overall body, spiciness, flavor intensity, and flavor persistency).

The Wine Sensory Anchor Scale (Figure B.2) is also divided into three main sections, but with a slightly different set of nine elements (dryness to sweetness, acidity, effervescence, tannin, alcohol level, overall body, spiciness, flavor intensity, and flavor persistency).

These references will be incorporated into the exercises throughout the following chapters.

The next two chapters focus on the components of food and wine, with exercises incorporating the wine and food examples shown in the anchor scales. Once these references are developed in your sensory memory bank, they will be valuable tools to increase the consistency of your wine and food rating across product and across time.

A word of caution: the reference items listed in the Sensory Anchor Scales are intended to provide relatively accurate examples of levels for each of the components, texture, and flavor elements. Many of these items are very consistent. For example, the sweetness references for food use prepackaged food items that vary little if at all. Dryness and sweetness for the wine references will on average be correct, but you should already be aware of variations that occur due to climate, winemaker, and region in which the wines are produced. The use of these anchors in most cases will require judgment and experience to increase your overall consistency in evaluating food and wine for each of these elements and predicting match levels based on your assessment.

	Components				Textures		Flavors		
	Sweetness	Acidity	Bitter	Saltiness	Fattiness	Overall Body	Spiciness	Flavor Intensity	Flavor Persistence
0		Pasta with extra-virgin olive oil only		Unsalted popcorn			No spice	No flavor	
1	Triscuit		Iceberg lettuce		Skim milk	Chicken en papillote			< 3 seconds
2		Milk					Weak spice	Weak flavor	
3	Wheat Thins	Pasta with balsamic vinaigrette	Celery Frise		2% milk				4–6 seconds
4				Popcorn 2 cups with 1/8 tsp salt					
5		Plain yogurt			Whole milk	Grilled pork loin		Moderately intense	7–9 seconds
6	Graham cracker	Pasta with balsamic vinaigrette and extra vinegar	Belgian endive						
7		Orange juice			Half-and-half		Intense spice	Intense flavor	10–12 seconds
8				Popcorn 2 cups with 1/4 tsp salt					
9	Pepperidge Farm Bordeaux cookie	Grapefruit Juice	Radicchio		Heavy cream	Braised beef	Powerfully spicy		13 + seconds
10		Pasta with vinegar only						Powerful flavor	

Figure B.1

Food Sensory Anchor Scale

Chapter 5 presents the impact of sweetness and acidity. While they are separate and distinct elements in wine and food, the close relationship between sweetness and acidity in wine means that these elements cannot be considered fully in isolation. Chapter 6 describes the effect of food bitterness, food saltiness, and wine effervescence. After completing the exercises in each chapter, you will be able to identify levels of food-and-wine components and discern the role each plays in food-and-wine match perception.

	Components			Texture			Flavor		
	Dry to Sweet	Acidity	Effervescence	Tannin	Alcohol Level	Overall Body	Spiciness	Flavor Intensity	Flavor Persistence
0	Brut Sparkling		Tap water Still wine	Riesling			No spice	No flavor	
1	Wine	Warm Climate Chardonnay			7%	Riesling			< 3 seconds
2	Chardonnay				8%		Weak spice	Weak flavor	
3					9%	Sauvignon			4–6 seconds
4	Gewürztraminer	Fume Blanc	Moscat d'Asti 50/50 seltzer & water	Pinot Noir	10%	Blanc			
5					11%	Pinot Noir	Moderately spicy	Moderately intense	7–9 seconds
6	White Zinfandel	New Zealand Sauvignon		Merlot	12%	Chardonnay			
7	Sauternes	Blanc			13%	Merlot	Intense spice	Intense	10–12 seconds
8		Sancerre			14%				
9	Cream Sherry		100% Seltzer	Cabernet	15% (Fortified Wines)	Cabernet	Powerful		13 + seconds
10			Champagne/Cava	Sauvignon	17%–22%	Port	Spicy	Powerful	

Figure B.2

Wine Sensory Anchor Scale

CHAPTER 5

THE IMPACT OF SWEETNESS AND ACIDITY LEVELS IN WINE AND FOOD

CHAPTER OUTLINE:

Introduction

Aperitif: Which to Choose First, Wine or Food?

The Impact of Sweetness Levels in Wine and Food

Sweetness Levels in Wine

Sweetness Levels in Food

Types of Sweeteners

Perceived Sweetness Levels

Interaction Between Wine and Food Sweetness

Acidity Levels in Wine

Acidity Level Descriptions

Acidity Levels in Food

Interaction Between Wine and Food Acidity

Summary

Exercises

KEY CONCEPTS:

- Dryness and sweetness in wine
- Perceptible levels of sweetness
- The impact of alcohol on perceived sweetness in wine
- Food sweetness levels less than or equal to wine sweetness levels
- The narrowing effects of food acidity in wine selection
- Identifying wine acidity levels
- Identifying food acidity levels
- Determining breaking points of acceptable food and wine acidity levels

INTRODUCTION

In wine, there is a balancing act between acidity and sugar that creates a sensation of structure and harmony. The basic structure in white wine is determined by the substances in it that are sweet and acid. In the case of red wine, a sense of balance is achieved predominantly through three characteristics: sweetness, acidity, and tannins (astringency). Tannin also provides a preserving characteristic in red wine—explaining why "big" reds are able to be aged for five, ten, twenty, or more years. Sugar too acts as a preservative. This is true in both food and wine. Sauternes and other wines with high levels of residual sugar can be aged well beyond what is possible for other, less sweet white wines. Just like big reds, quality dessert wines can be aged for many years, becoming darker in color and more honeyed in flavor, with dried fruit characteristics.

The balance of sugar and acid in whites and sugar, acid, and tannin in reds is related to perceptions of quality and harmony in wine. But the perception of balance varies substantially due to individual differences in sensitivity and acquired habits or traditions.[1] The following sections of this chapter focus on the impact of sweetness, acidity, and their interaction.

Aperitif | Which to Choose First, Wine or Food?

When you are selecting wine to consume with food in a restaurant, there are several strategies that can be helpful. If you are ordering off the menu, it is generally better to select the wine after you have made your food choices. The foundation elements in food can have a substantial impact on wine compatibility. Foods that are highly sweet, sour, bitter, or salty severely limit possible wine selection. By selecting the food first, you have a better chance of creating a good match with the food.

The natural sweetness of onions, tomatoes, plums, and other foods has important implications for wine selection.

Wine selection (or suggestion) can be intimidating, particularly when each guest selects a different dish. Most menus contain a variety of protein types, cooking methods, and, in many cases, ethnic or ethnic-influenced dishes. All of this variety can make wine selection confusing. Recall the strategies for a successful wine and food match discussed throughout this text. In the case where guests at a single table order a variety of items on the menu, try to discern the common elements of the items ordered. Is the common element sweetness or acidity level? Texture? Flavor? Wine and food components will in many cases be the driving factors for creating a refreshing to good match across a variety of dishes.

Also, consider the personal preferences of those at the table. If someone prefers red wine but a lighter white wine would be your recommendation, you can suggest a light red such as Lemberger or Beaujolais. Also, if you are unsure of particular wine producers on the menu, it is always a safe bet to order wines from known, consistent wineries. As a guest, this is a good time to learn from a well-trained wine server or sommelier. If you are a server, this is a good opportunity to share experiences with your fellow servers. What wines do they like with particular foods? Why do they believe these items go well together?

THE IMPACT OF SWEETNESS LEVELS IN WINE AND FOOD

The level of sweetness in food and wine can be difficult to judge. While North American tastes have a strong preference for sweet things (just look at the candy aisle at your closest food store), we are currently biased against sweet wines. In the United States, sweet wines are frequently associated with wines of low quality, but this is certainly not always the case. Canadian ice wines and Sauternes are very sweet, but few would suggest they are of low quality. In fact, these and other dessert wines are in many cases the most expensive and opulent wines in the world.

Thresholds of perceptible levels of sweetness in food and wine can vary substantially from one person to the next, and perceived sweetness levels in wine have been shown to vary significantly across cultures.[2] Perceived sweetness in food and wine can be affected by level of acidity present and alcohol (in the case of wine). Sweet and sour tastes in food items such as fruit sauces, catsup, and Asian sauces create a perceived balanced taste structure. The sweetness and acidity counterbalance each other and create a pleasant contrasting sensation. The same situation is true of wine: residual sugar counterbalances acidity to awaken the senses and reduce the sharply sour sensation, while acidity reduces the cloying sensation of a high sugar level. What remains is a balanced taste structure with a pleasant perceived level of sweetness and a crisp sensation from the acid present. Canadian ice wine would be sickeningly sweet without the balance of high acidity inherent in a cool-climate growing region.

Sweetness and acidity are not always easy to discern while tasting wine or food. Even trained sensory panel members can vary in their estimations of the sweetness or acidity of a particular food or wine. A complicating factor is the tangling of additional sensations in food and wine. Food items that are a combination of sweet, sour, salty, and bitter can provide a complex and balanced taste sensation, but it can be difficult for the beginner to estimate levels of each. To complicate matters further, when alcohol hits the tip of the tongue, it creates an initial sensation of sweetness, then warms the entire mouth; if the level of alcohol is fairly high, it can leave a lingering hot sensation. The palate-mapping exercises in Chapter 2 should assist you in this regard by clearly reinforcing where these sensations are perceived in your mouth.

SWEETNESS LEVELS IN WINE

Dry wines are those that have little or no residual sugar remaining after fermentation. Wine is generally described on a continuum from dry to sweet: bone dry, dry, medium dry, medium sweet, sweet, and very sweet. Wines that are much too sweet are described as cloying. The sweetness level of a wine depends on two main things—how ripe the grapes are at harvest and what the winemaker does during fermentation. As previously indicated, wine grapes grown in moderate and warm climate zones will have a tendency to be riper when harvested. But not all wines from warm zones are sweet, for the winemaker has a huge impact as well.

Many times grapes are deliberately left to become overripe and thus create a sweeter finished product. To achieve this, grapes can be left on the vine past the normal harvest time, which is the case for late-harvest wines, ice wines, and wines infected with "noble rot." Or grapes can be picked and left on straw mats in a wooden crate to become "raisined" (dried) prior to being turned into wine. (Italians call wines made from this process *passio*.) In all of these examples, a portion of the water evaporates, leaving a greater percentage of sugar in the grape, which upon fermentation creates very intense, complex, and sweet dessert wines.

The winemaker can control the amount of sugar and sweetness in a wine by lowering the temperature to 25°F (−4°C) or below, which stops fermentation. This method is used when some sweetness is desired to balance acidity (such as with Riesling), to offset the natural bitterness in the varietal (as with Gewürztraminer), or when slight sweetness is desired for the particular type of wine (for example, when making white Zinfandel or Asti Spumate). A second method is to add alcohol. When the alcohol level reaches more than 15 percent by volume, the yeast used in fermentation dies. This occurs naturally in very ripe grapes, and is the method used in fortified wines such as port, sherry, Marsala, and Madeira. The production of wine is constantly evolving. In Canada, ice wine producers are experimenting with the use of sulfur to stop fermentation. Toward the end of fermentation, high concentrations of sulfur are added. Because of this, the fermentation stops, the yeast dies, and the sulfur dissipates to an acceptable level while the wine remains sweet.[3]

Residual sugar in wine can be used to create a balance with acidity, to fit a particular style of wine, or to overcome wine fault. To create a good wine, the winemaker should provide a sense of harmony and balance. A quality wine is typically linked to a complex balance and counterbalance of tastes and smells. Balanced levels of acidity, tannin, and sweetness are important structural considerations.

Table 5.1 provides descriptions of evaluation bands for perceived wine sweetness levels on a 0-to-10 scale. The "Value Bands" column provides a range for the typical wine at each level. The "Level of Sweetness" column provides a description of the sensation for each category (bone dry through very sweet) and wine examples by type. The expected level of sweetness varies across wine types. Bone-dry wines include Sancerre, Barolo, and Barbaresco. About 85 percent of all red wines are considered dry (such as Cabernet Sauvignon and Merlot), and the majority of white wines are considered dry (for example, Chardonnay, Pinot Grigio, and Sauvignon Blanc). But fruity or floral white wines are generally assumed to have a higher level of residual sugar. Gewürztraminer, Riesling, and Vouvray usually have higher sugar levels and are described as medium dry. Late-harvest and white Zinfandel wines are generally described as medium sweet. Ice wines and fortified wines are described as sweet to very sweet. Residual sugar content varies widely and can range from .035 ounces per quart to over 7 ounces per quart.[4] Sample wines shown in the Wine Reference Anchor Sheet (Figure B.2) provide reference values for six levels. While the examples given generally fall within the suggested value bands, there are a number of factors (ripeness, climate, winemaking techniques) that impact whether the particular wine is slightly higher or lower in sweetness level.

SWEETNESS LEVELS IN FOOD

The level of sweetness in food can be derived naturally or with the addition of sugar or other sweetening agent. In general, sweet foods should be matched with sweet wines and non-sweet foods with dry wines. The sweetness level in the food should always be less than or at most equal to the level of sweetness in the wine. A sweet taste in a dish makes the wine taste drier. If the sweetness level in the dish is higher than the wine, the wine will taste thin and sour.

There is a definite difference between sweetness in foods and sugariness. Foods at the peak of freshness are nature's way of providing a product that is bursting with flavor, contains a sweet taste from more complex carbohydrates, and is wine-friendly to boot. Naturally sweet tastes can be found in everything from garden-fresh tomatoes, lettuce, carrots, and onions to scallops, cod, and lobster.[5] The naturally occurring sugars researchers have found in such foods are called fructooligosaccharides (FOSs). In FOSs, one sucrose molecule combines with two or three fructose units to form a more complex carbohydrate that increases sweetness without adding calories.[6]

Table 5.1 Wine Sweetness Level Descriptions

Value Bands	Level of Sweetness	Example Wines
0 1	**Bone dry.** The inability to pick up the sensation of sweetness on the tongue. Sweetness anchor: brut sparkling wines.	**Whites:** Sancerre, Pouilly-Fumé, Chablis, Germany's trocken wines, wines labeled "brut." **Reds:** Barolo, Barbaresco, Chianti Classico, most Médoc.
2 3	**Dry.** Any level of sweet characteristics are barely perceived and only with difficulty and hard work on the evaluator's part. Sweetness anchor: Chardonnay.	**Whites:** This is the biggest category and includes most Aligoté, Chardonnay, Sémillon, Sauvignon Blanc, Pinot Grigio, white Burgundy, whites labeled "sec." **Reds:** About 85 percent of all reds fall into this category. It includes most Cabernet Sauvignon, Merlot, Pinot Noir, Syrah and some Zinfandel.
4 5	**Medium dry.** A lightly sweet sensation is identified and perceived at a sufficient level. Sweetness anchor: Gewürztraminer.	**Whites:** Most Riesling, Viognier, Chenin Blanc, wines labeled "demi-sec" or "off-dry," most Alsace wines, Vouvray. **Reds:** Some Merlot and Pinot Noir, some New World Cabernet and Zinfandel, Lambrusco, some Australian Shiraz, Dolcetto, Lemberger, Gamay.
6 7	**Medium sweet.** A sweet sensation on the tongue that is clearly identifiable in a very defined way. Sweetness anchor: White Zinfandel.	**Whites:** Most late-harvest wines, wines labeled "moelleux," German Spätlese, Asti, most Moscato, Vin Santo. **Reds:** Sangria, sparkling Shiraz, Lambrusco, late harvest Zinfandel.
8 9	**Sweet.** Sugary, full, noticeable glycerin, containing residual sugar but pleasant in taste. Sweetness anchor: Sauternes.	**Whites:** Botrytized wines, selected late-harvest wines, Italian Passito, Muscat Beaumes de Venise. **Reds:** Kosher Concord wines.
9 10	**Very sweet.** Sweetness is at an unmistakably high level of perceptibility with a lot of emphasis. Sweetness anchor: Cream Sherry.	**Whites:** Orange Muscat, ice wine, Tokaji, Madeira, other fortified wines. **Reds:** Ruby Port, Tawny Port, Cabernet Franc ice wine.

Source: Adapted from J. Robinson, *How to Taste: A Guide to Enjoying Wine* (New York: Simon and Schuster, 2000).

TYPES OF SWEETENERS

In addition to sweetness provided by nature, there are a wide variety of sweeteners that can be added to food items. The largest group is the sugars. Granulated sugar makes up the bulk of production in this category, but the group also includes powdered sugar, brown sugar, maple sugar and syrup, molasses, corn syrup, and honey. Other non-sugar sweeteners include saccharin, aspartame, and sucralose. The sweetening power varies substantially by product and is an important consideration when formulating recipes.

PERCEIVED SWEETNESS LEVELS

Table 5.2 provides appraisal bands or values based on descriptions of perceivable levels of sweetness. These sensation descriptors apply to other taste sensations as well. In Table

Table 5.2 Sensation Levels in Foods and Wine Elements:
Appraisal Values

Value Bands	Description of Perception Level Used in Rating Food Elements
0 1 2	**Imperceptible:** If the particular sensation is not detectable or if this sensation fades almost immediately. No perception or barely perceptible. Sweetness anchor: Triscuit.
2 3 4	**Little perception:** A taste-smell sensation in which one succeeds in identifying or perceiving it in recognizable way, but the stimulus is not well defined. The level of perception is low. Sweetness anchor: Wheat Thins.
4 5 6	**Sufficiently perceived:** A taste-smell sensation in which one succeeds in identifying and perceiving it at a sufficient level. An intermediate level of perception. This score is not based on a hedonic (good or bad) evaluation or appraisal of the taste sensation but simply a quantitative appraisal.
6 7 8	**Abundant perception:** A taste-smell sensation in which one can clearly identify and perceive it in a defined way. The taste-smell sensation is at an emphasized level. Sweetness anchor: Graham cracker.
8 9 10	**Highly perceived:** A taste-smell sensation that can be unmistakably identified with much emphasis. One can identify a particular food or clearly characterize a complex preparation. High perceptibility with a lot of emphasis. Sweetness anchor: Pepperidge Farms Bordeaux Cookie.

5.1, wine descriptions followed the standards used by most wine evaluators in North America (bone dry to very sweet), but those labels are not used for food sweetness. Food items can form a continuous scale of sweetness level based on type and amount of natural and added sweetness.

The Food Reference Anchor table (Figure B.1) includes four food items that are readily available in the marketplace and provide standard measures of food sweetness levels. These items are included in Table 5.2 in the rating range under which they fall. Column 1 in Table 5.2 provides a numerical rating range for each sensation description. Column 2 of Table 5.2 provides a description of how the sensation is perceived by the taster at the particular level and the anchor sweetness example for each.

INTERACTION BETWEEN WINE AND FOOD SWEETNESS

Rule #1: Food sweetness level should be less than or equal to wine sweetness level.

Basically, wine and food experts suggest matching the level of perceived sweetness in food with the level of perceived sweetness in wine. This match creates a balance in taste and allows the remaining elements to interact in a positive way. When the sweetness in wine is greater than the food, the slightly higher wine sweetness creates a pleasant contrast with the savory, salty, and bitter characteristics of most foods. When the sweetness in the food item is greater than the wine, the interaction seems to accentuate and overemphasize the acidity present in the wine and any characteristics of bitterness or astringency inherent in the wine.

Many times, a savory dish will be prepared with a sauce or other accompaniment that has fruit or sweet elements (e.g., Duck with Sauce Bigarade). Sweeter wines work well with this type of dish, particularly medium-sweet Riesling. If you are preparing red meat or game with a fruit/sweet sauce, choose a wine that has a good sense of lush fruit of its own. In this situation, very ripe grapes from warm flavor zones will be appropriate (Zinfandel from California's warm zones or Australian Shiraz). It is a good idea to avoid serving heavily oaked white wines alongside savory dishes with sweet accompaniments. The fruit in whites aged in oak will be reduced, making the resulting food-and-wine combination taste harsh. As with reds, white wines in this situation should have ripe fruit flavors.[7] If the dish has sweetness and acid, you will want to use wines that both are sweet and have a higher acidity. Cool-climate whites from the Loire Valley or sweet German Rieslings are useful in this case.[8]

Foods that are served at the peak of freshness need to be matched with wines that have equally vibrant fruit flavors. Therefore, it is best to serve peak-season foods with lively young wines. These can be red or white but will generally be from New World locations (the United States, Chile, Argentina, Australia, South Africa, and New Zealand). Wines from these locations will have a fruit-forward, more lush tendency than their Old World counterparts (France, Germany, Spain, and Italy), which can have subtler, earthier profiles.[9]

ACIDITY: FROM FLAT TO TART (AND BEYOND)

The second main component of wine and food is the level of acidity and its relative level to sweetness in the wine or food. As discussed in Chapters 3 and 4, climate, culture, traditions, wine varietals, and preferred flavor profiles all impact sourness characteristics in wine and food. The use of acid is prevalent in food preservation methods (think of pickles, ceviche, sauerkraut, and marinades) as well as in the preparation methods in many cool-climate areas (examples include pickled herring, sourdough bread, stroganoff, and so on).

Any food item high in acidity makes pairing difficult. Vinegar in food can create unhappy marriages if not properly finessed. Acids used in food preparation are not created equal—many are harsher than others. The citric acid in oranges or lemons will be less likely to ruin the taste of a wine than the acetic acid of most vinegars. The lactic acid in yogurt and cheese will be even less destructive than the citric acid group. In fact, the creamy characteristics of cheese soften the palate and may have a flattering effect on the wine.

Which acids taste the most acid? While numerous organic acids exist in wine and food, common ones include malic (found, for example, in apples), tartaric (in grapes), citric (in citrus fruits), acetic (vinegar), and lactic (dairy). In solutions of equal strength, acetic acid is perceived as stronger than citric and lactic acids.[12] Malic acid is perceived as stronger than tartaric acid, which in turn is perceived as stronger than citric and lactic.[13] These general perceptions of acidity and the effects they can have on wine provide basic guidelines for selecting ingredients for salads, marinades, and accompaniments intended to be served with wine.

ACIDITY LEVELS IN WINE

Acidity in wine provides a feeling of crispness or freshness. Too much acidity creates a sour sensation in wine, and too little leaves a bland or flat impression. The right amount creates a pleasant, tingly sensation. A balance between sweetness and acidity (combined with tannin for reds) in all wines is essential to creating pleasant, cleansing, and contrasting sensations in the mouth.

Higher levels of acid in wine result in a "green" taste and may remind you of unripe fruit. Climate and geography can have a substantial impact on acidity levels in wine. Cooler-climate wines have a tendency to be crispier and tarter, while wines from warmer climates can be flat and bland. White grape varietals such as Sauvignon Blanc, Riesling, and Sémillon have higher acidity levels than Chardonnay and red wine varietals.

Much of the acidity level can be impacted by the winemaker. Decisions on when to harvest the grapes and the fermentation process can substantially impact final perceived acidity levels. While wine contains at least six organic acids (tartaric, malic, citric, succinic, lactic, and acetic), the principal natural acidity in grape juice comes from tartaric and malic acids.[14] One method for lowering total wine acidity is the process of malolactic fermentation. Basically, malolactic bacteria use the malic acid in wine as a source of energy and convert it into lactic acid. This process usually happens after the primary fermentation and has several effects on the finished wine. First, because malic acid is stronger in taste than lactic acid, wines that have undergone this process will taste less tart. Second, the malolactic fermentation process makes wine more stable and less likely to spoil during aging. Lastly, the process creates a compound called diacetyl; this produces the distinct buttery characteristic in Chardonnay that has undergone the malolactic process.[15]

ACIDITY LEVEL DESCRIPTIONS

The vocabulary used to describe wine acidity varies slightly from one era to the next and between wine-drinking cultures. Words used to describe highly acidic wines include *sharp*, *acidulous*, *stinging*, *tart*, *nervy*, *unripe*, and *green*. Words used to describe wines at the opposite end, with low acidity, include *flabby*, *flat*, *watery*, *soft*, *plump*, and *flaccid*.[16] Many wine evaluators classify wine acidity into three general categories: excessive, sufficient, and insufficient.

In addition to perceived levels of acidity in wine, acids can create positive and negative perceptions depending on the dominant acid type that is present. For example, acidity in wine derived from malic acid is generally associated with a sense of freshness and liveliness, while acidity derived from tartaric acid is perceived as harsh or hard and creates a less acceptable aftertaste at the back of the throat.[17]

Table 5.3 provides descriptions and wine and food examples of differing levels of acidity. The "Value Bands" column provides a range for the typical wines and food items at each level, using a 0-to-10 scale. The "Level of Acidity" column provides a description of the sensation for each category (flat through green/tart).

ACIDITY LEVELS IN FOOD

A sour taste in food can be from natural acids or from acid substances added to the food. Aside from the desired taste of sour in food, there are several reasons why acid items are used from a culinary perspective. Acids such as citrus or vinegar can be added to emulsified sauces such as hollandaise or beurre blanc to change the physiochemical properties of the emulsifying agent (allowing the protein to become more saturated with oil or fat). Acid-based marinades are used both to flavor the food item and to tenderize it. And acid (such as cream of tartar) is used in baking to relax the gluten in flour for many pastry applications.[18]

Just as acidity in wines varies based on climate and ripeness, raw food products vary in acidity based on where they were raised, climate, and other factors. The relative sourness in foods is determined by the amount of natural or added sugars used in their preparation and proportionally expressed relative to the pH scale. Cultural preferences for sour tastes in food vary widely. Individuals have differing levels of sensitivity to sour tastes in food. Many individuals are very sensitive, while others can detect sour tastes only when the acid level is moderately high.

Table 5.3   Acidity Level Descriptions

Value Bands	Level of Acidity Description	Example Wines and Foods
0 1 2	**Flat (flabby)—no to low acidity.** The inability to pick up the sensation of sourness on the tongue.	**Wines:** Inexpensive and poor-quality Chardonnay and some warm-climate whites **Foods:** Drinking water, plain pasta
2 3 4	**Lacking—little acidity.** Any level of sour characteristics is barely perceived and only with difficulty and hard work on the evaluator's part.	**Wines:** Warm-climate Chardonnay **Foods:** Pasta tossed with extra-virgin olive oil, cow's milk, sweet corn, lima beans, plain salmon
4 5 6	**Refreshing—Moderate Acidity.** A light/moderate sour sensation is identified and perceived at a sufficient level.	**Wines:** Moderate-climate (oaked) Fumé Blanc, moderate-climate (unoaked) Chardonnay, moderate/cool-climate reds **Foods:** Squash, yogurt, figs, pasta tossed with 1 part extra-virgin olive oil and 1 part balsamic vinaigrette
6 7 8	**Crisp—moderate / high acidity.** A sour sensation on the tongue that is clearly identifiable in a very defined way.	**Wines:** Many New Zealand whites, Loire wines, white Burgundy, most cool-climate whites, and many well made whites from moderate-climate zones **Foods:** Tree fruits (apricots, apples, peaches, cherries), applesauce, pasta tossed with balsamic vinaigrette
8 9 10	**Green or tart—very high acidity.** Sourness is at an unmistakably high level of perceptibility with a lot of emphasis.	**Wines:** Some Sancerre, Vinho Verde (Portugal), some Champagne **Foods:** Citrus juices, sauerkraut, plums, rhubarb, pasta tossed with balsamic vinegar

Source: Adapted from C. A. Rietz, *A Guide to the Selection, Combination, and Cooking of Foods* (Westport, CT: AVI, 1976); J. Robinson, *How to Taste: A Guide to Enjoying Wine* (New York: Simon and Schuster, 2000).

INTERACTION BETWEEN WINE AND FOOD ACIDITY

Rule #2: Food acidity level should be less than or equal to wine acidity level.

The sour tastes in food can create potential problems when combined with wine. The basic rule of thumb is that food acidity levels should be less than or equal to wine acidity. When high-acid foods are matched with high-acid wines, the acidities tend to cancel each other out, allowing the fruit and sweetness in the wine to come through. Classic examples of this approach include serving Salade Lyonnaise with French Beaujolais and goat cheese with French Sancerre (Sauvignon Blanc). This acid match can also let subtle food flavors become more prominent in dishes; without the wine accompaniment, they might taste sour at first bite.

Of course, not all acids are equally problematic for the culinary product, and the same acid in different foods can pose more or less of a problem. For example, citric acid from oranges and lemons can be combined with wine more successfully than citric acid from limes or grapefruits.[19] In order not to overwhelm the wine acidity with the food acidity, use less harsh acids in the food, and lower the total acid level if necessary.

It should be noted that vinegary tastes in wine and vinegar used in food do not provide a match. Tartaric and malic acids are produced by the grape as it develops, but these principal sources of natural acidity in wine are nonvolatile.[20] One of the most common winemaking faults is volatile acidity (VA). VA is the result of the growth of bacteria that produce acetic acid. Bacteria causing VA are found on the surfaces of grapes, winery equipment, and used oak barrels. The bacteria can also start in the vineyard, with grapes damaged by birds or mold. These bacteria need lots of oxygen to proliferate. When left unchecked, they produce enzymes that transform alcohol into the vinegary-smelling acetic acid. When wine has higher levels of oxygen exposure, is low in sulfur dioxide, and is low in tartaric, malic, and lactic acid, the wine becomes a likely breeding ground for volatile acidity.[21] This vinegary characteristic of poorly produced wine creates serious problems from a wine and food pairing perspective.

Because acid in wine can heighten flavors in a dish—much like adding a squeeze of lemon—the higher acidity in unoaked, fruity white wines allows them to work reasonably well with the tang and zest of many salads. Acid in wine also cuts the fat in food dishes, but the level of success in pairing wine acidity with food fattiness depends not only on the amount of wine acidity and the amount of fat but also on the type of fat. Plant-based fats such as olive oil and canola oil work well with wines that are moderately high to high in acidity. With cream or butter (dairy fats), the importance of body match (full-bodied wine with full-bodied food) becomes a better prediction of match than the acidity/fat relationship.[22] Because Chardonnays and other oak-aged whites generally have lower acid levels, an

Table 5.4   Example Acidic Foods with Wine Suggestions

Food Item	Suggested Wine(s)	Anticipated Level of Match
Artichokes or asparagus	A crispy white—New Zealand Sauvignon Blanc or white Rioja; if served with melted butter, a young, crisp Chardonnay	Neutral to good
Caesar salad	A full-flavored white such as cool/moderate-climate Chardonnay (New York or Washington)	Refreshment to neutral
Ceviche	A tart Sauvignon Blanc from New Zealand, Sancerre	Neutral
Crudités	Young dry whites such as Pinot Grigio, Chenin Blanc, or Pinot Blanc	Neutral to good
Fruit salad	A sparkling wine such as Moscato d'Asti	Good
Gazpacho	Sauvignon Blanc or Manzanilla Sherry	Good
Lemon tart	Canadian ice wine, Riesling	Good to synergistic
Chicken curry with lime	Gewürztraminer or Riesling	Neutral
Salads (general guidelines)	Sauvignon Blanc, Riesling, Pinot Grigio, dry rosé, or light reds such as Beaujolais, Dolcetto, or Gamay	Refreshment to neutral
Sauerkraut	Very crisp and dry white—Mosel Riesling, Canadian Riesling	Refreshment to neutral
Sorbets	Light sweet sparkling wine—Moscato d'Asti	Good
Savory dishes made with yogurt	California, Washington, or Australian Chardonnay	Good

Adapted from J. Simon, *Wine with Food* (New York: Simon and Schuster, 1996).

unoaked white is preferred when paired with yogurt or lighter creamy sauces. But an oaked Chardonnay also works well with high-fat, buttery sauces by matching body to body as well as bringing out the butter flavor in each.

Another strategy to match acidic foods with less acidic wines is to mask the acidity in the food item with added sweetness or fat. For example, creamed spinach or savory sauces made with fruit juices (as in Duck à l'Orange) can take the edge off the acidity in food.

Higher-acid wines such as Sauvignon Blanc, Sémillon, and Riesling generally work well with foods containing Asian flavors. The acidity in many Asian dishes cancels out the high acidity in wine, making both the food and wine taste sweeter.

Studies have indicated that squeezing lemon on a dish can reduce the perception of oak in full-bodied white or red wines.[23] But acid in food is likely to clash with the tannin inherent in many red wines. Thus, when choosing reds to go with higher-acid foods, select reds from cooler climates to more closely match the higher level of acidity and for their inherent lower tannin levels. Wines with lower acidity will taste flat when paired with higher-acid dishes. Most rosés are too soft for high-acid foods.[24] Also, Chardonnays and other oak-aged whites generally have lower acid levels and as a rule may not pair as well with high-acid foods.

While Old World examples such as Germany and Austria have successfully paired wines with high-acid foods, items such as pickles, sauerkraut, and similar foods can overwhelm many wines that have more subtle flavors and characteristics.

SUMMARY

This chapter has focused on sweetness, acidity, and their interaction in the relationship between wine and food. For sweetness, the general rule is that the food sweetness level should be less than or equal to the wine sweetness level. The perception of sweetness can be impacted by a variety of elements in wine or food such as acidity, alcohol, and salt. Wines range in sweetness from bone dry to very sweet. Food sweetness ranges from imperceptible to highly perceived. A number of other elements in wine can impact the match with food sweetness to increase a perception of match, including forward fruit, higher alcohol, and lower tannins.

Acidity in wine and food provides mouthwatering freshness and a spark in taste that would be noticeably absent if it was missing. The tanginess in wine and sour characteristics in food cancel one another when tasted together and allow other flavor and texture characteristics to shine. The key when matching wine and food acidity is balance—in acidity levels, sweetness levels, body styles, and flavor intensity (more on these last two issues in upcoming chapters).

High-acid food dishes such as salads with vinaigrette can be difficult to pair with wines. Some things that the chef can do are use acids that are less harsh (lemon or orange juice) and not overdo the amount of total acid in the dish when pairing with fine wine. Cool-climate and unoaked white wines are the most likely candidates for positive marriages with higher-acid food items.

DISCUSSION QUESTIONS

1. What are the foundation elements of wine and food (components)?

2. What sweetness level do the majority of wines fall into?

3. What is the standard pairing rule for sweetness?

4. What are other considerations in the sweetness pairing process?

5. What types of acid taste the most acidic?

6. What are the five acidity level descriptions? How would you describe the sensation of each?

7. What are three examples of higher-acid wines?

8. Describe a classic example of a high-acid wine and food marriage. Can you think of a New World example that is relatively high in acid?

EXERCISE 5.1

This exercise is designed to establish baseline measures of sweetness levels in wines ranging from bone dry to very sweet. The table below provides examples for white wines and red wines. Eighty-five percent of all red wines fall into the dry category. Thus, it may be easier to obtain white wines with a range of sweetness. The white wine suggestions are those shown in the Wine Sensory Anchor Scale (Figure B.2).

The numerical values on the Wine Sensory Anchor Scale are intended to provide you with a baseline to work with as you learn to assess sweetness in wine, but across these suggested wines, the level of sweetness may vary depending on the climate, the region where the grapes were grown, and the techniques/ preferences of the winemaker (the earlier discussions of climate zones, differences between Old World and New World, and traditions is applicable here). For example, while the Wine Sensory Anchor Scale indicates that Chardonnay will have a numerical value of about 2 on the dryness scale, it could range from somewhere between 1 to 3. The same is true for the other wine suggestions. Also, your perception of sweetness will vary depending on the wine selection, temperature at which it is assessed, your individual abilities in assessing residual sugar, and other interacting elements such as alcohol level, glycerin content, and acidity level.

OBJECTIVE

The primary objectives are to identify differences in sweetness levels in white and red wines and to establish a numerical baseline for reliable future assessment. This exercise also provides experience in wine evaluation as a whole and evaluation of sweetness in particular.

Mise en Place: Things to Do Before the Exercise

Prior to evaluation, become familiar with the numerical examples shown in the Wine Sensory Anchor Scale (Figure B.2). Keep this scale and an aroma wheel at your side as a reference during the evaluation process. While this exercise focuses on sweetness, don't miss this opportunity to do an informal evaluation of the other elements in each wine sample.

MATERIALS NEEDED

Table 5.5   Materials Needed for Exercise 5.1

1 white paper placemat per student with numbered circles to place wineglasses (Figures 2.4a, 2.4b)	Crackers to cleanse the palate
1 spit cup per student	Napkins
Corkscrew	Drinking water for each student
1 copy of the Aroma Wheel per student	6 (or 12 if both whites and red wines are used) wineglasses per student
Tasting instruction sheets for each student	1 (or 2) blank tasting form: wine sweetness only

Description	White Wine Suggestions	Red Wine Suggestions (optional)
Bone dry (numerical 0–1)	Sparking wine (brut)	Barolo
Dry (numerical 2–3)	Chardonnay	Cabernet Sauvignon
Medium-dry (numerical 3–4)	Gewürztraminer	Shiraz
Medium-sweet (numerical 5–6)	White Zinfandel	Late-harvest Zinfandel
Sweet (numerical 7–8)	Sauternes	Cabernet Franc ice wine
Very sweet (numerical 9–10)	Cream Sherry	Port

STEPS

1. Buy the wines.

2. Chill the white wines.

3. Distribute the placemats (Figures 2.4a and 2.4b) and set up the glasses.

4. Open the white wines and pour them in order of driest to sweetest.

5. Taste the wines in order and evaluate them (consider the six S's). Record your observations on the Wine Sweetness Level sheet (Figure 5.1).

Evaluator's Name: _____

Wine: _____ Producer: _____ Vintage:_____

0   5   10   Dry to Sweet

Wine: _____ Producer: _____ Vintage:_____

0   5   10   Dry to Sweet

Wine: _____ Producer: _____ Vintage:_____

0   5   10   Dry to Sweet

Wine: _____ Producer: _____ Vintage:_____

0   5   10   Dry to Sweet

Wine: _____ Producer: _____ Vintage:_____

0   5   10   Dry to Sweet

Wine: _____ Producer: _____ Vintage:_____

0   5   10   Dry to Sweet

Figure 5.1

Wine Sweetness Level

a. Focus on identifying the differences in sweetness level. Do the differences you perceive match those in Table 5.1? Is it difficult to determine differences in sweetness level?

b. What are the taste differences? Does acidity or alcohol impact your perception of sweetness?

6. In this exercise there are six whites (and/or six reds). Based on your analysis of each wine, rank the wines by level of sweetness from driest to sweetest.

Driest = 1. _____ 2. _____ 3. _____

4. _____ 5. _____ 6. _____ = Sweetest

Observations: _____

Retain the wine and setup for Exercise 5.3.

EXERCISE 5.2

RANKING SWEETNESS LEVELS IN FOOD

This exercise is designed to establish baseline measures of sweetness levels in food items. The foods used—from the Food Sensory Anchor Scale (Figure B.1)—are standardized items that can be purchased already prepared. These will provide consistent baseline measures of sweetness that will serve as points of reference in future tasting evaluations. However, as with the wine samples, your perception of sweetness in these food items may vary.

OBJECTIVE

The primary objective of this exercise is to establish baseline sweetness levels in food products.

Mise en Place: Things to Do Before the Exercise Prior to evaluation, become familiar with the numerical examples shown in the Food Sensory Anchor Scale. Keep this scale at your side as a reference during the evaluation process. While this exercise focuses on sweetness, don't miss this opportunity to do an informal evaluation of the other elements in each food sample (fattiness, saltiness, flavor intensity, etc.).

MATERIALS NEEDED

Table 5.6   Materials for Exercise 5.2

Prepackaged food items: Triscuits, Wheat Thins, graham crackers, Pepperidge Farms Bordeaux cookies	Napkins
1 copy Food Sensory Anchor References sheet per student	Drinking water for each student
1 food sweetness evaluation sheet per student	Glasses for water
Utensils for food items	Paper plates/bowls to serve items

STEPS

1. Purchase the food items and place a portion of each on a plate for each taster.

2. Taste the food items and rank them on the 0–10 scale. Focus on identifying the differences in sweetness level. Do the differences you perceive match those in Table 5.1? Is it difficult to determine differences in sweetness level? Record your observations on the Food Sweetness Level Sheet (Figure 5.2).

Evaluator's Name: _____

Food Item: _____

||||||||||||||||||||||||||||||||||||||||||||||| Sweetness
0   5   10

Food Item: _____

||||||||||||||||||||||||||||||||||||||||||||||| Sweetness
0   5   10

Food Item: _____

||||||||||||||||||||||||||||||||||||||||||||||| Sweetness
0   5   10

Food Item: _____

||||||||||||||||||||||||||||||||||||||||||||||| Sweetness
0   5   10

Food Item: _____

||||||||||||||||||||||||||||||||||||||||||||||| Sweetness
0   5   10

Food Item: _____

||||||||||||||||||||||||||||||||||||||||||||||| Sweetness
0   5   10

Figure 5.2

Food Sweetness Level

3. In this exercise there are four food items. Based on your impressions, rank-order the food items from least sweet to most sweet.
   Least sweet = 1. _____ 2. _____
   3. _____   4. _____ = Sweetest
   Observations: _____
   Retain the food for Exercise 5.3.

EXERCISE 5.3

SWEETNESS INTERACTIONS: TASTING WINES AND FOOD TOGETHER

This exercise incorporates the wine samples and food items from Exercises 5.1 and 5.2. You will taste each of the food items with each wine sample and determine whether the food is less sweet than, as sweet as, or sweeter than the wine sample. You will complete one Food Item and Wine Sweetness Comparisons sheet for each food item (a total of four).

The basic rule for wine and food pairing indicates that the food sweetness level should be less than or equal to the sweetness level of the wine to be perceived as a match. As you are tasting, you will want to think about this theoretical relationship and whether or not you believe it applies. Many people have individual preferences in terms of food flavor profiles and wine type preferences that may not accord exactly with the basic idea of sweetness matching. In a recent research project I performed, I found that while a sweetness match was a strong indicator of overall perceived match for wine and cheese pairing, significant differences occurred in perceived wine and cheese matches based on individual preferences for red wine or white wine, regardless of other theorized match relationships.

OBJECTIVE

The objective of this exercise is to assess sweetness levels of wine and food together and to evaluate the interaction of equal or different levels of sweetness of wine or food when tasted together.

Mise en Place: Things to Do Before the Exercise Prior to evaluation, make sure the wines are still at the appropriate tasting temperature and that you have a sufficient amount of each food item to taste a bite or two with each wine sample.

MATERIALS NEEDED

Table 5.7   Materials for Exercise 5.3

Prepackaged food items from Exercise 5.2	Napkins
Wines from Exercise 5.1	Drinking water for each student
1 copy Food and Wine Sensory Anchor Reference sheet per student	Glasses for water
Completed Wine and Food sweetness evaluation sheets	6 wineglasses on paper placemats
4 copies Food Item and Wine Sweetness Comparisons sheets per student	Paper plates or bowls to serve food
Utensils for food items	

Table 5.8   Wine and Food Sweetness Value Bands and Examples

Value Bands	Level of Wine Sweetness Description	Level of Food Item Sweetness Description
0 1	**Bone dry.** The inability to pick up the sensation of sweetness on the tongue. Sweetness anchor: brut sparkling wine.	**Imperceptible:** If the particular sensation is not detectable or if this sensation fades almost immediately. No perception or barely perceptible levels.
2 3	**Dry.** Any level of sweet characteristics are barely perceived and only with difficulty and hard work on the evaluator's part. Sweetness anchor: Chardonnay.	**Barely perceptible:** Any level of sweet characteristics are barely perceived and only with difficulty and hard work on the evaluator's part. Sweetness example: Triscuit.
4 5	**Medium-dry.** A lightly sweet sensation is identified and perceived at a sufficient level. Sweetness anchor: Gewürztraminer.	**Little perception:** A taste-smell sensation in which one succeeds in identifying or perceiving it in recognizable way, but the stimulus is not well-defined. The level of perception is still low. Sweetness example: Wheat Thins.
6 7	**Medium-sweet.** A sweet sensation on the tongue that is clearly identifiable and in a very defined way. Sweetness anchor: White Zinfandel.	**Sufficiently perceived:** A taste-smell sensation in which one succeeds in identifying and perceiving it in a sufficient level. An intermediate level of perception.
8 9	**Sweet.** Sugary, full, noticeable glycerin, containing residual sugar but pleasant in taste. Sweetness anchor: Sauternes.	**Abundant Perception:** A taste-smell sensation in which one can clearly identify and perceive in a very defined way. The taste-smell sensation is at an emphasized level. Sweetness example: graham cracker.
9 10	**Very sweet.** Sweetness is at an unmistakably high level of perceptibility with a lot of emphasis. Sweetness anchor: Cream Sherry.	**Highly perceived:** A taste-smell sensation that can be unmistakably identified with much emphasis. One can identify a particular food or clearly characterize a complex preparation. High perceptibility with a lot of emphasis. Sweetness example: Pepperidge Farms Bordeaux Cookie.

STEPS

1. Place a portion of each food item and an ounce of each wine sample (six total) on place settings for each taster.

2. Write your name and the name of the food item at the top of each Food Item and Wine Sweetness Comparisons sheet (Figure 5.3).

Name:_____ Sweet Food Anchor:_____

Level of Sweetness Match (Circle the level of match below):

Brut Sparkling Wine or _____

| −4 | −3 | −2 | −1 | 0 | +1 | +2 | +3 | +4 |

Food
Less Sweet   Equal
                                             Level   Food
                                                                                Sweeter

Chardonnay or _____

| −4 | −3 | −2 | −1 | 0 | +1 | +2 | +3 | +4 |

Food
Less Sweet   Equal
                                             Level   Food
                                                                                Sweeter

Gewurztraminer or _____

| −4 | −3 | −2 | −1 | 0 | +1 | +2 | +3 | +4 |

Food
Less Sweet   Equal
                                             Level   Food
                                                                                Sweeter

White Zinfandel or _____

| −4 | −3 | −2 | −1 | 0 | +1 | +2 | +3 | +4 |

Food
Less Sweet   Equal
                                             Level   Food
                                                                                Sweeter

Sauternes or _____

| −4 | −3 | −2 | −1 | 0 | +1 | +2 | +3 | +4 |

Food
Less Sweet   Equal
                                             Level   Food
                                                                                Sweeter

Cream Sherry or _____

| −4 | −3 | −2 | −1 | 0 | +1 | +2 | +3 | +4 |

Food
Less Sweet   Equal
                                             Level   Food
                                                                                Sweeter

Figure 5.3

Food Item and Wine Sweetness Comparisons

3. Taste the food items in order of sweetness (lowest to highest) and with each wine sample (driest to sweetest)—a Triscuit cracker with all wine samples (driest to sweetest), a Wheat Thins cracker with all wine samples (driest to sweetest), and so on. Record your observations and focus on ranking the comparative level of food item sweetness relative to the wine sample. For example, is the Triscuit less sweet than the White Zinfandel, and if so, by how much on a scale of 0 to −4? Do this for all of the food items with each wine.

4. Based on your sweetness impressions, rank-order the food items that you feel have the best match with each wine sample.

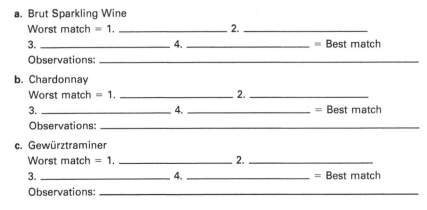

   a. Brut Sparkling Wine
   Worst match = 1. _____ 2. _____
   3. _____ 4. _____ = Best match
   Observations: _____

   b. Chardonnay
   Worst match = 1. _____ 2. _____
   3. _____ 4. _____ = Best match
   Observations: _____

   c. Gewürztraminer
   Worst match = 1. _____ 2. _____
   3. _____ 4. _____ = Best match
   Observations: _____

d. White Zinfandel

Worst match = 1. _____ 2. _____

3. _____ 4. _____ = Best match

Observations: _____

e. Sauternes

Worst match = 1. _____ 2. _____

3. _____ 4. _____ = Best match

Observations: _____

f. Cream Sherry

Worst match = 1. _____ 2. _____

3. _____ 4. _____ = Best match

Observations: _____

5. Did you find the best food-and-wine matches occurred when the food and wine sweetness levels were equal, when food sweetness was less than wine sweetness, or when food sweetness was greater than wine sweetness?

6. Did you identify other food or wine characteristics that contributed more to a sensation of match than sweetness did?

7. Other observations?

EXERCISE 5.4

RANKING ACIDITY LEVELS IN WINE

This exercise is designed to establish baseline measures of acidity levels in wines ranging from flat to tart. The table below provides examples of a range of acidity levels in white wines. The examples for this exercise are those shown as anchors in the Wine Sensory Anchor Scale. The wine sample with the lowest acidity in this exercise will be the warm-climate-zone Chardonnay. Chardonnay wines have less acidity than most white wines. The lower acidity will be partly due to the varietal, the warm climate (meaning riper grapes), and the aging process (if aged in oak). It is best to stick with New World selections for the Chardonnay sample in this exercise, such as warm areas of California (Central Valley, San Joaquin Valley), Texas, northern Chile (Aconcagua Valley), or parts of Australia (New South Wales, Hunter Valley). For the second level of acidity, a Fumé Blanc is suggested. The term Fumé Blanc was first used in the United States by Robert Mondavi in 1968. At the time, Sauvignon Blanc was a less popular varietal, and Mondavi coined the term to reflect a style similar to that of French Pouilly Fumé, which uses the same grape varietal. Fumé Blanc is grown in moderate-climate areas such as California and generally undergoes some aging in oak. Both of these issues should reduce the total acidity level below that of unoaked Sauvignon Blanc from cool-climate areas. The third level of acidity is reflective of Sauvignon Blanc produced in moderate-to cool-climate areas of New Zealand, California, and Washington. From New Zealand, select wines from Hawkes Bay, Auckland, or Gisborne. For the highest example of acidity, select Sauvignon Blanc from Sancerre or the Marlborough region of New Zealand. A second option for high levels of acidity is to try cool-climate Riesling from Germany or Canada.

While the Wine Sensory Anchor Scale indicates that the Chardonnay will have a numerical value of about 1–2, it could range from 0 to 3 on the acidity scale depending on your wine selection. This variability is true for the other wine suggestions as well. Your perception of acidity will vary depending on the wine selection, the temperature at which it is assessed, and your individual ability in assessing acidity (separating sweetness or bitterness from acidity). Therefore, during the tasting, you may find some of the wines to be closer or have a greater range of separation in acidity level than that shown in the Wine Sensory Anchor Scale. The numerical values are intended to provide you with a baseline to work from as you learn to assess acidity in wine.

OBJECTIVE

The primary objectives are to identify differences in acidity levels in wines and to establish a numerical baseline for reliable future assessment. This exercise also provides experience in wine evaluation as a whole and specifically in assessing the balance between sweetness and acidity.

Mise en Place: Things to Do Before the Exercise Prior to evaluation, become familiar with the numerical examples shown in the Wine Sensory Anchor Scale (Figure B.2). Keep this scale and an aroma wheel at your side as a reference during the evaluation process. While this exercise focuses on acidity, don't miss this opportunity to do an informal evaluation of the other elements in each wine sample.

MATERIALS NEEDED

Table 5.9 Materials Needed for Exercise 5.4

1 white paper placemat per student with numbered or labeled circles to place wineglasses (Figure 4.2)	Crackers to cleanse the palate
1 spit cup per student	Napkins
Corkscrew	Drinking water for each student
1 copy of the Aroma Wheel per student	4 wineglasses per student
Tasting instruction sheets for each student	1 copy Wine Acidity Level sheet per student

Table 5.10 Wine Suggestions for Exercise 5.4

Description	Wine Variety	Wine Suggestions
Low acidity (flat to lacking—if properly made it will be balanced with some tannin from oak aging), value band 0–3	Warm-climate Chardonnay	**California:** R. H. Philips, Toasted Head, Woodbridge, Talus, Kunde, Simi Reserve, Matanzas Creek **Australia:** Lindemans Bin 65, Rosemont Estates **Chile:** Concha y Toro, Errazuriz
Moderate acidity (refreshing), value band 4–6	Moderate/cool-climate Chardonnay or moderate-climate Fumé Blanc	**Chardonnay** **Burgundy:** Mâcon-Villages, Jadot **California:** Cambria, Gallo of Sonoma **Fumé Blanc** **California:** Robert Mondavi **Washington:** Covey Run, Hogue Cellars
Moderate-high acidity (crisp), value band 6–8	Moderate-climate California or Washington Sauvignon Blanc	**California:** Kenwood, Iron Horse, Morgan, Meridian **Washington:** St. Michelle, Columbia Crest, Arbor Crest
High to very high acidity (tart-green), value band 8–10	Cool-climate Sauvignon Blanc or Riesling	**Sauvignon Blanc** **Loire Valley Sancerre:** Lucien Crochet, Pascal Jolivet, Paul Cherrier **New Zealand, Marlborough:** Villa Maria, Stoneleigh, Brancott Reserve **Riesling** **German Riesling Kabinett, Mosel-saar-Ruwer, Rheingau:** J. J. Prüm, Schloss Johannisberg, Künstler, Wegeler **Canada:** Château des Charmes, Konzelmann, Inniskillin, Rief, Henry of Pelham

STEPS

1. Buy the wines.
2. Chill the wines.
3. Distribute the placemats (Figure 4.2) and set up the glasses.
4. Open the wines and pour them in order of lowest to highest acidity.
5. Taste the wines in order and evaluate them (consider the six S's). Record your observations on the Wine Acidity Level sheet (Figure 5.4).

Evaluator's Name: _____

Wine: _____ Producer: _____ Vintage:_____

[|||||||||||||||||||||||||] Low to High Acid
0   5   10

Wine: _____ Producer: _____ Vintage:_____

[|||||||||||||||||||||||||] Low to High Acid
0   5   10

Wine: _____ Producer: _____ Vintage:_____

[|||||||||||||||||||||||||] Low to High Acid
0   5   10

Wine: _____ Producer: _____ Vintage:_____

[|||||||||||||||||||||||||] Low to High Acid
0   5   10

Wine: _____ Producer: _____ Vintage:_____

[|||||||||||||||||||||||||] Low to High Acid
0   5   10

Wine: _____ Producer: _____ Vintage:_____

[|||||||||||||||||||||||||] Low to High Acid
0   5   10

Figure 5.4

Wine Acidity Level

a. Focus on identifying the differences in acidity level. Do the differences you perceive match those in Table 5.3? Is it difficult to determine differences in acidity level?

b. What are the taste differences? Does sweetness or bitterness impact your perception of acidity?

6. In this exercise there are four whites. Based on your analysis of each wine, rank the wines by level of acidity from lowest to highest.

Lowest = 1. _____ 2. _____

3. _____ 4. _____ = Highest

Observations: _____

Retain the wine and setup for Exercise 5.6.

Traditional pasta dishes such as this one of tomato and basil create a balance between the natural sweetness in the fresh tomato and its acidity. What wine would be a good match with this dish?

EXERCISE 5.5

RANKING ACIDITY LEVELS IN FOOD

This exercise is designed to establish baseline measures of acidity levels in food items. It includes both standardized food items that can be purchased already prepared and pasta preparations that range in acidity level. These will provide consistent baseline measures of acidity that will serve as points of reference in future tasting evaluations. The food items are those shown in the Food Sensory Anchor Scale (Figure B.1). As with the wine samples, your perception of acidity in these food items may vary. Acidity may also vary slightly based on ripeness of products used and regional differences.

OBJECTIVE

The primary objective of this exercise is to establish baseline acidity levels in food products.

Mise en Place: Things to Do Before the Exercise Prior to evaluation, become familiar with the numerical examples shown in the Food Sensory Anchor Scale. Keep this scale at your side as a reference during the evaluation process. While this exercise focuses on acidity, don't miss this opportunity to do an informal evaluation of the other elements in each food sample (sweetness, fattiness, saltiness, flavor intensity, etc.).

MATERIALS NEEDED

Table 5.11   Materials Needed for Exercise 5.5

Prepackaged food items: milk, yogurt, orange juice, grapefruit juice	Napkins
Items for pasta preparation (see recipes)	Drinking water for each student
1 copy Food Sensory Anchor References sheet per student	Glasses for water
1 copy food acidity evaluation sheet per student	Cooking utensils
Utensils for food items	Paper plates/bowls to serve items

Table 5.12   Examples of Food Acidity Levels for Exercise 5.5

Description of Sweetness	Food Items	Pasta Mixtures*
No to low acidity, value band 0–2		Pasta tossed with extra virgin olive oil
Little acidity, value band 2–4	Milk, cow's	
Moderate acidity, value band 4–6	Yogurt	Pasta tossed with balsamic vinaigrette
Moderate/high acidity, value band 6–8	Orange juice	Pasta tossed with equal parts balsamic vinaigrette and balsamic vinegar
Highly acidic, value band 8–10	Grapefruit juice	Pasta tossed with balsamic vinegar

Food Item: Pasta Mixtures

Yield: 4 servings of each of 4 types

Ingredients

Low Acid

2 cups (450 g) cooked pasta at room temperature
1/4 tsp (1 g) salt
1/4 tsp (1 g) black pepper
1 tbsp (15 ml) extra-virgin olive oil
Toss pasta with salt, pepper, and olive oil.

Moderate Acid

2 cups (450 g) cooked pasta at room temperature
1/8 tsp (0.5 g) salt
1/8 tsp (0.5 g) black pepper
2 tbsp (30 ml) balsamic vinaigrette (Newman's Own,
      another brand, or homemade)
Toss pasta with salt, pepper, and vinaigrette.

High Acid

2 cups (450 g) cooked pasta at room temperature
1/8 tsp (0.5 g) salt
1/8 tsp (0.5 g) black pepper
1 tbsp balsamic vinaigrette (Newman's Own, another
      brand, or homemade)
1 tbsp balsamic vinegar
Toss pasta with salt, pepper, vinaigrette, and vinegar.

Very High Acid

2 cups (450 g) cooked pasta at room temperature
1/4 tsp (1 g) salt
1/4 tsp (1 g) black pepper
2 tbsp (30 ml) balsamic vinegar
Toss pasta with salt, pepper, and vinegar.

STEPS

1. Purchase and prepare the food items and place a portion of each on a plate for each taster.

2. Taste the food items in order of acidity and rank them on a 0–10 scale (if tasting both liquid food items and pastas, taste and rank all of the liquids first, then the pastas). Focus on identifying the differences in acidity level. Do the differences you perceive match those in Table 5.3? Is it difficult to determine differences in acidity level? Record your observations on the Food Acidity Level sheet (Figure 5.5).

Evaluator's Name: _____

Food Item: _____

0   5   10   Low to High Acid

Food Item: _____

0   5   10   Low to High Acid

Food Item: _____

0   5   10   Low to High Acid

Food Item: _____

0   5   10   Low to High Acid

Food Item: _____

0   5   10   Low to High Acid

Food Item: _____

0   5   10   Low to High Acid

Figure 5.5

Food Acidity Level

3. In this exercise there are four food items (or two sets of food items). Based on your acidity impressions, rank order the food items from least acid to most acid.

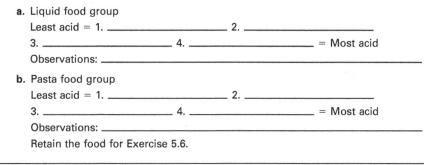

   a. Liquid food group
      Least acid = 1. _____ 2. _____
      3. _____ 4. _____ = Most acid
      Observations: _____

   b. Pasta food group
      Least acid = 1. _____ 2. _____
      3. _____ 4. _____ = Most acid
      Observations: _____
      Retain the food for Exercise 5.6.

EXERCISE 5.6

ACIDITY INTERACTIONS: TASTING WINES AND FOOD ITEMS TOGETHER

In this exercise, which incorporates the wine samples and food items from Exercises 5.4 and 5.5, you will taste each of the food items with each wine sample. Then, for each food item you will determine whether the food acidity level is less than the wine sample, equal to the wine sample, or more than the wine sample, completing one Food Item and Wine Acidity Comparison sheet (Figure 5.6) for each food item.

Name:_____ Acidity Food Anchor:_____

Level of Match (Circle the level of match below):

Warm Climate Chardonnay

-4	-3	-2	-1	0	+1	+2	+3	+4
Food				Equal				Food
Less Acid				Level				Higher Acidity

Moderate to Cool Climate Chardonnay or Moderate Climate Fumé Blanc

-4	-3	-2	-1	0	+1	+2	+3	+4
Food				Equal				Food
Less Acid				Level				Higher Acidity

Moderate climate New Zealand, California, or Washington Sauvignon Blanc

-4	-3	-2	-1	0	+1	+2	+3	+4
Food				Equal				Food
Less Acid				Level				Higher Acidity

Cool climate Sauvignon Blanc or Riesling

-4	-3	-2	-1	0	+1	+2	+3	+4
Food				Equal				Food
Less Acid				Level				Higher Acidity

Based on your evaluation of this food with the four wine samples, which wine element(s) **positively** impacted the wine and food match (check all that apply)? Please rank them in order of impact (1 = greatest impact).

___ Sweetness ____
___ Acidity ____
___ Tannin ____
___ Alcohol level ____
___ Overall Body ____
___ Wine flavor intensity level ____
___ Wine flavor persistence ____
___ Wine spiciness level ____
___ Wine flavor type ____

Based on your evaluation of this food with the four wine samples, which wine element(s) **negatively** impacted the wine and food match (check all that apply)? Please rank them in order of impact (1 = greatest impact).

___ Sweetness ____
___ Acidity ____
___ Tannin ____
___ Alcohol level ____
___ Overall Body ____
___ Wine flavor intensity level ____
___ Wine flavor persistence ____
___ Wine spiciness level ____
___ Wine flavor type ____

Figure 5.6

Food Item and Wine Acidity Comparison

The basic rule for wine and food pairing indicates that the food acidity level should be less than or equal to the acidity level of the wine to be perceived as a match. As you are tasting, you will want to think about this theoretical relationship and whether or not you believe it applies. In a recent research project, tasting panel members indicated that the perceived level of acidity of the warm-climate Chardonnay sample was somewhere between the level of cow's milk and yogurt. The perceived level of acidity of the Fumé Blanc was higher than yogurt but less than orange juice. The perceived level of acidity of a moderate-climate Sauvignon Blanc was about the same as orange juice, and cool-climate Sauvignon Blanc (in this case Sancerre) was higher than orange juice but less than grapefruit juice. What do these findings indicate in terms of matching wines with foods using vinaigrettes, marinades, and other sour additives?

Objective

The objective of this exercise is to assess acidity levels of wine and food together and to evaluate the interaction of lower, equal, or higher acidity when wine or food are tasted together.

Mise en Place: Things to Do Before the Exercise Prior to evaluation, make sure the wines are still at the appropriate tasting temperature and that you have a sufficient amount of each food item to taste a bite or two with each wine sample.

Materials Needed

Table 5.13   Materials Needed for Exercise 5.6

Prepackaged food items from Exercise 5.5	Napkins
Pasta mixture samples from Exercise 5.5	Drinking water for each student
Wines from Exercise 5.4	Glasses for water
1 copy Food and Wine Sensory Anchor Reference sheets per student	4 wineglasses on paper placemats
Completed Wine and Food Acidity evaluation sheets	Utensils for food items
4 or 8 Food Item and Wine Acidity Comparison sheets per student	Paper plates or bowls to serve food

Steps

1. Provide a portion of each food item and an ounce of each wine sample for each taster. Write the name of one food item at the top of each Food Item and Wine Acidity Comparison sheet.

2. Taste the food items in order of acidity (lowest to highest) and with each wine sample (least to most acid)—for example, milk (or pasta tossed with olive oil) with all wine samples (least to most acid); yogurt (or pasta tossed with balsamic vinaigrette) with all wine samples (least to most acid), and so on. Record your observations and focus on ranking the comparative level of food item acidity relative to the wine sample. For example, is the milk less acid than the Chardonnay, and if so, by how much on a scale of 0 to −4?

3. Based on your impressions, rank-order the food items that you feel have the best match with each wine sample.

   a. Warm-climate Chardonnay

     Worst match = 1. _____   2. _____

     3. _____   4. _____ = Best match

     Observations: _____

   b. Moderate- to cool-climate Chardonnay or moderate-climate Fumé Blanc

     Worst match = 1. _____   2. _____

     3. _____   4. _____ = Best match

     Observations: _____

   c. Moderate-climate New Zealand, California, or Washington Sauvignon Blanc

     Worst match = 1. _____   2. _____

     3. _____   4. _____ = Best match

     Observations: _____

d. Cool-climate Sauvignon Blanc or Riesling

Worst match = 1. _____   2. _____

3. _____   4. _____ = Best match

Observations: _____

4. Did you find the best food-and-wine matches occurred when the food and wine acidity levels were equal, when food acidity was less than the wine acidity, or when food acidity was greater than the wine acidity?

5. Did you identify other food or wine characteristics that contributed more to a sensation of match than acidity did?

6. Other observations?

NOTES

1. E. Peynaud, *The Taste of Wine: The Art and Science of Wine Appreciation*, 2nd ed. (New York: John Wiley & Sons, 1996).

2. Ibid.

3. Jeffery Stewart, personal communication, Niagara, Canada, November 28, 2005.

4. J. Robinson, *How to Taste: A Guide to Enjoying Wine* (New York: Simon & Schuster, 2000).

5. Andrea Immer, *Great Tastes Made Simple: Extraordinary Food and Wine Pairing for Every Palate* (New York: Broadway Books, 2002); M. McWilliams, *Food Fundamentals*, 6th ed. (Redondo Beach, CA: Plycon Press, 1995).

6. McWilliams, *Food Fundamentals*.

7. F. Beckett, *How to Match Food and Wine* (London: Octopus Publishing Group, 2002); J. Simon, *Wine with Food* (New York: Simon & Schuster, 1996).

8. Ibid.

9. Immer, *Great Tastes Made Simple*.

10. H. Charley and C. Weaver, *Foods: A Scientific Approach*, 3rd ed. (Upper Saddle River, NJ: Prentice-Hall, 1998); C. A. Rietz, *A Guide to the Selection, Combination, and Cooking of Foods* (Westport, CT: AVI, 1976).

11. Peynaud, *The Taste of Wine*, 94.

12. Robinson, *How to Taste*.

13. Peynaud, *The Taste of Wine*, 95.

14. Ibid.

15. J. C. Alexopoulos and J. P. Henderson, *About Wine* (Clifton Park, NY: Thomson Delmar Learning, 2006).

16. Andrea Immer, *Great Wine Made Simple: Straight Talk from a Master Sommelier* (New York: Broadway Books, 2000); S. Kolpan, B. H. Smith, and M. A. Weiss, *Exploring Wine*, 2nd ed. (New York: John Wiley & Sons, Inc., 2002); Peynaud, *The Taste of Wine*.

17. Peynaud, *The Taste of Wine*.

18. J. W. Chesser, *The Art and Science of Culinary Preparation* (St. Augustine, FL: Educational Institute of the American Culinary Federation, 1992).

19. M. W. Baldy, *The University Wine Course*, 3rd ed. (San Francisco: Wine Appreciation Guild, 2003).

20. A. J. Pandell, "*The Acidity of Wine*," http://www.wineperspective.com/the_acidity_of_wine.htm (accessed December 12, 2005).

21. R. Gawel, "Volatile Acidity in Wine," http://www.aromadictionary.com/articles/volatileacidity_article.html (accessed December 22, 2005).

22. See Kolpan, Smith, and Weiss, *Exploring Wine*.

23. Beckett, *How to Match Food and Wine*.

24. J. Simon, *Wine with Food* (New York: Simon and Schuster, 1996).

CHAPTER 6
SALT, BITTERNESS, AND BUBBLES

CHAPTER OUTLINE:

Introduction

Aperitif: Peller Estates Winery

Saltiness

Bitterness

Sparkling Wine and Pairing

Effervescence: The Great Equalizer?

Summary

Exercises

KEY CONCEPTS:

- The limiting effects of food saltiness and bitterness
- Effervescence lessens the negative effects of high salt
- Higher effervescence provides a cleansing effect on moderately high food bitterness
- Bitterness + bitterness = more bitterness

INTRODUCTION

The Peller Estates sparkling wines and food recommendations provide a good introduction to this chapter, which features a discussion of the impact of wine effervescence in food pairing decisions. The following sections introduce the impact of food saltiness and bitterness on the pairing process along with an overview of sparkling wine characteristics, levels of effervescence, and the relationship between effervescence and palate cleansing.

Aperitif | Peller Estates Winery

Peller Estates Winery, which produces some of North America's premium sparkling wines, is located on a forty-acre vineyard that is walking distance from the Old Town of Niagara-on-the-Lake in Ontario,

The entrance to Peller Estates Winery in the Niagara Region of Ontario, Canada (courtesy of Peller Estates Winery).

Canada. This family winery spans three generations and has captured the attention of knowledgeable consumers and critics alike. More than forty years ago, Andrew Peller, a Hungarian immigrant, opened a modest winery in British Columbia's Okanagan Valley. This humble beginning planted the roots of a dream that would be passed along to his son John and later to his grandson Joe.

The mission of Peller Estates is simply to produce high-quality premium wines combining the best vineyards and skilled winemaking with patience and dedication. The Niagara winery features a 5,000-square-foot underground barrel aging cellar (350 barrels) and a 5,000-square-foot press house (1,000 barrels) that is home to Peller's next-generation wines.

Peller Estates' renowned Ice Cuvee VQA is a traditional *méthode champenoise* sparkling wine made with Chardonnay and Pinot Noir grapes, naturally fermented and aged in the bottle. When the lees are disgorged, a *dosage* of Vidal ice wine is added. The intensity of the ice wine creates a sparkling wine of unique style and finesse. The finished product has very fine bubbles with a brilliant yellow straw color. A bouquet of apricot, yeast, and ripe apple with hints of honey is followed by tropical fruits on the palate and a refreshing sweet grapefruit finish.

This medium-dry sparkling wine (approximately 2.8 percent residual sugar) is noticeably sweet and is best enjoyed before a meal as an aperitif or after a meal with fresh fruit and cheese. Suggested foods to accompany this wine include oven-roasted plum tomatoes on toasted baguettes with goat cheese; phyllo spring rolls with plum sauce; fresh fruit such as mangoes, golden pineapple, Bartlett pears and strawberries; cream fruit cheeses with country bread; goat cheese terrine with a dried-fruit salad; harvest butternut squash soup with maple drizzle; and, of course, salty appetizers.

A more traditional approach to sparkling wine is found in the winery's Trius Brut VQA. The grapes for this *méthode classique* sparkling wine are hand-harvested and whole-bunch pressed with the special Champagne press cycle. A cuvée of 70 percent Chardonnay and 30 percent Pinot Noir receives a second fermentation in the bottle using Epernay yeast, up to two and a half years of aging *sur lie*, and time-honored riddling and disgorging for removal of spent yeast cells. This process produces a sparkling wine of great finesse and style. It has exceptional fizz and an appealing toasty/yeasty character, and it can hold its own against many well-made Champagnes.

This is a non-vintage brut sparkling wine with 0.8 percent residual sugar and is an excellent partner with a wide variety of foods, including pan-fried fresh perch or pickerel, chicken in a light lemon cream sauce, vegetarian spring rolls, glazed pork roast with apples, fresh strawberries, oven-roasted tomatoes with goat cheese on toasted baguettes, grilled salmon with zucchini and red peppers, and Gruyère and Emmenthal cheese fondue with a light rye bread.

Both of these sparklers have received numerous medals at regional and international competitions. The wine production at Peller is under the guidance of winemaker Lawrence Buhler. Born in Kingston, Ontario, Lawrence's family moved to Saudi Arabia where he spent the first 11 years of his life. Lawrence traveled growing up and visited great wine regions of the world. During his travels, his father's interest in wine grew stronger. Although Saudi Arabia was an alcohol free country, Lawrence's father used travel as a great excuse to try different wines.

After moving back to Canada in 1990, Lawrence entered into the Chemical Engineering program at the University of Ottawa in 1997, all the while pursing wine and winemaking as a hobby with his father who spent countless hours training for his Sommelier designation. It was when tasting his first Pinot Noir, that Lawrence's suspicions were confirmed; he was passionate about, and destined to work with, wine. As he contemplated his next move, he decided to follow the lead of his father and enroll in a Sommelier program at night. During his days he continued to attend University taking pre-requisite courses so he could apply to the Brock University Cool Climate Oenology and Viticulture Institute (CCOVI). The only program of its kind in Canada, Lawrence knew that he needed to do everything he could to be accepted as part of this elite group of future winemakers. Calling daily to the university's admission office paid off when Lawrence was told that he was accepted into the CCOVI program in 1999.

Graduating in 2002, with only one other, Lawrence knew he wanted to make wine in Canada; specifically Ontario. He was excited to see the progress of Ontario wines and how well they were standing up to some of the best wines in the world. He saw Ontario as a great opportunity for a young Canadian winemaker and saw no need to seek out any other wine region.

Interning at some of Niagara's most well known and respected wineries including Marynissen, Strewn, Vineland Estates, and Angels Gate provided Lawrence with a broad range of expertise from viticulture manager to assistant winemaker. He joined Peller Estates in April 2003 as an Assistant Winemaker to Rob Summers, and in the summer of 2005, was awarded the coveted position of Peller Estates Winemaker. Lawrence's passion for the vineyard, winemaking and wine continues to grow each day as he produces his own award-winning vintages.

The winery also features a dining room that overlooks the vineyards, creating a perfect location to experience the wines paired with cuisine indicative of the region. Additional information on Peller Estates and its wines can be found at www.peller.com.

SALTINESS

The level of salt in food has a profound impact on appropriate wine selections. Small to moderate levels of salt do not create huge problems when matching food with wine. In fact, savory foods with moderate levels of salt generally enhance the taste of many red wines. But foods with a high salt content are not compatible with most wines.

As with sweetness in food, salt can occur naturally or be added. Salty sensations are derived from three main sources: sodium chloride, sodium glutamate, and potassium chloride. It comes in various forms such as table salt, rock salt, kosher salt, sea salt, and flavored salts.[1] An important consideration of the use of salt in food is the temperature at which it will be served. The amount of salt is easily detectable at cooler temperatures and less pronounced at warmer ones.

While salt is the primary seasoning agent used to flavor foods, it is generally not present in wine at detectable levels, with the exception of perhaps dry sherry. The next time you get an opportunity, taste a very dry, light sherry (perhaps Tío Pepe or La Ina) and notice the impact on the part of your tongue that is sensitive to saltiness. You should find some salty characteristics in both Fino and Manzanilla sherry. Sometimes traces of salt are identifiable in Chilean reds and Rhône Valley Syrah, but salt traces are not an important wine characteristic as a whole.[2]

In food, salt magnifies our perception of tastes and flavors already present. Similarly, when salty foods are combined with wine, the salt magnifies the negative aspects inherent in wine when salt is present at a high level. This is particularly true for red wines—highly salty foods seem to accentuate any bitterness or astringency present in a wine. Salt magnifies the heat from alcohol and creates a bitter, unpleasant taste. And high salt in foods creates a metallic taste with wines of high acidity.

In general, high salt foods should be served with wines that have no tannins, have some residual sugar (sweetness), are fruit-forward, and have moderate levels of acidity.[3] Because of residual sugar and fruitiness, Rieslings or Gewürztraminers pair well with salty dishes. If reds are desired, choose cooler-climate reds that are low in tannins or red varietals from warm climates that have soft, ripe tannin characteristics. For traditional dishes such as baked ham, a rosé makes a good choice—the residual sugar, fruitiness, and low tannins work well with the saltiness in the ham as well as any fruit glazes that may be added during baking.[4]

Another suggestion is to create salty and sweet combinations such as Stilton and Port or Sauternes. Champagne is also regularly suggested as pairing fairly well with salty foods. The classic example is the marriage of Champagne and caviar. Due to its acidity and bubbles, Champagne is food-friendly in general, and the effervescence helps to cleanse the palate.

BITTERNESS

Most of us from North America do not have a strong tradition of enjoying distinctly bitter characteristics in our foods and beverages. Besides having hops added to the beer we drink or the occasional radicchio or frisée added to a salad, bitter elements are generally a rather subdued part of our daily sensory routines. Many European and Eastern cultures have a more positive relationship with bitter foods and beverages. Belgian endive, olives, and Campari are but three common examples of bitter tastes from Europe, where they are thought by many to stimulate the appetite and increase the flow of digestive juices.

A wine cellar in Monte Carlo, Monaco, containing Champagne bottles nearly two hundred years old.

The bitter sensation is derived from a reaction to the alkaloids in certain foods, and this sensation is usually detected on the back of the tongue. Bitter beverages include coffee, tea, and tonic water. Bitterness in foods can be slight, as in butter lettuce, iceberg, or romaine, or quite substantial, as in endive, citrus peel, and radicchio. Like saltiness, bitter alkaloids are far more discernible at cooler temperatures. This explains why cold coffee and cold Italian red wines (i.e. Barolo, Nebbiolo, and Chianti) taste so bitter.

Some people—perhaps 25 percent of the population, according to one study—are exceptionally sensitive to bitter tastes and tend to avoid them. This sensitivity to bitter tastes has a tendency to impact dietary choices and food selection, which may possibly have health consequences—in the study, women who disliked sharp and bitter foods limited their consumption of foods that are known to reduce cancer risk, such as broccoli and Brussels sprouts, citrus fruits (such as grapefruit), and other bitter berries and roots.[5]

In wine, tannin is often confused with bitterness, but they are different. Tannin is a feeling of astringency and is a tactile sensation felt throughout your mouth. Bitterness is a primary taste component detected on the back of the tongue. As with saltiness, bitterness is not a dominant characteristic in wine, and it is not included as a primary wine component.[6] When bitterness is present in wine, it can provide a pleasant additional layer of excitement (as can bitterness in food), but high levels of bitterness are not desirable in wine, and they are not a good thing in food-and-wine pairing. Unlike other matched components such as sweetness or acidity, matching a bitter food with a bitter wine just creates an intense bitter taste.

Bitterness in food magnifies the sensations of tannin in wine. Sweetness (residual sugar) in wine reduces the impact of food bitterness.

SPARKLING WINE AND PAIRING

Sparkling wine made in France outside of the Champagne region is labeled *vin mousseux*. Sparkling wines are called *spumante* in Italy, *Sekt* in Germany, *cava* in Spain, and *cap classique* in South Africa.[7] The effervescence in Champagne and other sparkling wines is often called bubbles, stars, or sparklers.

Sparkling wine can be created using several methods. The most common methods use two fermentations, with the second fermentation trapping dissolved carbon dioxide gas in the wine. The method used can substantially impact the sensory and quality characteristics of the wine (as well as the price of the wine). The traditional Champagne method (*méthode champenoise*) is considered by most to create the highest-quality sparkling wines.

The level of effervescence is defined by the amount of bubbles present in a wine product. Wine evaluators assess effervescence in four areas: the amount of bubbles (the number of bubbles in a bottle of good sparkling wine is estimated to be about 49 million),[8] their size (smaller bubbles provide evidence of skilled technique in the traditional Champagne method), their consistency (consistency in bubble size and intensity), and how long they last (bubbles should not dissipate quickly after the bottle is opened or the wine is poured). All of these areas are an indication of quality in a sparkling wine.

For the purpose of food-and-wine pairing, there are a number of criteria to consider when pairing food with sparkling wine. Sparkling wines come in a variety of body styles, acidity levels, sweetness levels, and effervescence levels.

Body style in sparkling wine is determined by the producer. Within the Champagne region, body styles vary from light to full-bodied. As with other wines, body style is determined by the type of grapes used, fermentation method, and growing region. Sparkling wines in the Champagne region are made from one of three types of grapes: Chardonnay, Pinot Noir, and Meunier. Most American producers of quality sparkling wines adhere to this list, but the varietals used vary by climate zone. Table 6.1 provides a list of varietals used by the majority of quality sparkling wine producers in cool, moderate, and warm climates.

Body The body style is determined by the producer and is dependent on the grapes used, fermentation, aging, and climate. The term *blanc de blancs* is used to designate white wine made only from white grapes, traditionally Chardonnay. The term *blanc de noirs* refers to white wine made only from black (red) grapes, traditionally Pinot Noir. Pinot Noir adds depth, complexity, and fullness to the sparkling wine. Chardonnay grapes grown in a cool climate such as Champagne allows the grapes to stay on the vine for a longer period. Cooler climates allow Chardonnay grapes to retain a desirable level of acidity, needed to achieve greater complexity during the aging process.[9]

Table 6.2 provides specific examples of sparkling wines produced in the Champagne region, grouped by increasing body. This list points out the influence of the house style on body even when the sparkling wines come from the same growing region.

Sparklers are usually made as a white or rosé wine. Rosé sparkling wines are less common than whites and have a fuller body style on average. Rosé sparkling wine can stand

Table 6.1   Varietals Used in *Méthode Champenoise* Production

Cool Regions	Moderate Regions	Warm Regions
Pinot Noir	Chenin Blanc	Parallada
Chardonnay	Chardonnay	Chardonnay
Meunier	Pinot Noir	Xarello
Gamay	Gamay	Mabaceo
Pinot Blanc	Meunier	Pinot Noir
		Chenin Blanc
		Meunier
		Sémillon

Source: B. Zoecklein, "A Review of Méthode Champenoise Production," Virginia Cooperative Extension and Virginia Polytechnic Institute and State University, Blacksburg, 2002.

up to pâtés, ham, beef, and game dishes. A unique sparkling wine is an Australian red made from Shiraz (Bancock Station). The full body and off-dry sweetness level of this sparkler make it a good choice with dishes such as lamb curry.

Body style in sparkling wine can have a substantial impact on wine and food matches. More specific issues of the importance of texture and body in wine and food are presented in the upcoming chapters. For now, be aware that sparkling wines vary substantially in body weight, and these differences are an important consideration in pairing choices.

Acidity   There are a number of environmental and viticultural factors that ultimately impact the palatability of a finished sparkling wine, including canopy climate, meso- and microclimates, rootstock, temperature, and pruning techniques. The complexity of these and other relationships creates difficulties for producers of sparkling wine beyond those of still wines.[10]

Champagne, France, is the most northern region for sparkling wine other than Mosel, Germany. As with still table wines, climate impacts the level of acidity in a finished product. Warm-climate Chardonnay has a tendency to have a narrow flavor profile and lacks a sense of freshness, liveliness, and length of finish. Sparkling wines that lack these factors will not have the ability of higher-quality sparkling wines to cleanse and refresh the palate, especially if foods are salty or bitter.

Sweetness   Unlike many other wine categories, sparkling wines are available in a wide range of sweetness levels from bone dry to very sweet. European countries have voluntary standards for levels of residual sugar in sparkling wines. There are six basic levels of sweetness, outlined in Table 6.3. Brut nature is less common, has a residual sugar level of 0–0.5

Table 6.2   Body Style of a Few Champagnes

Light-Bodied and Lovely	Medium-Bodied and Rich	Full-Bodied and Bodacious
Laurent-Perrier	Charles Heidsieck	Louis Roederer "Cristal"
Lanson	Piper-Heidsieck	Bollinger "Special Cuvée"
Duetz	Pol Roger	A. Gratien
G. H. Mumm	Henriot	Krug "Grande Cuvee"
Perrier-Jouët	Bruno Paillard	Veuve Clicquot
Taittinger	Paul Goerg	Gosset
Pommery	Moët et Chandon	

Table 6.3   Sweetness Levels in Sparkling Wines

Sweetness Levels	Descriptions
Brut nature	Bone dry with no hint of any sweet sensation.
Brut	An inability to pick up the sensation of sweetness on the tongue.
Extra Sec (Extra Dry)	Any level of sweetness is barely perceived and only with difficulty and hard work on the evaluator's part.
Sec	A lightly sweet sensation is identified and perceived at a sufficient level.
Demi-Sec	Sugary, full, noticeable glycerin, containing residual sugar but pleasant in taste.
Doux	Sweetness is at an unmistakably high level of perceptibility with a lot of emphasis.

percent, and should taste bone dry. Brut (residual sugar of 0.5–1.5 percent) should have no perception of sweetness and taste dry. Extra dry has a residual sugar level of 1.2–2.0 percent and tastes slightly sweet. Sec has residual sugar of 1.7–3.5 percent and is noticeably sweet (confusingly, *sec* translates as "dry"). Demi-sec is definitely sweet, with residual sugar of 3.3–5.0 percent. Doux sparkling wines, which are fairly uncommon in the United States, are very sweet, with a residual sugar level of over 5.0 percent. American sparkling wine producers don't conform to the European standards but follow the same hierarchy of dry-to-sweet organization in their terminology.[11]

How does sweetness level influence sparkling wine and food choices? As you remember from the previous chapter, sweetness in wine creates a match with the sweetness in food. Brut and extra-dry sparkling wines can be paired with a wide variety of foods, including light appetizers, seafood, fish, poultry, Asian foods, ham, and game. In general, sec, demi-sec, and doux wines are more appropriate with sweeter foods such as fruits and desserts.

Effervescence   A main criterion in wine consumed with salty or bitter food is the level of effervescence present. Wines can be still, slightly sparkling, semi-sparkling, or full sparkling. Slightly sparkling wine is called *pétillant* in French and *frizzante* in Italian. Table 6.4 provides some examples of wines in each of these categories.

Many wines are sometimes produced as slightly sparkling or have a "spritzer" character to them. Examples include Fendant, a white wine from the Valais region of Switzerland, and

Table 6.4   Sparkling Wine Effervescence Levels

Levels	Examples
Slightly sparkling	Fendant (Switzerland) Some Aligoté (Burgundy) Some Vinho Verde (Portugal) Some from the Prosecco grape (produced as still, slightly, semi-sparkling, and fully sparkling from the Veneto region of Italy)
Semi-sparkling	Clairette de Die (from Clairette and Muscat grapes—Rhône) Some Muscat (Oregon) Moscato d'Asti (Piedmont)
Full sparkling	Asti Spumante (Piedmont) Champagne (France) Crémant de Bourgogne (Burgundy) Cava (Spain) Rosa Regale Brachetto d'Acqui (red, from Italy)

Aligoté, a white wine from the Burgundy region of France that is the traditional wine used to create the classic aperitif Kir, in which the chilled wine is mixed with crème de cassis. A popular example of a semi-sparkling wine is Moscato d'Asti from the Piedmont region of Italy. It is produced with varying degrees of effervescence but is generally lighter than true sparkling wine. Fully sparkling wines are produced in a variety of locations. Champagne is the most well known, but Spain actually produces more sparkling wine than any other country.

In North America, good-quality sparkling wines are also produced in the cooler regions of California and in Washington, Oregon, and Canada (VQA Niagara Peninsula and VQA Okanagan Valley). Wine producers in Sonoma and Carneros are producing high-quality sparklers in these cool climate zones. Northwest producers such as Domaine Ste. Michelle (Washington) and Argyle (Oregon) are producing sparkling wines that have received much acclaim. Canadian wine producers are taking advantage of the cooler temperatures and developing a strong group of brut sparkling wines as well as some interesting specialties such as Inniskillin's sparkling ice wine.

EFFERVESCENCE: THE GREAT EQUALIZER?

Effervescence creates another sensation to consider beyond issues of sweetness, acidity, body, and flavor, and generally adds a significant food-friendly quality to wine. Effervescence is perceived on the tongue and in other areas of the mouth. It has a cleansing and refreshing effect on fat (cutting through it much like acidity in wine), salt, and bitterness, preparing the palate for the next bite.

Recently, I experimented with the impact of effervescence on low, medium, and high levels of salt (in air-popped popcorn) as well as four levels of bitterness in food (in iceberg lettuce, celery sticks, Belgian endive, and radicchio). Using a trained sensory panel and the exercises at the end of this chapter, the impact of bubbles was tested using straight effervescence in water (using three levels: still, a 50/50 mix of still water and seltzer, and 100 percent seltzer) and effervescence present in wine (again using three levels: a still Chardonnay, a Moscato d'Asti, and a Champagne).

The findings can be described by two guidelines:

Rule #3: Highly salty foods work better with wines that have high effervescence.

Rule #4: The negative impact of bitter food is lessened when combined with wines of moderate to high levels of effervescence.

For the tests of the impact with salty foods, effervescence in water lessened the negative affects of high salt and cleansed the palate, as suggested in food and wine literature. One hundred percent seltzer water had the greatest overall impact on cleansing the palate but

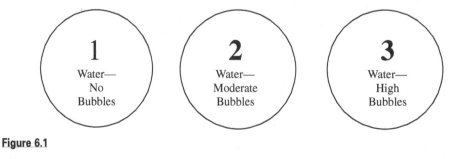

Figure 6.1

Water Effervescence Samples

Figure 6.2

Wine Effervescence Samples

did a slightly better job at the moderate salty level than at the high salt level. The 50/50 mix of seltzer and still water did a better job than still water alone.

For the wine samples, the findings basically mirrored the water samples, with a couple of exceptions. The Chardonnay wine was okay with moderate salt levels, lessening some of the saltiness. But with the high-salt popcorn, the match went from neutral to bad. The high salt in the popcorn seemed to magnify the bitter and astringent character in the wine. Chardonnay has a natural affinity with corn, particularly when you serve a buttery chardonnay with a corn dish that includes butter (including buttered popcorn). But care must be taken to make sure the salt level is not too high.

The Champagne did a better job of cleansing the palate at the moderate salt level, but the Moscato d'Asti performed equally as well with the high-salt sample. This finding points out the important interacting effects of effervescence, acidity, and sweetness with salty foods. The Moscato d'Asti had a high level of acidity (as did the Champagne) as well as a moderate level of sweetness (the Champagne was extra dry). This sweetness along with moderate effervescence and acidity in the Moscato d'Asti created an equal ability to refresh the palate in the case of salty foods.

In the tests of the impact of effervescence on food bitterness, similar relationships were found. Higher effervescence in water provided a cleansing effect on moderately high food bitterness. Once the food bitterness level reached that of radicchio, even 100 percent seltzer water did not create a total sense of refreshment for the palate. With the wine samples, the Chardonnay created a very poor match with the bitter food items. The Moscato d'Asti created the best matches overall and provided an equal level of refreshment for both the Belgian endive and radicchio items. Here again, in addition to the effervescence effect, the sweetness present in the Moscato helped to mask the perception of bitterness in the food items. The extra-dry Champagne was a better match than the Chardonnay but was not as good as the Moscato.

SUMMARY

This chapter discusses the main relationships between food saltiness and food bitterness and wine. In general, high levels of salt or bitterness in foods limit the ability to create a match with wine that refreshes the palate and severely constrains the ability to create a synergistic match. Salt characteristics are not dominant in wine, with very few opportunities to match salty characteristics of food and wine.

Unlike the canceling effects of matching sweetness or acidity, matching bitterness levels in food and wine just creates more bitterness. Bitterness in wine should not be a dominant characteristic in wine of good quality, and bitterness should not be confused with astringency (from tannins).

While effervescence can be a great equalizer when paired with foods, the interacting effects of body, sweetness, acidity and effervescence cannot be overlooked. The level of body is an important factor to move a match from the refreshment or neutral stage to the good match level. The importance of a body-to-body match is discussed in more detail in the next chapter. Sweetness has a tendency to mask bitterness and other negative tastes. Acidity acts much like effervescence to refresh the palate. Of course, remember that high salt in foods magnifies any negative effects in wine.

DISCUSSION QUESTIONS

1. What impact does high salt in foods have on the taste of wine?

2. Do food bitterness and wine bitterness cancel each other out when tasted together?

3. What are some of the wine elements that interact with food saltiness to impact the overall level of match?

4. What are the interacting factors in sparkling wine that impact the level of match with salty, bitter, and other types of foods?

5. What specific wines would you pair with a salad of frisée, radicchio, and Belgian endive?

EXERCISE 6.1

FOOD SALTINESS, BITTERNESS, AND WINE EFFERVESCENCE ANCHORS

In this exercise, you will test the impact of three levels of effervescence on three levels of saltiness and four levels of bitterness. To sort out the direct effects of effervescence from the interacting effects of acidity and residual sugar on food saltiness and bitterness, the three levels of effervescence in this exercise are provided in three water samples and then three wine samples.

As you taste the food items with the water and wine samples, you will evaluate the impact of effervescence on salty and bitter foods. Does effervescence cleanse away the negative effects of excessive salt or bitterness? Does the effervescence do a partial job? Or does the combination of high salt or high bitterness with wine characteristics make both items taste worse?

OBJECTIVES

The objective of this exercise is to train students to identify various scale values of food bitterness, food saltiness, beverage effervescence, and the interactions between them.

Mise en Place: Things to Do Before the Exercise Ensure that the water, seltzer water, still white table wine, Moscato d'Asti, and the fully sparkling wine (Champagne, Cava, sparkling wine from California, etc.) are properly chilled for tasting. Also, since timing is very important for the samples with effervescence—if poured too early, the bubbles will dissipate—do not pour the water or wine samples with effervescence until just before participants are ready to taste and evaluate.

MATERIALS NEEDED

Table 6.5   Materials Needed for Exercise 6.1

Food Saltiness Samples (1 sample per student)	Water Samples (1 sample per student)
2 c (480 ml) air-popped popcorn, no salt 2 c (480 ml) air-popped popcorn with ⅛ tsp (0.5g) popcorn or regular salt 2 c (480 ml) air-popped popcorn with ¼ tsp (1 g) salt	100% still water 50% still water and 50% seltzer 100% seltzer
Food Bitterness Samples (1 sample per student)	**Wine Samples (1 sample per student)**
Iceberg lettuce Celery or frisée Belgian endive Radicchio	Moscato d'Asti Champagne, Cava, or other sparkling wine
Corkscrew	
Sample cups or plates	6 wineglasses per student
1 white paper placemat per student for glass setup	
Food Saltiness and Food Bitterness Evaluation sheets	Drinking water for each student
1 copy Wine and Food Sensory Anchor Sheets per student	1 spit cup per student
1 copy Water/Wine Effervescence Evaluation sheet per student	
Napkins	
2 copies Effervescence and Food Saltiness comparison sheets per student	
2 copies Effervescence and Food Bitterness comparison sheets per student	

Name:_____ Wine/Water Anchor:_____

The impact of the wine/water sample on food saltiness (Place an **X** in the space in front of the description that matches the impact the wine/water effervescence level has on the palatability of the food sample):

Unsalted Popcorn   Comments: _____

____ The water/wine worsens the impact

____ No apparent impact

____ Slightly lessens the negative impact of salt

____ Lessens the negative impact of salt to a palatable level

____ Cleanses away the negative impact of salt and prepares it for another bite/mouthful

Popcorn with Moderate Salt   Comments: _____

____ The water/wine worsens the impact

____ No apparent impact

____ Slightly lessens the negative impact of salt

____ Lessens the negative impact of salt to a palatable level

____ Cleanses away the negative impact of salt and prepares it for another bite/mouthful

Popcorn with High Salt   Comments: _____

____ The water/wine worsens the impact

____ No apparent impact

____ Slightly lessens the negative impact of salt

____ Lessens the negative impact of salt to a palatable level

____ Cleanses away the negative impact of salt and prepares it for another bite/mouthful

Figure 6.3

Wine / Water Effervescence and Food Saltiness Comparison

Name:_____ Wine/Water Anchor:_____

The impact of the wine/water sample on food bitterness (Place an **X** in the space in front of the description that matches the impact the wine/water effervescence level has on the palatability of the food sample):

Lettuce   Comments: _____

____ The water/wine worsens the impact

____ No apparent impact

____ Slightly lessens the negative impact of bitterness

____ Lessens the negative impact of bitterness to a palatable level

____ Cleanses away the negative impact of bitterness and prepares the palate for another bite/mouthful

Celery/Frisée   Comments: _____

____ The water/wine worsens the impact

____ No apparent impact

____ Slightly lessens the negative impact of bitterness

____ Lessens the negative impact of bitterness to a palatable level

____ Cleanses away the negative impact of bitterness and prepares the palate for another bite/mouthful

Belgian endive   Comments: _____

____ The water/wine worsens the impact

____ No apparent impact

____ Slightly lessens the negative impact of bitterness

____ Lessens the negative impact of bitterness to a palatable level

____ Cleanses away the negative impact of bitterness and prepares the palate for another bite/mouthful

Radicchio   Comments: _____

____ The water/wine worsens the impact

____ No apparent impact

____ Slightly lessens the negative impact of bitterness

____ Lessens the negative impact of bitterness to a palatable level

____ Cleanses away the negative impact of bitterness and prepares the palate for another bite/mouthful

Figure 6.4

Wine / Water Effervescence and Food Bitterness Comparison

STEPS

Saltiness

1. Pop the popcorn in an air popper. When popped, divide it into three batches: one batch with no salt, a moderate-salt batch with ⅛ tsp salt, and a high-salt batch with ¼ tsp salt.

2. Provide a portion of each food saltiness sample for each student. Taste each popcorn sample and evaluate the level of saltiness on the Food Saltiness and Bitterness Evaluation sheet (Figure 6.6). Use the Food Sensory Anchor sheet (Figure B.1) and saltiness value bands for reference.

3. Provide each student with about 2 ounces of each water sample (still water, 50/50 mix, and 100 percent seltzer). Taste each water effervescence sample and evaluate the level of effervescence on the evaluation sheet. Use the Wine Sensory Anchor sheet (Figure B.2) and effervescence value bands for reference.

Evaluator's Name: _____

Water: _____

[|||||||||||||||||||||||||||]   Low to High Effervescence
0   5   10

Water: _____

[|||||||||||||||||||||||||||]   Low to High Effervescence
0   5   10

Water: _____

[|||||||||||||||||||||||||||]   Low to High Effervescence
0   5   10

Wine: _____ Producer: _____ Vintage:_____

[|||||||||||||||||||||||||||]   Low to High Effervescence
0   5   10

Wine: _____ Producer: _____ Vintage:_____

[|||||||||||||||||||||||||||]   Low to High Effervescence
0   5   10

Wine: _____ Producer: _____ Vintage:_____

[|||||||||||||||||||||||||||]   Low to High Effervescence
0   5   10

Figure 6.5

Water / Wine Effervescence Evaluation

4. Taste each popcorn sample with each water sample. Begin with the no-salt popcorn and taste it with the still water, then the 50/50 mix, then the pure seltzer. Do the same with the moderate-salt popcorn and then the high-salt popcorn. Record your observations on the Wine/Water Effervescence and Food Saltiness Comparison sheet (Figure 6.3).

5. Repeat the tasting procedure with the three wines, beginning by tasting the no-salt popcorn with the still, semi-sparkling, and sparkling wine, and repeating for the moderate-salt and high-salt batches.

6. Did you identify a relationship between the salt level in food and effervescence?

7. What was the impact of tasting the high-salt sample with each of the water samples?

8. Did you identify other food or wine characteristics that contributed to a sensation of match or non-match with this group of food and wine samples?

BITTERNESS

1. Prepare a portion of the four bitter food items for each participant: iceberg lettuce, celery or frisée, Belgian endive, and radicchio.

2. Taste each bitter food sample and evaluate the level of bitterness on the Food Saltiness and Bitterness Evaluation sheet (Figure 6.6). Use the Food Sensory Anchor sheet (Figure B.1) and bitterness value bands for reference. Begin with the lettuce, then move on to the celery or frisée, Belgian endive, and radicchio.

Food Item: _____

        [0   5   10]   Saltiness

Food Item: _____

        [0   5   10]   Saltiness

Food Item: _____

        [0   5   10]   Saltiness

Food Item: _____

        [0   5   10]   Bitterness

Food Item: _____

        [0   5   10]   Bitterness

Food Item: _____

        [0   5   10]   Bitterness

Food Item: _____

        [0   5   10]   Bitterness

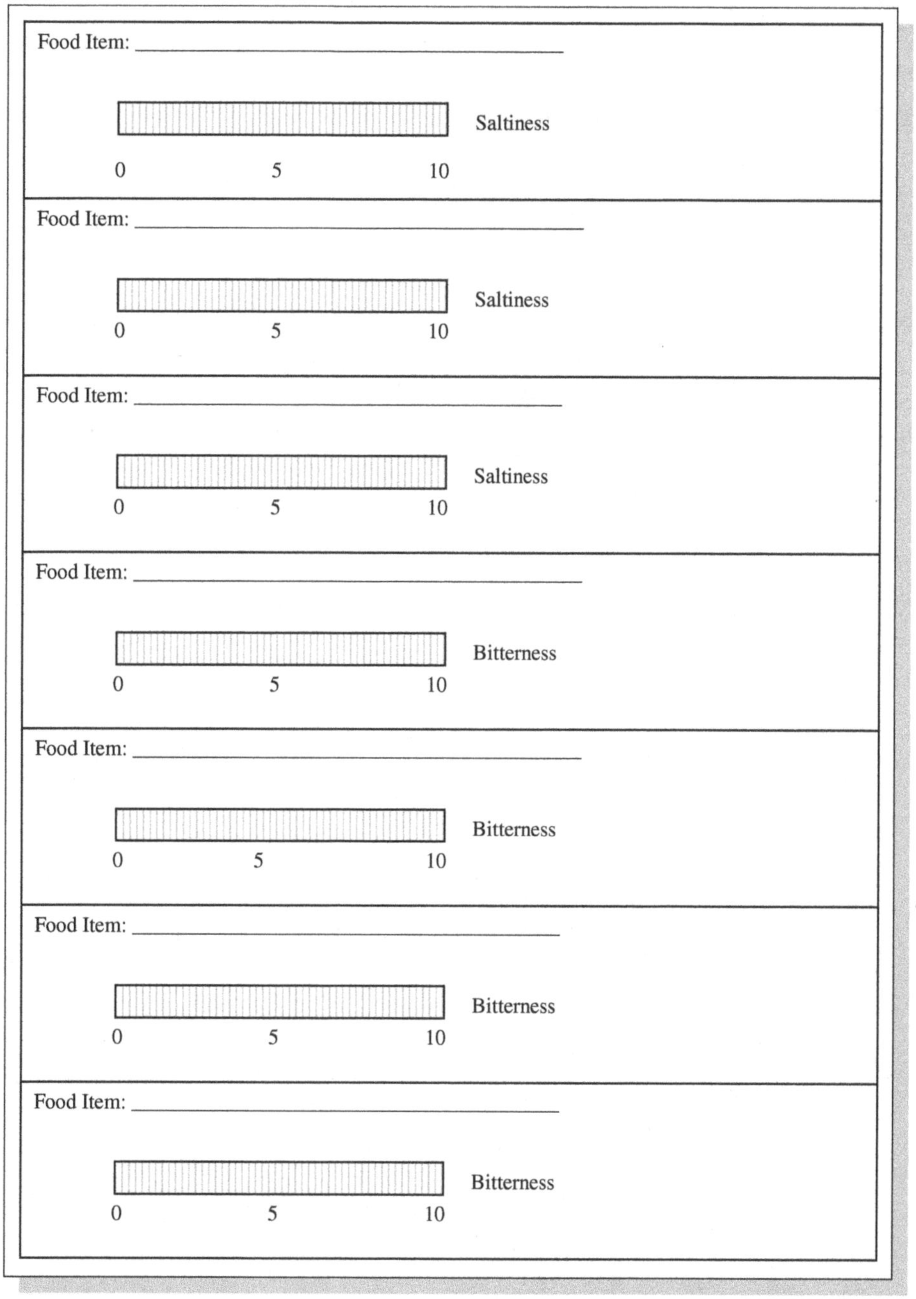

Figure 6.6

Food Saltiness and Bitterness Evaluation

3. Provide each student with about 11/2 ounces of each wine sample (still white wine, Moscato d'Asti, and sparkling wine). Taste each wine effervescence sample and evaluate the level of effervescence on the Water/Wine Effervescence Evaluation sheet (Figure 6.5), moving from no effervescence to high effervescence. Use the Wine Sensory Anchor sheet (Figure B.2) and effervescence value bands for a reference.

4. Next, taste each bitter food sample with each wine sample, beginning with the lettuce and tasting it with the still wine, then the Moscato, then the sparkling wine. Repeat with the other bitter foods, going from less bitter to more bitter. Evaluate the impact of the wine sample on each bitter food sample and record your observations on the Wine/Water Effervescence and Food Bitterness Comparison sheet (Figure 6.4).

5. Repeat the tasting procedure with the three waters, beginning by tasting the no-salt popcorn with the still water, 50/50 mix, and pure seltzer, and repeating for the moderate-salt and high-salt batches.

6. Did you identify a relationship between the bitterness level in food and effervescence in wine or water?

7. What was the impact of the highly bitter food sample when tasted with the wine samples? Water samples?

8. Did you identify other food or wine characteristics that contributed to a sensation of match or non-match with this group of food and wine samples?

NOTES

1. J. Robinson, *How to Taste: A Guide to Enjoying Wine* (New York: Simon and Schuster, 2000).

2. M. W. Baldy, *The University Wine Course*, 3rd ed. (San Francisco: Wine Appreciation Guild, 2003).

3. J. W. Chesser, *The Art and Science of Culinary Preparation* (St. Augustine, FL: Educational Institute of the American Culinary Federation, 1992).

4. Ibid.

5. D. Gilbert, "'Super-tasters' May Avoid Tart Vegetables, Fruits That Contain Cancer Preventive Compounds, Says U-M Researcher," http://www.umich.edu/~urecord/9697/Feb18_97/artcl03.htm (accessed December 23, 2005).

6. Robinson, *How to Taste*.

7. J. Lamar. "Sparkling Wines . . . Save the Bubbles," http://www.winepros.org/wine101/sparkling.htm (accessed December 22, 2005).

8. K. Zraly, *Windows on the World Complete Wine Course* (New York: Sterling, 2003).

9. Bruce Zoechlein. *A Review of Méthode Champenoise Production*, Virginia Cooperative Extension Publication 463-017W, 2002.

10. Ibid.

11. Lamar, "Sparkling Wines."

WINE AND FOOD TEXTURE CHARACTERISTICS

A second main category of elements to assess during the wine and food pairing process is the texture inherent in the wine or the dish to be paired with it. Texture has been described in a variety of ways: as part of a wine's body, as power, as weight, and as structure. Texture characteristics in food and wine provide a feeling of weight and create a sensation on a softness-roughness continuum. Texture matching by similarity or contrast becomes the "glue" that holds the paired food and wine together.

For the purposes presented in this text, texture is a characteristic in food or wine that creates a specific mouthfeel or tactile sensation in every corner of the mouth, rather than a perceptible flavor in the back of the throat or a taste component identifiable on specific parts of the tongue. Thus, textures are identified through the sense of touch rather than taste (components) or smell (flavors). Compared to components, textures are relatively easy to identify. But just like components and flavors, textures can be used to provide similarity or contrasts in matching.

Textures can be described in a variety of ways. In wine, texture can be characterized with words such as *thin*, *velvety*, *medium-bodied*, *viscous*, *drying*, or *rough*. Terms that can be used to describe texture in food include *grainy*, *loose*, *dry*, *oily*, or *rough*, among others. The most common texture description is a basic continuum ranging from light wines or food to rich wines or food. As with all wine and food elements, these combinations can be similar or contrasting in nature. Similar light or rich textures in food and wine are a safer bet and are at the heart of the notion that whites are served with fish and reds with meat. Contrasting light and rich wine or food can be effective if the rich wine or food doesn't overpower the lighter pairing item.

A secondary touch sensation that comes into play is the impact of temperature as a texture element. Temperature can serve as a texture contrast, with warm or hot foods served with cold wine to provide a refreshing and satisfying contrast. Figure C.1 provides a basic two-by-two matrix outlining the implications of matching similar or contrasting wine and food based on the level of lightness or richness in each. The light-wine-to-light-food match is the most reliable combination shown in the matrix. Matching rich wine and rich food is usually a good bet as long as the total richness is not too overwhelming. The light-to-rich matches can provide a pleasant contrast but normally don't offer synergy; rather, one of the players in this equation takes a supporting role.

		Light	Rich
Food	Rich	Take care to ensure the rich food does not overpower the light wine	Usually reliable unless the combination is too rich
	Light	Always a reliable combination	Take care to ensure the rich wine does not overpower the light food
		Light	Rich
		Wine	

Figure C.1

Light to Rich Pairing Implications

Main texture measures used in food evaluation include fattiness, cooking method, and an overall assessment of body/texture. Main texture measures used in the evaluation of wine include levels of tannin, alcohol, and oakiness, as well as an overall assessment of body. While oak aging of wine may impart color, body, flavor, and aroma, it should be considered in the wine texture section, as it is most likely to be a key contributor to the body of the wine when matching a wine with the body or power of the food item.

CHAPTER 7

WINE TEXTURE CHARACTERISTICS: TANNIN, OAK, AND BODY

CHAPTER OUTLINE:

Introduction

Aperitif: The Exemplary Nature of a Symbiosis Between Food Dishes and Cognacs

Texture in Wine

Tannin

Mouthfeel Wheel

Alcohol

The Impact of Oak

Overall Wine Body

Maturity, Micro-oxygenation, and Other Factors

Summary

Exercises

Key Concepts

KEY CONCEPTS:

- Smooth-to-rough mouthfeel continuum
- "Bigness" in wine: alcohol and other factors
- Oak as a "reverse marinade"
- Definitions and descriptions of body

INTRODUCTION

Wine and food have a number of elements that create touch sensations, perceived as texture, across the surfaces of the mouth. Texture provides an inclusive category for a number of terms used to describe these touch or mouthfeel sensations. While often referred to as a tactile sense, a broad definition of texture can include any attributes that are felt with all mouth surfaces (tongue, cheeks, teeth, palate, lips, etc.) and even the fingers. The sensation of carbonation (the tingly feeling of effervescence) is technically an attribute of texture but was included in the hierarchy under the components area due to its relationship with salt and bitterness in food.

Texture elements in wine can have positive or negative effects depending on expectations about the type of wine served and what it is being served with. Did the body of the wine match what is expected of the varietal? Did the amount of oak or alcohol match expectations (about Old World or New World traditions)? And did the astringency levels match expectations based on the varietal, climate zone, and maturity of the wine?

The following sections outline the primary texture elements of wine and how these elements interact with each other.

The decision on whether or not wine should be cellared is based on wine type, wine quality, personal preference, and other factors.

Aperitif | The Exemplary Nature of a Symbiosis Between Dishes and Cognacs: The Creation of a Unique Gala Dinner at the Paul Bocuse Institute

In this Aperitif, Professors Philippe Rispal and Yvelise Dentzer of the Paul Bocuse Institute, near Lyon, France, discuss how the creation of a gala dinner that featured unique pairings of Cognacs and food served as an exercise in multilayered sensory analysis. The project was carried out in partnership with Hennessy Cognac, who kindly made their best products available to the faculty and students of the Institute.

The Paul Bocuse Institute is a unique place where passionate and talented young students from around the world come together with teachers and professors recruited from among the best in Europe. The Institute's gastronomic training restaurant, Saisons, and the Sofitel Royal hotel-school welcome a range of guests, many of whom are well-informed food lovers who thoroughly enjoy the attentions of the students and the professional team of faculty.

How would you describe the mission of the Paul Bocuse Institute? And how is the process of innovation integrated across the curriculum (including the food and Cognac pairing experiment)?

At the launch of the Institute in 1991, it was decided that the school's mission should be to prepare the students for management posts in the complex yet inspiring professions of hotel management, catering management, and the culinary arts.

Hence, a three-stage pedagogy was created. To begin with, the students acquire theoretical and practical knowledge that is indispensable to the profession. Once in possession of these skills, they must then put them into practice, not least through group work, during which they are required to manage other students and demonstrate their ability to produce precision work by employing these fundamental skills. Finally, the students must demonstrate their own creativity, both in theory and in practice, the two being interdependent. Such opportunities include the creation of a series of temporary concept restaurants, a junior enterprise project, the organization of events, or the design and distribution of innovative products.

It is in this pedagogical context that a group of students worked to produce an innovative and effective range of pairings between food and Cognac. In essence, the research carried out led to an original and thorough sensory analysis, the results of which were immediately put into use and presented before a panel of experts during a special gala dinner hosted at the Saisons restaurant.

How would you describe the objectives of the food and Cognac pairing project?

It was effectively a question of creating the pairings and sensory symbioses between different foods and different Cognacs in order to present them to both professional and consumer audiences in an effort to determine how the consumption of Cognac might be broadened in the realm of gastronomy as a complement to the dishes offered, without distorting or depreciating their singularity.

Hennessy has at their disposal a Tasting Guide created for professionals such as chefs, restaurateurs, and sommeliers. It is clearly inspired by the methods defined by D. Hänig through his 1901 mapping of the tongue, because it establishes the basic flavors and then focuses on food types rather than their physiology.

Although this mapping is still studied today and considered as a useful basis, its limits have become apparent, and the students have been able to catalogue them before suggesting appropriate improvements. They have also catalogued some inaccuracies in the terminology, all the more regrettable because they tend to reduce the range of possible savory discovery.

In effect, the terms defining the tastes in the guide go beyond simple flavors. The students grouped them into four categories, each of which concerns different types of sensation: the simplest flavors (sweet, acid), olfaction and retro-olfaction (empyreumatical, herbaceous), the texture (soft, smooth, unctuous), and finally, other terms referring to the products (marine notes, chocolaty, etc.). Thus, we began by modifying the guide in order that it cease to be a simple guide to flavors and become a complete sensory guide. This guide was to present eight fields, each illustrated with a typical recipe.

Second, we were able to study the recipes suggested by way of illustration of each of the eight determined fields. Many of them contained errors, which we grouped into three categories: errors in terms of product choice, errors concerning the recipes, and finally some confusion relating to the distinction between certain tastes.

During their lessons in cuisine, the students were able to check the feasibility of the recipes and to suggest some appropriate modifications with regard to preparation and with regard to the choice of ingredients, in order for the recipes to be more precise sensory models.

Each of the pairings that we created through the modification or creation of a recipe and its suggested Cognac should illustrate a specific aspect of the taste experience. We have worked on the textures, the search for contrasts, and the olfactory and retro-olfactory qualities, and also on the capacity of these pairings to satisfy the demands of tradition as well as those of the new Asian consumer.

Because this chapter focuses on the texture elements of food and drink, can you provide an example of texture effects in your Cognac and food pairing examples?

By way of a texture example, here is the recipe designed to illustrate the field "soft, subtle, and iodized": Gratin of Sea Urchin and Scallops with Cognac. This pairing goes beyond a simple marriage of food and alcohol because the Cognac is an integral part of the dish: the sauce for the gratinée is made with the Cognac (basically, a savory sabayon or a mousseline sauce with Cognac). The olfaction of the Cognac is fully present. All aspects of the tasting are satisfied by the harmony and the continuity of the suggested pairing. The multiplicity of textures is present in the zabaglione liquid, which meets the lightly cooked, crisp yet tender caramelized scallops. We are aware of the audacity of this marriage—audacity being the best defense against boredom or indifference. This contrast is visually present with the softness of the zabaglione and the spikes of the sea urchin. The contrast is thus cognitive: the clients do not expect that a Cognac would be offered with sea urchin and scallops!

Having completed this work, we prepared the recipes for the other taste fields and presented them for a series of tastings and tests among the clientele of Saisons. The analysis of the tests showed us that the clients are not stuck in their ways, nor in their tastes. On the contrary, when they are offered new sensory experiences, their loyalty is often won—on condition, of course, that the products offered conform to the clients' expectations.

The concept of serving Cognac with food in a multicourse menu seems unique. What service issues did you find with this concept?

An important observation is the extent to which the quality of service can greatly help offerings of this type and ensure the clients' pleasure. Service rituals allow the setting of standards, of norms—a codification that ensures the quality of the service offered. During the early tastings and tests, we determined a method for offering these pairings designed to make them more accessible and pleasing to the audience.

The rituals are also very important for more tangible reasons. The table arts and all that they imply are an integral part of the gourmet's pleasure; it is therefore necessary to recognize their value to the guest and to give them prominence as a service element.

Finally, the clients who agree to partake of the offered pairings will be steered toward a world of surprise and discovery. The service rituals serve as a kind of guide to prevent the client from feeling lost in some kind of terra incognita. We know from studies into the psycho-sociology of taste that surprise is an important element. Yet when pushed to the extreme and beyond all familiar references, it rarely leads to satisfaction. Something of the familiar should always be present.

In the service of Cognac, we chose a classic tulip-shaped tasting glass from among the range of glasses proposed by Hennessy in order to afford this tasting such ceremonial ritual as might enhance the proposed products. For an optimal tasting experience, the glass must be maintained at the ideal temperature for tasting.

Additionally, the service is explained in order to guide the guests in their tasting experience:

1. Serve before each dish 2 cl (2/3 oz) of Cognac in a tasting glass.

2. Taste 1 cl (1/3 oz) of Hennessy Cognac before the dish in order to coat the taste buds with the flavors of the brandy, thereby having those flavors enter into the proceedings.

3. Taste the remaining 1 cl (1/3 oz) halfway through the dish in order to ensure that the alliance of flavors is complete.

4. Provide the client with a glass of fresh water to assist in the transition between dishes.

How was this pairing concept carried out to determine its success in terms of gastronomic pleasure?

To further assess the quality of the pairings and in order to present the results to professionals in the industry, we organized a dinner for professionals and the specialist national press that we titled "Le Dîner Symbiose." Conceived and orchestrated as a genuine gala dinner, the intention was to share and raise awareness of our research.

In order to offer the finest and most precise food and Cognac pairings, we limited the number of guests to thirty-five. It was equally important to establish an air of quality about the proceedings, an atmosphere in which service played a key ingredient. To offer a complete sensory impression with regard to the Cognacs, we created an ambiance entirely dedicated to brandy.

As an example, the aperitif was a Hennessy X.O on ice. The buffet table was decorated with two 250 kg ice blocks, each representing a bottle of X.O, and in which had been placed real magnums of X.O. Then the two students who served the aperitif sculpted individual ice cubes with a hammer and ice pick for the brandy glasses.

The omnipresence of Cognac allowed us to affirm the unique nature of the evening while radically transforming the classic image relating to this beverage. Indeed, the guests were immediately seduced by the originality of the spectacle mounted just for them.

How would you describe the outcome of this innovative process?

The tests carried out at Saisons during the first phase of the study and the Dîner Symbiose, owing to the demanding criteria, allowed us to go further. The omnipresence of the Cognacs, the manner of enhancing the dishes via decoration and quality service, as well as the way in which the whole had been executed, in complete contrast with the usual rituals related to Cognac, effectively maintained the interest of the clients through the construction of a powerful and enhancing sensory landscape.

This work has been particularly interesting. It allies a commercial perspective—of great benefit to the students—with the Paul Bocuse Institute's typical rigor and innovative spirit. Although the accent in the pairing process is more often than not put on taste, we have applied to Cognac, for the first time, an analysis from the richer and more exhaustive perspective of sensory fields, including the impact of textures, the search for contrasts, the olfactory and retro-olfactory qualities, and the capacity of these pairings to balance the demands of tradition with the need for innovation and surprise.

Overall, the tests carried out prove two fundamental points:

1. Clients are open to new offerings and are not, as we might often think, stuck in their traditional ways and conceptions.

2. The table arts and the service rituals play a huge role in the success of these marriages, especially when they are new and original.

This experience attests to the strength of the created sensory image. In effect, the service quality and the table arrangements, as well as the quality and precision of the cuisine and the marriages therein, effectively support the recommendations made to this demanding clientele, whether they are amateurs or professionals.

Finally, if not most importantly, the success of the Dîner Symbiose shows that the construction of a strong sensory image is fundamental in the quest for customers' trust, loyalty, and pleasure. In other words, individuals' own mental projections are essential in the definition of tastes.

Throughout this adventure, our students have been able to deepen their mastery of taste. They have carried out original culinary experiments; they have thought long and hard about the conception of a gala dinner, the key elements for success, and those elements that transmit the notion of the exceptional. Although it is sometimes difficult to appreciate during their training, the students achieved a greater understanding of the essential role service and the table arts play in the success of any dinner.

TEXTURE IN WINE

Texture in wine is described using a variety of terms, including *body, power, astringency,* and *structure*. While food texture can have a range of touch or mouthfeel characteristics,

Tannin in wine is derived in part by the amount of contact with oak during the aging process. Larger oak casks impart less oak flavor and less tannin than smaller oak barrels.

wine texture is basically limited to three main areas: a feeling of lightness or richness, a feeling of smoothness or roughness, and the impact of temperature. Textures are generally more easily and consistently identifiable than components or flavors. Wine lightness or richness character is derived from several elements, predominantly alcohol level, extract (particles of fruit that remain suspended in the finished wine), and the wine's viscosity. Wine smoothness or roughness derives from the tannic qualities of the wine being tasted. Grape varietals, crushing procedures, the fermentation process, the aging process, and the maturity of a wine all impact the smooth-rough sensation. Therefore, the overall wine texture is associated with a number of factors, including grape varietal, growing region, winemaking techniques, and the age of the wine. To break this down into a more meaningful form, the primary wine texture considerations in the pairing process are defined as tannin level, level of alcohol, presence and level of oak, and an overall feeling of body.

The Paul Bocuse Institute, an establishment of higher education as international in its partnerships as in its student intake, prepares students for careers in hotel and catering management and the culinary arts, leading to a professional degree after three years or a master's after five, both awarded by the Jean Moulin Lyon III University.

Philippe Rispal is a specialist in sensory analysis, professor of enology, and sommelier at the Paul Bocuse Institute. Yvelise Dentzer holds a doctor of arts degree and is a professor of history and social psychology of food at the Paul Bocuse Institute. Paul James Kirrage is a faculty member at the Institute and translated the discussion from French to English.

TANNIN

Tannin creates a sensation in wine known as astringency. It is separate from the sensation of bitterness and is often described as "puckeriness." Generally, tannin level is a defining factor in where a wine falls on the smooth-to-rough (or soft-to-hard) continuum.[1]

The feeling of tannin in wine is primarily based on the type of grape used but also is determined by the length of soak (with skins, stems, or seeds intact) during the winemaking process, the amount of aging in wood, and the age of the wine itself. Red wines made from thicker-skinned grapes generally have the most tannin. White wines generally have little or no tannin. When tannin is present in white wine, it is usually imparted during the aging process from newer oak barrels.

The length of soak and the pressing process can create an unpleasant bitter taste in wine as well. Wine bitterness virtually always creates pairing problems, for no matter what you serve with it, the wine will always taste bitter. A slightly bitter sensation is frequently present in red wines but is, in a sense, an acquired taste, with little negative impact if good pairing choices are made. The ability to assess astringency in wine is hampered by confusion about the differences between bitterness, acidity, and astringency as they are sensed in the mouth.[2] Secondarily, the perception of astringency may be hampered by sweeteners in wine or food. Residual sweetness in wine lessens the perception of astringency,[3] while sourness in wine heightens the perception of astringency.[4]

During the wine evaluation process, look for a drying or puckering sensation in your mouth as an indication of tannin level. Highly tannic wine provides a gripping mouthfeel and a coarse textural feeling. Tannin can range from barely perceived to mouth-grippingly rough. Very tannic reds such as Barolo or Cabernet Sauvignon are a major ally with steak and lamb. The higher fattiness and chewy texture of these meats makes the wine feel more supple, alluring, and enticingly complex. Many food textures are believed to block the taste buds and make the impact of tannin less than desirable. Some of these foods, including eggs, chocolate, and some cheeses, seem to have a mouth-coating effect when consumed with wine.[5] Although I find bittersweet chocolate and Cabernet Sauvignon to be a pleasant combination, semisweet and milk chocolate are both too sweet and mouth-coating to create a good combination with red wine. Most fish dishes provide an example of foods that can have negative effects with high-tannin wines. Tannic reds with strong wood flavors turn the taste of most fish metallic and nasty. Successful combinations of red wines with fish are more likely when choosing reds with lower tannins, such as Pinot Noir, Beaujolais, Dolcetto, or even Zinfandel. High salt in food has a negative interaction with wine tannins, making the tannins taste bitter and unpleasant.

MOUTHFEEL WHEEL

Mouthfeel is an important characteristic of wine evaluations. Evaluators have used a variety of terms and techniques to assess the level of astringency in wine, one of these methods being the idea of a mouthfeel wheel.[6] For the initial test of the mouthfeel wheel, samples of fabrics were used to serve as reference anchors for a variety of astringent sensations. Later research indicates that the original perspective of the mouthfeel wheel was too complex for even experienced wine judges, as it incorporated multiple characteristics including surface smoothness, drying sensations, dynamic elements, weight, complexity, and ripeness.[7]

The basic concept of using fabric samples for reference anchors has been supported. Fabric categories ranged from fine (silk, chamois, and satin) to medium (felt, velvet, emery, and suede) and coarse (corduroy, sandpaper, and burlap).[8] Following these findings, fabric sample descriptions are included in the wine anchor references shown in the Wine Anchor References Sheet (Figure B.2). These fabrics are included in the appropriate value band next to comparable levels of alcohol and wine varietals (Table 7.1).

ALCOHOL LEVEL

Alcohol generally is perceived as "bigness" or body in wine. While as a general rule the amount of alcohol in wine reinforces the perception of body, Peynaud suggests that body and alcohol strength are not the same; he describes the level of alcohol as "vinosity."[9] Regular table wines contain somewhere between 7 and 15 percent alcohol. Fortified wines such as Port, Sherry, Madeira, and Marsala contain somewhere between 17 and 22 percent.[10] Alcohol content is easily determined, as it is required by law in the United States to be printed on the wine label, and it is relatively easy to differentiate the feeling of light, moderate, and high alcohol by assessing the warming sensation in the mouth. Table 7.1 outlines general appraisal bands based on the level of alcohol present.

Warmer growing regions create riper grapes, which contain a higher level of sugar content. During the fermentation process, this higher sugar content converts to higher alcohol content and ultimately a "bigger" feeling of body in the finished wine. In the case of wine, bigger is not necessarily better—it depends on personal taste preferences and the food being served. As a rule, more robust or bold foods work well with bigger, bolder wines but your mood may also drive this matching decision. You may not prefer to drink big-feeling wines on a day-to-day basis; sometimes you may be in the mood for a lighter, more refreshing experience.

Pairing experts suggest that higher-alcohol wines work well with foods served at a higher temperature but should be avoided when eating or serving very spicy foods.[11] While high-tannin reds do not work well with some cheeses, alcoholic, flavorful, and lower-tannin red wines work well with cheeses as a rule. High alcohol in wine can also bring out any amount of fishiness present in fish dishes. Lower-alcohol wines should be served with most egg dishes, as higher alcohol tastes even hotter if served with eggs. Chocolate has a tendency to turn wines thin and acidic, but a higher alcohol content improves the relationship between wine and chocolate.[12]

Table 7.1   Values for Tannin Fabric References and Alcohol Levels in Wine

Value Bands	Tannin Fabric References	Alcohol Percentage Present
0 1	Silk	Less than 7%
1 2 3	Velvet	7 to 9%
4 5 6	Suede	10 to 12%
7 8 9	Corduroy	12.5 to 14.5%
9 10	Burlap	15% or higher

As indicated in the sweetness discussion (Chapter 5), high alcohol can also be perceived as sweetness and often can be a key element in food-and-wine pairing considerations. A California Chardonnay with its high level of alcohol will work in tandem with some sweetness (natural or added) present in many prepared dishes.

THE IMPACT OF OAK

The addition of oak can be thought of as a "reverse marinade" for wine. A marinade is a liquid that is used to flavor, tenderize, preserve, or "cook" a food item. Oak barrels provide a solid agent that imparts flavor, color, aroma, and body to a liquid (wine)—thus the concept of a "reverse marinade." As with any marinating technique, the longer and stronger the marinade, the bigger the impact on the final product. Just as the culinarian utilizes marinades for a variety of purposes, the winemaker may use oak during the fermentation and aging process to impart flavor, color, aroma, and texture to the finished wine. While oak aging may do all of these things, from a pairing perspective one of its largest impacts is on the texture or body style of the finished product. The long-standing tradition of serving white wine with fish has been viewed as a cardinal rule. But the addition of oak to a Chardonnay or Sauvignon Blanc can make them too rich for simply prepared fish dishes.

Wine is generally evaluated as having little, moderate, or heavy oak character, based on the multiple ways in which oak impacts the senses. Did it impact the color of the wine? Can you smell smoky, woody, or oaken aromas? Can you taste oak, wood, or smoke when you savor the wine? Or is the mouthfeel of the wine sample richer or more tannic than wines from the varietal that have not been aged in oak? Many whites and some reds will have no oak present; New World wines have a tendency toward stronger oak than many Old World wines, although the lines are definitely blurring between these traditions.

A final indicator of oak aging is price. All else being equal, wine that has been aged in oak will cost more than unoaked versions of the same varietal from the same region of the world and from a wine producer of equal reputation.

Unoaked fruity whites and reds with soft fruit work better with salads and other light or sour food items. Aging in oak reduces the acidity level in white and red wines. Oaked wines work well with cooking methods that impart a high degree of textures, such as grilling, broiling, smoking, roasting, or braising. Oak in wine also works with other types of heavier food textures such as grains or legumes—think of Cajun red beans and rice cooked with smoked sausage. Even as oak has a large impact on wine texture, it also imparts flavor and can interact with food flavors as well (the impact of flavors is discussed further in upcoming chapters). While the presence of oak is not included as a separate texture element in the wine and food pairing tool shown in the final section of this book, it is something to consider when writing comments during the wine evaluation process. Oak is included as part of the flavor type section of the pairing assessment tool. Earlier research indicates that an assessment of oak aging's effect on the texture of wine correlates strongly to judges' assessment of overall body.[13] A separate measurement of oak as texture would to some extent be redundant and was not included to simplify the pairing tool and increase its reliability.

OVERALL WINE BODY

Tannin, alcohol, oak, extract, and other elements work in tandem to provide a feeling of body and texture in wine. As previously noted, extract is basically particles of fruit that remain suspended in a finished wine; it creates a sense of body and adds a chewy character to wine. While all sweet wines are not full-bodied, sweetness in wine can also contribute to the overall weight and viscosity of certain wines (Sauternes and ice wines are examples).

Generally, a definition of body refers to the consistency or viscosity of wine, assessed through tactile sensations in the mouth. It provides an impression of weight, size, and volume in the mouth.[14] Wine evaluators use terms such as *substance* or *plenty of reserve* or *power* to describe a full-bodied wine.[15] A typical analogy to describe various levels of body in wine is to use a spectrum of milks and creams. These range from skim milk (light-bodied), whole milk (medium-bodied), half-and-half (full-bodied), and whipping cream (very full-bodied).[16]

One method to emphasize the differences between a full-bodied wine and a thin wine is to select a full-bodied wine (such as a good Cabernet Sauvignon or even an oaked Chardonnay) and create two samples: one that is the normal wine right out of the bottle and one that has been diluted with 10 percent water. This exercise will reinforce in a hurry what is meant by full-bodied wine.

Ranking wine on a perceived feeling of body can range from thin to robust. Value bands and descriptions are provided in Table 7.2 to guide you in this process. Also included are milk and cream samples to serve as references. Wine varietals that usually fall within these value bands are included as well. The wine examples provide good diversity in body levels, but as with other elements in wine, overall body can vary within the same wine varietal and may have slightly higher or lower values of body than those indicated in Table 7.2.

Experts on wine and food pairing do not agree about the importance of matching the body style of wine and food. Some authors suggest that it is the most important element to match, while others indicate it is just one of many factors that may impact good wine and food pairing. Given that wine and food have a natural affinity with each other, wine and food matching is not a win-or-lose proposition but instead is a win-or-synergize proposition. I believe that matching body style in wine and food is an important factor for creating great matches and, ultimately, transforming the gastronomic experience from a refreshing one to a memorable one. My belief is that texture elements play a secondary role only to components in their importance in creating a synergistic relationship with food. It is common sense to match lighter wines with lighter foods and robust wines with robust foods. When body styles are contrasted (light to rich or rich to light), the lighter member of this equation will generally serve as only a supporting actor on the gastronomic stage and doesn't create the ultimate goal of a synergistic wine and food match.

Table 7.2   Levels of Overall Body in Wine

Value Bands	Descriptions
0 1 2	**Thin.** Lacking in body—devoid of tannin, low in alcohol and, without oak. Resembles a watery consistency. Skim milk; some Riesling, Chenin Blanc, Gavi, Fendant, some sparkling wines.
2 3 4	**Light.** Agreeably light in body with relatively low tannin, alcohol, and oak. 1% or 2% milk; Sémillon, Sauvignon Blanc, Gewurztraminer, unoaked Chardonnay, Beaujolais Nouveau.
4 5 6	**Moderate.** Body that is identifiable at an intermediate level with sufficient amounts of tannin, alcohol, and/or oak. Whole milk; Pinot Noir, oaked Chardonnay, unoaked Barbera.
6 7 8	**Full.** Body in which elements of tannin, alcohol, or oak are unmistakably identified and are significantly emphasized. A feeling of big, and bold body and structure. Half-and-half; Cabernet Franc, Zinfandel, Syrah, Merlot, oaked Chianti.
8 9 10	**Heavy.** A very robust and rich body with high tannin, high alcohol, heavy oak and an unmistakable feeling of strong, heavy texture. Whipping cream; some Cabernet Sauvignon, Barolo, Port, late-harvest Zinfandel, Cabernet Franc ice wine.

MATURITY, MICRO-OXYGENATION, AND OTHER FACTORS

Many wine drinkers believe that aging or cellaring wine is always preferable to drinking a bottle that was just purchased from a local wine shop. This is certainly not the case. Champagne and other sparkling wines are ready for consumption when released and do not improve with age. Port improves with age only if it is vintage Port. Most New World wines are formulated to be ready to consume immediately upon their release (though this is not to say that wines from higher-quality producers will not benefit from additional aging). So why be concerned with aging of wine? The determination of any advantages to aging wine has to do with personal preferences in most white wines and the impact on wine texture and flavor in some red wines.

While quality Riesling and Chardonnay can be cellared for more than ten years, most whites shouldn't be aged for more than five to seven years (many even less). Aging of white wine has an impact on color and flavor. Young wines are pale and even green-tinged in color and are generally fruity in nature. Aged whites become darker in color (in many cases changing from yellow to gold to dark amber) and lose their fresh fruit character, taking on different flavors. This transition can be thought of similarly to the process of fresh fruit becoming aged and dried. For instance, if you cut open a fresh apple, it has a fresh, crisp apple taste and smell. If you leave it exposed to the air, it will darken in color and lose some of its original freshness and crispness. If you were to dry the apple, while its flavor, color, and taste would be different from the fresh apple, it would still be pleasurable, although in a quite different form. The same is true for aged wine.

Red wines change in color and flavor as well but also may change in terms of the amount of astringency. Color in red wine may change from bright red to brick red to brown as it ages. Color intensity also tends to decrease in red wine as it ages. Flavors may change from red or dark fruits to distinct flavors such as tobacco or leather. In many cases, the original wine varietal character is replaced with a more subtle and complex bouquet. One of the best-understood parts of the aging process is the smoothing of the tannins that are originally present. Most premium red wines will improve in flavor, bouquet, and smoothness as they age. Cabernet Sauvignon from premium vineyards will reach optimal drinkability after about ten years of proper handling and aging. Red wines that can be aged for substantial periods of time owe this ability to the tannins added during the winemaking process. Red wines with lower levels of tannin (such as Zinfandel and Pinot Noir) can age much like Cabernet but generally begin declining at an earlier stage. Thus, red wine's maturity can have a substantial impact on the forcefulness of its texture and ultimately impact pairing decisions. For instance, while a Cabernet will generally be more tannic than many other reds, a consideration of its aging is important when matching with foods to ensure a proper balance of textures. It would be a crime to overshadow a finely aged bottle of Cabernet with a food dish that is much too rich and powerful.

There seems to be two main advantages to aging wine. The first is the smoothing characteristics of aged, quality red wines. Second is the sense of exclusivity involved in drinking old wines. Very old wines are appealing to consumers more because of their historical appeal than because of gastronomic factors.[17] Clearly, the preferences of the consumer have a major impact on the value of wine aging.

Light, high temperatures, and air are the key enemies when aging wine. Few of us have the ability to create a light-, humidity-, and temperature-controlled cellar. If you decide to create a cellar (whether as a restaurant operator or in your home), it is important to consider whether the wines will be cellared for the short term, intermediate term, or long term. As pointed out above, not all wines benefit from aging, and only wines of higher quality and complexity will live longer and benefit from being cellared. There are several factors that impact a wine's ability to develop in the bottle and maintain a long life in the

Table 7.3   Wine Examples with Aging Potential

Cellaring Time	White Wines	Red Wines
Short-term Aging (1 to 5 years)	Burgundy, Chablis, Chardonnay, Gavi, Gewurztraminer, Graves, Pinot Grigio, Pouilly-Fumé, Riesling (dry and sweet), Rioja, Sancerre, Sauvignon Blanc	Barbera, Beaujolais, Bordeaux, Burgundy, Cabernet Sauvignon, Cahors, Chianti, Chianti Classico, Crozes-Hermitage, Dolcetto, Lemberger, Malbec, Merlot, Nebbiolo, Pinot Noir, Rioja, Syrah, Zinfandel
Intermediate Aging (5 to 10 years)	Burgundy, Chablis, Chardonnay, Châteauneuf-du-Pape, Gewurztraminer, Graves, Hermitage, Pouilly-Fumé, Riesling (dry and sweet), Rioja	Barolo, Barbaresco, Bordeaux, Burgundy, Cabernet Sauvignon, Cahors, Châteauneuf-du-Pape, Chianti, Chianti Classico, Côte Rôtie, Hermitage, Malbec, Merlot, Nebbiolo, Pinot Noir, Rioja, Syrah, Zinfandel
Long-term Aging (more than 10 years)	Barsac, Burgundy, Chablis, Chardonnay, Châteauneuf-du-Pape, Riesling, Sauternes	Amarone, Barolo, Barbaresco, Bordeaux, Burgundy, Cabernet Sauvignon, Châteauneuf-du-Pape, Chianti Classico, Côte Rôtie, Hermitage, Merlot, Nebbiolo, Pinot Noir, Rioja Reserva, Syrah, Zinfandel

cellar. Alcohol, tannin, acid, grape varietal, and methods of vinification all impact a wine's aging potential.

Short-term cellaring generally involves a period of one to five years. These are wines that can be consumed at any time during this period with some interesting changes over time. Intermediate-term cellaring ranges from five to ten years. Wines that fall into this category will provide rewards for moderate aging and will become more subtle and refined, developing a bouquet. Some wines need long aging to mature to a point where their depth of character is exposed. These are wines that will survive an aging process of more that ten years in a cellar with substantial smoothing of texture and change of character. The wines in this group should be from the best vintages and producers. Table 7.3 provides some suggested types of white and red wines that may benefit from each level of cellaring.[18]

A recent trend in both New and Old World wines is to use a modern technology known as micro-oxygenation to obtain softer tannins and easier drinking in young wines. In this process, oxygen is added to wine in two phases. The first is during the period lasting from the end of the primary alcohol fermentation until the start of the malolactic fermentation. This first stage is called polymerization and works to condense dry tannins, resulting in wine color stabilization and the elimination of harsh wine tastes. The second addition period follows the malolactic fermentation phase. This stage is called harmonization and creates a continuous softening of the tannins; it can also solve problems involving unpleasant odors. A main feature of this process is its ability to reduce the tannin levels in young red wines to levels of wines with greater maturity.

A further method of lowering tannin levels in younger wines is the practice of early harvest in warmer climates. Combining this process with the micro-oxygenation process creates a smoother, less harsh wine that retains deep and stable color typical of the varietals.

SUMMARY

Wine texture is driven by a number of factors. The most clearly identifiable ones are tannin, alcohol, and a sensation of body. Oak provides not only texture but also aroma, color, and flavor. These elements are important considerations when selecting wines based on personal preferences, the mood of the event, and foods with which the wine will be paired. The end-of-chapter exercises will allow you to reinforce your understanding of these elements and the tactile sensations they create.

DISCUSSION QUESTIONS

1. What are the key texture elements in wine?

2. How would you describe the astringent sensation of tannin?

3. Is tannin an element in white and red wines?

4. What are the key factors driving alcohol levels in wine?

5. Can you think of additional wine characteristics that provide a sense of texture?

6. Is an assessment of overall body related to tannin, alcohol, and oak levels in wine? Or are they separate characteristics?

EXERCISE 7.1

WINE TEXTURE ELEMENTS: TANNIN, ALCOHOL, OAK, AND OVERALL BODY

The purpose of this exercise is to focus on differences in the level of the primary elements in wine that make up tactile perceptions of texture. For this exercise, you may utilize many of the same varietals as the Basics of Wine Evaluation exercise in Chapter 2 (Exercise 2.2). These varietals provide a good spectrum of variation for all of the texture elements. Other varietals can be used to increase your knowledge if desired; some examples are provided in Table 7.2 in this chapter.

Using the Wine Sensory Anchor sheet (Figure B.2) and Tables 7.2 and 7.3, you will have basic reference points and descriptions for ascending levels of tannin, alcohol, and overall body. When selecting the wines for this exercise, be sure to consider the potential impact of Old or New World selections, climate zones, oak aging, and wine maturity.

OBJECTIVES

This exercise has four objectives. The first is to establish a baseline and sensory memory of the ascending mouthfeel characteristics of tannin in wine. The second objective is to reinforce your understanding of the impact of alcohol level on the perception of "bigness," hot after effects, and overall weight of a wine. The third is to be able to clearly identify the flavor, aroma, and texture impacts of oak.

The fourth objective is to instill a deeper knowledge of the typical textural elements of major wine varietals.

Mise en Place: Things to Do Before the Exercise Review the sections of this chapter describing the wine texture evaluation.

MATERIALS NEEDED

Select one wine sample for each overall wine body description shown in Table 7.2. You will wind up with five different varietals.

STEPS

1. Buy the wines.

2. Set up the glasses using the placemats (Figure 7.1) in the following order:

Table 7.4   Materials for Exercise 7.1

Body Style	Wine choice
Thin	
Light	
Moderate	
Full	
Heavy	
1 white paper placemat per student with numbered or labeled circles to place wineglasses	Crackers to cleanse the palate
1 spit cup per student	Napkins
Corkscrew	Drinking water for each student
1 copy of the Aroma Wheel per student	5 wineglasses per student
1 glossary of wine terms per student	Tasting instruction sheets for each student

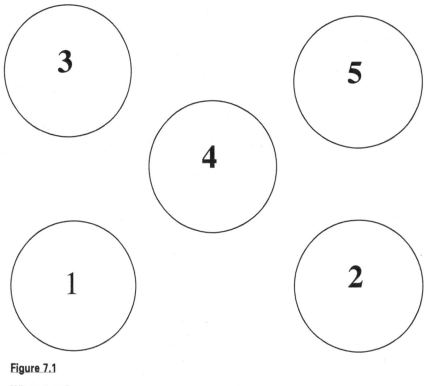

Figure 7.1

Wines 1 to 5

Table 7.5   Ascending Order of 5 Wine Varietals by Texture

1	2	3	4	5
Riesling, Chenin Blanc, Gavi, Fendant, sparkling wines	Sémillon, Sauvignon Blanc, Gewurztraminer, unoaked Chardonnay, Beaujolais Nouveau	Pinot Noir, oaked Chardonnay, unoaked Barbera	Cabernet Franc, Zinfandel, Syrah, Merlot, oaked Chianti	Some Cabernet Sauvignon, Barolo, Port, late-harvest Zinfandel

3. Open the wines and pour about 1-oz servings in number order.

4. On the Wine Texture sheet (Figure 7.2), complete the following information for each wine: wine type/category, wine producer, and vintage.

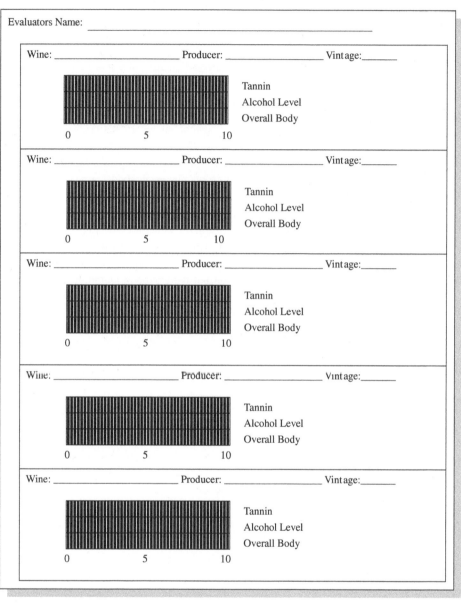

Figure 7.2

Wine Texture

5. Taste the wines in number order. Assess the six S's, paying particular attention to the texture elements of tannin, oak, alcohol, and overall body.

   a. *Sample number 1.* Do you pick up any astringent sensation in this sample? The typical color of Riesling and other wines in this group is pale yellow, sometimes with a greenish tinge. Does this sample give you a feeling of thin, light, or moderate weight or viscosity when swished about the mouth? Do you pick up any significant amount of chemical heat derived from alcohol? What is the alcohol percentage stated on the bottle? The varieties in the first group should have lower levels of alcohol, particularly those grown in a cool climate. Higher-quality Riesling comes from cooler climates. Make notes about your observations.

   b. *Sample number 2.* The varietals in this group will typically have more color and be more powerful than those in the first group. Is the alcohol percentage higher on the label for this sample than for sample 1? Can you detect any differences in tannin or alcohol levels in this sample? The wine selected for this sample should still have no oak character, little or no tannin, and a light to moderate body.

c. *Sample number 3.* If you selected an oaked Chardonnay, you should notice a significant change in the color and aroma compared to the other two samples. Generally, the Pinot Noir will have some oak aging, but it will not be as pronounced in its aroma compared to an oaked Chardonnay. The unoaked Barbera will have moderate levels of tannin, alcohol, and body, similar to those of a New World Pinot (though tannin level can vary significantly depending on the fermentation and aging process). Whatever the wine choice, this group will be more powerful in tannin and body than the previous groups. Is the alcohol percentage higher than the earlier samples? Can you detect any differences in tannin or alcohol levels in this sample? How strong are these characteristics? What stands out as dominant elements in this wine? Make notes about your observations.

d. *Sample number 4.* All of the wines in this group will be noticeably more substantial. Taste the difference in richness and power in terms of body, higher tannins, and alcohol. All of the wines in this group (Cabernet Franc, Zinfandel, Syrah, Merlot, and oaked Chianti) are of a richer color and weight. You should notice a significant change in the color and aroma as well. These wines will have darker, richer colors and more substantial aromas. Whatever the wine choice, this group will be more powerful in tannin and body than the previous groups. Is the alcohol percentage higher than the earlier samples? If there is a difference, are the climate zones a factor? Can you detect any differences in tannin or alcohol levels in this sample? How strong are these characteristics?

e. *Sample number 5.* The wines in this group will be substantially higher in weight, body, and usually tannins. Typically, Cabernet is naturally dark (it can be almost inky in color) and full-bodied. Inspect the viscosity and smell the aroma. What stands out as dominant elements in this wine? Taste and feel the difference in body. Is the puckery sensation greater than that of the wine from the previous group? If not, why not? Record your observations of its intensity and lingering effect on your mouth.

6. Once you have evaluated the five wines, go back and rank-order them on level of tannin, oak, alcohol, and overall body.

a. *Smooth to rough tannin.* Rank the wines from lowest to highest tannin levels. This is not always as straightforward as it might seem. The interaction of acidity and bitterness can alter our perception of tannin. Recall the palate mapping exercise in Chapter 2. Where did you identify the astringent sensation in your mouth? Try to separate the taste of acidity and bitterness from the mouthfeel of tannin. Visualize the fabric samples from smooth silk to rough burlap to assist you in this process.
Lowest (smoothest) = 1. _____ 2. _____
3. _____ 4. _____ 5. _____ = Highest (roughest)

b. *Oak.* Rank the wines from least oak to most oak. Many of the samples will have little or no oak. Rank them using your best judgment. Use the senses of sight, smell, and taste to identify oak level.
No oak = 1. _____ 2. _____ 3. _____
4. _____ 5. _____ = Most oak

c. *Alcohol.* Rank the wines from low alcohol to high alcohol. While the wine label provides an approximation of alcohol level, the alcohol content in the finished wine can be as much as 1.5 percent above or below the stated level. Focus on the initial perceived sweetness sensation on the tip of your tongue and the "hot" sensation throughout your mouth.
Low alcohol = 1. _____ 2. _____ 3._____
4. _____ 5. _____ = Highest alcohol

d. *Body.* Rank the wines from lightest body to heaviest body. Inspect the viscosity and color for clues. How heavy does the body feel in your mouth? Think of the dairy product examples in Table 7.2—is the mouthfeel similar to skim milk, 2 percent milk, whole milk, half and half, or heavy cream?
Lightest body = 1. _____ 2. _____ 3. _____
4._____ 5. _____ = Heaviest body

7. Write any other comments, thoughts, and observations that you identified during this evaluation process. Were there other factors that impacted your perception of wine texture? Extract? Spiciness in the wine? Viscosity?

EXERCISE 7.2
OAK IN WINE

OBJECTIVE

To explore wines with an oaky style.

Mise en Place: Things to Do Before the Exercise Select two wines that are both made using the white Chardonnay grape. The first sample should have no oak flavor, just the pure character of the Chardonnay grape. Good bets are many Chardonnays from Canada (Ontario region) or Mâcon-Villages from the Burgundy region of France. The second sample will have a distinct oaky character to it. Select a Chardonnay from California or Australia. Look for words on the label such as *barrel-aged* or *barrel-fermented* as well as the winemaker's description on the back of the label, which many times indicates oak aging or wood or smoky aromas.

STEPS

1. *Sight*. The oaked sample should be noticeably darker.

2. *Smell*. The dominant aroma in sample 1 will be pure Chardonnay. The dominant aroma in sample 2 will be much richer and have a smoked or woody character.

3. *Sip*. Sample 1 should provide a lighter to moderate sense of body and weight. The taste is all Chardonnay. Sample 2 will have a richer, fuller body and texture with a taste that is more complex and stronger. You should also notice a drop in the acidity level from sample 1 to sample 2.

4. *Spit/swallow and savor*. What differences are there in the lingering effects of these two wines? Is the oak aging worth the additional price in terms of providing more flavor persistence?

EXERCISE 7.3
TANNIN IN WINE

OBJECTIVE

To explore the differences in tannin levels between wines.

Mise en Place: Things to Do Before the Exercise Select a Pinot Noir (low tannin) and a Cabernet Sauvignon (high tannin) for this exercise. Be sure to choose two wines from the same general growing region to ensure substantial differences between them.

STEPS

1. *Sight*. The Cabernet should be noticeably darker—a deep reddish purple compared to the dark ruby color of the Pinot.

2. *Smell*. Note the character differences between the two. Tannin does not have an aroma, but the character of the Cabernet will be a good indicator of tannins to come.

3. *Sip*. The Pinot should be smooth and silky, while the Cabernet will be more puckery. This sensation should be apparent on the tongue, cheeks, and gums.

4. *Spit/swallow and savor*. What differences are there in the lingering effects of these two wines? Does the astringent effect from the tannin linger in your mouth?

EXERCISE 7.4
ALCOHOL IN WINE

OBJECTIVE

To compare high and low alcohol percentage and their impact on identifying the body of red and white wine.

Mise en Place: Things to Do Before the Exercise Select two whites (the same varietal) and/or two reds (the same varietal), with one wine from a cool climate zone and one from a moderate/warm climate zone. For example, you might select a lower-alcohol German Riesling and a Riesling from a warmer climate such as Washington State or California. For reds, select a red from the Burgundy region of France (Pinot Noir) and compare it against a Pinot Noir from California. Be sure to check the label to ensure alcohol level differences.

STEPS

1. *Sight.* The cooler-climate wines will have lighter colors than the warmer-climate wines (the Riesling from the cool climate may have a greenish tinge to it). The Burgundy will be more translucent than the California Pinot.

2. *Smell.* Note the character differences between the wines from the cooler and warmer climates. Can you smell more alcohol? What are the other aroma differences?

3. *Sip.* The cooler-climate wines will have more acidity and be more subtle. The warmer-climate wines with higher alcohol will be richer and more powerful. This sensation should be apparent on the tip of the tongue (initial sweetness), throughout the mouth, and in its aftereffects.

4. *Spit/swallow and savor.* What differences are there in the lingering effects of these wines? Are there prominent differences in body, alcohol, fruit character, and tannin?

NOTES

1. M. A. Amerine and V. L. Singleton, *Wine: An Introduction*, 2nd ed. (Berkeley: University of California Press, 1977).

2. M. C. King, M. A. Cliff, and J. Hall, "Effectiveness of the 'Mouth-feel Wheel' for the Evaluation of Astringent Subqualities in British Columbia Red Wines," *Journal of Wine Research* 14, 2–3 (2003): 67–78.

3. T. Ishikawa and A. C. Noble, "Temporal Perception of Astringency and Sweetness in Red Wine," *Food Quality and Preference* 6 (1995): 27–33.

4. S. Kallithraka, J. Bakker, and M. N. Clifford, "Effect of pH on Astringency in Model Solutions and Wines," *Journal of Agriculture and Food Chemistry* 45 (1997): 2211–6.

5. J. Simon, *Wine with Food* (New York: Simon and Schuster, 1996).

6. R. Gawel, A. Oberholster, and I. L. Francis, "A 'Mouth-feel Wheel': Terminology for Communicating the Mouth-feel Characteristics of Red Wine," *Australian Journal of Grape and Wine Research* 6 (2000): 203–7.

7. King, Cliff and Hall, "Effectiveness of the 'Mouth-feel Wheel.'"

8. Ibid.

9. E. Peynaud, *The Taste of Wine: The Art and Science of Wine Appreciation*, 2nd ed. (New York: John Wiley and Sons, 1996), 225.

10. A. Immer, *Great Tastes Made Simple: Extraordinary Food and Wine Pairing for Every Palate* (New York: Broadway Books, 2002).

11. F. Beckett, *How to Match Food and Wine* (London: Octopus, 2002).

12. D. Rosengarten and J. Wesson, *Red Wine with Fish: The New Art of Matching Wine with Food.* (New York: Simon and Schuster, 1989).

13. R. J. Harrington and R. Hammond, "Predicting Synergistic Matches in Wine and Food: Instrument Testing and Evaluation," *2005 Proceedings of International Council on Hotel, Restaurant and Institutional Education* (2005): 155–60.

14. B. Alexander, *Le Cordon Bleu Wine Essentials: Professional Secrets to Buying, Storing, Serving and Drinking Wine* (New York: John Wiley and Sons, 2001).

15. S. Kolpan, B. H. Smith, and M. A. Weiss, *Exploring Wine*, 2nd ed. (New York: John Wiley and Sons, 2001); Peynaud, *The Taste of Wine.*

16. A. Immer, *Great Wine Made Simple: Straight Talk from a Master Sommelier* (New York: Broadway Books, 2000); K. MacNeil, *The Wine Bible* (New York: Workman, 2001).

17. R. S. Jackson, *Wine Tasting: A Professional Handbook* (San Diego: Academic Press, 2002).

18. T. Maresca, *The Right Wine: Matching Wine with Food for Every Occasion* (New York: Grove Press, 1990).

CHAPTER 8

FOOD TEXTURE CHARACTERISTICS: FATTINESS, COOKING METHOD, PROTEIN, AND BODY

CHAPTER OUTLINE:

Introduction

Aperitif: Canoe Restaurant and Bar

Fattiness in Food

Cooking Method and Protein Interactions

Overall Food Body

Interaction of Wine and Food Textures

Summary

Exercises

KEY CONCEPTS:

- Food texture sensations
- Impact of animal or vegetable fats and oils
- Light-to-light and rich-to-rich matching

INTRODUCTION

A standard scientific definition of texture is "the arrangement of the particles or constituent parts of a material that gives it its characteristic structure."[1] Sensations such as smoothness, stickiness, graininess, fibrousness, and consistency can be detected as part of this tactile sense. Food textures can have a positive or negative impact on our perception of the food item. This perception depends on preconceived notions, context, and our state of mind at the time.

Textures in food can be an important element in food-and-wine pairing choices. The determination of whether a food item is light-, medium-, or full-bodied depends on a number of factors, including fat level in the protein or additional plate elements, the cooking method employed, and an overall feeling of body or texture across all of the food items included in a particular dish. These texture elements interact to impact the perception of the body, power, or weight of a particular dish.

It is important to note that texture preferences are partially driven by cultural and personal differences. Certainly we all have preferences in terms of texture expectations based on lifetime experiences. For instance, while tofu has a neutral flavor, the texture is very soft and almost gelatinous. This may be part of the reason tofu is not as popular in North American cultures as it is in many Asian cultures. Other common texture examples include preferences or dislike for eating raw oysters or sashimi.

A classic match of lamb and tannic red wine. The fattiness and power of the lamb dish provide a balance with the full-bodied and tannic characteristics of the red wine.

Aperitif | Canoe Restaurant and Bar

Canoe is a critically acclaimed restaurant located at the top of the TD Bank Building in Toronto, Canada. It is part of the Oliver Bonacini Restaurants group and was designed to reflect Canada's rich natural environment. The culinary team is led by executive chef Anthony Walsh and chef de cuisine Tom Brodi. The dinner menu highlights starters and main courses that feature regional Canadian-inspired dishes along with two food and wine tasting menus. There is both a six-course tasting menu (Taste Canoe) and four-course tasting menu (Canoe Taste Classics). Each menu presents creative regional dishes paired with appropriate wines. As an additional bonus, the tasting menus also include an amuse-bouche, an intermezzo, and a pre-sweet item. Additional information about Canoe and other Oliver Bonacini Restaurants can be found at www.oliverbonacini.com.

A recent tasting menu is provided below. The menu features Chef Walsh's inspired Canadian regional cuisine and highlights the unique interaction of the flavors and textures in food and wine. Ruben Elmer, the senior sommelier at Canoe Restaurant and Bar, has provided tasting notes for each match on this menu.

Canoe Taste Classic

Henry of Pelham Rosé Brut NV
Spice-Cured Salmon with Spring Radish, Melon, Yogurt, and Abiti Caviar

The inherent fattiness of the salmon demands a rich-textured white. Coupled with the heat of the radish and the sweetness of the melon, we find sparkling wine has both the high acidity and slight effervescent sweetness needed to refresh the palate and prepare it for the next bite.

Novala Recioto della Valpolicella 2001
Simmered La Ferme Foie Gras, Beluga Lentils, Celery Root, and Cocoa Nibs

This rich sweet red wine is reminiscent of a Port, only lighter and more savory. The unctuousness of the foie gras calls for an equally rich-textured wine. The sweetness of the wine contrasts well with the cocoa nibs, and the rich stock-flavored lentils dissipate any tannin left in the wine.

Martin Ray Merlot 2000
Grand River Venison Loin, Oka Poutine, Kumquats, and Mulled Red Cabbage

The beauty of wine and food matching lies in the fact that grand wines are not needed. (In fact, sometimes their personality is just too big.) This wine, a generous mature California Merlot, shares the same texture as the venison, while picking up the spices in the red cabbage and letting them change and enhance the wine.

Taylor Fladgate Ten-Year-Old Tawny Port
Dark Chocolate Truffle Tart, Roasted Pine Nuts, and Crème Fraîche

Good dark chocolate is one of wine's greatest allies, letting the sweetness or the ripeness of the wine complement the bitterness of the chocolate. This tawny Port plays off the rich chocolate bitterness while the pine nuts bring out a side of the wine that wouldn't have been noticed otherwise. The fat in the crème fraîche smoothes out any edges that remain.

The food selections matched with the wines create interesting layers of taste, texture, and flavors. The tasting notes provide many specific examples of food-and-wine texture interactions: the fattiness in the salmon with the rich, textured rosé brut sparkling wine, the natural texture in the lentils smoothing any tannin in the Recioto della Valpolicella, the texture match of the venison and Merlot, and the fat in the crème fraîche smoothing the edges of the Port. Based on your experience, can you think of other wines you might pair with these dishes? Are there any other texture interactions not pointed out here that may come into play in these examples?

The Canoe Restaurant and Bar dining room in preparation for the next meal period.

FATTINESS IN FOOD

Fats can be divided into a number of categories (saturated/unsaturated, fats/oils, invisible/visible, vegetable/animal, etc.). For pairing purposes, it is meaningful to determine whether the fat is natural or an added textural element. Natural fats are found in foods such as dairy products, meats, seeds, and nuts. Added fats include oils, shortenings, lard, butter, and margarine. Added fats are used for flavoring and mouthfeel. The main objective of assessing fattiness in food from a texture perspective is determining mouthfeel characteristics such as smoothness, richness, and moistness. The use of milk and cream as references for wine body in the previous chapter provide a good example of how levels of fat affect the tactile sensation experienced in the mouth.

Generally, a richer, fatter dish will require a richer, more full-bodied wine to complement it. Wine elements can be used to cut through the food fattiness levels. A classic match is lamb or beef with young Cabernet Sauvignon; the fat in the meat has a natural affinity for the higher tannins present in the wine, mellowing them.

While an in-depth discussion of cheeses is provided in Chapter 12, it is important to note that fattiness levels vary substantially due to cheese type. Fresh cheeses (ricotta or fresh goat cheeses) and aged hard cheeses (Parmigiano Reggiano, Asiago) have a much lower fat content than high-fat cheeses such as Brie and Brillat-Savarin. Lower-fat cheeses generally match better with light wines, and fattier cheeses are a better match with stronger wines.

High acidity in wine can also be effective in cutting the fat in foods with higher fat content. As discussed in Chapter 5, acidity in wine generally works best with vegetable-based fats rather than animal-based ones. For the creamy sauces commonly served with fish, an unoaked Chardonnay is preferred to an oaky Chardonnay. The unoaked version will retain a higher level of acidity, and the closer body match will pair better with this dairy-based sauce.

Matching acidity in wine with food fattiness is an example of an exception to the rule of similar body styles in food and wine. When matched with fatty foods, white wines need to be crisp and intensely flavored, but when paired with meaty items, white wines should have an element of sweetness to them (such as German Spätlese or Auslese).

COOKING METHOD AND PROTEIN INTERACTIONS

While an important texture element is the level of fat present in the protein portion of the finished dish, the cooking method also has significant effects on the texture of prepared food items. For example, poaching or steaming maintains a light texture, while frying or grilling provides additional texture. Table 8.1 provides examples of proteins and cooking methods in ascending order based on the level of body they provide to finished dishes. The cooking method used and the level of fat in the protein interact to modify the overall body of the protein in its finished form.

Using the ascending levels of cooking method styles in Table 8.1 will assist in ranking food items based on cooking method, protein, and final texture. Body can range from very

Table 8.1   Ascending Levels of Body in Proteins and Cooking Methods

Protein	Moist Cooking Method	Anticipated Body Levels	Protein	Dry Cooking Method	Anticipated Body Levels
White fish	Poached, steamed	Very light			Very light
Chicken	Poached, steamed	Light	White fish	Grilled	Light
Veal	Stewed, braised	Light to moderate	Chicken	Grilled, pan-seared	Light to moderate
Game birds	Braised	Moderate	Veal	Pan-fried, grilled, fried	Moderate
Pork	Stewed, braised	Moderate to full	Game birds	Roasted	Moderate to full
Beef	Stewed	Full	Pork	Roasted, grilled	Full
Lamb	Stewed, braised	Robust	Beef	Roasted, grilled	Robust
Venison, elk	Stewed, braised	Powerful Very powerful	Lamb Venison, elk	Roasted, grilled Grilled, blackened	Powerful Very powerful

light in the case of poached or steamed white fish to very powerful in the case of grilled or blackened venison or elk. This relationship is impacted by the protein type, fattiness level, and cooking method.

Moist heat cooking methods are those where heat is conducted to the food item by a liquid and include methods such as steaming, boiling, and braising. Cooking methods defined as dry heat methods are those where heat is conducted to the food item by hot air (roasting, baking), hot metal (grilling, blackening), radiation (broiling), and hot fat (stir-frying, sautéing, pan-frying, deep-frying). These cooking methods impact not only the amount of fat retained in the finished dish but also the protein and collagen structure. When a dry heat method is utilized, the structure of the dish can be very different than if moist heat is used. A dry heat cooking method often allows excess fat to run off (grilling is an example), whereas moist heat often reincorporates the fats that melt off back into the food as part of the sauce, such as in a rich beef stew. Conversely, some dry heat methods such as pan-frying and deep-frying increase the fat content in the finished food item. In many cases the browning or charring that is sometimes a part of dry heat cooking creates a more powerful structure than a moist cooking method would. This explains how a lighter protein prepared using a more robust cooking method will have a more powerful texture than the protein type alone would suggest. For instance, sea bass cooked on a grill has a more powerful texture than chicken done by a moist heat method (poached, for instance).

In Table 8.1, the protein listed in the first column and the moist cooking method in the second column interact to create the anticipated body level indicated in the third column (Anticipated Body Levels). The interaction of the dry cooking method in the Dry Cooking Methods column with the protein type in the fourth column creates the anticipated body level shown in the far right-hand column. These are but a few examples, but as you can imagine, there are numerous other protein type and cooking method interactions, and you may also find yourself eating a dish prepared using a variety of cooking methods.

Meats prepared with robust cooking methods such as roasting or grilling should be paired with young reds with high tannin to match robustness with robustness. Robust cooking methods require wine with a strong enough personality to balance the powerful textures added to the dish. Bigger reds or big whites pair well with dishes prepared using robust cooking methods. White wines that provide an effective contrast with robust cooking methods range from dry Fino or Manzanilla sherry to German Kabinett. The opposite end of the cooking method continuum (poaching, steaming, etc.) requires a similarity match, which can be achieved by pairing these finished dishes with neutral, light-bodied wines.

OVERALL FOOD BODY

The overall food body is a texture element based on your perception of the overall power or body of the prepared dish. This evaluation takes the following factors into consideration: protein type, fat level, cooking method, and what the item is served with—basically the range of texture factors that provide a feeling of weight or structure throughout your mouth. The most basic assessment of food body is based on a continuum from light to very rich.

The type of food item and the temperature at which it is served impact the definition and perception of its body. For warm and cool items, body characteristics may include the consistency, viscosity, richness, and toughness of the food. For frozen items such as ice cream, body may be associated with the melting characteristics in your mouth. Does it quickly melt away and give the impression of lightness? Or does it resist melting and create a rich feeling in the mouth?

The examples of overall food body included in the Food Sensory Anchor Sheet (Figure B.1) presented in this chapter's exercises provide ascending levels of body derived from a combination of protein type, cooking method, and fattiness of the prepared dish. These provide a good example of variation in overall body and texture in finished food dishes.

INTERACTION OF WINE AND FOOD TEXTURES

Rule #5: Wine tannin levels should be equal to animal-based food fattiness levels.

Rule #6: Wine acidity levels should be equal to vegetable-based food fattiness levels.

Rule #7: Wine overall body should be equal to food overall body.

In a recent study, a trained panel provided support for the theory that wine tannin levels and food fattiness have a strong relationship with regard to the level of match when pairing wine with food. Panel members associated a higher level of match when tannin and food fattiness level were relatively equal.[2] The tannin-fattiness relationship works better when the fat is animal-based. The greater mouth-coating character of cream, natural fat in meats, and some cheeses mellows the harshness in tannin, while the tannin cuts through the fat. Vegetable fats and oils seem to pair better with the natural acidity in wine and can stand up to a wine with moderate to high acidity.

As previously noted, oak and alcohol are also important characteristics for determining overall body in wine. For instance, a big and oaky California Chardonnay could be a perfect match with grilled salmon because the riper grapes produce higher alcohol and a more powerful body in this style of Chardonnay. The more robust cooking method (grilling) and more powerful character of salmon creates a bigger, bolder, meaty taste that begs for a more substantial wine (in this case, a Pinot Noir or even Merlot might also be appropriate). Add a compound butter to finish the salmon (herb butter, for example) and you could create an additional match with the buttery character of the Chardonnay (assuming it has undergone malolactic fermentation); these aspects will be discussed further in the upcoming discussions on flavor.

SUMMARY

Tannin, oak, alcohol level, and body impact the perception of wine texture. Fattiness, protein type, cooking method, and body impact the perception of food texture. Matching these wine and food elements moves the level of match from refreshment to neutral or good. Once the wine and food components and texture elements have been properly matched, we can generally be assured that we will achieve a pleasant gastronomic sensation when the items are tasted together. The flavor elements will then provide the crowning touches for the potentially good and synergistic wine and food matches.

DISCUSSION QUESTIONS

1. What are the texture elements in food?

2. How is food texture traditionally defined?

3. What wine elements interact with food fattiness and body?

4. What impact do cooking method and protein type have on the texture sensation in finished food dishes?

EXERCISE 8.1

FOOD FATTINESS AND WINE TANNIN MATCHING

This exercise allows you to assess the interactions among five food fattiness levels and five tannin levels using five different wine varietals. For this exercise, you may utilize many of the same varietals used in Exercise 7.1 on wine texture. While these varietals provide a good spectrum of all the texture elements in wine, this exercise's primary focus is on tannin. Using the Food Sensory Anchor Scale (Figure B.1) and Wine Sensory Anchor Scale (Figure B.2), you will have basic reference points for ascending levels of wine tannin and food fattiness. When selecting the wines for this exercise, be sure to consider the potential impact of Old or New World origins, climate zones, oak aging, and wine maturity.

OBJECTIVES

To distinguish differing levels of food fattiness and assess the relationship between wine tannin and food fattiness levels in terms of perceived match.

Mise en Place: Things to Do Before the Exercise
Review the texture sections of Chapter 7 (wine texture evaluation) and Chapter 8 (food texture evaluation), particularly the sections on wine tannin and food fattiness.

A formal place setting with bread, butter, and red wine. These elements provide a simple test of the relationship between food fattiness and wine tannin.

MATERIALS NEEDED

Table 8.2   Materials Needed for Exercise 8.1

1 white paper placemat per student with numbered or labeled circles to place wineglasses (Figure 7.3)	1 spit cup per student Corkscrew Drinking water for each student
1 copy of the Aroma Wheel per student	Napkins
Tasting instruction sheets for each student (Figures 8.1, 8.2, and 8.3)	5 wineglasses per student
1 copy Food and Wine Sensory Anchor Scales per student	Cutting board
Plastic knives	Bread knife
1 paper plates per student	Pastry brush
Commercially made French bread cut into 1-inch slices, 4 slices per student	

Wine Options	Ascending Levels of Food Fattiness
Riesling, Chenin Blanc, Gavi, Fendant, sparkling wines	Plain French bread
Sémillon, Sauvignon Blanc, Gewurztraminer, unoaked Chardonnay, Beaujolais Nouveau	Butter-flavored cooking spray on French bread
Pinot Noir, oaked Chardonnay, unoaked Barbera	Extra-virgin olive oil brushed lightly on French bread
Cabernet Franc, Zinfandel, Syrah, Merlot, oaked Chianti	Smart Balance Light spread, 1 tsp on French bread
Cabernet Sauvignon	Unsalted butter, softened, 1 tsp on French bread

STEPS

1. Slice the French bread and prepare one slice of bread with each sample of spread for each student.

2. Pour a sample of each wine for each student to try with each sample of bread.

3. Taste the wine samples and assess the level of tannin in each. Record tannin levels in Figure 8.1.

Evaluator's Name: _____

Wine: _____ Producer: _____ Vintage:_____

| | | | | | | | | | | | | | | | | | | | | | | | | | Tannin

0   5   10

Wine: _____ Producer: _____ Vintage:_____

| | | | | | | | | | | | | | | | | | | | | | | | | | Tannin

0   5   10

Wine: _____ Producer: _____ Vintage:_____

| | | | | | | | | | | | | | | | | | | | | | | | | | Tannin

0   5   10

Wine: _____ Producer: _____ Vintage:_____

| | | | | | | | | | | | | | | | | | | | | | | | | | Tannin

0   5   10

Wine: _____ Producer: _____ Vintage:_____

| | | | | | | | | | | | | | | | | | | | | | | | | | Tannin

0   5   10

Figure 8.1

Wine Tannin

Evaluator's Name:

Food Item: _____

Fattiness

0   5   10

Food Item: _____

Fattiness

0   5   10

Food Item: _____

Fattiness

0   5   10

Food Item: _____

Fattiness

0   10

Food Item: _____

Fattiness

0   5   10

Figure 8.2

Food Fattiness Level

4. Taste the bread samples and assess the level of fattiness in the following order (record on Figure 8.2):

   a. Plain French bread

   b. Bread with butter-flavored cooking spray

   c. Bread brushed with extra-virgin olive oil

   d. Bread with Smart Balance Light Buttery Spread

   e. Bread with butter

Name:_____ Food Item:_____

Circle the level of match below:

Wine Sample 1:_____

| −4 | −3 | −2 | −1 | 0 | +1 | +2 | +3 | +4 |

Food Has   Equal   Food Has
Lower Fattiness   Level   Higher Fattiness

Wine Sample 2:_____

| −4 | −3 | −2 | −1 | 0 | +1 | +2 | +3 | +4 |

Food Has   Equal   Food Has
Lower Fattiness   Level   Higher Fattiness

Wine Sample 3:_____

| −4 | −3 | −2 | −1 | 0 | +1 | +2 | +3 | +4 |

Food Has   Equal   Food Has
Lower Fattiness   Level   Higher Fattiness

Wine Sample 4:_____

| −4 | −3 | −2 | −1 | 0 | +1 | +2 | +3 | +4 |

Food Has   Equal   Food Has
Lower Fattiness   Level   Higher Fattiness

Wine Sample 5:_____

| −4 | −3 | −2 | −1 | 0 | +1 | +2 | +3 | +4 |

Food Has   Equal   Food Has
Lower Fattiness   Level   Higher Dattiness

Overall feeling of Food & Wine Match (Circle the level of match below):

Wine Sample 1   1——2——3——4——5——6——7——8——9
                      No Match   Average Match   Synergistic Match

Wine Sample 2   1——2——3——4——5——6——7——8——9
                      No Match   Average Match   Synergistic Match

Wine Sample 3   1——2——3——4——5——6——7——8——9
                      No Match   Average Match   Synergistic Match

Wine Sample 4   1——2——3——4——5——6——7——8——9
                      No Match   Average Match   Synergistic Match

Wine Sample 5   1——2——3——4——5——6——7——8——9
                      No Match   Average Match   Synergistic Match

Figure 8.3

Level of Match Between Food Fattiness and Level of Wine Tannin

5. Taste each bread sample with the five wine samples. Using the scale in Figure 8.3, rank the relationship between food fattiness and wine tannin. This scale is a bipolar line scale, with 0 representing a combination in which neither the food fattiness nor the wine tannin dominates. A negative value indicates that the wine tannin dominates, and a positive value indicates that the food fattiness dominates. Record any sensory observations based on the relationship between wines and food fattiness.

6. Rank the bread samples from lowest to highest in fattiness levels. This is not always as straightforward as it might seem. Do your assessment levels match the value bands provided in the Food Sensory Anchor Scale (Figure B.1)? Where did you identify the fattiness or fullness sensation in your mouth?

Lowest fat = 1. _____ 2. _____ 3. _____
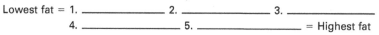
4. _____ 5. _____ = Highest fat

7. Rank the wines from lowest to highest in tannin level. Remember that the interaction of acidity and bitterness can alter your perception of tannin. Recall the palate mapping exercise in Chapter 2—where did you identify the astringent sensation in your mouth? Try to separate the tastes of acidity and bitterness from the mouthfeel of tannin. Visualize the fabric samples from smooth silk to rough burlap to assist you in this process.

Lowest (smoothest) = 1. _____ 2. _____ 3. _____

4. _____ 5. _____ = Highest (roughest)

8. Write down any other comments, thoughts, and observations that you identified during this evaluation process. Were there other factors that impacted your perception of wine tannin? What was your perception of the relationship between food fattiness and wine tannin? Was there a relationship? Did it differ depending on whether the fat was animal-based or vegetable-based? Did the acidity in the wine have an impact on food fattiness?

EXERCISE 8.2

FOOD BODY AND WINE BODY MATCHING

The purpose of this exercise is to showcase the impact of matching food body and wine body based on similarity or contrast. This exercise includes three finished food dishes and five wines providing a range of body levels and alcohol levels. The food items provide examples of how protein type and cooking method interact with each other and impact the overall perception of food body. While all of these food items are very wine-friendly, you should find substantial differences in your perception of body, power, and texture.

For this exercise, you may utilize many of the same varietals in Exercise 8.1 or experiment with other wines or varietals. Using the Food Sensory Anchor Scale (Figure B.1) and Wine Sensory An-

chor Scale (Figure B.2), you will have basic reference points for ascending levels of alcohol level, wine body, fattiness, and food body. When selecting the wines for this exercise, be sure to consider the potential impact of Old or New World origins, climate zones, oak aging, and wine maturity.

OBJECTIVES

To distinguish differing levels of food fattiness, food body, alcohol level, and wine body; to explore the relationships between food body and wine body; and to explore the relationship between alcohol level and food and its impact on perceived match.

Mise en Place: Things to Do Before the Exercise Review the sections of Chapter 7 describing the wine texture evaluation and the sections in this chapter on food texture. Time the food preparation around the desired tasting time. Recipes are included at the end of this chapter. The braised beef dish should be prepared well in advance to ensure that the flavors are well blended and the beef tips are tender. The chicken en papillote can be prepared ahead of time and cooked prior to the tasting session. The grilled pork dish can be seasoned and marinated in advance, grilled just prior to tasting. Care must be taken to ensure the food items are served at the proper temperature.

MATERIALS NEEDED

Table 8.3   Materials Needed for Exercise 8.2

1 white paper placemat per student with numbered or labeled circles to place wineglasses (Figure 7.3)	1 spit cup per student Corkscrew Drinking water for each student
1 copy of the Aroma Wheel per student	Napkins
Tasting sheets for each student (Figures 8.4, 8.5, and 8.6)	5 wine glasses per student
1 copy Food and Wine Sensory Anchor Scales per student	Cutting board
Plastic forks and knives	Bread or crackers to cleanse palate
Plates for tasting samples of each food dish	

Wine Options	Food Items
Riesling (or substitute Chenin Blanc, Gewürztraminer, Gavi, Sémillon, or Sauvignon Blanc if desired)	Chicken en Papillote
Pinot Noir (or substitute oaked Chardonnay, Barbera, Dolcetto, or Beaujolais if desired)	Grilled Pork Loin
Merlot (or substitute Cabernet Franc, Zinfandel, Syrah, or Chianti if desired)	Braised Beef in Red Wine
Cabernet Sauvignon, a New World example such as California, Australia, or Washington State (or substitute Nebbiolo or Barolo if desired)	
Port, Tawny or Ruby (or substitute other fortified examples such as sherry, Madeira, or Marsala if desired)	

STEPS

1. Prepare the food items and distribute samples of each food item—a sufficient amount to evaluate level of fattiness and body as well as enough to taste with all five wines.

2. Pour a sample of each wine for each student—enough to evaluate and to try with each food sample.

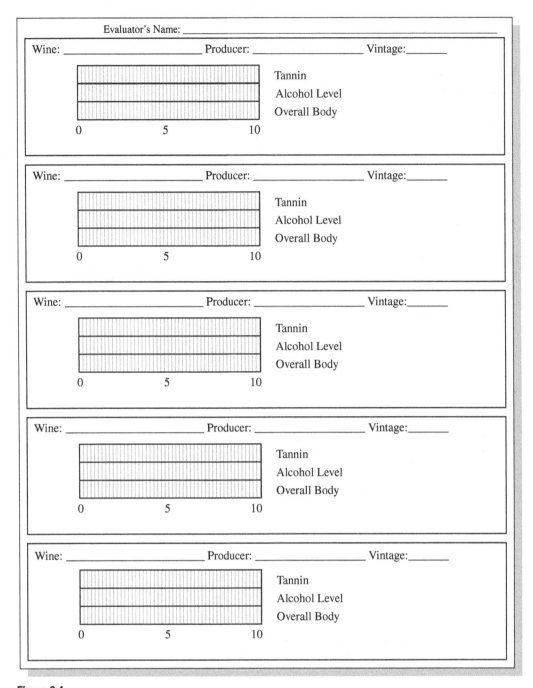

Figure 8.4

Wine Texture

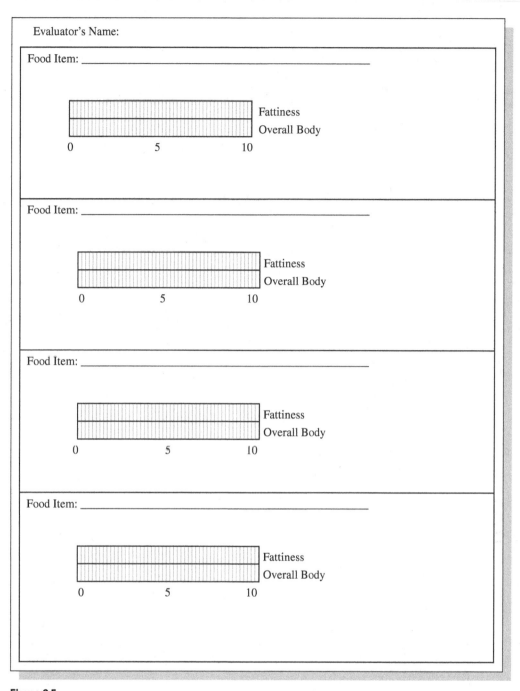

Figure 8.5

Food Overall Body

3. Taste the wine samples and assess the level of tannin, alcohol, and overall body in each. Record in Figure 8.4.

4. Taste each food sample and assess the level of fattiness and overall body in the following order (record on Figure 8.5):

   a. Chicken en papillote

   b. Grilled pork loin

   c. Braised beef

Name:_____ Food Item:_____

Circle the level of match below:

Riesling (dry) or Other _____

  −4   −3   −2   −1   0   +1   +2   +3   +4
Food Has   Equal   Food Has
Weaker Body   Level   Stronger Body

Chardonnay, Pinot Noir or Other _____

  −4   −3   −2   −1   0   +1   +2   +3   +4
Food Has   Equal   Food Has
Weaker Body   Level   Stronger Body

Merlot or Other _____
  −4   −3   −2   −1   0   +1   +2   +3   +4
Food Has   Equal   Food Has
Weaker Body   Level   Stronger Body

Cabernet Sauvignon or Other _____

  −4   −3   −2   −1   0   +1   +2   +3   +4
Food Has   Equal   Food Has
Weaker Body   Level   Stronger Body

Port or Other _____

  −4   −3   −2   −1   0   +1   +2   +3   +4
Food Has   Equal   Food Has
Weaker Body   Level   Stronger Body

Overall feeling of Food & Wine Match (Circle the level of match below):

Wine Sample 1   1——2——3——4——5——6——7——8——9
                      No Match   Average Match   Synergistic Match

Wine Sample 2   1——2——3——4——5——6——7——8——9
                      No Match   Average Match   Synergistic Match

Wine Sample 3   1——2——3——4——5——6——7——8——9
                      No Match   Average Match   Synergistic Match

Wine Sample 4   1——2——3——4——5——6——7——8——9
                      No Match   Average Match   Synergistic Match

Wine Sample 5   1——2——3——4——5——6——7——8——9
                      No Match   Average Match   Synergistic Match

Figure 8.6

Level of Body Match

5. Taste each food sample with the five wine samples. Using the scale in Figure 8.6, rank the relationship between food body and wine body. This scale is a bipolar line scale, with 0 representing a combination where neither the food nor the wine dominates with regard to body. A negative value indicates that the wine body dominates, and a positive value indicates that the food body dominates.

6. Discuss and record any sensory observations regarding the relationship between wines and food body. What impact did alcohol level and tannin have on this relationship? What impact did protein type and cooking method have on the relationship? Would the outcomes be different if different cooking methods were used?

7. Rank the food items from lightest to fullest body. Do your assessment levels match the value bands provided in the Food Sensory Anchor Scale (Figure B.1)? What were the key drivers of body or power in each food dish?

Lightest body = 1. _____ 2. _____ 3. _____

4. _____ 5. _____ = Fullest (most powerful) body

8. Rank wine texture in terms of alcohol and body.

   a. *Alcohol.* Rank the wines from lowest to highest alcohol levels. Does your rank order match the stated level of alcohol on the bottle? What impact did high or low alcohol have on the sensation of wine body? What impact did high or low alcohol have on perceived match with these food items?

   Lowest alcohol = 1. _____ 2. _____ 3. _____

   4. _____ 5. _____ = Highest alcohol

   b. *Wine body.* Rank the wines from lightest to fullest body. Do your assessment levels match the value bands provided in the Wine Sensory Anchor Scale (Figure B.2)? What were the key drivers of body or power in each wine?

   Lightest body = 1. _____ 2. _____ 3. _____

   4. _____ 5. _____ = Fullest (most powerful) body

9. Write any other comments, thoughts, and observations that you identified during this evaluation process. Were there other factors that impacted your perception of match between the food dishes and the wine? What was your perception of the relationship between food and wine alcohol? What impact did dry or moist cooking methods have on these relationships?

Food Item: Chicken en Papillote

Yield: 4 servings

En papillote is a traditional preparation literally meaning "in a parcel." The cooking method of the final product resembles steaming but provides the opportunity to create a unique tableside release of intense aromas as the parcel is opened and the steam is released. While the traditional parcel material is parchment paper, the chicken en papillote recipe can be prepared using aluminum foil if desired. This preparation allows for the use of a wide variety of sauces, vegetables, herbs, and butters to be added to the parcel prior to cooking.

Ingredients

1 medium leek, washed and sliced into thin strips

1 medium carrot, peeled and sliced into thin julienne strips

1 medium zucchini, sliced into thin julienne strips

4 medium-sized skinless chicken breasts

1/4 c (60 ml) melted butter or olive oil

2 tbsp fresh herbs (thyme, chives, oregano, cilantro, etc.)

1/4 c (60 ml) white wine

Salt

Pepper

Preparation

Heat oven to 400°F (205 °C). Divide the leeks, carrots, and zucchini between four 12-inch (30 cm) squares of parchment or aluminum foil, placing the vegetables about a quarter of the way from the bottom. Place a chicken breast on top of the vegetables. Brush with butter or oil and evenly distribute the fresh herbs. Drizzle each packet with white wine and season with salt and pepper.

For each parcel, fold the parchment paper over the top of the chicken and tightly fold the edges so the chicken and vegetables are enclosed in a pouch. Place the parcels on a baking sheet and bake for about 20 minutes. Carefully remove the parcels from the oven and place them on serving plates. Normally, the packets are opened at the table so that the aroma is part of the experience.

**Pork provides a good example
of a protein with great
flexibility for the chef to
impact the overall weight or
body of the dish based on
cooking method, the fattiness
of the cut selected, and other
ingredients.**

Food Item: Grilled Pork Loin with Mustard and Molasses

Yield: 8 servings

Ingredients

12 oz (355 ml) dark beer

1/3 c (80 ml) dark molasses

1/4 c (60 ml) Dijon mustard

1/4 c (60 ml) olive oil

1 tbsp (15 ml) chopped mixed fresh thyme,
    rosemary, and chives

2 cloves garlic, minced

One 3-pound (1.4 kg) boneless pork loin, cut
    into 3/4-inch (2 cm) slices

Preparation

In medium bowl, combine the beer, molasses,
mustard, oil, herbs, and garlic. Pour this
mixture over the sliced pork and
refrigerate for 1 to 4 hours. Preheat a
grill or char-broiler. Remove pork from
the marinade and grill over medium-
high heat until it reaches an internal
temperature of 155 to 160°F (68 to 71°C).
Use the reserved marinade to baste the
pork during cooking if desired.

Food Item: Braised Beef in Red Wine Sauce

Yield: 8 servings

Beef Bourguignon is a classic French dish known for its slow, moist cooking technique and deep rich sauce. The dish features the rich, meaty characteristics of beef with the substantial cooking method of braising. This item is very wine-friendly and provides an opportunity to marry the wine used in its preparation with the wine served as its accompaniment. This is one reason why red Burgundies go so well with Beef Bourguignon. The traditional preparation calls for red Burgundy (Pinot Noir), but other red varietals can be substituted to produce a fine final product.

Ingredients	Preparation
4 lb (1.8 kg) trimmed beef, cut into 1-inch (2.5 cm) cubes Salt Black pepper Flour for dredging 6 oz (170 g) bacon, diced 1/4 c (60 ml) olive oil 1 1/2 c (355 ml) sliced onions 1 1/2 c (355 ml) peeled baby carrots 1/4 c (60 ml) peeled and thinly sliced garlic 2 c (470 ml) button mushrooms 2 c (470 ml) dry red wine 3 c (710 ml) beef stock or canned beef broth 1 c (240 ml) diced tomatoes, fresh or canned 2 bay leaves 4 sprigs thyme 1/4 c (60 ml) parsley, chopped 1 tbsp (15 ml) chopped thyme	Season the beef cubes generously with salt and black pepper. Dredge the seasoned beef in the flour. In a heavy skillet or rondo, sauté bacon in the olive oil until lightly browned over medium-high heat. Remove the crisp bacon from skillet and drain on paper towels. Brown the beef in the hot fat in batches, being careful not to crowd the pan or burn the beef. When nicely browned, add the onions, carrots, garlic, and mushrooms to the pan. Continue cooking over medium-high heat for 8–10 minutes, until the vegetables are caramelized. Add the red wine, beef broth, tomato, bay leaves, thyme sprigs, and cooked bacon to the pan. Incorporate the browned bits into this mixture by scraping the bottom of the pan. Bring the mixture to a boil, then reduce to a simmer. Cover the skillet and cook slowly for 2 1/2–3 hours, until meat is very tender. Before serving, add chopped parsley and thyme and adjust the seasoning with salt and black pepper, if needed.

NOTES

1. M. Bennion and B. Scheule, *Introductory Foods*, 12th ed. (Upper Saddle River, NJ: Pearson–Prentice Hall, 2004), 142.

2. R. J. Harrington and R. Hammond, "Which Wine with Chicken, Pork or Beef? The Impact of Food and Wine Texture Elements on Perceived Match," *Proceeding of the 2006 I-CHRIE Conference*, in press.

FLAVORS: ARCHITECTURAL ELEMENTS IN THE WINE AND FOOD PAIRING PROCESS

Flavors in food and wine are the third category of elements that we will discuss in this text. Flavors are closely tied to our perceptions of specific characteristics inherent in food or wine and are derived from both aroma and taste sensations. Matching the flavor elements in wine and food is one of the defining steps in the pairing process and helps to move the level of match from good to synergistic.

The concepts of aromas and flavors have received a substantial amount of both anecdotal and empirical study. Unfortunately, much of the anecdotal research comes across as elitist, with wine and food experts articulating convoluted descriptions with obscure references. Stories abound of supposed experts who claim to be able to identify the exact vintage, variety, winemaker, and terroir—only to find out that what's in the glass is a blend of several different wines. Nonetheless, identifying aromas and flavors is a skill that can be developed and improved substantially based on experience and hard work, so you should not be intimidated. The exercises provided throughout this book are intended to help you to further develop this ability. But beware of the self-proclaimed expert—Alex Eberspaecher's amusing definition of a wine expert in *Vino Veritas* is "a person who has an inferiority complex or some other personality disorder."

For the purposes of wine and food pairing, the concept of flavor follows Baldy's definition of flavor as retronasal or "in-mouth" smells. Basically, flavor in any food or wine substance can be defined as the collaboration between the sense of smell and the sense of taste in the back of the mouth. When selecting wines to pair with food, the concept of flavor encompasses the following attributes: dominant identified flavor(s), intensity of flavor, persistency of flavor, and whether or not the wine or food has any spicy characteristics.

Chapter 9 provides on overview of the impact and implications of spiciness in food and wine. This element of flavor is discussed first because spicy food can have a substantial limiting effect on the wines that will pair well with it. Spiciness in food is a wild card in the pairing process—while a food and wine may match well in the component and texture relationships, food spiciness may trump this relationship and return us to the no match or refreshment match level.

Chapter 10 provides an overview of flavor categories or types and their intensity and persistency. For both the food and wine items to become equal partners in the pairing relationship, they must have similar or contrasting flavor types, similar levels of flavor intensity, and similar levels of flavor persistence.

CHAPTER 9
THE IMPACT OF SPICE

CHAPTER OUTLINE:

Introduction

Aperitif: Bayou La Seine: An American Restaurant in Paris

Wine Varietals and Styles

Food Types and Styles

How Spice Is Assessed: Identifying Hot, Savory, or Sweet

Impact on Pairing Possibilities

Summary

Exercises

KEY CONCEPTS:

- Adapting ethnic foods to local tastes
- Prominent spice flavors
- Differences between herbs and spices
- Spice flavor levels
- Savory spices
- Sweet spices
- Hot spices
- Potential wine killers
- Limiting effects of spice on wine pairing

INTRODUCTION

Flavor layering adds more elements to taste components and texture. Trying to consider all of these elements simultaneously can create confusion about the best wine choice for a given food item. Therefore, one objective of the food-and-wine pairing process is to isolate these flavors and identify the most prominent ones. Major flavor character categories include fruity, nutty, smoky, herbal, spicy, cheesy, earthy, and meaty. Spicy flavors in food and wine can be particularly important for matching purposes.

Spices have a long and colorful tradition, having been used for centuries in cooking, for medicinal purposes, and for other reasons. In ancient Greece, bay leaves were made into crowns for scholars and victorious athletes to wear. Capsicum peppers have been eaten by New World Indians since about 7000 BC. In past centuries, fennel was traditionally hung over doorways because the plant was believed to ward off evil spirits.[4]

Technically, spices are distinguished from herbs based on the part of the plant from which they are derived. Spices come from roots (for example, ginger), bark (cinnamon), flowers (saffron), seeds (cumin), fruit (allspice), or buds (cloves), while herbs are the fresh or dried leaves. We can classify seasonings based on their taste: sweet-spicy, savory-spicy, hot-spicy, and herbal, for example.[5]

While many experts suggest pairing food and wines by matching flavors, evaluators need to keep in mind that spicy or herbal flavors in wine do not come from actual spices and herbs, and spiciness in food and wine does not by itself guarantee a good match between the two.[6] While both Gewürztraminer and many Asian and Indian dishes are frequently described as spicy, this particular match is more likely to work because of similar levels of acidity and sweetness, not because of the spiciness. To create a match using flavors and spiciness, it is important to define the type of spice in the wine and food to ensure a satisfying match.

The wine and food pairing instrument that will be presented and discussed in Chapters 11 and 12 includes a separate line to assess the level of spice in both wine and food as part of the evaluation process. The flavor of spice is listed as a separate category because of its likely impact on pairing decisions when a significant level is present in food dishes. The following sections explore the issue of spice and its potential impact on pairing decisions.

Aperitif | Bayou La Seine: An American Restaurant in Paris

Chef and co-owner Judith Bluysen opened the restaurant, originally called Thanksgiving, along with her husband, Frédéric, in 1993. The restaurant evolved into a full-service operation after a three-year stint selling American packaged food and homemade take-out foods such as Chili con Carne, Barbecued Ribs, and Jambalaya, and running an American-cuisine catering service in Paris. The packaged-food store, Thanksgiving American Grocery Store, still operates directly behind the restaurant, selling baking needs, basic American groceries, spices, Louisiana specialties, Tex-Mex ingredients, and other specialty items.

For the first year, their restaurant served dishes based on a variety of regional American cuisines, including New England Baked Beans, North Carolina Barbecue Pork, Kentucky Burgoo, guacamole, pastrami, coleslaw, a few California-inspired salads, and Louisiana's gumbos, jambalayas, and étouffées. Although the restaurant was relatively successful, they quickly determined that the various cooking styles, ingredients, and range of accompaniments were too confusing for the Parisian clientele. Judith and Frederic decided to choose one cuisine and stick with it. Partially because Louisiana cuisine is particularly relevant to France, but mostly because of its rich history and its quality, they chose the Cajun and Creole cuisines of Louisiana. As part of this focus, they decided to change the name of the restaurant to Bayou La Seine to utilize the Cajun term for a small river and identify its location near the Seine River in Paris.

In this chapter, the focus is on the impact of spicy flavors on wine and food pairing decisions. An assumption of Cajun and Creole cuisine is that it is spicy. While this is not always the case, the level of spice and seasoning does tend to be higher than what is generally served in traditional French cuisine. Judith shares some of the challenges she encountered in adapting this ethnic cuisine to French tastes and French wines.

"When adapting ethnic or foreign cuisine to the French market, the most difficult obstacle to overcome is the preconceived notion of the food, which generally is negative or patronizing at best. The predominant prejudice expressed regarding our Cajun cuisine was that the cuisine is too spicy. To reduce a number of possible negative associations with the term *Cajun cuisine*, we decided to describe our food as *Louisiana cuisine*. This description is a more inclusive term (encompassing both the Cajun and Creole cuisines as well as the influences of African, French, Spanish, German, and Italian cultures in Louisiana), takes it out of the realm of "home cooking" and into cuisine (an important selling factor in France), and reduces the connotations of spiciness associated with the term *Cajun*.

"Spice usage being perhaps the single most important identifying component of this cuisine, I felt that it was crucial to learn to balance the taste notes of the different spices. This can be accomplished in many fashions: the combination of the spices in complementary and contrasting interactions, the timing of the addition of the spices during the cooking process, and different techniques of getting flavor from the spices, such as heating, grinding, mashing, or infusing in a water-based potion or in an oil.

"In creating the menu, I found there were many aspects to consider apart from the actual flavor of the item served on the plate. How the taste would develop as one worked through a bowl of Jambalaya? Would the first sting of cayenne pepper deaden the taste buds to the tangy slivers of marinated pepper used in the sausage? Would the murky spiciness of Dirty Rice (made with roasted mustard seeds and cumin as well as three powdered peppers and herbs) complement the smoky, piquant Blackened Rib Eye Steak, dusted with a sweet paprika, cayenne, and thyme concoction and then seared in a white-hot dry pan? Or would one overwhelm the other? And, of course, what would these spices do to the flavor of the wines offered?

"In the best of all possible worlds, a dry but fruit-forward white wine such as a good California Chardonnay or an Arbois from the Jura region of France is a perfect complement for the spicier Cajun dishes, such as Jambalaya, Dirty Rice, or Barbecue Shrimp. But in France, red wine outsells white wine in restaurants such as ours by ten to one, and price is a major factor. Also, many of our customers who are native or have traveled through Louisiana order beer. Beer is great to accompany fried food on a sweltering day, but a well-chosen wine accentuates the flavors in our more complex dishes."[1]

One of Judith's menu items is a dish she calls Cajun Matriochka, which is a takeoff on a traditional Cajun dish called Turducken. Turducken is basically a roasted whole turkey that has been stuffed with a whole duck, which has been stuffed with a whole chicken. Prior to this stuffing process, all of the poultry bones are removed. This delicacy is becoming popular as a holiday dish throughout much of the southern United States.[2]

A matriochka is a Russian nested doll set that consists of a wooden figure that can be pulled apart to reveal a smaller figure inside, which can be pulled apart to reveal a smaller figure, and so on. Her Cajun Matriochka adapts the traditional Turducken into a menu item that can be prepared as an individual portion. It features red-wine-poached fig quarters rolled in a thin slice of duck breast, which is rolled in a thin slice of turkey breast, dusted with a mixture of ginger, coriander, sweet paprika, and cinnamon, and browned in butter. Sliced into rounds, it is served with smothered greens, wild rice, and a Burgundy/balsamic vinegar caramel sauce.

"Sauces offer a dramatic medium for the dichotomy of flavor," says Judith. "In the wine-based sauce for my Matriochka, I infuse star anise, Szechuan pepper, and cinnamon stick in a sweetened, vanilla-scented merlot that was used to poach the figs and also pears. Reduced to nearly a syrup, the sweetness cut by a dash of balsamic vinegar, this sauce awakens the fruitiness of the fig as it assuages the meatiness of the duck and turkey. The Asian spices in the poultry react differently in the meat than they do in the sauce. The finished dish creates a combination of contrasting sweet, spice, fruity, meaty, and lightly sour elements.

"On the other end of the flavor spectrum is a brown beer Cajun roux-based sauce that I use for Cajun Boudin Blanc, a fresh sausage made with pork, poultry, rice, and lots of sage. To accentuate the beer flavor, juniper berries simmer in the sauce as it thickens. To balance the acid note, I replace the green pepper in the sauce's traditional 'Cajun trinity' (chopped onion, celery, and green bell pepper) with carrot—a bit like the proverbial pinch of sugar in tomato sauce. A light red wine that can be served slightly chilled, such as Beaujolais or Saumur Champigny, nicely complements this dish."[3]

The challenges of adapting ethnic food dishes to local tastes require thought, experimentation, and knowing your customer. Many ethnic cuisines include a variety of spices and herbs that can limit our ability to match these food dishes with wines that create a good or ideal match. Chef Bluysen also points out that in her situation, wine selection is limited by her customers' overwhelming preference for red wines. All of these issues point to the importance of considering how menu items can be delivered in line with consumer taste while using savvy methods to provide unique experiences for customers that simultaneously shape their preferences. Judith and her husband, Frédéric, used a variety of techniques to adapt menu items, menu descriptions, and service styles to meet the tastes of their local clientele. This adaptation process allowed them to create traditional Louisiana dishes that can be successfully paired with French wines.

Up-to-date information on Judith and Frédéric's restaurant, Bayou La Seine, can be obtained by visiting their Web site at www.thanksgivingparis.com.

Food Item: Cajun Matriochka (courtesy of Bayou La Seine)

Yield: 6 servings

Ingredients for Spice

3 tbsp (45 ml) ground ginger
1 tbsp (15 ml) white pepper
1/2 tbsp (8 ml) paprika
1 tbsp (15 ml) cayenne pepper
1 tbsp (15 ml) herbes de Provence,
    crumbled, or 1 tsp each thyme, sage,
    and rosemary
1 tbsp (15 ml) oregano, crumbled
1 tbsp (15 ml) tarragon, crumbled
1 tbsp (15 ml) salt
1 tbsp (15 ml) cinnamon
1 K tsp (5 ml) onion powder
1 tsp (5 ml) nutmeg

Ingredients for Matriochka Rolls

6 thin turkey scallops, cut diagonally from
    the breast, about 4 oz (120 g) each
1 duck breast, fat and skin pulled off and cut
    into 6 very thin diagonal slices, about
    1–1 1/2 inches (2.5-4 cm) wide
6 poached figs, each cut into thirds (reserved
    from the sauce preparation above)
2 oz (60 ml) butter
1–2 tbsp (15–30 ml) balsamic vinegar

Preparation

If necessary, carefully pound the turkey scallops until uniformly thin (about 1/16 inch [1.6 mm]) and about 6 inches by 4 inches (15 cm by 10 cm). Lay one scallop on a cutting board, the longer sides horizontal. Trim the left and right sides if necessary. Sprinkle with some of the spice mix. Place a slice of duck on the turkey scallop, slightly lower than the center, and place 3 fig pieces on the duck slice. From the bottom, roll the turkey to enclose the duck and figs. Slip 3 pieces of twine under the roll and tie to form a cylindrical shape. Set aside and repeat with the other 5 turkey scallops. Coat each of the rolls with the spice mix. Heat the butter until foaming in a large skillet and briefly brown all of the rolls at once, turning so that they color and firm uniformly. (This should take no longer than 3 minutes.) Remove the rolls and deglaze the skillet with 4 cups (about 1 liter) of the poaching liquid from the pears and figs. Bring to a boil and reduce for 2–3 minutes. Add the balsamic vinegar to taste and boil another 1–2 minutes. The duck should be rosy in color. (At this point the rolls and the sauce can be cooled, covered, and held under refrigeration. If the rolls have been chilled, sauté them briefly in a skillet with butter, then cover and bake at 400°F [205°C] for 7 minutes.) Turn and allow to rest 2 minutes off heat in the covered skillet. Strain the sauce through a cheesecloth-lined sieve and boil until syrupy. Slice the uneven ends off the duck rolls and cut the remainder into 5 or 6 rounds. Pour a little of the sauce onto the plate and place the rounds cut side up on the sauce; drizzle a little more sauce on the rolls.

Ingredients for Sauce	**Poaching Preparation**
28 oz (800 g) sugar 3 cups (710 ml) red wine 3 cups (710 ml) water 1 orange, sliced ½ vanilla pod, split 3 star anise 2 cinnamon sticks Pinch of Szechuan pepper 6 pears, still firm to the touch 12 dried figs	Dissolve the sugar in the red wine and water. Add the sliced orange, split vanilla pod, star anise, cinnamon, and Szechuan pepper and bring to a boil. Peel the pears and poach them and the dried figs in this liquid until the pears are tender but still firm. Cool the pears and figs in the liquid and reserve. (The pears and half the figs are not used in this recipe, but you will have a great dessert.)

WINE VARIETALS AND STYLES

In both food and wine, spice flavors can take on a variety of characteristics—for example, being sweet, savory, or hot. A number of white and red varietals are described as having spice characteristics. The classic spicy white varietal is Gewürztraminer. This wine tends to have exotic fruit flavors as well as flavors of many sweet spices, including nutmeg, cloves, ginger, or allspice. (The name of the wine, in fact, most likely means "aromatic Traminer," where Traminer is the name of the grape from which it is made. In Fruili, Italy, you can still find a wine called Traminer Aromatico, another regional name for Gewürztraminer.)[7] The exotic fruit flavors and sweet spices associated with Gewürztraminer make it the go-to wine recommendation with Asian, Mexican, and Indian food. Spicy Gewürztraminers are available from the Alsace area of France, Germany, Washington State, Oregon, Idaho, and California.

The classic spicy red varietal is Syrah or Shiraz (two different names for the same grape). Shiraz wines provide flavors of both savory and sweet spices. A signature scent is black pepper, but you may also find spices such as cumin, dried chiles, or cinnamon. Red wines made from the Syrah grape in the Rhône valley of France have this natural characteristic of spiciness. The Shiraz from Australia is a full-bodied red with peppery and spicy characteristics that match the full-bodied and peppery character of Aussie-style grilled steak.

Examples of wines that potentially contain spice and herbal elements are described in Table 9.1. Several white and red wines echo sweet spices such as cinnamon, cloves, and ginger. Many of these same wines will have notes of peppery and savory spice, such as black pepper, mustard seed, or a bite of horseradish. These flavors can be combined with similar foods as long as food tanginess (acidity) or hot spice (heat) are not too overpowering. In the case of sour foods, ensuring higher acidity in the wine is of greater importance. (What does this suggest for the possibility of using oaky Chardonnay with these foods?) Column 3 of Table 9.1 provides some suggestions for wines that tame the hot and spicy impact of the food and prepare the palate for the next bite.

White wines that go well with hot, spicy foods are typically off-dry, have relatively low alcohol, and retain a good amount of acidity. Off-dry or semi-dry Rieslings are a particularly good choice in this regard. Rieslings are generally grown in cool climates, so they retain a substantial level of natural acidity. Many wine experts believe the Riesling grape is

The spicy red grape Syrah (also known as Shiraz) in the Côtes du Rhône, France (courtesy of Carroll Falcon).

Table 9.1   Wines with Spice, Herbal, and Taming Characteristics

Wines with Spice Notes	Wines with Herbal Notes	Wines that Tame Hot-Spicy Foods
Whites: Gewurztraminer, Viognier, oaky Chardonnay, Austrian Grüner-Veltliner, Mosel Riesling (Germany), Portuguese Vinho Verde	**Whites:** Sauvignon Blanc, Fumé Blanc, Sémillon, New World Viognier, white Bordeaux, Sancerre, Pouilly-Fumé, Alsace Riesling	**Whites:** Italian Moscato d'Asti, German Riesling Kabinett, Gewürztraminer, Portuguese Vinho Verde
Reds: Shiraz, Syrah, Côtes du Rhône, red Zinfandel (California and Washington), Greek reds, Petite Sirah (California), Sangiovese	**Reds:** Merlot, Cabernet Sauvignon, Cabernet Franc, Shiraz, Syrah, red Rioja, Italian Chianti	**Red:** Reds with low tannins, lower alcohol, and a fruity nature (e.g., Beaujolais, Gamay, Italian Dolcetto, Lemberger, Valpolicella, Spanish Tempranillo)

capable of producing some of the highest-quality white wines on the planet, with good aging potential. Because the current fashion is to drink dry red wines (or big, oaky Chardonnays if forced to drink whites), off-dry Rieslings are currently a great wine value. Riesling with spicy foods can be a refreshing to good match due to the acidity, a slight sweetness in the off-dry versions, and a great contrast of fruit and floral flavors with the food's hot or peppery spices.

For a red wine to go with hot and spicy foods, choose one with lower tannin, lower alcohol, and a fruity character. Lemberger, Beaujolais and Dolcetto are good examples of fruity, lower-tannin, higher-acid red wines. For both reds and whites, however, with hot, spicy foods the best you can generally hope for is a refreshing match, one that doesn't fan the flame of the food's heat.

Spices in food are more difficult to pair with wine than herbs. Depending on the level of spice in a food dish, many spices can clash with oak and wine tannins. Excessive heat from horseradish, hot mustards, and chiles can numb your palate prior to even tasting the wine. Herbs are much more wine-friendly than most spices. Column 2 of Table 9.1 provides examples of wines that have herbal notes in them—again, not from the herbs themselves, but from growing conditions at the vineyard, the characteristics inherent to the varietal, or the winemaking process. The key to matching herbal foods is to use a wine that echoes herbal notes as well. Many of these wines also have spice characteristics.

FOOD TYPES AND STYLES

Spice and seasoning use in food has evolved dramatically over the past thirty years. Overall consumption of spice has increased substantially over this period, with greater use of herbs, fusion flavors, robust and bold flavors, chile varieties, and ethnic flavors.[8] Spices with a sweet character include cinnamon, clove, nutmeg, ginger, and tamarind. Savory spices and seasonings are those such as pepper, cumin, cardamom, fish sauce, and so on. Hot spices include mustard seed, hot peppers, and horseradish.

The first spice brought to Europe from the East was pepper. Peppers and other hot spices (including black pepper, white pepper, red pepper, and mustard seed) account for 41 percent of total U.S. spice usage. Though chiles or hot peppers originated in the Americas, they have become a basic ingredient in many cuisines around the globe. Many of the ethnic cuisines we enjoy today, such as Indian, Asian, Mexican, African, and Caribbean, rely on hot peppers. Common varieties include habanero (also known as scotch bonnet), poblano, ancho, serrano, jalapeño, Anaheim, and chipotle. Calling the sensory reaction to these peppers "hot" refers not to an actual thermal reaction but rather to a chemically induced irritation.[9]

To determine a natural wine pairing for spicy foods, it is very useful to look at what people drink with the dish in the region of the world where it originates. For example, in Italy, Italian pasta with pesto is served with Soave, Bianco di Custoza, Gavi, or Lugana. These white wines are light, acidic, and refreshing, which works well with the basil and garlic elements in this pasta dish. Japanese food served with sake or a Louisiana seafood boil served with beer provide additional beverage examples that work well in terms of taste components, texture, and flavor matches.

Thai cuisine presents a unique situation where all of the elements and spice types may be incorporated into a single dish: sweet spices, hot spices, savory spices, and a variety of herbs. In this case, slightly sweet, light, acidic, and refreshing white wines provide a counterbalance in the relationship.

HOW SPICE IS ASSESSED: IDENTIFYING HOT, SAVORY, OR SWEET

As discussed earlier, flavors are closely tied to our perceptions of specific characteristics inherent in food or wine, and are derived from both aroma and taste sensations. These sensations can be described as in-mouth smells.

In assessing spice in wine or food, it is important to differentiate between herbs and spices as well as among hot, savory, and sweet spices. While many foods include more than one type of spice or herb, the evaluation process is about determining the dominant spice types that will have an impact on wine choices. Once the dominant spice types are determined, the level of intensity of the specific spice flavor has important implications for wine choices.

The term *intensity* refers to concentration, power, or force[10] and applies to all flavor types. The evaluation of spice intensity defines the relative level of intensity or force of the characteristic spice(s) in the wine or food. These levels can be verbally described on a scale ranging from no spice to weak spice, moderate spice, intense spice, and powerful spice.

These descriptions are defined and ranked utilizing the appraisal values described in Table 9.2. At the no spice level (the 0–2 value band in Figure 9.1 for wine spice and 9.2 for food spice), the sensation of spice either is undetectable or fades almost immediately. At the weak spice level (the 2–4 value band), the spice sensation is recognizable but the stimulus is not very strong. At the moderate spice level (the 4–6 value band level), the sensation of spice is defined as "sufficient"—the spice sensation is amply defined. At the intense spice level (the 6–8 value band), the spice sensation can be clearly identified in a very distinct way; foods in this range begin to push the limit in terms of wine matching possibilities. Finally, at the powerful spice level (the 8–10 value band), the spice sensation is intense and can be identified unmistakably; only a limited number of wines can be matched with foods in this range.

Each spice type has differing acceptable levels in regard to wine and food pairing. Sweet spices in food are more wine-friendly—they can be matched with a wider variety of wines, and higher match levels are more likely. In food, some savory and hot spices, as well as the more intense spice levels, make it increasingly difficult to create a good match. Potential "wine killers" are ingredients that have an unusually high level of sweetness, sourness, saltiness, bitterness, or hot spiciness.[11]

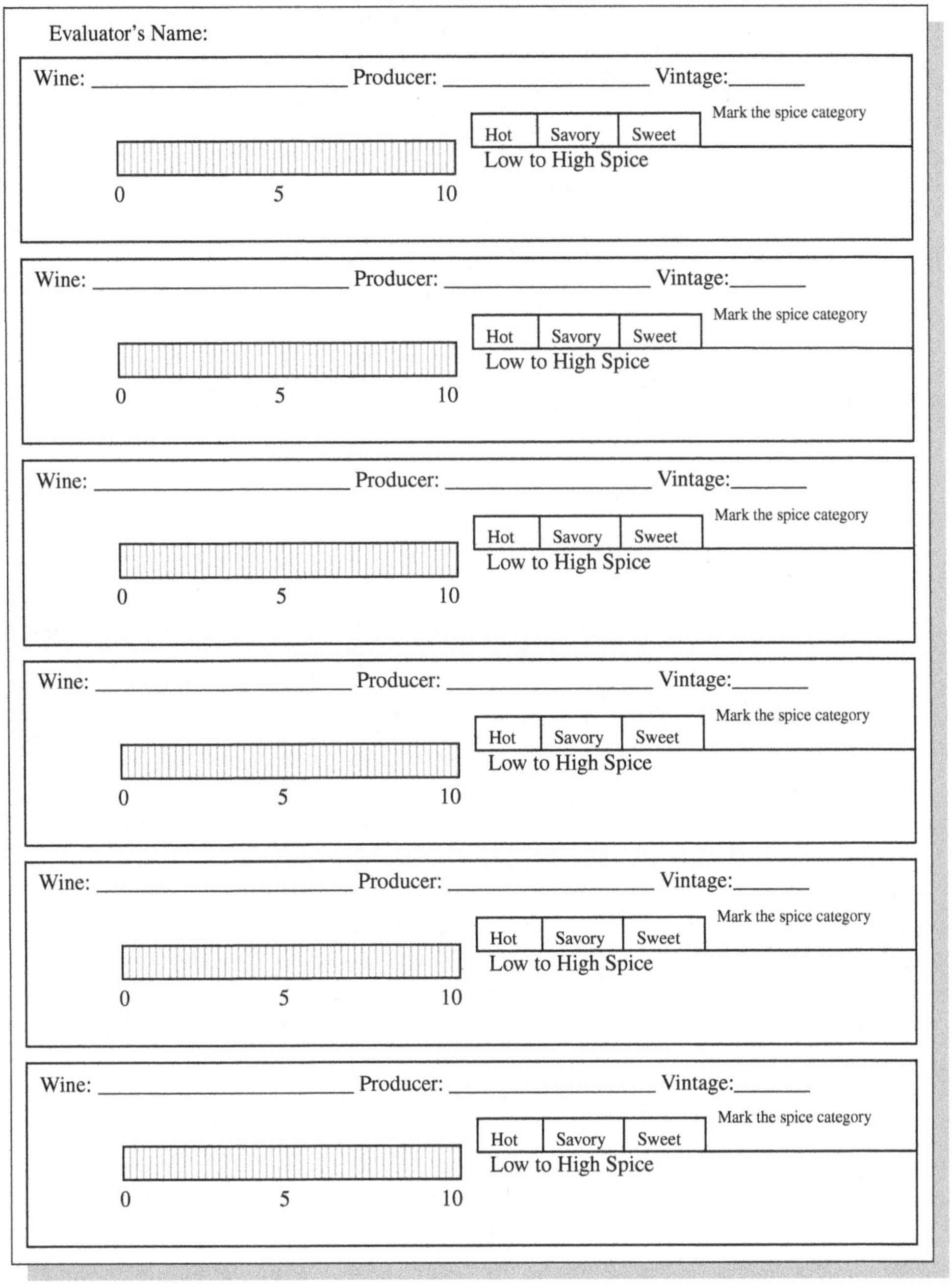

Evaluator's Name:

Wine: _____ Producer: _____ Vintage:_____

| | Hot | Savory | Sweet | Mark the spice category |

Low to High Spice

0   5   10

Wine: _____ Producer: _____ Vintage:_____

| | Hot | Savory | Sweet | Mark the spice category |

Low to High Spice

0   5   10

Wine: _____ Producer: _____ Vintage:_____

| | Hot | Savory | Sweet | Mark the spice category |

Low to High Spice

0   5   10

Wine: _____ Producer: _____ Vintage:_____

| | Hot | Savory | Sweet | Mark the spice category |

Low to High Spice

0   5   10

Wine: _____ Producer: _____ Vintage:_____

| | Hot | Savory | Sweet | Mark the spice category |

Low to High Spice

0   5   10

Wine: _____ Producer: _____ Vintage:_____

| | Hot | Savory | Sweet | Mark the spice category |

Low to High Spice

0   5   10

Figure 9.1

Wine Spice Level

Evaluator's Name:

Food Item: _____

Mark the spice category below

Hot	Savory	Sweet

Low to High Spice

0   5   10

Food Item: _____

Mark the spice category below

Hot	Savory	Sweet

Low to High Spice

0   5   10

Food Item: _____

Mark the spice category below

Hot	Savory	Sweet

Low to High Spice

0   5   10

Food Item: _____

Mark the spice category below

Hot	Savory	Sweet

Low to High Spice

0   5   10

Food Item: _____

Mark the spice category below

Hot	Savory	Sweet

Low to High Spice

0   5   10

Food Item: _____

Mark the spice category below

Hot	Savory	Sweet

Low to High Spice

0   5   10

Figure 9.2

Food Spice Level

Table 9.2   Evaluating Spiciness in Food and Wine

Perceived Ratings Range	Description of Perception Level Used in Rating Food/Wine
0 1 2	**Imperceptible (no spice):** If the particular sensation is not detectable or if this sensation fades almost immediately. No perception or barely perceptible levels.
2 3 4	**Little perception (weak spice):** A taste-smell sensation in which one succeeds in identifying or perceiving it in a recognizable way, but the stimulus is not well defined. The level of perception is still low.
4 5 6	**Sufficiently Perceived (moderately spicy):** A taste-smell sensation in which one succeeds in identifying it and perceiving it at a sufficient level. This score should not be based on a hedonic (good or bad) evaluation or appraisal of the taste sensation but simply a quantitative appraisal. There is an intermediate level of perception.
6 7 8	**Abundant perception (intense spice):** A taste-smell sensation in which one can clearly identify and perceive in a very distinct way. The taste-smell sensation is at an emphasized level.
8 9 10	**Highly perceived (powerful spice):** A taste-smell sensation that can be unmistakably identified. One can identify a particular food or clearly characterize a complex preparation. High perceptibility with a lot of emphasis.

IMPACT ON PAIRING POSSIBILITIES

Rule #8: Food spiciness should be equal to wine spiciness.

Rule #9: Spicy food should be paired with off-dry, acidic white wines.

A wine's flavors can complement a food's spicy character or provide a contrast to it with fruity, earthy, oaky, or herbal layers. In either case, take into account the richness and acidity of the food and wine as well. Some pairing experts suggest that spice matches best with white wines.[12] Others suggest that spicy foods should be paired with fruity, young, low-tannin reds or whites with moderate alcohol, some sweetness, and light acidity. What these suggestions have in common is the idea that in many cases hot spicy foods are best paired with a wine that provides a refreshing reprieve to prepare the palate for the next bite. Full-bodied, high-alcohol reds create a sensation of additional heat on the palate rather than a refreshing change. Hot and spicy foods accentuate obvious oak flavors, make dry reds taste astringent, and reduce our perception of sweetness in any wine accompanying them. Therefore, wines with no or light oak and plenty of ripe, juicy fruit flavor are suggested to accompany most hot and spicy foods.[13]

Ground pepper and other savory spices can obscure many of the nuances and complexities of an old, high-quality, and complex wine; such wines should be paired with simple but high-quality foods prepared to perfection. But these spices can interact with simple, light wine to bring it alive and to a higher level of enjoyment. Savory spices can provide a pleasant match when the spice levels are not over the top. If we consider Old World examples of wine and food matches, we can see that traditional foods in places such as France and Italy are not overly spicy—the food is well seasoned but matches in intensity levels with the wines of the region. Spicy characteristics that work in these regions are things such as garlic, herbs, and moderate levels of savory spices (mustard, pepper, horseradish, etc.).

Because New World wines are bigger, bolder, and more fruit-forward, foods from these regions are also bolder and more powerful. Grilled foods with Zinfandel from California,

Name_____ Spice Food Anchor_____

Level of Match (Circle the level of match below):

Riesling

–4	–3	–2	–1	0	+1	+2	+3	+4
Food Less Spicy				Equal Level				Food Higher Spiciness

Gewürztraminer

–4	–3	–2	–1	0	+1	+2	+3	+4
Food Less Spicy				Equal Level				Food Higher Spiciness

Pinot Noir

–4	–3	–2	–1	0	+1	+2	+3	+4
Food Less Spicy				Equal Level				Food Higher Spiciness

Syrah

–4	–3	–2	–1	0	+1	+2	+3	+4
Food Less Spicy				Equal Level				Food Higher Spiciness

Based on your evaluation of this food with the four wine samples, which wine element(s) **positively** impacted the wine and food match (check all that appy)? Please rank them in order of impact (1 = greatest impact)
___ Sweetness ___
___ Acidity ___
___ Tannin ___
___ Alcohol level ___
___ Overall body ___
___ Wine flavor intensity level ___
___ Wine flavor persistence ___
___ Wine spiciness level ___
___ Wine spice type ___

Based on your evaluation of this food with the four wine samples, which wine element(s) **negatively** impacted the wine and food match (check all that apply)? Please rank them in order of impact (1 = greatest impact)
___ Sweetness ___
___ Acidity ___
___ Tannin ___
___ Alcohol level ___
___ Overall body ___
___ Wine flavor intensity level ___
___ Wine flavor persistence ___
___ Wine spiciness level ___
___ Wine spice type ___

Figure 9.3

Wine and Food Spice Match

Malbec with beef from Argentina, and Aussie Shiraz and peppery barbecued steak are examples of this relationship.

Table 9.3 provides some examples of safe bets in wine and food pairings based on the prominent spice flavor. However, do not limit yourself only to these wine selections. What should be apparent from the suggestions in Table 9.3 is that a safe bet for spicy food is a lighter wine with a higher level of acidity. These create a range of matches, from refreshment to neutral to good, depending on the other levels of components and textures in the wine and food. Off-dry wines have a tendency to mask powerful seasonings such as pepper and other hot spices. Acidity and effervescence in wine provide a cleansing effect, preparing the palate for the next bite.

Table 9.3   Safe Bets for Food Spices and Herbs

Herb or Spice	Possible Wines
Coriander and dill	Sauvignon Blanc
Mint	Cabernet Sauvignon
Fresh chiles	Crisp, fruity whites
Dried chiles	Try fruity, lightly acidic whites or lighter reds
Garlic	Sauvignon Blanc, unoaked Chardonnay
Ginger	Alsace Gewürztraminer, Riesling, Champagne
Mustard	Solid acidic whites (Sancerre, Riesling), lighter Chardonnays (unoaked), lighter Pinot Noir, Rioja
Saffron	Dry whites, young Tempranillo
Pepper	Tannic or rustic reds such as Cabernet Sauvignon, Shiraz, Côtes du Rhône
Horseradish	Fruity, lightly acidic white or light red (Sancerre, Dolcetto, Beaujolais)

The exception to this rule is the impact of fruit-forward wines from the New World. While these will not be a great match with highly peppery and hot spicy foods, they will hold their own in this relationship up to moderate or intense spice levels.

The good to synergistic match is determined by the level of spice and basic spice flavor matching in both food and wine, with acidity, sweetness, and texture as other important factors.

SUMMARY

Spices can be categorized into three main groups: sweet, savory, and hot. These categories represent prominent spice flavors that impact the match relationship between wine and food. This relationship is impacted not only by the type of spice but also by the level of spice. Sweet spices are inherently more wine-friendly than hot spices. The level of potential match and wine-friendliness is influenced by the level of savory spices, hot spices, and sweet spices as well as whether the wine selected creates a similar or contrasting match with the food item.

Spices and herbs are distinguished by where these items are derived from on a plant; herbs come from the leaves, while spices come from other parts of the plant. Herbs and herbal characteristics are important in the wine and food match. Herbs are more wine-friendly than spices as a rule.

Spices can have a substantial limiting effect on matching levels of wine with food. High levels of savory and hot spices are potential "wine killers" as much as excessive food sweetness, acidity, saltiness, and bitterness. An assessment of food and wine spiciness is an essential element in predicting the possibility and level of match between a wine and food item.

DISCUSSION QUESTIONS

1. What are the prominent spice categories?

2. How are the different spice sensations defined?

3. What wine elements interact with food spice?

4. What impact do wine tannin, sweetness, and acidity have on food spice?

EXERCISE 9.1

For this exercise, I suggest using neutral white and red jug wines to eliminate any possible spice character interactions—I would use a bulk-produced, unoaked Chardonnay and a bulk-produced Merlot.

OBJECTIVES

To identify and define spice characteristics in white and red wine; to categorize the type of spice as sweet, savory, or hot; to assess and rank the level of spiciness for each wine sample.

Mise en Place: Things to Do Before the Exercise
Review the sections of Chapter 9 describing the wine spice sensations. Assemble the food ingredients, wines, and other materials. Prepare one sample per student (about 1 ounce) of each of the following wine samples laced with spices as shown in Table 9.4 and described in step 3 below.

Table 9.4 Wine Samples with Spice for Exercise 9.1

Wines	Plain	Sweet	Savory	Hot
White jug wine	1 No spice	2 Nutmeg	3 White pepper	4 Jalapeño
Red jug wine	5 No spice	6 Cinnamon or cardamom	7 Black pepper	8 Cayenne

Table 9.5 Exercise 9.1 Materials

2 white paper placemats per student, with numbered or labeled circles to place wineglasses (Figures 9.4a and 9.4b)	Crackers to cleanse the palate
1 spit cup per student	Napkins
Corkscrew	Drinking water for each student
1 copy of the Aroma Wheel per student	8 wineglasses per student
2 copies Figure 9.1 per student	

STEPS

1. Purchase the wines.
2. Chill the white wine prior to the tasting.
3. Divide both the white and red wines into four equal parts. One part is to be left plain and not spiced. The remaining three parts are to be spiced as shown in Table 9.4. The spice levels should be brought to a point where an aroma is detectable to the knowledgeable wine evaluator. Allow the spiced wines to sit long enough for the flavors to infuse the wine.
4. Set out placemats and wine glasses and distribute the wine samples.

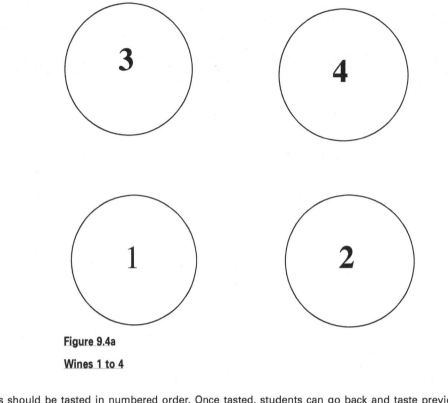

Figure 9.4a

Wines 1 to 4

5. Wine samples should be tasted in numbered order. Once tasted, students can go back and taste previous samples. Students should identify the spice, categorize it, and rank the level of sensation according to Figure 9.1. Discuss the findings with the group.

6. Rank the white wine samples from lowest to highest spice levels.
   Lowest spice = 1. _____ 2. _____ 3. _____
   4. _____ = Highest spice

7. Rank the red wine samples from lowest to highest spice levels.
   Lowest spice = 1. _____ 2. _____ 3. _____
   4. _____ = Highest spice

8. Write any other comments, thoughts, and observations that you identified during this evaluation process. How did you identify spice flavors? Was the identification primarily driven by the aroma or in-mouth smells? Was it more or less difficult to identify the spice type and level in white wine compared to red wine? Did the plain wine samples have any herbal or spice characteristics?

EXERCISE 9.2

RANKING AND MATCHING SPICE LEVELS IN FOOD AND WINE

In this exercise, which involves identifying spice types and levels in both food and wine and assessing their interaction, two of the wine samples are traditionally described as spicy: the Gewürztraminer and the Shiraz. The other wine samples are relatively low in spicy characteristics. The Riesling should have an acidity that helps to provide a cleansing impact and which masks any sweetness in the wine. The Pinot Noir is a medium-bodied wine that can have a variety of flavor characteristics depending on the climate, terroir, and production techniques used. These flavors can range from jammy to minerally or spicy, or the wine can be relatively neutral. Research suggests that Pinot Noir works best with less spicy cheeses,[14] but other authors have suggested Pinot Noir is a good match with certain types of spicy foods;[15] you will need to judge for yourself.

The aroma wheel can be helpful in identifying specific spices or herbs within general categories.

OBJECTIVES

To identify the type of spice and rank spice level in four wine varietals; to identify the spice type and rank spice level in five food samples; to determine level of perceived match for each food sample with all four wine samples.

Mise en Place: Things to Do Before the Exercise Review the sections of Chapter 9 describing the wine and food spice sensations. Assemble the food ingredients, wines, and other materials. Prepare one sample per student (about 1 ounce) of the wine samples as shown in Table 9.6. Prepare the popcorn samples as in step 2 below, tossed with the spices shown in Table 9.7.

Table 9.6   Wine Samples for Exercise 9.2

White	Dry Riesling	Gewürztraminer
Red	Pinot Noir	Shiraz

Table 9.7   Spiced Food Samples for Exercise 9.2

Popcorn Sample 1	Popcorn Sample 2	Popcorn Sample 3	Popcorn Sample 4	Popcorn Sample 5
Plain salted	Spiced with Cajun or Creole seasoning	Spiced with taco seasoning	Spiced with curry	Spiced with Chinese 5-spice seasoning

Table 9.8   Materials Needed for Exercise 9.2

1 white paper placemat per student with numbered or labeled circles to place wineglasses (Figure 9.4a)	Crackers to cleanse the palate
1 spit cup per student	Napkins
Corkscrew	Drinking water for each student
1 copy of the Aroma Wheel per student	4 wineglasses per student
5 copies of Figure 9.3 per student	1 copy of Figure 9.1 and 1 copy of Figure 9.2 per student

STEPS

1. Purchase the wines and chill the white wines prior to tasting.

2. Using an air popper, pop the popcorn. Divide the popcorn into five parts. Leave one part plain and toss the remaining four parts with one spice type each. The spices used can be commercially prepared spice mixes or created using your favorite recipe.

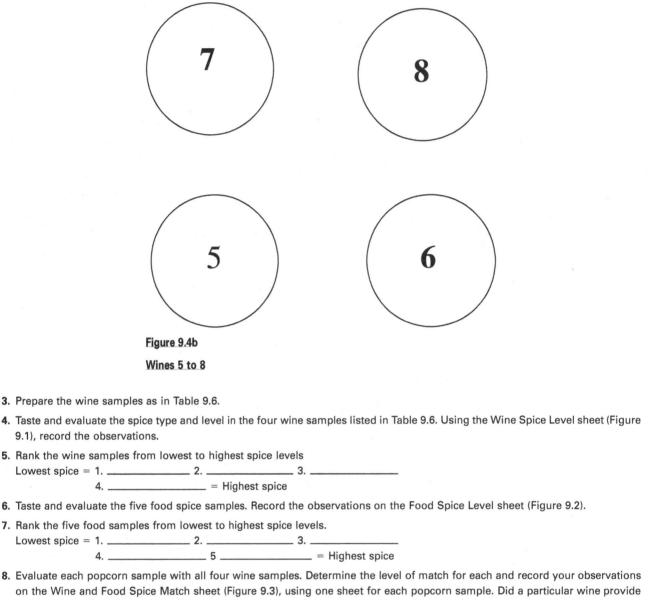

Figure 9.4b

Wines 5 to 8

3. Prepare the wine samples as in Table 9.6.

4. Taste and evaluate the spice type and level in the four wine samples listed in Table 9.6. Using the Wine Spice Level sheet (Figure 9.1), record the observations.

5. Rank the wine samples from lowest to highest spice levels
   Lowest spice = 1. _____ 2. _____ 3. _____
   4. _____ = Highest spice

6. Taste and evaluate the five food spice samples. Record the observations on the Food Spice Level sheet (Figure 9.2).

7. Rank the five food samples from lowest to highest spice levels.
   Lowest spice = 1. _____ 2. _____ 3. _____
   4. _____ 5 _____ = Highest spice

8. Evaluate each popcorn sample with all four wine samples. Determine the level of match for each and record your observations on the Wine and Food Spice Match sheet (Figure 9.3), using one sheet for each popcorn sample. Did a particular wine provide a good overall match across all spice types? Did a particular wine provide a poor overall match across all spice types? Which wines created a similarity match with food samples with regard to spice type or level? Which wines created a contrasting match with food samples with regard to spice type or level? Which spice type was the most difficult to match? Was one or more spice type(s) particularly wine-friendly? Was one or more spice type(s) a "wine killer?"

EXERCISE 9.3

OPTIONAL EXERCISE

Try a variety of wine styles (white and red) with everyday items such as chips and salsa, barbecue potato chips, chorizo, and pepper jack cheese. Or try your favorite ethnic and regional recipes for Thai, Indian, Cajun, Tex-Mex, Caribbean, Japanese, or hot and spicy Chinese cuisine. Wines that have a greater likelihood of matching with these foods are those with crisp acidity, slight sweetness, light to medium body, low to moderate alcohol, smoother tannins, and a relatively neutral flavor.

NOTES

1. Judith Bluysen, personal communication, January 15, 2006, Paris.
2. John D. Folse, *The Encyclopedia of Cajun & Creole Cuisine* (Gonzales, LA: Chef John Folse and Co., 2004).
3. Bluysen, personal communication.
4. D. R. Tainter and A. T. Grenis, *Spices and Seasonings: A Food Technology Handbook*, 2nd ed. (New York: John Wiley and Sons, Inc., 2001).
5. Andrea Immer, *Great Tastes Made Simple: Extraordinary Food and Wine Pairing for Every Palate.* (New York: Broadway Books, 2002); C. A. Rietz, *A Guide to the Selection, Combination, and Cooking of Foods* (Westport, CT: AVI, 1961).
6. D. Rosengarten and J. Wesson, *Red Wine with Fish: The New Art of Matching Wine with Food* (New York: Simon and Schuster, 1989).
7. Immer, *Great Tastes Made Simple*; J. Robinson, *Concise Wine Companion.* (Oxford, UK: Oxford University Press, 2001).
8. Tainter and Grenis, *Spices and Seasonings*.
9. M. Bennion and B. Scheule, *Introductory Foods*, 12th ed. (Upper Saddle River, NJ: Pearson–Prentice Hall, 2004).
10. *The American Heritage College Dictionary* (New York: Houghton Mifflin Company, 1997), p. 707.
11. F. Beckett. *How to Match Food and Wine* (London: Octopus, 2002).
12. Rosengarten and Wesson, *Red Wine with Fish*.
13. Beckett, *How to Match Food and Wine*.
14. R. J. Harrington and R. Hammond, "A Change from Anecdotal to Empirical: An Alternative Approach to Predicting Matches Between Wine and Food," *Proceedings of the EuroCHRIE Conference* 23 (2005): 1–8.
15. Immer, *Great Tastes Made Simple*.

CHAPTER 10

FLAVOR INTENSITY AND FLAVOR PERSISTENCY

CHAPTER OUTLINE:

Introduction

Aperitif: Release Weekend Wine and Food Menu from On the Twenty

Identifying Flavor Types in Wine and Food

Food Flavor Categories

Wine Flavor Categories

Assessing Flavor Intensity

The Interaction of Wine and Food Flavor Intensity

Assessing Flavor Persistency

The Interaction of Wine and Food Flavor Persistency

Summary

Exercises

Key Concepts

KEY CONCEPTS:

- Retronasal flavors
- In-mouth flavor evaluation process
- Umami
- Flavor intensity levels
- Wine length, finish, and aftertaste

INTRODUCTION

For me there is no better aroma than the fragrance of a well-prepared veal stock that has been simmering in the kettle all night. There is also something special about the smell of freshly baked bread or homemade pie. But the experience of aromas and flavors goes beyond the present moment—they can evoke memories and emotions of past experiences. Because of this, we use flavor and smells constantly to evoke responses from consumers in a variety of settings. For example, real estate agents trying to sell a home suggest baking bread, burning scented candles, or simmering apples on the stove so that the aromas evoke a "homey" feeling in potential buyers.

Flavor research has made significant progress during the past few decades and has helped to provide a greater understanding of the flavor chemistry in food and beverage products. Most food and beverage flavors are very complex, with human perception impacted by both context and inter-

---

Evaluato's Name: _____

Wine: _____ Producer: _____ Vintage: _____

Flavor Intensity & ID _____
Flavor Persistency

| | 0 | 5 | 10 |

Mark all flavor categories that apply in the boxes below

Flavor Type:

Fruity	Nutty	Smoky	Buttery	Herbal	Floral	Earthy	Other

Wine: _____ Producer: _____ Vintage: _____

Flavor Intensity & ID _____
Flavor Persistency

| | 0 | 5 | 10 |

Mark all flavor categories that apply in the boxes below

Flavor Type:

Fruity	Nutty	Smoky	Buttery	Herbal	Floral	Earthy	Other

Wine: _____ Producer: _____ Vintage: _____

Flavor Intensity & ID _____
Flavor Persistency

| | 0 | 5 | 10 |

Mark all flavor categories that apply in the boxes below

Flavor Type:

Fruity	Nutty	Smoky	Buttery	Herbal	Floral	Earthy	Other

Wine: _____ Producer: _____ Vintage: _____

Flavor Intensity & ID _____
Flavor Persistency

| | 0 | 5 | 10 |

Mark all flavor categories that apply in the boxes below

Flavor Type:

Fruity	Nutty	Smoky	Buttery	Herbal	Floral	Earthy	Other

Figure 10.1

Wine Intensity and Persistency Level

actions with competing flavors and other factors.[1] These interactions are both physiological and psychological.

Flavor is perceived through both aroma inhaled nasally and the retronasal smell when the food or wine is in the mouth. For our purposes, the term *flavor* refers to the retronasal, or in-mouth, smells associated with food and beverage products.

There is a wide range of specific and identifiable flavors, but the major flavor categories include *fruity, nutty, smoky, herbal, spicy, cheesy, earthy,* and *meaty.* In terms of the pairing process, the specific flavor of a food or wine and its degree of persistence as well as the intensity of the flavor affect the level of a particular match. In wine and food pairing, the dominant flavors can be either similar or contrasting.

The food and wine flavor categories used in the evaluation system (see Figures 10.1 and 10.2) include dominant flavor(s), flavor intensity, flavor persistency, and spicy flavors. The full evaluation form (see Chapter 11) also provides space for the evaluator to note other important flavor descriptions. This option is particularly useful when the flavor of the food or wine packs a relatively high level of intensity.

Evaluato's Name: _____

Food Item: _____

0   5   10

Flavor Intensity & ID_____
Flavor Persistency

Mark all flavor categories that apply in the boxes below

Flavor Type:	Fruity	Nutty	Smoky	Cheesy	Herbal	Umami	Earthy	Other

Food Item: _____

0   5   10

Flavor Intensity & ID_____
Flavor Persistency

Mark all flavor categories that apply in the boxes below

Flavor Type:	Fruity	Nutty	Smoky	Cheesy	Herbal	Umami	Earthy	Other

Food Item: _____

0   5   10

Flavor Intensity & ID_____
Flavor Persistency

Mark all flavor categories that apply in the boxes below

Flavor Type:	Fruity	Nutty	Smoky	Cheesy	Herbal	Umami	Earthy	Other

Food Item: _____

0   5   10

Flavor Intensity & ID_____
Flavor Persistency

Mark all flavor categories that apply in the boxes below

Flavor Type:	Fruity	Nutty	Smoky	Cheesy	Herbal	Umami	Earthy	Other

Figure 10.2

Food Intensity and Persistency Level

While flavors in food or wine may not be the most important element driving pairing decisions, they are generally the most interesting. It is important to note that flavors in wine come from different sources than flavors in food, and so wine flavor words such as *fruity, spicy,* or *herbal* are generally metaphoric in nature. As noted in Chapter 9 in regard to spiciness, do not assume that a wine and food make a good match just because they can be described with the same adjectives. In most cases, it is easier to match food with wine based on contrasting flavors—for example, matching smoky foods with flowery wines such as Riesling, or matching spices such as cinnamon, clove, or saffron in food with the herbal or grassy character of Sauvignon Blanc. If a food and wine truly have similar flavors, they will usually go well together.

Matching the flavor intensity of food and beverage items is an important element in creating a synergistic match. Matching intensity creates a sense of balance and equal footing between the wine and the food. Flavor intensity may be perceived at a variety of levels, ranging from virtually nonexistent to extremely strong.

Assessing flavor attributes in food and beverages is less straightforward than evaluating taste components (sweet, sour, salty, bitter) or tactile elements (texture). The measuring instrument used to assess flavor intensity—a human being—is an extremely sensitive device, but it also is relatively unreliable due to a variety of psychological factors, physiological factors, and individual differences, among other reasons. Have you ever tasted something that reminded you of a certain time or event? Do you have a memory of flavor that inspires you? Disgusts you? Or makes you feel excited? All of us have specific and individual reactions to flavors based on past experiences.

Complicating this task further is the fact that food and wine flavors are unstable. The food and beverage products being examined are in a dynamic state and are impacted by changes in temperature and exposure to the external environment.[2]

The following sections provide an overview of what to consider when determining flavor identification, flavor intensity, and flavor persistency of food and wine items. This discussion and the exercises that follow will provide you with a better understanding of the measurement process and the associated potential pitfalls to help you to fine-tune your personal human measurement instrument.

Aperitif I Release Weekend Wine and Food Menu from On the Twenty

On the Twenty, Ontario's first and best-known estate winery restaurant, is consistently rated as one of the finest restaurants in Canada. The culinary team is led by Kevin Maniaci and is committed to the flavors of Niagara's bountiful harvest. The restaurant is located in the Inn on the Twenty, which comprises a twenty-four-room main inn, Vintage House, Winemaker's Cottage, and full-service spa. The Inn on the Twenty is located in the village of Jordan on the Niagara Peninsula, Ontario. The wine list features Vintner's Quality Alliance (VQA) wines from Cave Spring Cellars as well as other VQA wines of Canada.

Cave Spring Cellars is located across the street, and visitors are welcome to tour the winery and sample its well-regarded wines. Cave Spring Cellars was founded in 1986 by grape grower Leonard Pennachetti and winemaker Angelo Pavan. The vineyards are nestled along Niagara's Beamsville Bench at the heart of the Niagara Escarpment. Cave Spring has one of Niagara's oldest vinifera plantings.

Additional information about On the Twenty or Cave Spring Cellars can be obtained by visiting their Web sites at www.innonthetwenty.com and www.cavespringcellars.com.

The food-and-wine menu shown here is from a recent release weekend, when new Cave Spring Cellars wines are released for sale. It features three tastings per course to create multiple sensations with the featured wines. This menu underscores the concepts introduced in this chapter regarding flavor type, flavor intensity, and flavor persistency. This provides a great experience for the guest, highlighting a variety of synergistic food-and-wine matches in every course.

Welcome to Inn on the Twenty
Release Weekend

Amuse-Bouche

Pear-cardamom chutney in prosciutto
Petit quiche of squash and Geai Bleu
Scallop ceviche on pickled cucumber
Cave Spring Cellars 2003 Brut

~~~

Leek and camembert soup
Pomegranate-glazed quail on baby arugula
Pork tenderloin on quince purée
CSV Riesling 2004

~~~

Insalata bianco
Duck confit and pistachio with truffled greens
Pan-seared Arctic char with vanilla corn beurre blanc
Chardonnay Reserve 2003

~~~

Monkfish Bourguignon
Grilled lamb chop with preserved lemon and white beans
Seared veal tenderloin with tomato risotto
Pinot Noir 2004

~~~

Smoked wild boar and wild rice agnolotti in veal broth
Garlic and anchovy shrimp Provençal
Bone marrow custard with sel de mer
Gamay Reserve 2004

~~~

Balsamic crème caramel
Riesling-and-spice-poached pear
Crème fraiche almond tart
Indian Summer Late Harvest Riesling 2004

Which dishes do you believe will have complementary or contrasting flavor types? Which combinations do you think should have the best match in flavor intensity and persistency? Why?

IDENTIFYING FLAVOR TYPES IN WINE AND FOOD

The first step in evaluating the flavor factors in food is to determine the dominant flavor(s) present. As previously noted, there is a range of flavor types that includes flavors such as *fruity, nutty, smoky, cheesy, buttery, herbal, meaty, umami,* and *earthy*. While this may seem straightforward, the perception of flavor is impacted by the interrelationships of salt, sugar, acids, and texture as well as by the in-mouth flavor identification process. For example, without sufficient levels of acid and sweetness, fruit flavors such as strawberry fall flat when tasted in the mouth.[3]

In-Mouth Process Determining flavor type and intensity is based on aroma perception and retronasal olfaction (the smell of a food or wine once it's in your mouth, which is due to the connection between the oral and nasal cavities). Much of what you perceive as taste or flavor is primarily driven by your ability to smell.

To maximize your potential when identifying aromas in wine and food, you need to follow the simple nosing steps described in Chapter 2. When evaluating wine, fill the glass no more than one-third full. This will allow you to properly swirl the wine and fully release aromas. Tilt the glass toward you and place your nose inside the bowl. Take one deep sniff or three or four short sniffs, then remove your nose from the glass to consider the aromas. This is what is considered the "first nose" of the wine, providing you with your first impressions of the aroma. After swirling the wine a second time and allowing the aromas to open up more fully, follow the same smelling procedure. Many times, in this "second nose," you will notice aromas different from those you detected in the first nose. This process can be done for food while it is on a plate, in a cup, or on a fork.

A challenge when identifying and assessing the intensity of in-mouth flavors is maximizing the ability to detect specific flavors and their intensity. Numerous research studies have evaluated the impact that talking, swallowing, exhaling through the nose, chewing, and tongue movements have on an evaluator's perception of in-mouth flavors.[4] When identifying flavors in food and wine, the main objectives are to release the flavor components while in the oral cavity, and to ensure that the back-of-the-mouth nasal cavity is open. As you swallow and talk, the nasal cavity closes, limiting access to retro-nasal flavors.

To release the flavor components in wine and other liquids, it is helpful to retain the product in the oral cavity for several seconds (up to a minute) with normal breathing. Once the time has passed, the air is deliberately exhaled through the nose. This process ensures that the nasal cavity is open to help you to better assess types of flavors and their intensity. Some wine evaluators will suck in additional air through the mouth to intensify flavor sensations.

Chewing releases flavor compounds in some foods, assisting in maximizing in-mouth flavors and identification. As with liquids, experiments have demonstrated that food molecules released into the airspace of the oral cavity will proceed to the nasal cavity if air is exhaled through the nose while the lips are closed.[5]

FOOD FLAVOR CATEGORIES

Once you have tasted a food item, note the dominant flavor(s) present. Also note any other flavors present in the food. Most of the major food flavors are fairly self-explanatory. However, one that may need additional discussion is umami, identified by Japanese flavor researchers. In Japanese, the word *umami* basically translates as "deliciousness." Most wine and food pairing books suggest that umami is not generally a key driver when matching food and wine.[6] Further, pairing experts suggest umami is a concept similar to savoriness or meatiness in terms of a pairing characteristic.[7] For our purposes, umami is described as the flavor associated with sources such as soy products, mushrooms, MSG, meat glazes, and tomatoes. While umami is not a main factor in wine and food matching, it does create a wine-friendly characteristic in food that makes certain foods more versatile with regard to matching them with various wines. A suggestion for pairing wines to foods with umami flavors is to use medium- to full-bodied red wines depending on the strength of the umami flavor present in the food item. Highly intense umami flavor will overshadow light whites, but less intense umami-flavored dishes work well with all types of white wines.

Earthy food flavors provide a positive, wine-friendly element in many foods, including garlic, potatoes, mushrooms, truffles, some cheeses, rainbow trout, beans, and many grains. Earthy foods work particularly well with wines that have earthy elements. Wines from the

Old World have a tendency toward greater levels of earthiness. Specific wine examples are provided in Table 10.1.

Smoky foods need wine that has a strong enough personality to cope with this more powerful flavor. Smokiness generally works well with oaked, rich, and fruity whites or spicy reds. Smoked fish, pork, and other meats can also be paired with German Kabinett Riesling. Smoky barbecue sauces generally work well with powerful reds such as Shiraz or Zinfandel, but you must make sure that the sweetness and acidity levels in the sauce are not too extreme. Smoky barbecue sauces with higher sweetness can be served with reds that have plenty of fruit—New World reds and Old World examples such as Beaujolais, Dolcetto, and Tempranillo.

As discussed in Chapter 9, foods with prominent herbal flavors can generally be paired with Sauvignon Blanc, but the type of herbal flavor in the food will have an impact on the affinity of this potential match. Refer to Tables 9.1 and 9.3 for some suggestions in this area.

WINE FLAVOR CATEGORIES

Identifying and categorizing wine flavors tends to be more difficult than food flavors. For food, you have the physical product (such as a bell pepper) to cue you about what you are about to taste and smell. For wine and other beverages, we are forced to rely on our aroma memory and the quality of our sensory abilities. Practice is the only way to improve your ability to identify the various wine flavors.

The aroma wheel is an industry standard used to identify and categorize wine aromas. While there are a number of possible aromas in wine, there are seven dominant categories that seem to have a direct correlation to the wine and food pairing process. These are included in the lower boxed in area of each section in Figure 10.1 and include *fruity, nutty, smoky, buttery, herbal, floral,* and *earthy.* The *other* category includes flavors such as meaty, vegetative, chemical, and so on. Spiciness is not included here because it is assessed separately, as discussed in Chapter 9.

Table 10.1 provides examples of wines that typically fall into the seven major flavor categories. This table can be used as a basic guide for pairing when wine flavor serves as a driver for wine and food matching.

A young Riesling is the classic fruity example. While many of the wines on the market have fruity aromas and flavors, these aromas and flavors vary by varietal and climate zone. Most wine made with the Riesling grapes has an intensely fruity and in some cases floral characteristic.

Nutty aromas and flavors in wine are less common. Some types of sherry have nutty characteristics and are a natural match, as an aperitif, with salted nuts. Fino and Amontillado sherries have a nutty character that creates a similarity match with almonds.

Smoky characteristics in wine are common in some New World Chardonnays and particularly in oaky Australian ones.

The classic herbal example is Sauvignon Blanc from New Zealand. Sauvignon Blanc wines are generally quite herbaceous as well as occasionally grassy or vegetal.

Oaky Chardonnays from California, Washington, and Australia that have undergone malolactic fermentation provide classic buttery characteristics.

Moscato d'Asti, an Italian sparkling wine from the Piedmont region, has an inherent floral flavor. Earthy flavors are more likely in Old World wines and particularly likely in French white wines and French reds from Burgundy, Bordeaux, or Côte Rôtie.

Two additional flavors can sometimes be found in wine: cheesy and meaty. Aged Greco di Tufo (white) and some Chianti, Brunello, or Valpolicella (reds), which are all Italian wines, are likely to have cheesy flavors. Sometimes wines can be described as meaty. Young Pomerol (France) and young Merlot from California or Washington tend to be meaty wines.[8]

Table 10.1   Examples of Wines Likely to Have Particular Flavors

Wine Flavor	Whites	Reds
Fruity	Gewürztraminer Muscat Pinot Grigio Pinot Gris Riesling Soave	Barbera Beaujolais Dolcetto Lemberger Merlot (some young from California, Oregon, Washington) Pinot Noir (young) Valpolicella
Nutty	Fino Sherry Amontillado Sherry	
Smoky	Aged Burgundy Oaky Chardonnay (New World, Australia, California and Chile in particular)	Aged Barolo and Barbaresco Some aged Cabernet Sauvignon (Australian, Chilean) Aged Rioja
Herbal	Fumé Blanc (California, Washington) Pouilly-Fumé Sancerre Sauvignon Blanc (New World, New Zealand in particular)	Bordeaux (young) Cabernet Franc (Ontario) Some Meritage reds Cabernet Sauvignon (young from California, Washington, Okanagan)
Buttery	Many oaky New World Chardonnay (California, Australia, Washington)	Perceptible in some reds that have undergone malolactic fermentation Some Spanish Tempranillo and Rioja
Floral	Moscato d'Asti Muscat Some Gewürztraminer	
Earthy	French whites in general Aged Burgundy (France) Some aged Chardonnay	Aged Bordeaux Aged Burgundy Some Pinot Noir (Oregon in particular) Côte Rôtie Some Syrah (Washington, Côtes du Rhône, some South Africa)

ASSESSING FLAVOR INTENSITY

As defined in Chapter 9, flavor intensity is the level of concentration, power, or force of the prominent flavors: spicy, herbal, earthy, or fruity. These levels can be described verbally on a scale ranging from no flavor to weak flavor, moderately strong flavor, strong flavor, and powerful flavor.

When evaluating flavor intensity, there are a number of issues to consider. First, you must consider the order in which a series of wines and a series of food dishes are tasted. You should also make note of which is tasted first, the wine or the food, since this tasting sequence can have some impact on perceived intensity levels of flavor in both the food and wine. Research indicates that when items with a moderate concentration of flavor intensity are preceded by items with lower concentration levels, the moderate-concentration item always rates higher in intensity than when it is preceded by an item of higher concentration.[9] A solution to this issue is to do a reversed-pair test within the tasting group or for evaluators to taste the items both before and after lower or higher concentrations before determining their final assessment of intensity.

When identifying flavors and intensity, context matters. To avoid many problems, you should follow the suggestions in the "Setting up a Tasting Session" section of Chapter 2, or

Table 10.2 Flavor Intensity Levels in Food and Wine

Perceived Intensity Range	Description of Perception Level Used in Rating Intensity
0 1 2	**Undetectable (no flavor):** If the particular sensation is not detectable or if this sensation fades almost immediately. No perception or barely perceptible levels.
2 3 4	**Little perception (weak flavor):** A taste-smell sensation in which one succeeds in identifying or perceiving it in a recognizable way, but the stimulus is not well-defined. The level of perception is still low.
4 5 6	**Sufficiently perceived (moderately strong):** A taste-smell sensation in which one succeeds in identifying and perceiving it at a sufficient level. Perception is at an intermediate level.
6 7 8	**Abundantly Perceived (strong):** A taste-smell sensation in which one can clearly identify and perceive it in a well-defined way. The taste-smell sensation is at an emphasized level.
8 9 10	**Highly perceived (powerful):** A taste-smell sensation that can be unmistakably identified. One can identify a particular food or clearly characterize a complex preparation. High perceptibility with a lot of emphasis.

research sensory evaluation methods in books at your school or public library. Aside from the external context issues, the internal context of how the wine or food item is presented can impact retronasal assessments. Other taste components (sweetness, sourness, saltiness, and bitterness) can have an impact—for example, as noted earlier, sweetness interacts with strawberry flavors to increase the overall perceived flavor intensity.[10] Texture in food and liquids—tannin, alcohol, oak, fattiness, viscosity, and body—has also been shown to impact overall perceptions of intensity.[11]

When the sensation of flavor intensity of wine or food is described as "no flavor" or is at an undetectable level (the 0–2 value band), the flavor is imperceptible or fades almost immediately. In wine and food with weak flavor (the 2–4 value band), there is a recognizable flavor sensation, but the stimulus is not very strong. With moderately strong flavor intensity in wine or food (the 4–6 value band), the flavor is "sufficient"—that is, it can be clearly defined. The sensation of strong flavor (the 6–8 value band) means that the flavor sensation can be clearly identified. With powerful flavor intensity (the 8–10 value band), the flavor can be unmistakably identified and is strongly emphasized.

THE INTERACTION OF WINE AND FOOD FLAVOR INTENSITY

Rule #10: Food and wine flavor types can be matched using similarity or contrast.

Rule #11: Wine and food flavor intensity should be equal.

It is important to note that each flavor type has differing acceptable levels and combinations for an ideal match in wine and food. In general, flavor types can be matched using similarity or contrast. Contrast can be particularly interesting. For instance, the fruit flavors in mango relish contrast with and complement the smoky, meaty flavors in grilled swordfish.

Fruity wines paired with smoky foods can create the same type of pleasant flavor contrast. Of course, the key to a successful flavor contrast match is to also ensure the components, texture, and spice characteristics are a match.

Finally, achieving a flavor intensity match plays an important role in the quest for a synergistic relationship between wine and food. Research indicates that tasting foods with a high level of flavor intensity prior to drinking wines of lower flavor intensity lowers the perceived flavor characteristics of the wine. For example, the flavors in blue cheese substantially decrease perception of flavors in white wine such as apple, citrus, oak, and herbal.[12] Without a flavor intensity match, the relationship at best will be one in which either the food or the wine is only a supporting actor; at worst, it can be a total mismatch.

ASSESSING FLAVOR PERSISTENCY

Flavor persistency is the final criterion used in the pairing decision process. Defined as "continuance of an effect after the cause is removed,"[13] persistence can be a pleasant and important indicator of wine and food quality, or it can create a negative aftertaste. Aftertaste is defined as "a taste that remains in the mouth after a food has been swallowed."[14] In wine terminology, persistency is described as length (*longueur* in French and *longitude* in Spanish) or finish (*fin de bouche* in French and *final de boca* in Spanish).[15]

Wine Flavor Persistency Several terms have been used synonymously for persistency in wine tasting. *Finish* is defined as the final sensations of wine on the palate, *length* is defined as persistency in flavor,[16] and *aftertaste* as the impressions that linger after the wine is swallowed or spit out.

Flavor persistency is an indicator of the quality of wine and may also reveal flaws that might not have been apparent in the initial stages of tasting. For instance, a bitter aftertaste may be initially perceived as astringency. Improper storage or handling of wine can create unpleasant aftertastes, or they may occur due to the presence of spent yeasts or lactic acid left in a wine that has not been properly fermented or stabilized.[17] By contrast, one indicator of a good wine is when the length has a clean, balanced, and complete structure and the complete flavors linger in a long finish. A wine with good flavor persistency provides more bang for your buck—you get more flavor out of each sip.

Flavor persistency is an evolutionary process that occurs during the final phases of the tasting process. A common method of assessing flavor persistency is to time how long the flavor lingers and how long the aromatic sensations are apparent after swallowing or spitting. The measurement of flavor persistency begins with the concept of finish and moves on to the persistence of flavor, which generally lasts for approximately 3 to 15 seconds. Finally, there is potential for an unpleasant taste or aftertaste, which may indicate a faulty wine.[18] In terms of the aftertaste of wine, a good white wine leaves the mouth scented and gently motivated by fresh acidity; a good red wine fills the mouth with its retronasal smells and the rich character of its tannin.[19]

An important consideration of wine quality is the aromatic element in a wine's finish. Aromatic persistence is likely created by the least volatile and most durable flavor compounds inherent in a wine. It can be difficult to isolate this aspect from the other sensations.[20] In my study, flavor intensity and flavor persistence were shown to be closely and strongly connected by the majority of the tasting panel.[21] While the flavor intensity and flavor persistence of wine and food can be closely connected, they are separate issues. Intensity relates to initial power or force, while persistence relates to the length and aftertaste of the sensation. Other issues related to flavor quality are the refinement of flavor and aromas and their appeal.[22]

Many wine writers propose measuring and classifying flavor persistence on a hierarchical basis, using 3-second intervals (i.e., less than 3 seconds, 4–6 seconds, 7–9 seconds, 10–12 seconds, 13 or more seconds).[23] This hierarchical basis is used in the measurement method presented in this text and is discussed further at the conclusion of this section.

Food Flavor Persistency   Flavor profile analysis is a process in which "the judge is asked to record aromas, flavors, and aftertastes in the order perceived and their intensities using a constant rating scale."[24] Sensory analysts use the concept of the time-intensity curve to tie intensity and persistency together in food products. The typical time-intensity curve includes assessing maximum intensity, time to maximum, total duration, maximum rates of onset and decay, lag time, plateau time, and areas before and after maximum intensity.[25]

Persistency in food is part of an overall assessment of intensity, duration, and aftertaste. While persistency in wine provides an indication of quality, persistency in food flavor is more closely related to the intensity of ingredients included in the finished dish. The relationship with wine persistency is one of creating dishes that do not overpower the wine served with them.

How Persistency Is Measured   The basic process for assessing persistency is similar for both wine and food. However, food requires chewing to release flavor compounds and induce retronasal smells in the oral cavity. Steps in the process for assessing food-and-wine flavor persistency are described below:

1. Take a good-sized sip of wine or small taste of food.
2. If you are tasting a liquid, roll the liquid around your gums, cheeks, and the roof of your mouth for 2–3 seconds. If you are tasting a solid food, chew the food to release the flavors and to cover all of the mouth surfaces, ensuring complete contact with taste receptors.
3. Swallow or spit. (Don't talk—talking closes the nasal cavity.)[26] Keep your mouth closed and force the air out through your nose.
4. Count the number of seconds that the wine or food flavors persistent. Finish in wine can last up to a minute in some cases.[27]

Following are the value bands for the number of seconds in a wine or food's finish (see Figures B.1 and B.2):

3 seconds or less = 0–2 on the 10-point scale

4–6 seconds = 2–4 on the 10-point scale

7–9 seconds = 4–6 on the 10-point scale

10–12 seconds = 6–8 on the 10-point scale

13 or more seconds = 8–10 on the 10-point scale

THE INTERACTION OF WINE AND FOOD FLAVOR PERSISTENCY

Rule #12: Flavor persistency of wine and food should be equal.

A general definition for persistence is when the flavor continues to be perceptible for a period of time after swallowing. While the basic level of persistence seems relatively straightforward in terms of the number of seconds the flavor persists, the evaluator needs to separate component and texture elements from the flavor characteristics of the wine or food. In wine, the persistence of flavor is a primary indicator of quality. In terms of wine and food pairing, the objective is to marry wine and food flavors that enhance each other to increase the overall gastronomic experience. An appropriate lingering of these flavors will provide the guest with a longer period of sensory stimulation to enjoy the marriage—and neither food nor wine will overpower or underwhelm the other.

SUMMARY

An assessment of flavor type and intensity is not as straightforward as the assessment of taste components or texture in wine and food. Flavor analysis and research is a complex endeavor that draws from a variety of disciplines: psychology, physiology, sensory analysis, and chemistry. The nature of flavor compounds, contextual issues, and individual differences create challenges for assessment. Students of wine and food pairing can overcome many of these challenges by identifying potential obstacles and creating settings that minimize their effects.

Food and wine are made up of a web of flavor compounds. As evaluators, our job is to determine and quantify the most prominent ones. These are the ones that will impact the level of match when wine and food are consumed together. To assist in the identity of flavor types and intensity levels in wine and food, this chapter has presented suggestions for maximizing in-mouth flavor identification, lists of wines that are likely to have the various flavor categories, and descriptions of flavor intensity at a range of levels.

The main goal of flavor type identity and flavor intensity assessment is to move the wine and food match from a neutral or good match to a synergistic one. Similarity or contrasting approaches to food-and-wine matches with respect to flavor type and flavor intensity add a sense of refinement and interest to the final gastronomic product.

Persistency in food-and-wine flavor create an additional sensation for the match. Persistency in wine flavor is an important indicator of quality and provides more value to the consumer. Food flavor persistency is driven by the food products included in the finished dish and its preparation. Ingredients, cooking method, and protein type have an impact on flavor persistency.

DISCUSSION QUESTIONS

1. What are the prominent flavor categories?

2. What contextual issues should you be aware of prior to and during flavor assessment?

3. What is the suggested process for assessing in-mouth flavors?

4. What impact does flavor type matching have on the wine and food pairing process?

5. What is the relationship between wine and food flavor intensity?

6. What does the length of persistency in wine flavor indicate?

7. What is the relationship between wine and food persistency?

EXERCISE 10.1

WINE FLAVOR INTENSITY AND PERSISTENCY

For this exercise, I suggest comparing a jug Chardonnay and jug Cabernet Sauvignon with a moderately priced Chardonnay and Cabernet Sauvignon. The moderately priced Chardonnay can be selected from a variety of producers, but some possible suggestions include Beringer, BV, Cambria, Chateau Ste Michelle, Clos du Bois, J. Lohr, Kendall-Jackson, Robert Mondavi, and Simi, to name a few. For a moderately priced Cabernet Sauvignon, try Beringer, BV, Chateau Ste Michelle, Clos du Bois, Franciscan, Gallo Estate, Kendall-Jackson, Robert Mondavi, or Simi. In tasting these samples, it should become obvious that the wine-maker has spent a substantial amount of extra effort in the preparation of the moderately priced samples compared to the lesser priced samples.

Use an aroma wheel to sort out the specific flavors, and refer to the descriptions of wine flavor intensity in Table 10.2 and the value bands of flavor persistency shown in Figure B.2 to assess each sensation range.

OBJECTIVES

To identify specific flavors and define main flavor categories in white and red wines; to assess flavor intensity and persistency in wine; to practice the in-mouth flavor evaluation process.

Mise en Place: Things to Do Before the Exercise Review the sections of this chapter describing the flavor intensity and persistency sensations. Review the sections on context issues in identifying flavors, flavor intensity, and flavor persistency. Review the in-mouth flavor assessment process.

Table 10.3   Wines for Exercise 10.1

	White Wine	Red Wine
Low End	Jug (bulk) Chardonnay	Jug (bulk) Cabernet Sauvignon
High End	Moderately priced, quality Chardonnay	Moderately priced, quality Cabernet Sauvignon

Table 10.4   Materials Needed for Exercise 10.1

White paper placemats, 1 per student, with numbered or labeled circles to place wineglasses (Figure 9.4a)	Crackers to cleanse the palate
1 spit cup per student	Napkins
Corkscrew	Drinking water for each student
1 copy of the Aroma Wheel (students bring)	4 wineglasses per student
1 copy of Figure 10.1 (Wine Intensity and Persistency Level) per student	

STEPS

1. Choose and purchase the wines.
2. Chill the white wines prior to the tasting.
3. Distribute the placemats (Figure 9.4a) and set up the wine glasses.
4. Open the wines and pour them in order: jug Chardonnay, moderately-priced Chardonnay, jug Cabernet Sauvignon, and moderately-priced Cabernet Sauvignon.
5. Taste the wine samples, focusing on the specific flavor characteristics of each sample. Identify the key flavor. On the Wine Intensity and Persistency Level sheet (Figure 10.1), place an X in each flavor category box that applies to each wine sample. Discuss your observations.
6. Taste each Chardonnay (sample 1, then sample 2) and retaste (sample 2, then sample 1) for flavor intensity and persistency. Repeat this process for the two Cabernet samples.

8. Rank the four wine samples from lowest to highest flavor intensity.
   Weakest flavor intensity = 1. _____ 2. _____
   3. _____ 4. _____ = Strongest flavor intensity

9. Rank the four wine samples from lowest to highest flavor persistency.
   Shortest flavor persistency = 1. _____ 2. _____
   3. _____ 4. _____ = Longest flavor persistency

10. Write any other comments, thoughts, and observations that you identified during this evaluation process. How did you identify specific flavors? Was the identification primarily driven by aroma or by in-mouth smells? Was it more or less difficult to identify the spice type and level in white wine as opposed to red wine? Did any wine have a long but negative aftertaste?

EXERCISE 10.2

FRUITY, FLORAL, HERBAL, AND BUTTER FLAVORS

Mise en Place: Things to Do Before the Exercise Review the sections of Chapter 10 describing the flavor intensity sensations. Review chapter sections on context issues in identifying flavors, flavor intensity, and flavor persistency. Review the in-mouth flavor assessment process.

PART A: FRUITY AND FLORAL

OBJECTIVE

To identify the differences and similarities in flavor types, flavor intensity, and flavor persistency in wine and food.

MATERIALS NEEDED

Table 10.5   Materials Needed for Exercise 10.2A

White paper numbered placemats (Figure 2.4a), 1 per student	Crackers to cleanse the palate
1 spit cup per student	Napkins
Corkscrew	Drinking water for each student
1 copy of Figure 10.1 (Wine Intensity Level) per student	2 wineglasses per student
1 copy of Figure 10.2 (Food Intensity Level) per student	1 Champagne flute
3 copies of Figure 10.3 (Wine and Food Flavor Intensity Match) per student	3 2-ounce cups and 1 tasting spoon per student
Wine Requirements	**Food Requirements**
Dry Riesling	Strawberry yogurt
Sweet Riesling (late harvest)	Smoked salmon
Moscato d'Asti	Salted mixed nuts

Name:_____ Food Item:_____

Level of match between food intensity and wine intensity (circle the level of match below):

Wine Sample 1:_____

    -4   -3   -2   -1   0   +1   +2   +3   +4
  Food Is   Equal   Food Is
Less Intense   Level   More Intense

Wine Sample 2:_____

    -4   -3   -2   -1   0   +1   +2   +3   +4
  Food Is   Equal   Food Is
Less Intense   Level   More Intense

Wine Sample 3:_____

    -4   -3   -2   -1   0   +1   +2   +3   +4
  Food Is   Equal   Food Is
Less Intense   Level   More Intense

Overall feeling of food and wine match (circle the level of match below):

Wine Sample 1   1-----2-----3-----4-----5-----6-----7-----8-----9
                      No Match   Average Match   Synergistic Match

Wine Sample 2   1-----2-----3-----4-----5-----6-----7-----8-----9
                      No Match   Average Match   Synergistic Match

Wine Sample 3   1-----2-----3-----4-----5-----6-----7-----8-----9
                      No Match   Average Match   Synergistic Match

Based on your evaluation of this food with the wine samples, which wine element(s) **positively** impacted the wine and food match (check all that apply)? Please rank them in order of impact (1 = greatest impact)	Based on your evaluation of this food with the wine samples, which wine element(s) **negatively** impacted the wine and food match (check all that apply)? Please rank them in order of impact (1 = greatest impact)
___ Sweetness ____ ___ Acidity ____ ___ Tannin ____ ___ Alcohol level ____ ___ Overall body ____ ___ Wine flavor intensity level ____ ___ Wine flavor persistence ____ ___ Wine spiciness level ____ ___ Wine spice type _____	___ Sweetness ____ ___ Acidity ____ ___ Tannin ____ ___ Alcohol level ____ ___ Overall body ____ ___ Wine flavor intensity level ____ ___ Wine flavor persistence ____ ___ Wine spiciness level ____ ___ Wine spice type _____

Figure 10.3

Wine and Food Flavor Intensity Match

STEPS

1. Buy the wines.

2. Chill the wines prior to the tasting session.

3. Distribute the placemats (Figure 2.4a) and set up the glasses.

4. Provide a small cup of each of the food items for each student (about 1–1½ oz [30–45 ml] per person). Provide a tasting spoon for each student.

5. Open the wines and pour about 1–1½ oz (30-45 ml) per person. Pour the Moscato d'Asti just prior to evaluation to retain effervescence during the tasting session.

6. Taste the wines in the following order: dry Riesling, sweet Riesling, and Moscato d'Asti. Evaluate the wines for flavor type, intensity, and persistency, documenting the results on the Wine Intensity and Persistency Level sheet (Figure 10.1).

7. Taste each of the food items, cleansing your palate with water and crackers between food items to ensure that there is no carryover of flavors from one item to the next. Evaluate the flavor type, intensity, and persistency of each food item, documenting the results on the Food Intensity and Persistency Level sheet (Figure 10.2).

8. Taste each food item with all three wine samples and record the results on the Wine and Food Flavor Intensity Match sheet (Figure 10.3). Use a separate sheet for each food item.

   a. Sip the dry Riesling sample.

   b. Chew, taste, and swallow a little of the strawberry yogurt.

   c. Take a sip of the same wine sample.

   d. Determine the relative levels of intensity for the strawberry yogurt and the dry Riesling. Is the food flavor more intense or less intense than the wine flavor?

   e. Repeat this process with the strawberry yogurt and the late-harvest Riesling. Then repeat again with the Moscato d'Asti.

   f. Repeat steps a–e using the smoked salmon as the food item with the three wines.

   g. Finally, repeat steps a–e using the mixed nuts as the food item with the three wines.

9. Assess the flavor types.

   a. *Dry Riesling*. What is the flavor of this wine? Does the lack of sweetness in this wine have an impact on your perception of fruit flavor intensity? What types of food would you serve with this wine? Why?

   b. *Sweet Riesling*. What is the flavor of this wine? How does the fruit flavor in this wine differ from the dry Riesling? Do you think the sweetness level in this wine had an impact on your perception of fruit flavor intensity? What types of food would you serve with this wine? Why?

   c. *Moscato d'Asti*. How would you describe the flavor in this wine? Floral? Orange blossom or honeysuckle? Any fruit flavors such as grape, tangerine, mandarin orange, or apricot? How about sweet spice such as ginger? Do you think the sweetness level in this wine had an impact on your perception of fruit flavor intensity? What types of food would you serve with this wine? Why?

10. Rank the samples of wine for flavor intensity.

   Least intense = 1. _____ 2. _____ 3. _____ = Most intense

Poached salmon and sorrel is a classic combination. Acidic greens such as sorrel can present a challenge for pairing if too overpowering (courtesy of PhotoDisc, Inc.).

11. Rank the samples of wine for flavor persistency.

    Least persistent = 1. _____ 2. _____ 3. _____ = Most persistent

12. Rank the food samples for flavor intensity.

    Least intense = 1. _____ 2. _____ 3. _____ = Most intense

13. Rank the food samples for flavor persistency.

    Least persistent = 1. _____ 2. _____ 3. _____ = Most persistent

14. Write any other comments, thoughts, and observations that you identified during this evaluation process. How did you identify flavor type? Was the identification primarily driven by the aroma or in-mouth smells? Was it difficult to assess flavor intensity? After tasting the food and wine together, did these tests confirm any ideas regarding wine and food pairing? Did these tests create any surprises regarding wine and food pairing? Did the tests support the idea of matching by flavor type and flavor intensity?

PART B: HERBAL, GRASSY, OR VEGETAL

OBJECTIVE

To identify differences and similarities in several flavor types: herbal wine flavors, herbal food flavor, spicy food flavor, and vegetal food flavor; to identify differing levels of flavor intensity and persistency in the same varietal.

MATERIALS NEEDED

Table 10.6   Materials Needed for Exercise 10.2B

1 white paper numbered placemat (Figure 2.4a) per student	Crackers to cleanse the palate
1 spit cup per student	Napkins
Corkscrew	Drinking water for each student
1 copy of Figure 10.1 (Wine Intensity Level) per student	3 wineglasses per student
1 copy of Figure 10.2 (Food Intensity Level) per student	3 copies of Figure 10.3 (Wine and Food Flavor Intensity Match) per student
Wine Requirements	**Food Requirements**
Sauvignon Blanc (California or Chile)	Steamed Asparagus
Sauvignon Blanc (French or Ontario, Canada)	Pasta with Pesto
Sauvignon Blanc (New Zealand or other Southern Hemisphere)	Hot dog or sausage with mustard

STEPS

1. Buy the wines.

2. Chill the wines prior to the tasting session.

3. Distribute the placemats (Figure 2.4a) and set up the glasses.

4. Provide a sample of each of the food items for each student (about 1–1½ oz [30–45 ml] per person). Provide a tasting fork for each student.

5. Open the wines and pour about 1½ oz (45 ml) per person.

6. Taste the wines in the following order: warm-climate Sauvignon Blanc, Old World Sauvignon Blanc, and Southern Hemisphere Sauvignon Blanc. Evaluate the wines for flavor type and intensity, documenting the results on the Wine Intensity and Persistency Level sheet (Figure 10.1).

7. Taste each of the food items, cleansing your palate with water and crackers between food items to ensure that there is no carryover of flavors from one item to the next. Evaluate the food item for flavor type and intensity, documenting the results on the Food Intensity and Persistency Level sheet (Figure 10.2).

8. Taste each food item with all three wine samples and record the results on the Wine and Food Flavor Intensity Match sheet (Figure 10.3). Use one sheet for each food item.

   a. Sip the warm-climate sample.

   b. Chew, taste, and swallow a little of the asparagus.

   c. Take a sip of the same wine sample.

   d. Determine the relative levels of intensity for the asparagus and the warm-climate Sauvignon Blanc. Is the food flavor more intense or less intense than the wine flavor?

   e. Repeat this process with the asparagus and the Old World Sauvignon Blanc. Then repeat again with the Southern Hemisphere sample.

   f. Repeat steps a–e using the Pasta with Pesto as the food item with the three wines.

   g. Finally, repeat steps a–e using the hot dog or sausage with mustard as the food item with the three wines.

9. Assess the flavor types.

   a. *Warm-climate Sauvignon Blanc.* What is the flavor of this wine? What types of food would you serve with this wine? Why?

   b. *Old World Sauvignon Blanc.* What is the flavor of this wine? How does the flavor of this wine differ from the warm-climate sample? What types of food would you serve with this wine? Why?

   c. *Southern Hemisphere Sauvignon Blanc.* How would you describe the flavor of this wine? Herbal? Grassy? Any other flavors, such as canned asparagus, hay, tarragon, green bean, green tomato, or gooseberry? What types of food would you serve with this wine? Why?

10. Rank the wine samples from least to most intense flavor.
    Least intense = 1. _____ 2. _____ 3. _____ = Most intense

11. Rank the wine samples from least to most persistent flavor.
    Least persistent = 1. _____ 2. _____ 3. _____ = Most persistent

12. Rank the food samples from least to most intense flavor.
    Least intense = 1. _____ 2. _____ 3. _____ = Most intense

13. Rank the food samples from least to most persistent flavor.
    Least persistent = 1. _____ 2. _____ 3. _____ = Most persistent

14. Write any other comments, thoughts, and observations that you identified during this evaluation process. How did you identify flavor type? Was the identification primarily driven by the aroma or in-mouth smells? Was it difficult to assess flavor intensity?

Asparagus is one of several naturally acidic foods (others are spinach, sorrel, and artichokes) that can be a challenge when pairing with wine. One method to lessen the negative impact of these acidic foods on wine is to serve them with additional fat or sweetness to mask the natural acidity. Creamed spinach and asparagus with hollandaise or beurre blanc are examples of this tactic.[28] Taste the asparagus with each of the wines and judge for yourself if it is a food that should be avoided when drinking wine with your meal. You can also experiment by putting sweet butter on the asparagus and testing the new relationship.

Sparkling wine is a good accompaniment with asparagus or artichokes with hollandaise sauce. Asparagus can be successfully paired with several less common selections such as Austrian Grüner-Veltliner, Italian Verdicchio, or Italian Vermentino. These Old World white wines have a substantial amount of earthiness, acidity, and spice that subdues the acidity and negative taste, altering the impact of the asparagus.[29]

Pasta with Pesto is easy to prepare, and if the raw garlic taste is not overpowering, this dish is generally very wine-friendly. As you taste this dish with the three wines, think about the impact of flavor matching and intensity matching. Would this dish also hold up to some red wines? Are there any clues from the Chapter 9 discussion and exercises on spiciness?

The hot dog or sausage with mustard is a simple example of the impact of a savory and spicy food item on wine. The classic beverage match might be beer while watching a baseball game at the ballpark, but this type of food is similar to other savory and spicy prepara-tions such as Pork Tenderloin with Creole Mustard Sauce, Shrimp Remoulade, or Filet of Beef with Sauce Robert. Does the Sauvignon Blanc wine work with this savory and spicy combination? Why or why not? What wine suggestions would you make for this food item?

After tasting the food and wine together, did these tests confirm any ideas regarding wine and food pairing? Did these tests create any surprises regarding wine and food pairing? Did the tests support the idea of matching by flavor type and flavor intensity?

PART C: BUTTER FLAVOR

OBJECTIVE

To identify differences in butter flavor; to identify differences in intensity and persistency.

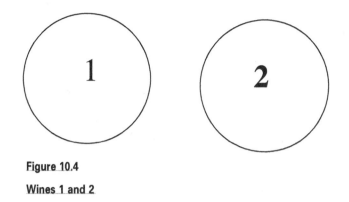

Figure 10.4

Wines 1 and 2

MATERIALS NEEDED

Table 10.7   Materials Needed for Exercise 10.2C

1 white paper numbered placemat (Figure 10.4) per student	Crackers to cleanse the palate
1 spit cup per student	Napkins
Corkscrew	Drinking water for each student
1 copy of Figure 10.1 (Wine Intensity Level) per student	2 wineglasses per student
1 copy of Figure 10.2 (Food Intensity Level) per student	3 copies of Figure 10.3 (Wine and Food Flavor Intensity Match) per student
Wine Requirements	**Food Requirements**
Non-buttery Chardonnay (Burgundy, Ontario, Canada)	Buttered popcorn
Buttery Chardonnay (California or Australia)	Grilled fish
	Hollandaise sauce

STEPS

1. Buy the wines.

2. Chill the wines prior to the tasting session.

3. Distribute the placemats (Figure 10.4) and set up the glasses.

4. Provide a small cup of each of the food items for each student (about 1–1½ oz [30–45 ml] per person): buttered popcorn, grilled fish without Hollandaise sauce, and grilled fish with Hollandaise sauce. Provide a tasting spoon for each student.

5. Open the wines and pour about 1½ oz (45 ml) per person.

6. Taste the wines in the following order: non-buttery Chardonnay, then buttery Chardonnay. Evaluate the wines for flavor type, intensity, and persistency, documenting the results on the Wine Intensity and Persistency Level sheet (Figure 10.1).

7. Taste each of the food items, cleansing your palate with water and crackers between food items to ensure that there is no carryover of flavors from one item to the next. Evaluate each food item for flavor type, intensity, and persistency, documenting the results on the Food Intensity and Persistency Level sheet (Figure 10.2).

8. Taste each food item with the wine samples and record the results on the Wine and Food Flavor Intensity Match sheet (Figure 10.3). Use one sheet for each food item.

   a. Sip the non-buttery Chardonnay sample.

   b. Chew, taste, and swallow a little of the buttered popcorn.

   c. Take a sip of the same wine sample.

   d. Determine the relative levels of intensity for the buttered popcorn and the Chardonnay. Is the food flavor more intense or less intense than the wine flavor?

   e. Repeat this process with the buttered popcorn and the buttery Chardonnay.

   f. Repeat steps a–e using the plain grilled fish as the food item with the wines.

g. Finally, repeat steps a–e using the grilled fish topped with Hollandaise sauce as the food item with the wines.

9. Assess the flavor types.

    a. *Non-buttery Chardonnay.* What is the flavor of this wine? What types of food would you serve with this wine? Why?

    b. *Buttery Chardonnay.* The in-mouth buttery flavor is more subtle than the aroma. The acidity in the buttery wine sample is less crisp and the body fuller than the non-buttery Chardonnay sample. What are the prominent flavors of this wine? How does the fruit flavor in this wine differ from the non-buttery sample? Do you perceive other flavors in this wine such as vanilla, smoke, spice, or herbs? What types of food would you serve with this wine? Why?

10. Rank the wine samples from least to most intense flavor.

    Least intense = 1. _____ 2. _____ = Most intense

11. Rank the wine samples from least to most persistent flavor.

    Least persistent = 1. _____ 2. _____ = Most persistent

12. Rank the food samples from least to most intense flavor.

    Least intense = 1. _____ 2. _____ 3. _____ = Most intense

13. Rank the food samples from least to most persistent flavor.

    Least persistent = 1. _____ 2. _____ 3. _____ = Most persistent

14. Write any other comments, thoughts, and observations that you identified during this evaluation process. How did you identify flavor type? Was the identification primarily driven by the aroma or in-mouth smells? Was it difficult to assess flavor intensity?

Corn food items have a natural affinity with Chardonnay wines. The butter should beef up the body of the popcorn to more closely match the Chardonnay. The fattiness of the butter should match the tannins in the Chardonnay with oak aging. Finally, the buttery Chardonnay should create a flavor match with this dish.

    Grilled fish creates a quandary with regard to the level of match with these two wines. The non-buttery Chardonnay has higher acidity, creating a sour punch (like a squeeze of lemon) with the fish. But the cooking method is more robust and may demand a more robust wine such as the Chardonnay with oak aging. You decide which match you think is better.

    Finally, the Hollandaise sauce is perceived as a classic match with a buttery chardonnay, but research indicates that the Hollandaise actually overpowers the Chardonnay by coating the tongue, making the wine taste weak and watery.[30] Here again, the combination of grilled fish and Hollandaise creates an interesting sensory test for you. If you are tasting the items in this part of the exercise at the same time as Part B, you could evaluate the impact of Hollandaise sauce on the asparagus. Does the Hollandaise sauce make the asparagus more wine-friendly? What wine is best served with the grilled fish and Hollandaise, or with the asparagus and Hollandaise?

    After tasting the food and wine together, did these tests confirm any perceived ideas regarding wine and food pairing? Did these tests create any surprises regarding wine and food pairing? Did the tests support the idea of matching by flavor type and flavor intensity?

Food Item: Pasta al Pesto

Yield: 6 servings

The basic ingredients and preparation of pesto sauce are similar in all recipes. Standard ingredients include fresh basil leaves, Parmesan cheese, pine nuts, garlic, and olive oil. Pesto can be made in advance and stored in the refrigerator or freezer. There are many uses for pesto: as a pasta sauce, as an accompaniment for grilled or poached chicken or fish, as a flavoring for salad dressings and soups, and as a condiment for sandwiches. Variations in the preparation of pesto can be achieved by substituting other herbs instead—for instance, cilantro or a combination of herbs such as thyme, sage, oregano, and rosemary. Further, a variety of nuts can be substituted for pine nuts to create a different twist—walnuts, pecans, pistachios, and so on.

Ingredients for Pesto Sauce	**Preparation**
2 c (475 ml) basil leaves, fresh 2 cloves garlic, peeled 1/2 c (120 ml) pine nuts 3/4 c (180 ml) grated Parmesan cheese 3/4 c (180 ml) extra-virgin olive oil Salt Pepper	Put basil leaves and garlic in a food processor and process until they are finely chopped. Add the pine nuts and process until finely chopped. Add Parmesan cheese and process until combined. With the machine running, add the olive oil in a slow, steady stream. When the oil is incorporated, turn off the machine and season to taste with salt and pepper. The finished pesto will keep under refrigeration for at least a week.

Ingredients for Pasta	**Preparation**
1 lb (.45 kg) dried pasta (such as fettuccine) 1 1/2 c (350 ml) Pesto Sauce 1/2 lb (230 g) fresh green beans, cut into 2-inch pieces (optional) 1/2 lb (230 g) new potatoes, cut into medium dice (optional) Freshly grated Parmigiano Reggiano cheese (optional)	In a large pot, bring salted water to a rolling boil. Add the pasta and cook until al dente. If you are adding the optional ingredients, add the green beans and diced potatoes to the pot about 5 minutes before the pasta is cooked. When done, reserve a small amount of the cooking liquid, then drain the pasta and vegetables. Place the pasta (and vegetables, if using) in a large bowl; toss with the pesto sauce. Add some of the reserved cooking liquid to the bowl, allowing the pesto to coat the pasta. Top with Parmigiano Reggiano cheese if desired.

Food Item: Grilled Fish

Yield: 6 servings

Grilled fish can be prepared very simply or with a variety of ingredients, marinades, and sauces. This preparation is intentionally simple to highlight the relationship grilled fish has with the wines in the exercise. Any type of firm fish can be used.

Ingredients	**Preparation**
2 lb (.90 kg) firm fish fillets 1/4 c (60 ml) extra-virgin olive oil Juice of 1 lemon or lime Salt Freshly ground black pepper	Brush fish fillets with olive oil and sprinkle with the citrus juice. Place the fish fillets on a well-oiled grill or in a well-oiled grill basket. Grill the fish over moderately high heat until just cooked. Serve immediately.

Food Item: Classic Hollandaise Sauce

Yield: 1 cup (240 ml)

Hollandaise is a classic sauce made from an emulsification of egg yolks and butter. The sauce is typically served over vegetables or fish, and is a main element of Eggs Benedict. It is important that the sauce not be prepared more than a few minutes prior to service to ensure food safety. The sauce can only be held at room temperature after preparation, and given the ingredients involved, bacteria can grow rapidly in this environment. During preparation, it is important to use a double boiler to keep from ending up with scrambled eggs or having the sauce "break" during preparation. Instant Hollandaise sauce can be purchased in most grocery stores. While in my opinion it is nothing like the real thing, instant Hollandaise has similar flavor characteristics and will do in a pinch for the purposes of this exercise.

Ingredients	Preparation
2 tbsp (30 ml) fresh lemon juice 1/4 c (60 ml) boiling water 3 egg yolks (from large eggs) 1/2 c (120 ml) unsalted butter 1/2 tsp (2 ml) salt 1/4 tsp (1 ml) cayenne pepper	Melt the butter in a small pan and keep warm. Place the egg yolks in the top part of a double boiler over boiling water. Whisk the egg yolks briskly until they begin to thicken. Add a splash of boiling water to the egg yolks (about 1 tablespoon of the boiling water). Continue to beat the egg yolk mixture until thickened and lemon-colored. Remove the top part of the double boiler from the heat. Add the lemon juice to the egg yolk mixture and beat the sauce briskly with a wire whisk. Continue beating the mixture while slowly pouring in the melted butter, one ladle at a time. When all of the melted butter is incorporated, season to taste with the salt and cayenne pepper. Serve immediately.

NOTES

1. S. E. Ebeler, "Sensory Analysis and Analytical Flavor Chemistry: Missing Links," in K. D. Deibler and J. Delwiche (eds.), *Handbook of Flavor Characterization* (New York: Marcel Dekker, 2004), 41–50.

2. G. Reineccius, *Source Book of Flavors*, 2nd ed. (New York: Chapman and Hall, 1994).

3. Ibid.

4. B. P. Halpern, "When Are Oral Cavity Odorants Available for Retronasal Olfaction?" in K. D. Deibler and J. Delwiche (eds.), *Handbook of Flavor Characterization* (New York: Marcel Dekker, 2004), 51–63.

5. Ibid.

6. Andrea Immer, *Great Tastes Made Simple: Extraordinary Food and Wine Pairing for Every Palate* (New York: Broadway Books, 2002); D. Rosengarten and J. Wesson, *Red Wine with Fish: The New Art of Matching Wine with Food* (New York: Simon and Schuster, 1989).

7. F. Beckett, *How to Match Food and Wine* (London: Octopus, 2002).

8. Rosengarten and Wesson, *Red Wine with Fish*.

9. B. M. King, P. Arents, and C. A. A. Duineveld, "Difficulty in Measuring What Matters: Context Effects," in K. D. Deibler and J. Delwiche (eds.), *Handbook of Flavor Characterization* (New York: Marcel Dekker, 2004), 119–34.

10. Ibid.

11. K. G. C. Weel, A. E. M. Boelrijk, A. C. Alting, G. Smit, J. J. Burger, H. Gruppen, and A. G. J. Voragen, "Effect of Texture Perception on the Sensory Assessment of Flavor Intensity." In K. D. Deibler and J. Delwiche (eds.), *Handbook of Flavor Characterization* (New York: Marcel Dekker, 2004), 105–18.

12. I. T. Nygren, I. B. Gustafsson, and L. Johansson, "Perceived Flavour Changes in White Wine after Tasting Blue Mould Cheese," *Food Service Technology* 2 (2002): 163–71.

13. *The American Heritage College Dictionary* (New York: Houghton Mifflin, 1997), 1019.

14. M. Bennion and B. Scheule, *Introductory Foods*, 12th ed. (Upper Saddle River, NJ: Pearson–Prentice Hall, 2004), 20.

15. C. Cadiau, *LexiWine*, 3rd ed. (Pernand-Vergelesses, France: Cadiau, 1998); J. Robinson, *Concise Wine Companion* (Oxford, UK: Oxford University Press, 2001).

16. Ibid.

17. Italian Trade Association, "Finish and Aftertaste" (2003), www.italianmade.com/wines/primer35.cfm (accessed January 12, 2006).

18. E. Peynaud, *The Taste of Wine: The Art and Science of Wine Appreciation*, 2nd ed. (New York: John Wiley and Sons, 1996).

19. Ibid., 102.

20. Ibid.

21. R. J. Harrington and R. Hammond, "A Change from Anecdotal to Empirical: An Alternative Approach to Predicting Matches between Wine and Food," *Proceedings of the EuroCHRIE Conference* 23 (2005): 1–8.

22. Peynaud, *The Taste of Wine*.

23. Ibid., 103.

24. H. Charley and C. Weaver, *Foods: A Scientific Approach*, 3rd ed. (Upper Saddle River, NJ: Prentice-Hall, 1998), 9–10.

25. Ibid.

26. D. Markham Jr., *Wine Basics: A Quick and Easy Guide* (New York: John Wiley and Sons, 1993).

27. K. MacNeil, *The Wine Bible* (New York: Workman, 2001).

28. M. W. Baldy, *The University Wine Course*, 3rd ed. (San Francisco: Wine Appreciation Guild, 2003).

29. Immer, *Great Tastes Made Simple*.

30. Nygren, Gustafsson, and Johansson, "Perceived Flavour Changes."

PART E

THE WHOLE ENCHILADA: PUTTING IT ALL TOGETHER

The previous chapters have presented a variety of ideas on wine and food elements and how they react to each other. Chapters 5 through 10 provided twelve basic rules to consider in wine and food pairing decisions. These are not hard-and-fast laws, but they do provide guidance in making better wine and food matching decisions.

These rules provide a tool chest of considerations when pairing. The exercises thus far have focused on evaluating specific elements of wine and food and their interactions when tasted together. This process provides you with a taste, texture, and flavor memory that will be useful during the remaining exercises and in future pairing decisions. This experience also adds to your tool chest when assessing food-and-wine elements in the future.

Rule #1: Food sweetness level should be less than or equal to wine sweetness level.

Rule #2: Food acidity level should be less than or equal to wine acidity level.

Rule #3: Highly salty foods work better with wines that have high effervescence.

Rule #4: The negative impact of bitter food is lessened when combined with wines of moderate to high levels of effervescence.

Rule #5: Wine tannin levels should be equal to animal-based food fattiness levels.

Rule #6: Wine acidity levels should be equal to vegetable-based food fattiness levels.

Rule #7: Wine overall body should be equal to food overall body.

Rule #8: Food spiciness should be equal to wine spiciness.

Rule #9: Spicy food should be paired with off-dry, acidic white wines.

Rule #10: Food-and-wine flavor types can be matched using similarity or contrast.

Rule #11: Wine and food flavor intensity should be equal.

Rule #12: Flavor persistency of wine and food should be equal.

Tasting wine and food can be done either sequentially or in a mixed procedure. The sequential process allows the taster to evaluate the wine or food on its own merits. Is it high or low in acidity? What is the overall body? How intense is the flavor? A mixed process occurs when the wine and food items are tasted simultaneously. This type of tasting allows the taster to assess the interaction of the wine and food elements. Did one of the items overpower the other? Did the wine make the food taste exceedingly bitter or vice versa? Did the sweetness level in the food cause the wine to taste thin and acidic?

In the next three chapters (Chapters 11–13), you will evaluate, taste, and analyze wine and food items using both the sequential and mixed tasting processes. These assessments will combine all of the elements of food and wine presented in the earlier chapters. For this assessment, you will be using an instrument that brings together all of these elements into three pages.

Chapter 11 presents the concept of a wine and food pairing decision tree. This decision tree follows the hierarchy-of-taste philosophy, with taste components as the foundation, texture as the secondary match element, and flavor as the refining element. The exercises in the next three chapters will help you to determine pairing situations where this hierarchy of taste holds true and pairing situations where there are exceptions to this concept. Chapter 12 focuses on pairing wine with cheese, and Chapter 13 provides an in-depth look at dessert and dessert wine.

Chapter 14 provides some concluding thoughts and exercises on the food-and-wine pairing processes. It also covers some broader topics related to a bundle of activities associated with a successful food-and-wine program.

CHAPTER 11

MENU PLANNING: HORIZONTAL AND VERTICAL PAIRING DECISIONS

CHAPTER OUTLINE:

Introduction

Aperitif: Food and Wine of the Pacific Northwest

General Menu Planning Suggestions

Basic Wine Sequencing Recommendations

Pacific Northwest Menu Item Discussion and Recipes

Wine and Food Pairing Instrument

Wine and Food Match Decision Tree

A Profiling Approach to Match Level Assessment

Summary

Exercises

KEY CONCEPTS:

- Horizontal or vertical pairing choices
- Integrating indigenous ingredients, ethnic cooking styles, and regional wines into a menu theme
- Using judgment to predict level of perceived food-and-wine match
- The twelve primary pairing decision rules and integrating them into pairing decisions

INTRODUCTION

Until this point, the exercises in this book have focused on specific elements in food and wine or categories of elements—taste components, texture, and flavors. In this chapter, a more holistic approach is used with the introduction of the Wine and Food Pairing Instrument (Figures 11.2a, 11.2b, and 11.2c). This instrument is based on a three-step process—a sequential assessment of wine, a sequential assessment of the food item, and then a mixed tasting of the wine and food to determine the perceived level of match. Each of these three parts represents a layer of the complete matching process.

Individual profiles of the wine and food are prepared (Figures 11.2a and 11.2b), and then the two are put side by side and compared (Figure 11.2c).

Before we get the discussion of how to use the Wine and Food Pairing Instrument, this chapter first presents an Aperitif on the wine and food of the Pacific Northwest, including a multicourse menu, recipes, and a discussion on designing a menu with several courses. This focus on food-and-wine planning then leads into the sections about the instrument.

Aperitif I Food and Wine of the Pacific Northwest

For this discussion, I focus on Washington, Oregon, Idaho, and British Columbia. Unlike the Cajun and Creole example presented in Chapter 4, this region does not have as distinct or clearly defined a gastronomic identity. Even so, the climate and ethnic influences in the region provide some interesting and unique products. The cuisine in this region is continually evolving and derived from a variety of ethnic influences (Native American, Asian, and European), indigenous ingredients (salmon, clams, venison, duck, and huckleberries, to name a few), and agricultural products (such as apples, potatoes, cherries, and rhubarb).

The Pacific Northwest menu presented in this chapter incorporates many of these products and influences. The overview of the history in this region is based on research and my interpretations from thirty-six years of living in the Pacific Northwest. History and stories can provide a value-added element to any menu. Whether guests are tourists from afar or local residents from down the street, they are curious about the region, its foods, and its influences. When planning a menu, think about your particular location and how its gastronomic identity can be utilized as part of the menu or in the server's discussion with the guests about nightly specials to project a sense of knowledge and uniqueness to the customer.

The Pacific Northwest is very diverse in climate, with mild, rainy weather on the western side of the region, dry, hot summers and cold winters in the central part, and harsh, snowy winters in the northeastern portion. These differences result in a wide variety of food products, preparation methods, and eating habits across the northwestern states. The ethnic influences of Asian populations, migrant workers from Mexico, German and French settlers, and the native people provide further diversity and generate an evolving fusion cuisine.

THE FOOD OF THE PACIFIC NORTHWEST

The western side of Washington State is known for its abundant fish and seafood products: salmon, halibut, lingcod, mussels, razor and geoduck clams, Olympia oysters, and Dungeness crab. Further, this area has had a significant influence from the Pacific Rim, resulting in an abundance of Japanese, Vietnamese, Chinese, and Thai restaurants and shops. The central and eastern parts of the state are primarily an agricultural region. Famous for its apples, this area is also a major producer of asparagus, rhubarb, hops, and barley. Other fruits (such as pears, raspberries, strawberries, cherries, and grapes) and vegetables (including potatoes, corn, and onions) are produced in large quantities, thanks to irrigation in the area. Protein in this area comes from a large number of cattle ranches and feedlots, a variety of fish (rainbow trout, crappie, bass, and steelhead), and game (pheasant, quail, ducks, geese, and venison). Large numbers of Mexican immigrants and migrant workers along with early German settlers have influenced the central and eastern areas of the state.

The coastal side of Oregon has an abundance of fish and seafood similar to Washington. Oregon produces tremendous scallops, Dungeness crab, and Coho and king salmon. About 40 miles south of Portland is the Willamette Valley. This area is known for its rich soil and large amounts of rainfall, which produce high-quality berries, wild mushrooms, and Pinot Noir grapes; the valley is also known for its cheddar cheese. The central and eastern portions of the state have a topography similar to the northern part of Washington and produce many of the same products. The area just below the Columbia River in the central portion of the state is known for its high-quality melons. As in Washington and Idaho, the influence of Native American smoking techniques can be seen here, with an abundance of smoked salmon and trout available in restaurants and shops. This Native American smoking technique uses a "hot smoke" style, which creates a drier finished product. For their smoking, Native Americans traditionally used wood from a variety of sources, from alder wood to wild rose wood, based on availability.

Famous for its potatoes, Idaho was settled after the Civil War by many disenfranchised southerners who brought with them the techniques and foods that were used in pioneer fare (cooking in cast iron, cornbread, fried foods, and a variety of dried legumes). In addition, Idaho is home to a large Chinese population who came to the area around the turn of the century to mine and build the railroads. These Chinese immigrants stayed in Idaho, where they maintained gardens near the Boise River and opened early Chinese restaurants known as "noodle houses." Idaho is also home to the highest concentration of Basque population in the United States. In addition to potatoes, Idaho is a large producer of farmed rainbow trout, tilapia, lamb, and a variety of fruits and vegetables. The Palouse Hills (the northwest portion of the state and an eastern portion of Washington) are home to the most productive wheat and lentil farms in the country. The region produces soft white wheat that is best used for pastries because of its relatively low gluten content.

Wine growers throughout the Pacific Northwest have achieved success growing the finicky Pinot Noir grape.

Not unlike Washington and Oregon, British Columbia has coastal and noncoastal regions as well as a variety of ethnic influences on its cuisine. On the coastal side of the province, the importance of salmon to the First Nations people and other early settlers to the region cannot be overstated. Even with a constant drive to "break all the rules" in British Columbian cuisine, salmon is still central to this region's cooking. In addition, a wide variety of other fish and seafood are prominent in the cuisine, including prawns, scallops, clams, Dungeness crab, rockfish, halibut, and black cod (a.k.a. sablefish).

Canada's only indigenous cooking method hails from British Columbia and is known as bentwood box cookery. Well-known Canadian food writer Anita Stewart explains the process: "Handmade cedar boxes were filled with water to soak and tighten for three or four days. A fire was lit and potato-sized beach rocks were placed in it to heat. The hot rocks were then picked out of the fire with a split alder branch, washed briefly in one box, then placed in a second filled with water and salmonberry shoots. In moments the water foamed and boiled. Seafood was added . . . and a woven mat was placed over top to hold the steam. Within minutes the pure, sweet tastes of the sea were retrieved from the box and the feast began."[1]

Since the 1970s, the region's fusion cuisine has been influenced by a blend of Asian, European, Indian, and Native American flavors combined with British Columbian ingredients. Hydroponically grown tomatoes and peppers, indigenous hazelnuts, huckleberries, and pine mushrooms as well as a variety of orchard fruits are just some of the bounty available in B.C.

WINE IN THE PACIFIC NORTHWEST

With the exception of California, Washington produces more grapes than any other state in the United States. Until 1967, Washington was an important source of Concord grapes for juice, jelly, and wine but grew a relatively small amount of vinifera grapes. In 1967, André Tchelistcheff (California's most prominent winemaker at the time) "went to Washington and tasted a homemade Gewürztraminer from the cellar of Washington State University Professor Philip Church. Tchelistcheff called it the finest white wine made from Gewürztraminer in the U.S."[2] Since that time, growers have replaced their Concords with vinifera, and Washington now supplies grapes not only to its own wineries but also to California, Oregon, Idaho, Michigan, and Canada.

Washington is endowed with the ideal combination of climate and soil, with the warm days and cool nights combining to produce well-balanced grapes (flavorful, sweet, and high in acid). The main appellation is known as Columbia Valley, which covers a large region in the central part of the state as well as vineyards in the Yakima Valley and the Walla Walla Valley. This area lies just north of 46 degrees north latitude on the map, the same latitude that cuts across the Bordeaux and Burgundy regions of France. In the summer, ripening grapes receive an average of 17.4 hours of sunlight per day. This is about two hours per day more than in the premier grape-growing areas of California. The resulting wines can compete with any in the world, and vintners have had particular success with Gewürztraminer, Riesling, Chardonnay, Sauvignon Blanc, Sémillon, Lemberger, Syrah, Cabernet Sauvignon, Pinot Noir, and Merlot.

Oregon has produced a substantial amount of wine dating back to the turn of the century (the majority from fruit other than grapes). Most of the vineyards are near the Oregon coast in the north along the Willamette River near Portland, and in the south along the Umpqua and Rouge Rivers near Roseburg. Statistically, much of the growing region is nearly identical to Burgundy's Côte d'Or region in France. Not surprisingly, many Oregon growers have found a match between the climate and soil with the finicky Pinot Noir grape. Some of America's finest examples of Pinot Noir come from Oregon. In 1979, Oregon Pinot Noir beat out a large group of red Burgundies in France during a blind tasting.[3]

The primary Oregon viticulture areas include the Willamette, Umpqua, and Rogue Valleys, as well as the lower Columbia and Walla Walla Valleys, which extend from Washington into Oregon. Wine production consists of about an equal split between red and white wines, with principal varieties including Gewürztraminer, Riesling, Chardonnay, Sauvignon Blanc, Pinot Gris, Pinot Noir, Merlot, Zinfandel, and Cabernet Sauvignon.

For the most part, Idaho winters are too cold for viticulture. But growers have had great success near Boise in the southwestern corner of the state and in the Clearwater River Valley near Lewiston. Several boutique wineries have emerged in this region, but few are large enough to have any commercial significance to date. The largest is Sainte Chapelle Winery in Caldwell (just north of Boise). Most of the wine is consumed locally, and producers have had success with Chardonnay, Gewürztraminer, Riesling, Sauvignon Blanc, Sémillon, Cabernet Franc, Merlot, Pinto Noir, and Cabernet Sauvignon.

An Oblate priest, Father Charles Pandozy, planted grapes in the Okanagan Valley in British Columbia as early as the 1860s. More recently, the region is being recognized internationally for its wine-growing potential.[4] This region has a diverse growing climate that ranges from cool to moderately warm. The Okanagan Valley has several major wineries as well as a growing number of high-quality bouquet wine producers. With the diversity in climate, the region produces everything from opulent ice wines to bold and complex reds. The region has had good success with a variety of varietals including Riesling, Chardonnay, Sauvignon Blanc, Pinot Blanc, Pinot Noir, Merlot, and Cabernet Sauvignon.

The quality of the Pacific Northwest's wine regions will continue to improve as the vineyards age and through continued trial and error. The concept of terroir, new production methods, and less traditional varietals will differentiate specific growing regions from those of California and other parts of the New World.

Of course, any discussion of the Pacific Northwest cannot end without at least some mention of the fine handcrafted beers from this region. Small and large commercial breweries as well as innovative brew pubs abound everywhere from Victoria, British Columbia, to Portland, Oregon, and Boise, Idaho. Many of these great local and regional beers are a delightful accompaniment to the Pacific Northwest's Asian-, Indian-, and Mexican-influenced dishes.

The menu and recipes later in this chapter integrate many of the foods, preparation methods, and ethnic ingredients that are part of Pacific Northwest cuisine.

GENERAL MENU PLANNING SUGGESTIONS

Prior to planning any menu, several questions need to be considered:

1. *Who is the audience?* This is an important consideration when determining the types of food, preparation, and wines that will be most appreciated.

2. *What is the purpose of the dinner or event?* The reason for the event will be a key driver of many decisions. Menu and wine choices for a wedding, for example, will be quite different from those for a corporate meeting.

3. *Is there a theme?* The theme in this chapter's menu focuses on the Pacific Northwest—but other themes may be tied to a special occasion, holiday, ethnic culture, or cuisine.

4. *What are the equipment, staff, and location constraints?* Each location has its limitations, and careful consideration is needed to maximize value and creativity while ensuring that the menu can be successfully presented in the given situation. These constraints should also be considered if you are hosting a dinner party in your home—you may want to decide how much time you want to spend in the kitchen rather than interacting with your guests, and how much can be done in advance.

5. *How many guests will be there? What are the price and cost issues?* Certainly, a menu for a group of 8–10 people has different needs than one for 50, 100, or 500 people. Also, knowing the price limitations and cost constraints up front can help you to find creative ways to present great food and wine but with great value.

6. *Are there any special diet needs?* For example, in Louisiana, with its large Catholic population, it's often important to eliminate meat from menus during Lent. It is not uncommon for the hosts of many catered dinners to specify particular needs.

7. *What is the "ebb and flow" of the menu?* This has to do with a smooth transition from one course to the next. One method is to alternate more complicated dishes with simpler ones. The menu below begins with a more complicated appetizer, which includes both hot and cold elements, and follows with a soup that can be ready to go and just needs to be dished up. This ebb-and-flow idea comes in handy in situations where unexpected issues arise, as the simpler dishes give you time to adjust.

BASIC WINE SEQUENCING RECOMMENDATIONS

Wine and food pairing can be thought of as having horizontal choices and vertical choices. Horizontal pairing is the simplest kind and involves pairing one wine with a particular food dish. Vertical pairings are more complicated and refer to matching with multiple wines in a multicourse, progressive dinner.

"Fire and Ice" Northwest Oysters

Baked Olympia Oysters Topped with Roasted Shallots, Ginger and Proscuitto. Served with a Savory

Sorbet of Fennel, Lime, and Riesling

Wine: Chateau Ste. Michelle Eroica Riesling 2004

Asian Chowder of Coconut, Lingcod, and Geoduck Clam

Smoked Lingcod, Coconut Milk, Galangal and Tomato, Served with Geoduck Clam Sashimi

Wine: Columbia Winery Gew rztraminer 2004

Roasted Columbia Basin Pheasant

Marinated in Grappa, Served with German Bread Dumplings and Reduction of Lemberger Wine,

BlackPepper, Mustard, and Molasses

Wine: Kiona Lemberger 2002

Cedar-Planked Idaho Rainbow Trout

Served with Lemon-Dusted Asparagus Tips and Micro-greens

Wine: Continue with Lemberger

Roasted Loin of Venison

With Smoked Trio of Beets, Mashed Idaho Potatoes, and Syrah Demiglace

Wine: McCrea Cellars, Boushey Grand C te Vineyard Syrah 2002

Rouge Creamery Oregonzola and Washington State Cougar Gold Cheddar

Served with Thyme-Infused Honey, Apricot-Orange Conserve, and Dried-Cherry Compote

Wine: Continue with Syrah or begin dessert wine

Sweet Flavors of the Northwest

Walnut Lacey Cookie Cup Filled with Homemade Vanilla Ice Cream and Strawberry-Rhubarb

Sauce

Wine: David Hill Vineyard Muscat Port

Figure 11.1

Menu: Food and Wine of the Pacific Northwest

A basic vertical pairing rule of thumb is that wine and food pairs should increase in intensity with each successive course. In addition, several other suggestions are centered on fundamental rules related to our sensory impression of wine taste, texture, and flavor.

1. *Light-bodied wine before medium-bodied wine before full-bodied wine.* This rule is based on the fact that lighter-bodied wines tasted after fuller-bodied ones have a tendency to be perceived as thin and weak. Therefore, follow this rule whenever possible. If this is not possible, try to maximize the time between the fuller-bodied wine and the lighter one by serving some sort of palate cleanser between them. A sorbet is a classic example, but a green salad or sparkling wine would also cleanse the palate.

2. *Dry wines before sweet wines.* This ordering suggestion is similar to the ordering of savory items before sweet food items such as dessert. Dry wines do not leave a lingering taste of sweetness in your mouth. Sweet wines and particularly forti-fied wines can deaden the palate. While this rule serves as a general guideline, there are many exceptions to it. Many times you will want to serve an off-dry table or sparkling wine as an aperitif. You could serve a Gewürztraminer or off-dry Riesling with an appetizer or seafood course—or even the classic Sauternes with foie gras.

3. *Lower-alcohol wines before higher-alcohol wines.* As alcohol is an indicator of body, this ordering suggestion follows the same idea of lighter-bodied wines before fuller-bodied ones. Most table wines are between 10 and 14 percent alcohol, but al-cohol content may become an issue if you are serving a wine that is significantly lower in alcohol (7–8 percent) or higher (greater than 14 percent).

4. *Lower-quality wines before higher-quality wines.* It stands to reason that wines of a lower quality taste less impressive af-ter those of higher quality. This can also be an issue when serving young versus mature wines. Younger wines usually lack complexity and nuance. Therefore, if you plan to splurge on a more expensive bottle or serve a mature one that you have been cellaring for some time and it will be part of a multicourse meal, it makes sense to choose one that will be served later rather than earlier in the meal as a rule. Many times, the highest-quality wine is served with the main course, but it can also be appropriate to serve the most dramatic wine with the cheese course or dessert. Of course, you should be careful not to serve it too late, when the diners may have succumbed to sensory fatigue.

A more traditional Pacific Northwest dish featuring salmon, asparagus, and edible flowers.

5. *Low-tannin wines before high-tannin wines.* This follows the normal progression that wines and foods are served in order of intensity from light to full. The general rule is to serve white wines before red wines with some exceptions such as a light red (e.g., Beaujolais-Villages) and an oaky Chardonnay. In this case, the oak adds body and tannin to the Chardonnay and it may be appropriate to serve it after a light red wine. A food exception is the cheese course; whites usually go best with the majority of cheeses, but the cheese course is served after the main course and typically with a full-bodied red wine. Of course, this basic guideline may some-times contradict the previous one. As quality red wines age, the inherent tannins mellow, creating a smoother but more complex sensation. In a situation where you might serve two reds (one well-aged and one still young), I would generally

suggest that the fourth suggestion should supersede the fifth, as the well-aged red in this example will be perceived as the higher-quality wine.

These basic ordering guidelines are useful to keep in mind when planning a menu with multiple courses and multiple wines. Fortunately, in most cases, you can use time and creativity to get around these guidelines to some extent. You are encouraged to keep these issues in the back of your mind while planning vertical choices and to make adjustments accordingly.

PACIFIC NORTHWEST MENU

Appetizer This course features Olympia oysters served with hot and cold contrasting elements. Olympia oysters are known for their intense and minerally flavor, and this dish combines these oysters, served baked, with a savory sorbet. The idea is to add a little of the wine, citrus, and fennel sorbet with each bite of oyster—layering additional flavors, acid (like a squeeze of lemon), and temperature differences. This non-sweet sorbet takes some getting used to, as tradition provides us with a preconception that sorbet should be sweet. Some people can move past this sensory "script," while others cannot.

The ingredients in this dish combine some Asian elements (gingerroot and Japanese red pepper seasoning) with traditional European preparation methods and ingredients. For the sorbet, a Washington Riesling with a relatively high acidity and fruity flavor was used—an off-dry version that contrasts the mineral flavor of the oysters, the salty components of the prosciutto and sea salt, and the spicy flavors of the gingerroot and red pepper seasoning. For this dinner, a Chateau Ste. Michelle Eroica Riesling was served. It has been described as lively (plenty of acidity) with off-dry fruit flavors and a tangy mineral edge. These flavors create both similarity and contrasts to the finished dish. You might also try a Sauvignon Blanc or unoaked Chardonnay, which are classic matches with oysters.

Food Item: "Fire and Ice" Northwest Oysters

Yield: 6 servings

Ingredients for oysters

2 oz (60 ml) extra-virgin olive oil
2 shallots, peeled and sliced into fine
    julienne
2 oz (60 g) ginger root, peeled and sliced
    into fine julienne
36 Olympia oysters, washed and ready to
    shell
1½ oz (40 g) prosciutto, sliced thin, then
    finely diced (brunoise)
Sea salt
Ichimi togarashi (Japanese red pepper
    seasoning)
Juice of 1 lemon

Ingredients for sorbet

1 c (220 ml) Riesling
Juice of 1 lemon
1 tbsp (15 ml) chopped fennel
Salt
Pepper

Preparation

Combine all of the sorbet ingredients. Freeze in an ice cream freezer according to directions. Heat a little of the olive oil in a saucepan. Add shallots and gingerroot and lightly caramelize. Reduce the heat and cover the shallot/ginger mixture with the remaining olive oil. Simmer over low heat until the shallots and ginger are tender. Open the oysters and place them in the half shell on a baking sheet. Top them evenly with the shallot/ginger mixture and diced prosciutto and drizzle with the oil from the shallot/ginger mixture. Season with sea salt, ichimi togarashi, and lemon juice. Bake at 375°F (190°C) for 6–8 minutes. Serve immediately with a small scoop of the frozen sorbet.

Soup Course This menu item incorporates regional ingredients (lingcod and geoduck clams), local cooking methods (smoking), and ethnic influences (Asian culture). The chowder can be served in a regular bowl or, for an added twist, in a carved-out green papaya. The geoduck sashimi is basically a ceviche. Geoduck clams are huge—a single one weighs between 3 and 5 pounds (about 2 kg) and can be purchased fresh or as frozen meat. For this item, the geoduck sashimi should be stirred into the hot chowder at the last minute to make sure that it does not get tough. For this event, the clam was served in an Asian soup spoon next to the soup bowl, and then the guests stirred it into the chowder when it arrived at the table. Lingcod is a popular and modestly priced regional fish. It is not technically a cod but a white fish that looks similar to cod once filleted.

The wine selection is the classic match of Gewürztraminer. Washington Gewürztraminer is of high quality and a good value. In general, the wine has a spicy character and good acidity and is off-dry. All of these elements work well with this moderately spicy dish (which contains sweet spice and hot spice). The wine acid cuts through the coconut milk and balances the food acidity from the geoduck and tomatoes. The wine's slight sweetness contrasts with the saltiness of the smoked fish and fish sauce. The selected wine for this course (Columbia Valley Gewürztraminer) is semi-dry, has crisp acidity, and has an interesting blend of fruit flavors, lime, and minerals. It holds its own with the spiciness and acidity in the soup.

Food Item: Asian Chowder of Coconut, Smoked Lingcod, and Geoduck Clam Sashimi

Yield: 6–8 servings

Ingredients

5–6 oz (150–160 g) geoduck clam (both siphon and body meat), trimmed and thinly sliced

1/3 c (75 ml) fresh lime juice

2 tsp (20 ml) soy sauce

2 tbsp (25–30 ml) thinly sliced onions

Salt

White pepper

One 3–4-inch piece of fresh galangal (available at most Asian markets)

4 c (900 ml) coconut milk

2 c (450 ml) chicken stock

2 tsp (20 ml) finely chopped red chilies

12 oz (340 g) smoked lingcod (you can substitute other smoked fish)

3 tbsp (40 ml) Thai fish sauce

2 tsp (20 ml) brown sugar

1/2 c (115 ml) chopped cilantro

1 c (225 ml) diced tomatoes (concassé)

Preparation

Place the clam meat in a glass bowl or platter. Combine the lime juice, soy sauce, onions, and salt and white pepper to taste and pour over the clam meat. Let marinate for several hours or overnight. Peel the galangal and cut it into thin slices. Combine the galangal with the coconut milk and chicken stock in a 2- or 3-quart saucepan. Bring it to a boil, reduce the heat, and simmer uncovered for about 10 minutes. Stir the mixture occasionally while simmering. Add the diced chilies to the mixture and simmer for an additional 8 minutes. Cut the smoked fish into small strips, add it to the soup mixture, and heat through. Add the fish sauce and brown sugar. Taste for seasoning and adjust as desired. To serve, add the chopped cilantro and tomato concassé. Add the geoduck sashimi at the time of service or present it tableside and allow the guests to add it themselves.

Poultry Course The region around my hometown (Moses Lake, Washington) is well known for its pheasant hunting. This pheasant dish integrates the German influence of the central and eastern region of the state with an upgraded version of German bread dumplings (known as *Servietten Knödel*). The grappa is added to the marinade to tenderize and flavor the pheasant (you can substitute wine, beer, or other distilled beverages). This dish can be served as a main course or as one of several smaller courses as part of a multicourse menu, as was done here. I like to serve it with a garnish of a little basil oil and a brush of carrot and green pea purees for a splash of color.

The cooking method (roasting), the marinade, the type of bird, and the marrying of a red wine in the sauce reduction allow this dish to be served with a red wine as long as it is not too big and tannic. The selection of a lighter red wine was made for several reasons: to not overpower the pheasant, to allow the wine to match reasonably well with the next course, and to create a progression of intensity with the red wine served with the main course. A couple of choices from the Northwest come to mind. The menu recommends a less common wine known as Lemberger (or Limburger). The name comes from the same town in Germany as the famous (and odorous) cheese. The wine is a light- to medium-bodied, fruity, and lightly tannic red wine. The grape it is made from is known as Blaufränkisch in Austria and Kekfrankos in Hungary. The best producers in the United States are in Washington State, primarily in the Yakima Valley. Kiona Lemberger was selected to be served with this course. While Lemberger vines have been grown in Washington since 1964, Kiona was the first commercial winery to plant the grape in 1976 and is considered by many to be the gold standard for Washington Lemberger. Lemberger is a modestly priced wine with a surprising amount of character. This Kiona Lemberger is grown in the Red Mountain appellation and has a deep ruby color, lots of fruit, relatively low tannin, and a slightly spicy character. The intensity of this wine allows it to hold up to this dish without overpowering it. Its spicy and fruity character plays well with the molasses, mustard, and black pepper in the sauce.

You can also substitute an Oregon Pinot Noir or Chardonnay, which would provide a nice combination due to an approximate body match with the dish.

Food Item: Roasted Columbia Basin Pheasant Marinated in Grappa with German Bread Dumplings

Yield: 6 servings (12 in a multicourse menu)

Ingredients for Pheasant

1 c (225 ml) grappa
1–2 oz (30–60 g) fresh thyme
3 bay leaves
Salt
Black pepper
3 whole pheasants
1/2 bottle Lemberger or other red wine
3 c (675 ml) veal stock
1 tbsp (15 ml) Dijon mustard
1 tbsp (15 ml) molasses
Salt
Coarsely ground black pepper
Cornstarch

Ingredients for German dumplings

6 oz (170 g) bacon, small dice
3 oz (85 g) onions, finely diced
4–5 kaiser rolls, thinly sliced
3/4 c (170 ml) milk
3 eggs
1 tbsp (15 ml) finely chopped parsley
Salt
Pepper
Breadcrumbs as needed
2 tbsp (30 ml) butter

Preparation

To make the dumplings, cook the bacon until crisp and drain well. Sauté the onions in the bacon fat until tender. Remove from heat and allow to cool. Combine the bacon, onions, and rolls. Soak them in the lukewarm milk for 30 minutes. Add the eggs, parsley, and salt and pepper to taste and mix well. If the mixture is a little too wet, add some breadcrumbs to give it the same consistency as a bread dressing for Thanksgiving. Divide the mixture into two equal portions. Roll each portion into tube shapes in clean cloth napkins. Tie the napkin ends so that the bread dumpling tubes are evenly distributed and firm. Carefully put the napkin tubes into salted, barely simmering water. Cook for about 25 minutes. Remove from the cooking liquid and allow to cool completely. Once cold, unwrap the napkins and place the cooked dumpling tubes on a cutting board. Slice them into 1/2-inch-thick medallions. Melt the butter and sauté the sliced bread dumplings until golden brown just prior to serving.

For the pheasant, combine the grappa, thyme, bay leaves, and salt and pepper to taste. Marinate the pheasant in this mixture for several hours or overnight. Preheat the oven to 400°F (200°C). Remove the pheasant from the marinade and season the cavity with additional salt and pepper. Place in a roasting pan and roast for 1 to 1 1/2 hours until the meat is tender, the internal juices run clear, and the internal temperature reaches 165°F (75°C). Remove the roasted pheasant from the pan and keep warm. Deglaze the roasting pan with the red wine. Add the stock and reduce by half. Season the liquid with the mustard, the molasses, and salt and pepper to taste. Thicken the sauce to a jus lie consistency with a little cornstarch mixed in water. Split the pheasants in half and remove all of the interior bones, leaving only the outer bones of the leg and wing. Serve one-half of a pheasant as a main course portion; cut the birds into quarters for a smaller portion. Serve each pheasant portion atop one or more sautéed slices of dumpling. Drizzle each portion with sauce.

Fish Course This is a fish course with some characteristics of a light salad course. It has a minimal amount of acidity, which allows it to be successfully served with wine. Cedar-planking salmon is a traditional cooking technique derived from the Northwest's Native American tribes. Cedar planks can be purchased online or in many specialty cooking stores. The cooking technique is really a combination of baking, steaming, and light smoking. The cedar plank is soaked in water prior to using. The fish is placed directly on the plank and baked in a hot oven. During the cooking, the moisture in the plank steams the fish and provides a slight cedar-smoked flavor, while the top develops a firm baked texture. Many restaurants serve the planked fish directly on the plank. In this case, it was presented in a more "refined" fashion at this upscale event.

The finished dish has a stronger body due to the cooking method and fattier fish, light acidity, and light smoky and citrus flavors. This dish lends itself well to a wide range of wine possibilities depending on whether it is part of a multicourse meal, where in the menu sequence it is served, and how acidic you make the final dish. Here, the wine was served with the same Lemberger that had been served with the pheasant, because the wine's fruitiness and mild tannins worked well with the natural acidity in the asparagus.

If this dish is served on its own or in a different order, there are a number of effective match choices—everything from Sauvignon Blanc and Fumé Blanc to Chardonnay and Beaujolais. The Sauvignon Blanc selection would match the acidity of the dish with the wine and the grassiness of the wine with the character of the asparagus and micro-greens. The Fumé Blanc choice would have similar characteristics, but if a Fumé Blanc with some oak aging is selected, it would also match the light, smoky flavor of the trout. A Chardonnay would work if it is not too big and oaky. A cool-climate Chardonnay with some oak will have sufficient acid and match the body of this relatively fatty fish. Much like a Lemberger, a Beaujolais would be medium-bodied with light tannins and have sufficient fruitiness and acidity to pair with this fish.

Food Item: Cedar-Planked Idaho Rainbow Trout Served with Citrus-Dusted Asparagus Tips and Micro-Greens

Yield: 3 servings

Ingredients

3 Idaho rainbow trout, boned and filleted
Cedar planks
Zest of 2 lemons
Zest of 2 oranges
2–4 tbsp (30–60 ml) extra-virgin olive oil, divided
Juice of 2 lemons
Salt
Pepper
2 lbs (1 kg) fresh asparagus, peeled, blanched, and cut into 1-inch pieces
1½ c (350 ml) micro-greens
1–2 tbsp (15–30 ml) herb-infused oil
1 tbsp (15 ml) aged traditional balsamic vinegar (modern balsamic vinegar can be used as a substitute if reduced by half)

Preparation

Skin the boned trout fillets and set aside. Soak the cedar planks in water for a couple of hours prior to using. To prepare the citrus "dust," separately pulverize the lemon and orange zests in an electric coffee grinder until each is a fine dust. Set aside. Drizzle the trout fillets with 1–2 tbsp of olive oil and the lemon juice and season to taste with salt and pepper. Place the trout skin side down on the cedar planks. Roast in a hot oven (400–450°F or 200–230°C) for 7–10 minutes. Meanwhile, sauté the asparagus in the remaining 1–2 tbsp olive oil and season with salt and pepper to taste. Using a ring or other small form as a base, place a portion of asparagus in the center of each plate. Top with a portion of trout (each fillet cut in half to fit on top of the asparagus ring). Next, place an equal portion of micro-greens on each portion of trout. Drizzle each serving with herb-infused oil and balsamic vinegar. Sprinkle each with a little lemon dust and orange dust.

Meat Course Deer hunting and venison are common in Idaho, eastern Washington, and eastern Oregon. The venison for this dish is marinated in buttermilk to remove some of the gamy flavor and to tenderize the meat. It is wrapped in strips of bacon (known as barding) prior to being roasted. This technique adds fat and flavor to this otherwise low-fat meat. For the side items, fresh baby beets were served, but you can also use full-size beets that are sliced or quartered after smoking (the smoking is done the same way as for meat or fish and takes about 15 to 20 minutes, depending on how much smoke flavor you want). For this event, a little bit of pureed, smoked red beet was added to the sauce. This addition gives a bright color to the sauce as well as a little smoky and earthy flavor.

This finished dish is full-bodied, lightly smoky, and somewhat peppery. The buttermilk marinade creates a smoother flavor and texture in the finished product. The use of the Syrah in the marinade and sauce reduction marries the flavors when served with the same type of wine. Syrah was selected because it usually has flavors of black pepper and is full-bodied, and many of the winemakers in Washington produce some great examples using this varietal. Of course, you can easily substitute a Cabernet Sauvignon or a wine based on the Syrah grape from another region such as Côte du Rhône or Australia (where it's called Shiraz). However, the Syrahs from Washington State are unique in comparison to those of California, Australia, or the Rhône Valley, since the terroir of the Columbia Valley creates wines with their own characteristics and integrity. The soil and areas selected to grow Washington Syrah are similar to those in the Côte du Rhône—south-facing, composed of shallow soil, pebbles, stones, and lava pumice. This situation forces the Syrah vines to struggle, resulting in wines with layers and layers of character. Good Washington Syrah will have earth, fruit, and spice. Washington Syrah typically has less tannin, and its flavor can be anywhere from lean to big, "velvet hammer" to tannic and coarse.

The quality of these Syrahs is quite amazing given the fact that the first Syrah vineyard was planted only in 1985 by David Lake. Lake liked Rhône wines and had faith that the varietal would flourish in Washington. In 1988, Lake and Red Willow Vineyard owner Mike Sauer produced Washington's first Syrah under the Red Willow label. Today Syrah is grown across the state. The quality and style of Syrah in the region varies: those grown in relatively cool climates have a leaner structure, spice, pepper, and berry fruits; grapes from more moderate climates make wines with a fuller structure and black fruits; and Syrah grapes grown in warmer climates may exhibit a jammy character.

The Syrah selected for this menu was from McCrea Cellars. Doug McCrea was the first to follow Lake's lead in producing Syrah in Washington. His first Syrah was released in 1994. The McCrea Syrah selected for this menu is made from grapes from the Boushey Vineyard, located on a steep, south-facing slope along the Rattlesnake Hills. The wine is reminiscent of the Côte Rôtie in style with "a meatier side, almost bacon fat, and with a core of sweet fruit."[5] This wine is from the 2002 vintage, which was a relatively warm year in Washington State, resulting in fruit-forward and slightly higher-alcohol table wines. This wine is well balanced with fruit intensity, tannins, and excellent acidity.

Food Item: Roasted Loin of Venison with Smoked Trio of Beets and Syrah Demiglace

Yield: 6 servings

Ingredients

1¼ c (280 ml) buttermilk

2¼ c (510 ml) Syrah, divided

1½ c (340 ml) mirepoix (large dice of 2 parts onion, 1 part carrot, and 1 part celery)

1 tsp (10 ml) juniper berries

1 tbsp (30 ml) fresh thyme plus sprigs for garnish

Salt

Black pepper

2½ lb (1.1 kg) boneless loin of venison

6–8 oz (200 g) small red beets

6–8 oz (200 g) small gold beets

6–8 oz (200 g) small striped beets

2 cloves garlic, minced

2 tbsp (50–60 ml) extra-virgin olive oil

¾ lb (340 g) smoked bacon

2 bay leaves

¾ c (170 ml) demiglace (a mixture of half brown stock and half brown sauce that is reduced by half)

3 c (700 ml) mashed Idaho potatoes, seasoned with a little cream, butter, salt, and pepper

Preparation

Combine the buttermilk, 1 cup (240 ml) of Syrah, juniper berries, thyme, bay leaves, 2 tsp (10 ml) salt, and 1 tsp (5 ml) pepper. Add the venison loin to the marinade and allow to marinate overnight. Boil the beets until they are cooked; when cool enough to handle, remove the skins by rubbing them with your fingers, and completely cool the beets. Trim the beets to remove the bottom ends and remaining green tops, as desired. Place the beets in a smoker for 15–20 minutes (up to 30 minutes for full-sized beets). Remove from the smoker. The beets can be left whole if they are baby beets or quartered/cut into wedges if they are a larger size. Season with garlic, salt, pepper, and olive oil. Place on a roasting pan and roast at 425°F (245°C) for about 15–20 minutes just prior to service. Remove the venison from the marinade. Wrap the loin with bacon slices. Remove the mirepoix from the marinade, place the vegetables on the bottom of a roasting pan, and set the barded venison loin(s) on top. Preheat the oven to 425°F (245°C). Roast the venison for about 30 minutes or until the internal temperature reaches the desired doneness. Remove from the roasting pan and allow the venison roast to rest while you are preparing the sauce. Deglaze the roasting pan with the remaining 1¼ c (300 ml) of Syrah and reduce by half. Add the demiglace, bring to a boil, then reduce to a simmer and cook until it reaches the desired thickness (nappé—it coats the back of a spoon). Season to taste with salt and pepper. Slice venison and serve with roasted beets, mashed potatoes, Syrah demiglace, and a sprig of thyme as a garnish.

Cheese Course The next chapter provides a more in-depth look at pairing wines with cheeses and desserts. The addition of a cheese course or using it to replace dessert has been a growing trend in restaurants in North America. One reason for this growth is the simultaneous growth of artisan cheesemakers throughout the United States and Canada. For this particular menu, two well-known Northwest cheeses were selected: Oregonzola and Cougar Gold Cheddar. The Oregonzola is produced by the Rouge Creamery in Oregon, which has won numerous international awards for its blue-veined cheeses. This particular one is a Gorgonzola-style cheese that has sweet and savory characteristics. Cougar Gold Cheddar is produced by Washington State University Creamery and is a white cheddar featuring a sharp, nutty flavor that resembles Swiss or Gouda. To add a little excitement to this course, I include thyme-infused honey, apricot-orange conserve, dried cherry compote, and aged balsamic vinegar.

The wine selection depends on the sequencing of this item. If it is the final course, you can choose from a wider variety of wines. If a dessert course follows, in my mind the selections are a little more limited. When this course was served, we continued service of the Syrah that was served with the main course. A Washington Syrah, an Aussie Shiraz, or Cabernet/Shiraz blend would fit the bill in this case. The Washington Syrah is not as full-bodied as a Cabernet but has a smoother tactile sensation and more fruit-forward character.

While aged cheddar complements just about any wine, Stilton and vintage Port is the classic match for blue-veined cheese and wine. The combination of cheeses, infused honey, and fruit compote provides an opportunity to serve something a little sweeter with more acidity and flavors of honeyed, dried fruits. Late-harvest wines, ice wines, and Sauternes come to mind. A demi-sec sparkling wine or a Port would also fit the bill nicely here. Another option is to give the diners a choice—pour the dessert wine and leave the red wine on the table if they are not finished with it. This option gives them the opportunity to experiment and see which combination they prefer.

Food Item: Rouge Creamery Oregonzola and Washington State Cougar Gold Cheddar with Thyme-Infused Honey, Apricot-Orange Conserve, and Dried Cherry-Hazelnut Compote

Yield: 6 servings

Ingredients

3 tbsp (40 ml) honey
2 oz (30–60 g) bunch of fresh thyme (other herbs such as lavender can also be used)
3 fresh apricots (can substitute dried if desired)
Zest and juice of 1 orange
1/4 c (60 ml) sugar
2 oz (60 g) dried cherries
2 oz (60 g) hazelnuts, shelled and coarsely chopped
2–3 oz (60–80 ml) Port
Aged (15–25-year-old) balsamic vinegar
8 oz (225 g) Oregonzola
8 oz (225 g) Cougar Gold Cheddar

Preparation

Place the honey and thyme in a saucepan. Steep the honey mixture over low heat for about 45 minutes or until the herb flavor is infused in the honey. Remove from heat and strain out the thyme. For the conserve, blanch the apricots in boiling water to loosen the outside peel. Remove the peel and pit. Chop the peeled apricots into medium dice. Combine the diced apricots with the orange juice and the sugar. Bring to a boil and cook to 9°F above the boiling point (221°F [105°C]) or until thick. Remove from heat and skim. Chill and refrigerate until ready to serve. For the compote, combine the dried cherries, chopped hazelnuts, orange zest, and Port in a small bowl. Allow these to soak to blend the flavors and soften the cherries. To serve, drizzle a little of the infused honey and balsamic vinegar on the bottom of the plate. Cut the cheeses into wedges of about 1–1 1/2 oz (30–40 g) and arrange on top of the honey and vinegar. Place a small spoonful of the conserve and compote next to the cheeses.

Dessert Course The dessert course features a small cookie bowl filled with vanilla ice cream and a sauce made by combining strawberries and rhubarb. The cookie is like a Florentine, with a caramel-nutty flavor. It is made with walnuts, a popular nut in the Northwest, but you can substitute other nuts such as almonds or pecans. Vanilla ice cream is a favorite everywhere in North America, but the addition of strawberry-rhubarb sauce adds a regional touch. Washington and British Columbia are significant commercial producers of rhubarb, and strawberries are an abundant fruit crop in the Willamette Valley of Oregon, Idaho's Treasure Valley, and the Columbia Valley in Washington.

The custard base of the ice cream, the nuttiness of the cookie, and the fresh acidity of the fruit provide for several possible wine matches. A late-harvest Riesling, Sauternes, or ice wine would create a nice match of acidity and sweetness. The nutty character in the cookie shell would provide a match with a tawny Port. And the crisp acidity and bubbles of a demi-sec sparkling wine would provide a stimulating match for this ending to the meal.

For this menu, an Oregon white Port by David Hill was selected. The David Hill Vineyard is located near Forest Grove in the northern Willamette Valley. While traditional ports are made from red grapes, this Port is made from Muscats. The grape imparts a strong, sweet flavor, which is fortified with high-proof brandy and aged in French oak barrels. The finished wine contains 20–21 percent alcohol with flavors of peach, sweet orange, and soft caramel. The tastes of honey and nutmeg are also present; the total package creates a nice complement to the nutty, vanilla custard, and fruity dessert.

Food Item: Lacy Walnut Cookie Cup with Homemade Vanilla Ice Cream and Strawberry-Rhubarb Sauce

Yield: 12 servings

Ingredients for Cookies

1 c (225 ml) finely ground walnuts
3/4 c (170 ml) sugar
3 oz (85 g) unsalted butter, softened
4 tsp (18 ml) all-purpose flour
2 tbsp (28 ml) milk

Preparation

Preheat the oven to 350°F (175°C). Place all of the ingredients in a bowl and combine into a smooth paste. Place parchment paper on a baking sheet or use silicone baking mats. Use a heaping tablespoon of the dough for each cookie, allowing 4 to 6 inches on each side for the cookie dough to spread out (you should be able to get about 6 cookies on each large commercial sheet pan, 3 or 4 on a smaller baking sheet). Wet your fingers in a little cold water and gently flatten each spoonful of dough into rounds about 3 inches in diameter. Bake the cookies for 12–13 minutes until they are golden brown and about 6 inches in diameter. Remove the cookies from the oven and allow them to rest at room temperature for 1 minute. Lift each cookie from the parchment paper and drape it over a small glass bowl. Press the cookie over the bowl to mold the cookie in the shape of the bowl. You will need to work fast, as the cookies become brittle as they cool off. If they get a little too brittle, put them briefly back in the oven to soften. Remove the molded cookie from the bowl once it is hardened.

Ingredients for Ice Cream

1 1/2 c (340 ml) whole milk
1 1/2 c (340 ml) heavy or whipping cream
2 tsp (10 ml) vanilla
2 eggs
1/2 c (115 ml) sugar

Preparation

Combine the milk, cream, and vanilla in a saucepan and scald over medium-high heat (about 190°F or 88°C); do not boil. In a mixing bowl, whisk the eggs and sugar together until blended. Slowly add the heated milk mixture into the egg mixture, whisking constantly until thoroughly blended. Return the ice cream mixture back to the saucepan and return to the heat. Cook, stirring constantly, until it returns to about 190°F (88°C); again, be careful not to boil. Strain the mixture through a fine sieve and refrigerate until fully chilled. Freeze the mixture in an ice cream freezer.

Ingredients for Strawberry-Rhubarb Sauce

2 c (450 ml) diced fresh rhubarb
Juice of 1 lemon
1 c (225 ml) sugar
1/2 c (110 ml) water
1 pint (450 ml) fresh strawberries, washed, stemmed, and sliced

Preparation

Combine the rhubarb, lemon juice, sugar, and water in a saucepan. Bring to a boil and allow to simmer until the rhubarb is tender. Allow to cool. This can be made in advance and stored in the refrigerator for several days. Just prior to service, combine the sliced strawberries with the rhubarb sauce.

Assembly

Place a lacy cookie cup in the center of each plate. Put a scoop of ice cream in the center of each cookie cup. Top with the strawberry-rhubarb sauce. Garnish as desired with additional berries, mint, whipped cream, or nuts. Serve immediately.

WINE AND FOOD PAIRING INSTRUMENT

Figures 11.2a–11.2c constitute a three-page instrument that is useful in profiling wine and food items and determining whether or not these items are a match. It incorporates sequential tastings of the wine and the food and then a mixed tasting. As in the earlier discussion of the hierarchy of taste and the wine and food sensory pyramid, the wine and food elements are separated into three main categories: components, texture, and flavor elements.

As in earlier exercises, the sensory reference anchors will be useful to more consistently analyze wine and food elements using a 0-to-10-point scale (see Figure B.1, Food Sensory Anchor Scales, and Figure B.2, Wine Sensory Anchor Scales).

Step 1: Wine Evaluation

1. Fill in the descriptive information at the top of the Key Wine Pairing Elements sheet (Figure 11.2a).
2. Note the visual characteristics: color, clarity, consistency, and other observations.
3. Evaluate the wine components: sweetness level, acidity level, and amount of effervescence present, if any.
4. Evaluate the level of tannins present, alcohol level, and overall body.
5. Assess the level of spiciness, flavor intensity, and flavor persistence in the flavor section. Identify the dominant flavor(s) and put checks in the flavor check boxes where appropriate. If any spiciness is present, indicate if it is primarily hot spice, savory spice, or sweet spice.

Finally, write down any additional thoughts or observations based on your evaluation of the wine (general impressions, maturity, balance, food friendliness, quality, etc.).

Step 2: Food Evaluation

1. Fill in the descriptive information at the top of the Key Food Pairing Elements sheet (Figure 11.2b). Check the box indicating whether it is served hot or cold.
2. Just as you did with the wine, evaluate the food based on visual characteristics: color, shape, visual textures, height, portion size, and so on.
3. Evaluate the food components: sweetness, acidity, saltiness, and bitterness.
4. For texture, evaluate the fattiness level and overall body. Overall body is the power in the mouthfeel for the entire dish and will be impacted by protein type, cooking method, and the ingredients used.
5. Assess the level of spiciness, flavor intensity, and flavor persistence. Also, identify the dominant flavor(s) and put checks in the flavor check boxes where appropriate. If any spiciness is present, indicate if it is primarily hot spice, savory spice, or sweet spice.
6. Finally, write down any additional thoughts or observations based on your evaluation of the food (general impressions, balance, wine friendliness, quality, etc.).

Step 3: Food and Wine Final Evaluation

1. Transfer the descriptions and ratings from Figures 11.2a and 11.2b to the Food-and-Wine Pairing Evaluation sheet (Figure 11.2c).

Wine: _____ Producer_____ Vintage _____

Wine visual: Color[1]_____
                Clarity[2]_____

Wine Aroma[3]:   _____

```
              0              5              10
```

C O M P O N E N T S

| W 1 |

Dry to Sweet
Acidity
Effervescence

T E X T U R E

| W 2 |

Tannin
Alcohol Level
Overall Body

F L A V O R S

| W 3 |

Mark the spice category below

Spicy: | Hot | Pepper | Sweet | _____

Flavor Intensity & ID: _____

Flavor Persistence _____

```
0              5              10
```

Mark all flavor categories that apply in the boxes above

Wine Flavor Type:

| Fruity | Nutty | Smoky | Buttery | Herbal | Floral | Earthy | Other |

Wine Observations: _____

1. White color scale: Colorless—Green-tinge—Straw-Yellow—Yellow/Gold—Deep Gold—Amber/Brown
    Red color scale: Purple—Ruby Red—Deep Red—Red/Brown—Mahogany—Brown
2. Clarity scale: Cloudy---About Clear---Clear---Crystal Clear---Brilliant
3. See descriptions on Aroma Wheel.
4. Describe dominant flavor(s) and rate overall level of flavor intensity.

Comments: _____

Figure 11.2a

Key Wine Pairing Elements

Food Item: _____

| Hot | Cold |

Mark the temperature

Food visuals[1]:
_____
_____
_____

	0	5	10	

C O M P O N E N T S

F 1

Sweetness
Acidity
Saltiness
Bitterness

T E X T U R E

F 2

Fattiness   Type: _____
Overall Body

Mark the spice category below

F L A V O R S

F 3

| Hot | Pepper | Sweet |

Spicy:
Flavor Intensity & ID[2]:_____
Flavor Persistence _____

| 0 | 5 | 10 |

Food Flavor Type:

| Fruity | Nutty | Smoky | Cheesy | Herbal | Umami | Earthy | Other |

X All flavor categories that apply in the boxes above.

Food Observations: _____

1. Describe the basic visual impression of the prepared dish: color, shape, texture, general appeal, etc.
2. Describe the dominant flavor(s) and rate the overall level of flavor intensity

Comments:_____

Figure 11.2b

Key Food Pairing Elements

Food Item: _____ | Hot | Cold |

Wine: _____ Producer _____ Vintage _____

Food visuals: _____   Wine visual: Color _____
_____   Clarity _____
_____
_____   Wine Aroma: _____

		0	5	10	
COMPONENTS	**F 1**				Sweetness
					Acidity
					Saltiness
					Bitterness
	W 1				Dry to Sweet
					Acidity
					Effervescence
TEXTURE	**F 2**				Fattiness Type: _____
					Overall Body
	W 2				Tannin
					Alcohol Level
					Overall Body
FLAVORS	**F 3**				Spicy:	Hot	Pepper	Sweet	
					Flavor Intensity & ID: _____
					Flavor Persistence
	W 3				Spicy:	Hot	Pepper	Sweet	
					Flavor Intensity & ID: _____
					Flavor Persistence _____

0   5   10

Food Flavor Type:	Fruity	Nutty	Smoky	Cheesy	Herbal	Umami	Earthy	Other
Wine Flavor Type:	Fruity	Nutty	Smoky	Buttery	Herbal	Floral	Earthy	Other

Food Observations: _____

Wine Observations: _____

Level of Food & Wine Match: Match based on: Complementary   Contrast

          0---1---2---3---4---5---6---7---8---9---10   Components   _____   _____
     None Refreshment Neutral Good Synergistic   Texture   _____   _____
                                                           Flavors   _____   _____

Comments:

Figure 11.2c

Wine and Food Pairing Evaluation

2. Beginning at the left end of each scale (components, textures, and flavors), shade in the space on the scale up to your marked ranking of the food item and wine for each element on the scale.

3. Circle the food element descriptions on the right-hand side of the scale that are at or beyond the middle point of the scale. These are likely to be the key elements that will drive wine pairing decisions. Evaluate the likely impact of these food elements based on their magnitude and likely reactions with wine elements. Is there one key element? More than one?

4. Circle the wine element descriptions on the right-hand side of the scale that are at or beyond the middle point of the scale. These are likely to be the key elements that will drive food matching decisions.

5. Look at the profiles and decide whether this is likely to be a good food-and-wine match or not. (Additional guidance on the use of these profiles is provided in the upcoming sections.)

6. Taste the wine and food item together. Based on this mixed tasting, rank the level of perceived match using the 0–10 scale at the bottom of the page. The level of match can range from no match to a synergistic match. Indicate whether this match is based on similar or contrasting characteristics of components, texture, or flavors by placing an X in the appropriate box.

This evaluation system is designed so that you can keep the individual evaluations of food dishes with the recipes for future reference and the individual wine evaluations with the wine menu for future pairing selections and recommendations. The completed third page combining both food-and-wine evaluations can be saved for future reference. If a poor match was achieved with the wine and food item, additional wines can be evaluated or recipe adjustments can be made to create a better fit with a desired wine.

WINE AND FOOD MATCH DECISION TREE

Chapters 5 through 10 present twelve rules that impact the level of perceived match when wine and food are tasted together. These relationships are incorporated into the Wine and Food Pairing Decision Tree (Figure 11.3). This decision tree allows you to quickly walk through an assessment of the anticipated level of match based on the profiles created for the wine and food in steps 1 and 2 of the wine and food pairing instrument.

The three main categories of wine and food elements—components, texture, and flavor—are at the top of the decision tree. The level of match is at the bottom of the decision tree. In between, there are a series of decisions based on the twelve decision rules presented in Chapters 5 through 10. These decision rules provide likely assessments of match level when taken in an additive fashion. "Additive fashion" means that the relationships in the decision tree are hierarchical in nature (components to texture to flavors), and as more and more of these relationships indicate a match, the overall perception of match increases.

A PROFILING APPROACH TO MATCH LEVEL ASSESSMENT

How can wine and food profiles based on the Wine and Food Pairing Instrument and decisions based on the Wine and Food Pairing Decision Tree allow you to predict levels of

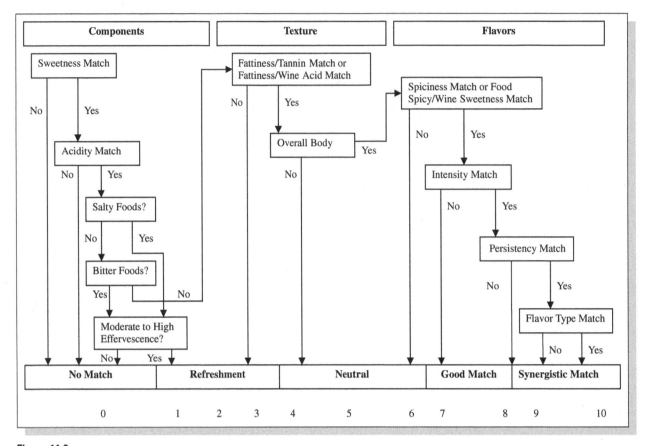

Figure 11.3

Wine and Food Pairing Decision Tree

match? Figure 11.4 provides a format for quantifying the wine and food associations based on the relationships shown in the decision tree (Figure 11.3), the twelve matching rules discussed in earlier chapters, and the visual profiles of the wine and food items developed in the first two parts of the pairing instrument.

In the following examples, two wine and food pairing profiles are presented. These items were selected from a five-course menu created by students in one of my previous wine and food pairing classes. When the menu was prepared, the entire class tasted and evaluated it, along with two wine and food experts. The match scores generated by the students using the Wine and Food Pairing Instrument strongly correlated with the wine and food experts' scores of perceived level of match. This finding provides support for this method of predicting match based on profiles and quantifying relationships.[6]

The five-course menu and wine matches selected by the student groups are presented in Figure 11.5. Under each menu and wine item description, there is a match score based on the 0–10 scale shown in the Wine and Food Pairing Decision Tree; it was calculated as the average level of perceived match across fifteen participants. As you can see, the average match scores ranged from a low of 3.5 (the cheese course) to a high of 9 (for the lamb course).

Example 1   First, let us consider the pasta course. The food item was a combination of smoked corn, grilled chicken, Alfredo sauce, and penne pasta. The wine was a New Zealand Sauvignon Blanc. Figure 11.6 provides a profile of the component, texture, and flavor relationships for this dish and the wine.

Figure 11.7 provides a score following the Quantifying Wine and Food Profiles to Predict Match Level sheet (Figure 11.4) using the Wine and Food Pairing Decision Tree as a guide.

Food Item:_____

Wine:_____ Producer_____ Vintage _____

Components	Similarity	Contrast	Score
Sweetness Match	_____	_____	_____
(Food Sweetness < or = Wine Sweetness: Yes = 1, No = 0)			
Acidity Match	_____	_____	_____
(Food Acid < or = Wine Acidity: Yes = 1, No = 0)			
Low to Moderate Levels of Food Saltiness			_____
(Yes = .5, No = 0)			
Low to Moderate Levels of Food Bitterness			_____
(Yes = .5, No = 0)			
Moderate-High Food Saltiness or Bitterness and Wine Effervescence Level Match			
(Yes = 1, No = 0)			_____
High Levels of Food Salt or Bitterness (Yes = No Match)			**No Match**

Texture	Similarity	Contrast	Score
Food Fattiness and Wine Tannin Match			_____
(Food Fattiness = Wine Tannin: Yes = 1, No = 0)			
Food Fattiness (Vegetable Fat) and Wine Acidity Match			_____

Figure 11.4

Quantifying Wine and Food Profiles to Predict Match Level

The first step is to evaluate the match relationships for the components. You can see from Figure 11.7 that this food item is slightly sweeter (due to the sweet cream and fresh corn in the dish) than the Sauvignon Blanc. At this point, you need to make a judgment call. Is the food sweetness level difference high enough to lower the level of perceived match? Or will it balance out with a contrast to the acidity in the wine? As you can see, the sweetness match could be given a 0 or a 1 depending on your judgment. The acidity component indicates a match, as the wine acidity is much higher than the food item. The pasta has low to moderate levels of salt and bitterness, resulting in a value of .5 for each. There is no need to match this item with a sparkling wine, as it does not have moderately high levels of salt or bitterness—although this does not mean a sparkling wine would not be a good match.

(Food Fattiness = Wine Acid: Yes = 1, No = 0)

Food and Wine Body Match   _____   _____   _____

(Food Overall Body = Wine Overall Body: Yes = 1, No = 0)

Flavor	**Similarity**	**Contrast**	**Score**

Low to Moderate Spice Level Match   _____   _____   _____

(Food Spiciness = Wine Spiciness: Yes = 1, No = 0)

Moderate Food Spice and Wine Sweetness   _____   _____   _____

(Food Spiciness = Wine Sweetness: Yes = 1, No = 0)

High Levels of Food Spice (Yes = No Match)   **No Match**

Flavor Intensity Match   _____

(Food Intensity = Wine Intensity: Yes = 1, No = 0)

Flavor Type Match   _____   _____   _____

(Flavors similar or contrasting: Yes = 1, No = 0)

Flavor Persistency Match   _____

(Food Persistence = Wine Persistence: Yes = 1, No = 0)

Total Score   _____

Figure 11.4

(Continued)

Next, you should consider the texture relationships based on the food and wine profiles. Sauvignon Blanc has no tannin, so it does not create a match with food fattiness. The wine acidity could create a match with food fattiness, but in this case the fat is animal (dairy) rather than vegetable. Finally, in looking at the body-to-body match, it is obvious that the body of the pasta is substantially higher than that of the Sauvignon Blanc.

In terms of flavor, the pasta and wine have a match based on similar spice levels, intensity levels, flavor type contrasts, and persistency levels. The spice levels are about the same in both items; the wine is slightly more intense, while the pasta flavor is slightly more persistent. The main flavors in the food are lightly smoky and cheesy. The main flavor in the wine is herbal and grassy. This creates a contrast match between them.

Overall, the predicted level of match would be a 6 or 7, depending on your interpretation of the sweetness match. The students' average perceived match when they tasted the pasta and wine together was 6.5—very close to the predicted level. This score is on the border between a neutral and good match for this particular wine and food combination. When students tasted them together, the combination was adequate but could have been improved with some other possibilities. For instance, a Chardonnay with some oakiness to

Smoked Corn & Chicken Pasta

Penne pasta tossed in a creamy Alfredo sauce with delicate hints of smoked corn

and chicken

Wine: 2002 Villa Maria Sauvignon Blanc

Match Score: **6.5**

Salad

Salad of charred beef filet, arugula, cherry tomatoes, & roasted garlic vinaigrette

Wine: 2000 Bouchard Père & Fils, Le Chamville, Beaujolais

Match Score: **8**

Lamb Two Ways

Grilled lamb chop & braised lamb shoulder meat with golden whipped potatoes

and forest mushrooms

Wine: 2001 Baron Philippe Rothschild, St. Emillion, Bordeaux Rouge

Match Score: **9**

Cheese Course

Grilled Brie with spiced pecans and apple compote

Wine: 2001 Wynn's Coonawarra Australia Cabernet Sauvignon

Match Score: **3.5**

Cassati alla Siciliana

Sicilian cake with ricotta icing & candied orange peel

Wine: 2003 Nivole Moscato d'Asti

Match Score: **7**

Figure 11.5

Wine and Food Menu Example

Food Item: _Smoked Corn and Chicken Pasta_ | ~~Hot~~ | Cold

Wine: _Sauvignon Blanc_   Producer: _Villa Maria_   Vintage: _2002_

Food visuals:
Creamy, red, yellow and white in
color

Wine visual: Color: _Straw Yellow_
                Clarity: _Crystal Clear_

Wine Aroma: _Grassy/Herbaceous_

0   5   10

COMPONENTS	F1		Sweetness
			Acidity
			Saltiness
			Bitterness
	W1		Dry to Sweet
			Acidity
			Effervescence

TEXTURE	F2		Fattiness Type: _____
			Overall Body _____
	W2		Tannin
			Alcohol Level
			Overall Body

FLAVORS	F3		Spicy: Hot Pepper Sweet _Basil_
			Flavor Intensity & ID: _Light smoke, cheese_
			Flavor Persistence
	W3		Spicy: Hot Pepper Sweet _Herbs_
			Flavor Intensity & ID: _Grassy, vegetal_
			Flavor Persistence

0   5   10

| Food Flavor Type: | Fruity | Nutty | ~~Smoky~~ | ~~Cheesy~~ | Herbal | Umami | Earthy | Other |
| Wine Flavor Type: | Fruity | Nutty | Smoky | Buttery | ~~Herbal~~ | Floral | Earthy | Other |

Food Observations: _Creamy and lightly smoky_

Wine Observations: _Crisp acidity and grassy_

Level of Food & Wine Match:

0---1---2---3---4---5---6---~~7~~---8---9---10
None Refreshment Neutral Good Synergistic

Match based on: Complementary   Contrast
Components   _____   _____
Texture   _____   _____
Flavors   _____   _____

Comments:

Figure 11.6

Wine and Food Pairing Example 1

Components	Similarity	Contrast	Score
Sweetness Match	_____	___X___	0 or 1
(Food Sweetness < or = Wine Sweetness: Yes = 1, No = 0)			
Acidity Match	_____	_____	1
(Food Acid < or = Wine Acidity: Yes = 1, No = 0)			
Low to Moderate Levels of Food Saltiness			.5
(Yes = .5 No = 0)			
Low to Moderate Levels of Food Bitterness			.5
(Yes = .5, No = 0)			
Moderate-High Food Saltiness or Bitterness and Wine Effervescence Level Match			
(Yes = 1, No = 0)			N/A
High Levels of Food Salt or Bitterness (Yes = No Match)			**No Match**

Texture	Similarity	Contrast	Score
Food Fattiness and Wine Tannin Match			0
(Food Fattiness = Wine Tannin: Yes = 1, No = 0)			
Food Fattiness (Vegetable Fat) and Wine Acidity Match			0
(Food Fattiness = Wine Acid: Yes = 1, No = 0)			
Food and Wine Body Match	_____	_____	0
(Food Overall Body = Wine Overall Body: Yes = 1, No = 0)			

Figure 11.7

Smoked Corn and Chicken Pasta and Sauvignon Blanc Predicted Match Level

it would create a match in terms of body, smoke, and oak, and offer a little tannin to provide a better match with the dairy fat in the Alfredo sauce.

Example 2 Figure 11.8 provides a profile of the dish served for the salad course, Salad of Beef and Arugula with Roast Garlic Vinaigrette, and the wine served with it, a Beaujolais. Figure 11.9 shows the quantified score based on the assessment of this profile. As with any dish, the first step is to evaluate the match relationships of the components. With this course,

Flavor	Similarity	Contrast	Score
Low to Moderate Spice Level Match	X	_____	1
(Food Spiciness = Wine Spiciness: Yes = 1, No = 0)			
Moderate Food Spice and Wine Sweetness	_____	_____	0
(Food Spiciness = Wine Sweetness: Yes = 1, No = 0)			
High Levels of Food Spice (Yes = No Match)			**No Match**
Flavor Intensity Match			1
(Food Intensity = Wine Intensity: Yes = 1, No = 0)			
Flavor Type Match	_____	X	1
(Flavors similar or contrasting: Yes = 1, No = 0)			
Flavor Persistency Match			1
(Food Persistence = Wine Persistence: Yes = 1, No = 0)			
Total Score			6–7

Figure 11.7

(Continued)

there is a match regarding the sweetness levels and acidity levels. There are no problems with excessive saltiness or bitterness. Thus, for the components section, this combination receives 3 points.

For the texture section, this combination receives 2 more points. The beef tenderloin was not particularly fatty and the Beaujolais has relatively little tannin, so the rule relating tannin to animal fat is not very relevant here. Since the fattiness in this dish comes mostly from the olive oil in the vinaigrette, there is a match between that and the acidity level in the wine. There is also a body-to-body match for the beef salad and the Beaujolais.

In the flavor section, the combination picks up 3 additional points, creating a predicted match score of 8. The spice levels in the wine and salad are similar, and there is a match in flavor intensity and flavor types. The flavor types in the salad are mainly smoky (due to the charred beef) and earthy (due to the garlic and arugula). The smoky flavor creates a contrast with the fruity flavor of the wine, and the earthy flavor of the salad creates a similarity match with the earthy flavor of the Beaujolais. The predicted match score of 8 is the same as the average match score of 8 provided by the fifteen participants.

Collectively, the profiles, the Wine and Food Paring Decision Tree, and the Quantifying Wine and Food Profiles to Predict Match Level scoring sheet provide some tools and guidelines for predicting potential matching levels. This process forces you to think about all of the wine and food elements as you determine the impact of a match or non-match between the various elements on perceived level of overall match when the food and wine are tasted together. The exercises at the end of this chapter offer you an opportunity to walk through this process and to become more familiar with this holistic evaluation method.

Food Item: _Salad of Beef, Arugula, and Roast Garlic Vinaigrette_   Hot | ~~Cold~~

Wine: _Beaujolais_   Producer: _Bouchard Père & Fils_   Vintage: _2000_

Food visuals:
Colorful, contrasting tenderloin with crisp greens

Wine visual: Color: _Medium red_
Clarity: _Crystal Clear_

Wine Aroma: _Fruity and earthy_

		0	5	10	

COMPONENTS

F1
- Sweetness
- Acidity
- Saltiness
- Bitterness

W1
- Dry to Sweet
- Acidity
- Effervescence

TEXTURE

F2
- Fattiness   Type: _Primarily olive oil_
- Overall Body

W2
- Tannin
- Alcohol Level
- Overall Body

FLAVORS

F3
- Spicy: | Hot | Pepper | Sweet | _Peppery_
- Flavor Intensity & ID: _Light smoke & garlic_
- Flavor Persistence

W3
- Spicy: | Hot | Pepper | Sweet |
- Flavor Intensity & ID: _Red fruit & earthy_
- Flavor Persistence

		0	5	10	

Food Flavor Type: | ~~Fruity~~ | Nutty | ~~Smoky~~ | Cheesy | Herbal | Umami | ~~Earthy~~ | Other

Wine Flavor Type: | ~~Fruity~~ | Nutty | Smoky | Buttery | Herbal | Floral | ~~Earthy~~ | Other

Food Observations: _Grilled beef, peppery greens, and light vinaigrette_

Wine Observations: _Fruity, light tannin, and light earthiness_

Level of Food & Wine Match:

0---1---2---3---4---5---6---7---~~8~~---9---10
None   Refreshment   Neutral   Good   Synergistic

Match based on: Complementary   Contrast

- Components   _____   _____
- Texture   _____   _____
- Flavors   _____   _____

Comments:

Figure 11.8

Wine and Food Pairing Example 2

Components	Similarity	Contrast	Score
Sweetness Match	X	___	1
(Food Sweetness < or = Wine Sweetness: Yes = 1, No = 0)			
Acidity Match	X	___	1
(Food Acid < or = Wine Acidity: Yes = 1, No = 0)			
Low to Moderate Levels of Food Saltiness			.5
(Yes = .5, No = 0)			
Low to Moderate Levels of Food Bitterness			.5
(Yes = .5, No = 0)			
Moderate-High Food Saltiness or Bitterness and Wine Effervescence Level Match			
(Yes = 1, No = 0)			N/A
High Levels of Food Salt or Bitterness (Yes = No Match)			**No Match**

Texture	Similarity	Contrast	Score
Food Fattiness and Wine Tannin Match			0
(Food Fattiness = Wine Tannin: Yes = 1, No = 0)			
Food Fattiness (Vegetable Fat) and Wine Acidity Match			1
(Food Fattiness = Wine Acid: Yes = 1, No = 0)			
Food and Wine Body Match	___	___	1
(Food Overall Body = Wine Overall Body: Yes = 1, No = 0)			

Figure 11.9

Beef Salad and Beaujolais Predicted Match Level

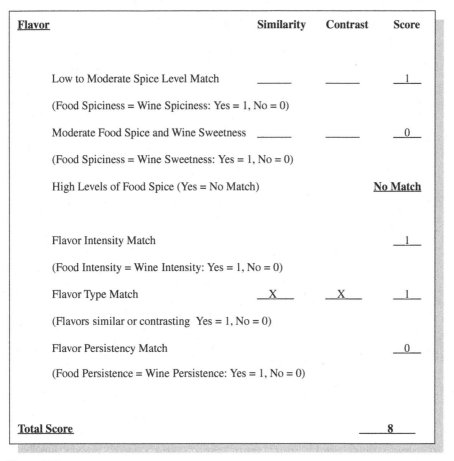

Flavor	Similarity	Contrast	Score
Low to Moderate Spice Level Match	_____	_____	_1_
(Food Spiciness = Wine Spiciness: Yes = 1, No = 0)			
Moderate Food Spice and Wine Sweetness	_____	_____	_0_
(Food Spiciness = Wine Sweetness: Yes = 1, No = 0)			
High Levels of Food Spice (Yes = No Match)			**No Match**
Flavor Intensity Match			_1_
(Food Intensity = Wine Intensity: Yes = 1, No = 0)			
Flavor Type Match	X	X	_1_
(Flavors similar or contrasting Yes = 1, No = 0)			
Flavor Persistency Match			_0_
(Food Persistence = Wine Persistence: Yes = 1, No = 0)			
Total Score			_8_

Figure 11.9

(*Continued*)

SUMMARY

This chapter focuses on the wine and food pairing instrument and how the profiles developed can be used to predict levels of match between certain foods and wines. The instrument and decision tree are designed so that food items and wines can be assessed separately to identify their profiles, and then the wine and food match decision tree and scoring sheet provide a structure to evaluate the impact of various elements on the potential match.

The final page of the wine and food pairing instrument (Figure 11.2c) can be used without the first two pages if you are planning a mixed tasting. If you want to save the results for future reference for potential pairs with other wines or food items, you can complete all three pages.

The Pacific Northwest menu is an example of how many more variables come into play when you are plan-

ning a vertical pairing of multiple wines with various food courses. As a general rule, as you progress through successive courses, the food and wine increase in intensity. The discussion of the Pacific Northwest menu and recipes provides examples of the reasoning behind pairing decisions. Why were these particular food items selected? Why were these particular wines selected? Do you believe they are each good to ideal matches?

The following exercises will reinforce the wine and food pairing concepts and the process illustrated throughout this chapter. The food items and wines have been selected to illustrate the spectrum of match levels. Your job will be to determine if you agree with the expected match level after tasting these items together. Did you find any surprises? Were there any differences based on your individual preferences?

DISCUSSION QUESTIONS

1. What issues should be considered before planning any menu?

2. What are the five basic rules for wine sequencing decisions?

3. What are the twelve general guidelines for wine and food matches that are outlined in the decision tree?

4. Are these twelve general guidelines hard-and-fast rules to follow, or is there some judgment involved?

5. Are there situations where it is advantageous to use a sequential tasting approach as opposed to a mixed tasting approach?

EXERCISE 11.1

FOOD-AND-WINE MATCH LEVELS

For this exercise, you may utilize many of the same varietals used in previous chapters or experiment with other wines. Use the Food Sensory Anchor Scale (Figure B.1) and Wine Sensory Anchor Scale (Figure B.2) to create basic reference points for ascending levels of components, texture, and flavor as you complete the questions posed by the Wine and Food Pairing Instrument. When selecting the wines for this exercise, be sure to consider the potential impact of Old or New World selections, climate zones, oak aging, and wine maturity.

OBJECTIVES

To distinguish and rank differing levels of elements present in wine and food; to compare food and wine profiles to predict match level; to assess whether the predicted level of match mirrors the perceived level of match.

Mise En Place: Things to Do Before the Exercise Review the Wine and Food Pairing Decision Tree and the sections explaining how to use Figures 11.2a–11.2c and Figure 11.4 in this

chapter. Schedule the food preparation to meet the desired tasting time. The shrimp and melon dish can be assembled at the last minute if all of the mise en place is gathered and the shrimp is poached, chilled, and peeled ahead of time. The Caesar salad can be assembled at the last minute using either bottled dressing or homemade dressing. The grilled sirloin needs to be cooked and served right before the tasting. The cheese and chocolate should be ready to go whenever needed. Of course, care must be taken to ensure the food items and wines are served at the proper temperature.

MATERIALS NEEDED

Table 11.1   Materials Needed for Exercise 11.1

1 white paper placemat per student, with numbered or labeled circles to place wineglasses (Figure 9.4a)	1 spit cup per student Corkscrew Drinking water for each student
1 copy of the Aroma Wheel per student	Napkins
4 copies of Figures 11.2a, 11.2b, and 11.2c per student	5 wineglasses per student
1 copy Food and Wine Sensory Anchor Scales per student	Cutting board
4+ copies of Figure 11.4 (Quantifying Wine and Food Profiles to Predict Match Level) per student	Bread or crackers to cleanse palate
Plates for tasting samples of each food item	Plastic (or other) forks and knives

Table 11.2   Wines, Food Items, and Anticipated Match Levels

Wines	Food Items	Anticipated Match Level
Moscato d'Asti	Chilled Shrimp and Melon with Mint-Curry Cream	Good plus
Cool/moderate-climate Chardonnay	Caesar Salad	Refreshment to neutral
Cabernet Sauvignon, Meritage, or Bordeaux	Grilled Sirloin	Good plus
Tawny Port	Stilton	Good plus
Moscato d'Asti, Cabernet Sauvignon, or Port	Bittersweet chocolate	These should all work, but for different reasons, and preferences will vary

STEPS

1. Prepare and distribute the food items.

2. Pour a sample of each wine for each student.

3. Taste the wine samples and assess all wine elements. Record your observations on Figure 11.2a (and/or Figure 11.2c).

4. Taste each food sample and assess all food elements. Record your observations in Figure 11.2b (and/or Figure 11.2c).

5. Taste the food items in the following order. You can then go back and forth between them later if needed.

   a. Shrimp and Melon with Mint-Curry Cream

   b. Caesar Salad

   c. Grilled Sirloin

   d. Cheese

   e. Dark chocolate

6. Using Figure 11.4, calculate a predicted level of match for each item, and match each item with at least one wine using the profiles created with Figures 11.2a and 11.2b.

7. Taste each food sample with each of the four wine samples. Using the perceived level of match scale at the bottom of Figure 11.2c, rank your perception of the match using the 0–10 scale. Compare this match score with the one you predicted using Figure 11.4.

8. Discuss and record any sensory observations you make about the relationship between the wines and food items. Which wine and food had the best match? Was it what you predicted? Which wine and food had the lowest match? Did any items have a no match rating? If so, why? Were any of the matches truly synergistic?

9. Rank the level of match for each food item with each wine from lowest to highest level of predicted match using the score from Figure 11.4.

   a. Shrimp and Melon with Mint-Curry Cream
      Lowest score = 1. _____   2. _____   3. _____
                      4. _____ = Highest score

   b. Caesar Salad
      Lowest score = 1. _____   2. _____   3. _____
                      4. _____ = Highest score

   c. Grilled Sirloin
      Lowest score = 1. _____   2. _____   3. _____
                      4. _____ = Highest score

   d. Stilton Cheese
      Lowest score = 1. _____   2. _____   3. _____
                      4. _____ = Highest score

   e. Dark chocolate
      Lowest score = 1. _____   2. _____   3. _____
                      4. _____ = Highest score

10. Write any other comments, thoughts, and observations that you identified during this evaluation process. Did the predicted level of match coincide with your perceived level of match when the food and wine were tasted together? Was there a pre-

dominant category of elements that impacted the level of match across all of the food-and-wine combinations? If so, was it components, texture, or flavors? Were there any surprises based on the resulting matching relationships?

Food Item: Shrimp and Melon with Mint-Curry Cream

Yield: 8 appetizer servings

Ingredients

24 shrimp (20–25 per lb [40–50 per kg])
1/2 gal (2 l) water
1 lemon, cut in half
1 tbsp (15 ml) Old Bay seasoning (or seasoning of your choice)
1 tbsp (15 ml) dill, chopped
1 honeydew
1 cantaloupe
6 oz (170 ml) heavy cream
2 tsp (10 ml) finely chopped mint
1/2 tsp (2 ml) curry powder
Salt
Pepper

Preparation

Combine the water, Old Bay, and dill in a 1-gallon (4 l) pot. Squeeze the lemon into the water and place the lemon halves into the pot. Bring to a boil. Add the unpeeled shrimp to the boiling liquid. Once the liquid returns to a simmer, turn off the heat, leaving the shrimp in the hot liquid. Allow to sit about 15 minutes. Remove the cooked shrimp from the liquid and chill with ice or in a shallow pan in the refrigerator. Discard the liquid. Once the shrimp are completely chilled, peel and devein the shrimp. Keep the peeled shrimp chilled until ready for service. Cut the melons in half; remove and discard the seeds. Using a melon baller, scoop all of the honeydew and cantaloupe flesh into round balls. Place in a small bowl and lightly season with salt and pepper. Place the cream in a bowl and whisk lightly until it is thickened enough to coat the back of the spoon. Fold in the chopped mint and curry powder. Season to taste with salt and pepper. To assemble, place a tablespoon of mint-curry cream in the center of each appetizer plate. Add a small mound of melon balls to the center. Dip the shrimp in the remaining mint-curry cream and place 3 shrimp on each plate, partially leaning them on the mound of melon balls. Garnish as desired and serve.

Food Item: Caesar Salad Recipe

Yield: 4 servings

There are numerous versions of Caesar Salad, from the traditional to those that barely resemble one. This recipe is of the traditional style. For this exercise, you can easily use a bottled dressing or substitute your favorite Caesar dressing recipe.

Ingredients

1 head romaine lettuce
4 anchovies
2 cloves garlic
2 tsp (10 ml) Dijon mustard
2 tsp (10 ml) Worcestershire sauce
4–5 dashes Tabasco sauce
2 whole eggs, room temperature
Juice of 1 lemon
1/2 c (115 ml) extra-virgin olive oil
1/2 c (115 ml) grated Parmesan cheese
2 c (450 ml) croutons
Salt
Pepper

Preparation

Trim any bruised or browned leaves from the romaine. Thoroughly wash and drain the lettuce; pat the lettuce dry. Cut or tear the cleaned lettuce into 1 1/2-inch pieces and refrigerate it for about 30 minutes to make it crispy. In a large bowl, grind anchovies and garlic to a pastelike consistency with the back of a spoon. Stir in mustard, Worcestershire sauce, Tabasco, eggs, and lemon juice. Drizzle the olive oil into the mixture while continuously whisking. Season to taste with salt, pepper, and additional Tabasco or Worcestershire, if desired. Just before service, toss the dressing, lettuce, croutons, and Parmesan cheese together. Serve on chilled dinner plates. Garnish with additional croutons and Parmesan, if desired.

Food Item: Grilled Sirloin

Yield: 6 servings

For this recipe, you can use either beef or lamb sirloin. While the flavors in lamb are generally more intense than beef, both selections help demonstrate wine matching relationships.

Ingredients	Preparation
3 tbsp (40 ml) olive oil 1 tbsp (10–15 ml) Worcestershire sauce 2 tsp (10 ml) soy sauce 1 clove garlic, minced 1 tbsp (15 ml) fresh thyme Salt Pepper 3 lb (1.4 kg) beef or lamb sirloin, in 6 steaks	Combine olive oil, Worcestershire sauce, soy sauce, garlic, thyme, and salt and pepper to taste. Brush this mixture over the surface of the steaks. Cover and refrigerate for at least 1 hour. Preheat grill or barbecue. Grill the steaks to desired doneness.

NOTES

1. Anita Stewart, *The Flavours of Canada* (Vancouver, BC: Raincoast Books, 2000), 17.
2. Alexis Lichine, *Alexis Lichine's New Encyclopedia of Wines and Spirits* (New York: Alfred A. Knopf, 1987), p. 583.
3. J. Arkell, *New World Wines: The Complete Guide* (New York: Sterling, 1999).
4. Stewart, *The Flavours of Canada*.
5. R. Mayfield, "Washington Syrah—Set in Stone" (2002), www.thewinenews.com/augsep02/cover.html (accessed February 1, 2006).
6. R. J. Harrington and R. Hammond, "Predicting Synergistic Matches in Wine and Food: Instrument Testing and Evaluation," *Proceedings of the International CHRIE Conference* (2005): 155-60.

CHAPTER 12

WINE AND CHEESE: A NATURAL AFFINITY?

CHAPTER OUTLINE:

Introduction

Aperitif: Cheese, An Inspiration and an Education

Wine and Cheese Pairing

Cheese Categories

Summary

Exercises

KEY CONCEPTS:

- Balance and harmony between wine and cheese
- Limitations of red wine with cheese
- The impact of cheese type and wine friendliness

INTRODUCTION

The old wine merchant's tenet is that when you buy wine, taste it with apples, as it will be at its worst, and sell wine when buyers taste it with cheese, as it will be at its best. What is it about wine and cheese that creates such a positive gastronomic response?

In its simplest role, wine acts to cleanse the palate. This occurs due to a basic "washing" action as well as increased saliva production caused by tannic wines and ethanol (alcohol). This cleansing process minimizes sensory fatigue. Alternating wine with food helps to freshen the palate for more wine.

Further, the fat, proteins, and acid inherent in cheese combine with acids and tannin in wine to soften the impact of acid, bitter, and astringent sensations that are typical of most white and red wines. The dilution of alcohol when wine is consumed with food in general and cheese in particular is thought to promote the release of wine aromatics and create a more pleasant finish.

Despite these characteristics (or perhaps in part because of them), the main reason people consume wine and cheese together is that they enjoy the combination. Artisanal cheese makers and knowledgeable restaurateurs create an opportunity for us to maximize this enjoyment. The following description by Etienne Boissy of his experience in the French competition Meilleur Ouvrier de France provides an interesting example not only of the innovative process used in cheese production and service but also of pushing the envelope in a competitive environment.

Aperitif | Cheese, an Inspiration and an Education

Le Concours du Meilleur Ouvrier de France is an annual competition in France that has as its goal the search for professional excellence, bringing together individual performance and economic adaptation. The competition, whose name literally translates as "the contest of the best workmen in France," is a symbol of excellence and is held every three years, with over two hundred trades represented. Values that are rewarded in this contest include manual skills, intelligence, imagination, taste, technicality, courage, and perseverance.

The category of "trades of the mouth" includes cuisine, pastry, baking, and cheese. Etienne Boissy is the coordinator of pedagogy and a professor of table arts at the Paul Bocuse Institute near Lyon, France. He received a Meilleur Ouvrier de France award in cheese in 2004. For the competition, Etienne included a variety of cheeses made from cow's, goat's, or sheep's milk as well as a variety of styles (fresh, semisoft, hard, blue). Below he describes the theme and creative process he used to create his winning presentation for the competition.

"The competition that I won in order to become Meilleur Ouvrier de France de Fromage 2004 [Best Cheese Craftsman in France 2004] was based on the subject of time. What better theme is an invitation to think deeply about fine cheeses? It is this reflection about time that finally led me to create the cheese installation that ultimately became the winning entry.

"In order to imagine this winning structure, I turned first toward clock faces for inspiration and second toward the two materials insisted upon by the 2004 competition: beech wood and Plexiglas.

"When speaking of cheese and its history, time and the maturation process are key, given that, the period of maturation varies according to the type of cheese. It is both human factors and storage conditions that allow a cheese to assert itself owing to the lactic cultures, mold, fungi, and yeasts that form. The changes are apparent with each passing day: the color, the texture, the smell and the taste become stronger, the whole cheese develops toward excellence—over time. In thinking about time, I was aware that time and space have long been understood to be relative and, in a sense, unified. The solar system in which our planet moves situates the earth in a wider galaxy appropriately known as the Milky Way. This enormous Milky Way and all that it represents brings us to the heart of the subject: the ability of man to work in harmony with nature and her cycles in the transformation of milk into cheese during time.

"I chose to retain the materials imposed by the competition—beech wood and Plexiglas—in order to give the structure a contemporary design. The wood brings a certain warmth; its roughness and its natural aspect invites us to look back to a rural and natural past. The Plexiglas affords a certain luminosity and transparency. As the product of modernity, it sends us forward to the future. This juxtaposition is successful owing to the inherent contrast of elements such as can be found in various gastronomic partnerships today.

"In the past, tradition held that the earth was the center of the universe. Once created, the earth had to be organized into days, months, seasons, and years. The seasons, thereafter, are naturally associated with vegetation, nature, and life cycles, not least with regard to spring and the associated notion of rebirth.

"It was my intention to present the notion of renewal represented by the seasons in the context of cheese. In the display, each season was illustrated by a subtle change of color, by nature's shifting symbols, and by appropriate extracts from the world of literature.

"As time passes, the tick-tock of the pendulum counts out the seconds. This idea of motion is illustrated by the presence at the center of the room of clock parts placed on a plinth that slowly turns clockwise. As cog wheels transmit their movement from one to the other, so we see a representation of the transmission of knowledge and know-how between generations of cheese producers. Finally, the notion of movement reaches its apogee in the form of a model solar system mounted at the top of the structure as a representation of the planets' cycle in time around the sun.

"In order to illustrate time in a historical way, I have chosen to illustrate the passing of time via developments in the equipment used in the production of cheese, notably the changes in the manufacture of cheese vats during the centuries, be they pottery, wood, iron, aluminum, or plastic.

"Finally, as label holders for each cheese, I chose wood-base hourglasses, through which time passes slowly in homage to the best of my cheese samples. For the smaller cheese examples, I was inspired by antique pocket watches. On the label, besides the name of the cheese and its origin, is the duration of the maturation, which is stressed.

"Each of the three different colors of paper used to make the labels represent a different milk, be it cow's, goat's, or sheep's."

As you can see from this description, winning a competition of this stature requires substantial thought and planning in regard to not only the cheese but also additional elements that relate to its production, innovation, and ultimately enjoyment. The creative and innovative process can be inspiring and educational for all for the participants (including the competitors).

WINE AND CHEESE PAIRING

This chapter focuses on cheeses and pairing them with wine. Many people assume that all wines go with all cheeses—but do they? If this is not the case, do red wines taste better with most cheeses or do white wines? This chapter answers these questions by providing some basic guidelines in wine and cheese pairing and dividing cheeses into general categories that are relevant to overall wine-friendliness.

In many cases, wine and cheese have a couple of things in common that create a natural match. First, both are created by using a fermentation process. This process creates a variety of attributes in cheese that relate to their components, texture, and flavor. In cheese, this

---

Etienne Boissy is the coordinator of pedagogy and professor of table arts at the Paul Bocuse Institute. The description of the competition was written in collaboration with Yvelise Dentzer, professor of history and social psychology of the food at the Paul Bocuse Institute.

process may create a salty, tangy, sweet, or bitter product. The texture can vary from smooth and velvety to hard and crumbly. Cheese flavors vary substantially from mild to sharp, subtle to intense, grassy to spicy and pungent. These differences may be the result of either the fermentation and ripening process or the aging process, but usually involve both. A second similarity of wine and cheese is that they are both living things that change substantially during aging. These changes take place as they are aged (or not) by the producer as well as when they are in their final package waiting to be consumed. This situation creates wines and cheeses that range from fresh, young, and simple to aged, mature, and complex.

As with other foods, there are no hard-and-fast rules to pairing; much is based on personal preferences. A number of people believe that red wine goes best with cheese, but many wine professionals disagree with this assumption.[1] In two recent studies, the ideal match in wine and cheese pairing was put to the test. King and Cliff found that in general, white wines were judged as closest to an ideal match across a variety of cheeses.[2] Red wines and specialty wines such as ice wines, late-harvest wines, and ports were more difficult to match with a spectrum of artisanal cheeses. Harrington and Hammond tested the relationship between the elements of six wines (Riesling, Sauvignon Blanc, Chardonnay, Pinot Noir, Merlot, and Cabernet) and the food elements of four types of cheeses (soft, firm, hard, and blue-veined). In their study, Pinot Noir was shown to be the most cheese-friendly of the reds, and an off-dry Riesling was the most cheese-friendly of the whites. The hard cheese (Gruyère) was the most wine-friendly of the four cheese types.[3] A consistent finding across both studies was a substantial amount of variation in perceived level of match across the panel of trained judges—which supports the notion that personal preferences have a substantial impact on perceived level of match when tasting wine and cheeses.

Similar to the theory "red wine with meat and white wine with fish," an old adage of wine and cheese pairing is that "red wines go with hard cheeses and white wines go with soft cheeses."[4] Just as there are exceptions to the "red wine with meat" rule, there are also exceptions to this rule. In her book *The New American Cheese*, Laura Werlin recommends white wines with a variety of artisanal cheeses produced in the United States. Some of her specific suggestions include:

- Pairing light white wines with light cheeses, such as goat's or sheep's milk cheeses with a Chenin Blanc
- Pairing high-acid white wines with high-acid cheeses, such as an aged chèvre with a cool-climate Sauvignon Blanc
- Pairing low-acid wines with lower-acid cheeses, such as a Gouda with a California Chardonnay
- Pairing strong wines with strong cheeses, such as aged cheddar with Syrah or Rhône reds
- Pairing dessert wines with strong, salty cheeses, such as blue-veined cheeses and Sauternes or Port[5]
- Pairing wines and cheeses from the same region

These rules are a good starting point, but cheeses and wines are constantly changing due to aging, vintage, and processing techniques. Therefore, our own judgments should be a guide through this maze of matching uncertainty. Fortunately, the natural affinity between most wines and cheeses allows a match to work most of the time, but additional experimentation will need to be done to achieve an ideal or synergistic match.

The main goal is to create a balance and harmony between the cheese and the wine. You should aim to create similar intensity levels, matches using interesting contrasts, and simple-to-simple or complex-to-complex relationships. There are several categories of cheese, and within these categories, styles can range from delicate to mushroomy to down-right funky.[6] The following wine and cheese suggestions range from very general to very specific and are intended to provide a variety of wine and cheese choices. This is particularly valuable when serving a variety of cheeses on a cheese board. You can minimize any wine and cheese clashes when serving multiple cheeses by selecting a wine that is generally cheese-friendly, selecting cheeses that are generally wine-friendly, or selecting cheeses that are different styles but a good match with the wine being served.

One final note regarding wine and cheese has to do with serving temperature. As suggested earlier, cold temperatures can mask tastes and flavors from our senses. This is particularly true of cheeses. To fully enjoy the nuances in cheese, it is best served at room temperature. Second, be sure not to overchill your white wines. Lighter sweet wines are best served between 41 and 50°F (5–10°C); light and dry white wines should be served between 46 and 54°F (8–12°C).

CHEESE CATEGORIES

There are a number of ways to categorize cheeses, such as country of origin, type of milk used, aging or ripening procedure, fat content, and texture. For the purposes of wine and food pairing, it seems logical to create a classification scheme that maintains a (relatively) consistent focus on components (saltiness, sweetness, acidity, and bitterness), texture (fattiness and body/power), and flavor (intensity, persistence, and types). To achieve this, cheeses are classified as fresh, semisoft, soft ripened, firm, hard, or blue-veined.[7]

Each section discussing cheese categories includes a table that outlines some of the common cheeses by type along with descriptions of their texture, flavor, and color. The last column in each table provides some examples of wines that could be served successfully with these cheeses. Some cheeses have a wide range of wine possibilities and are very wine-friendly, while others are more limiting in pairing relationships, but please do not limit your possible wine selections to only these recommendations. The recommendations are intended to give you some examples, but you are encouraged to try any of the numerous other possibilities.

Fresh and Soft Cheeses   Fresh cheeses are relatively mild and creamy and are neither cooked nor ripened (Table 12.1). These cheeses have a high moisture content, 40–80 percent, and should not taste overly acidic or bitter. Many fresh and soft cheeses are not intended to be served as part of a cheese course but instead are used as an ingredient in other cold or hot food items. Cottage cheese, cream cheese, fromage blanc, mascarpone, Neufchâtel, and ricotta usually fall into this category. Cheeses in this group usually can be matched effectively with lighter, dry to off-dry whites and some low-tannin, higher-acid reds. The level of match depends on the aging of the cheese and any flavorings that have been added to it. For instance, aged chèvre works well with a high-acid Sauvignon Blanc. In this match, the acidity levels cancel each other out and allow the creamy, sweet taste of the cheese to shine through. As you make each wine and cheese matching decision, consider the following questions: What are the key elements of the cheese (sharpness, tanginess, intensity, etc.)? What are the key elements of the wine (sweetness, acidity, tannin, body, intensity, etc.)? How will these interact? Is there a harmony between the two?

Semisoft Cheeses   These cheeses, whose origin can generally be traced back to monasteries of the Middle Ages,[8] include a variety of mild, buttery types that have a sliceable texture. The moisture content of this style of cheese ranges from 40 to 50 percent, and the cheeses can be mild to funky. This category provides a lot of versatility from a pairing perspective.

This group of cheeses retains a buttery flavor and, in many cases, takes on some nutty character. The texture is semisoft and in most cases not as pungent as other general styles. Semisoft cheeses are relatively wine-friendly as long as the wines do not overpower them.

Table 12.1   Examples of Fresh and Soft Cheeses

Type	Milk Used and Color	Components, Texture, and Flavors	Wine Suggestions
Boursin (France)	Cow's Cream to pale yellow, no rind	Triple-cream, smooth, creamy. Usually flavored with herbs, garlic, and pepper.	Dry white wines, such as Sancerre; fruity low-tannin reds such as Beaujolais, Lemberger.
Chèvre	Goat's White	Usually tangy (good acidity), soft to crumbly. May be flavored with ash, herbs, or peppercorns. When aged, it can be quite pungent and intense.	Sauvignon Blanc, Fumé Blanc, Pouilly-Fumé, Sancerre, Vouvray, Chablis, Beaujolais Cru, Pinot Noir.
Cottage	Cow's White	Mild, low salt, low tanginess, soft and moist.	A dry or off-dry white. Cottage cheese is rarely eaten on its own and the wine choice is likely to be determined by what accompanies it.
Cream	Cow's White	Mild, slightly tangy and slightly sweet, soft and creamy.	Cream cheese is rarely eaten on its own and can be part of savory or sweet food items. The wine choice will be determined by what accompanies it.
Feta	Sheep's, goat's or cow's White	Tangy and salty, soft and crumbly. Can have intensely sharp flavor.	Feta can be eaten by itself or as part of a food item. Try a dry Greek wine such as those made from the Muscat grape in regions such as Samos or Lemnos of the Aegean Islands. Or try some classic reds (Merlot or Bordeaux Rouge) or Manzanilla Sherry.
Fromage blanc	Cow's White	Mild and tangy, soft and slightly crumbly.	Used similarly to cream cheese.
Mascarpone	Cow's Pale yellow	Slight tanginess, soft and smooth, buttery.	Off-dry Champagne or sparkling wine, Moscato d'Asti, most dessert wines.
Montrachet	Goat's White	Slightly tangy, soft and creamy. Moderately intense with some pungency.	White or Red Burgundy, cool-climate Chardonnay or Pinot Noir.
Mozzarella	Cow's or buffalo's White	Mild, ranges from tender to elastic. Sometimes smoked.	New World Chardonnay, Gavi, young Barbera.
Neufchâtel	Cow's White	Slightly tangy, soft and creamy, mild.	Semi-dry Riesling, Fendant.
Queso Oaxaca	Cow's White	Mild, slightly tangy, and slightly salty. Smooth and semisoft with a stringy texture. Sometimes blended with herbs, spices or chiles.	If plain, the wine choice should be more subtle, such as dry white wine. If flavored with herbs or spices, it can be contrasted with an off-dry Riesling or create a similar match with a dry Alsace Riesling.
Ricotta	Cow's White	Mild, soft, ranges from moist to grainy.	Ricotta is not generally eaten by itself and can be part of both savory and dessert food items—wine choices will reflect this.

Table 12.2   Semisoft Cheese Examples

Type	Milk Used and Color	Components, Texture, and Flavor	Wine Suggestions
Bel Paese (Italy)	Cow's Light yellow	Mild and semisoft. A light, milky aroma, ranges from bland to buttery and young to earthy depending on the age.	As an appetizer, it works well with Chardonnay and fruity whites. It is also served as a dessert and goes with dried-grape and late-harvest dessert wines
Brick (U.S.)	Cow's Light yellow	Mild to moderately sharp depending on the age. Semifirm in texture, elastic.	New World Chardonnay.
Doux de Montagne (France)	Cow's Pale yellow interior with brown wax	Semisoft texture. Mellow, slightly sweet, buttery and nutty flavor. May be studded with green peppercorns.	Ales, light sparkling wines, dry rosé, Sancerre.
Edam (Netherlands)	Cow's Pale orange/ yellow	Semisoft to firm with a smooth texture. Mellow and nutlike in flavor.	Riesling, dry sparkling wine, Pinot Noir.
Fontina (Italy)	Cow's or sheep's Medium yellow	Firm, elastic and smooth. A nutty flavor and strong aroma. May have a slightly grassy flavor.	Sangiovese, light fruity Pinot Noir, Pinot Grigio, Nebbiolo, Barolo, or Barbaresco.
Havarti (Denmark)	Cow's Medium yellow	Mild, creamy, and mellow. May be flavored with garlic and herb, dill, jalapeño, caraway, or chives.	Sauvignon Blanc, fruit-forward New World Merlot or Cabernet Sauvignon, red Bordeaux, Rioja.
Livarot (France)	Cow's Orange rind with golden yellow center	Semisoft, pungent, intense flavor and slightly piquant.	Tokaji, Pinot Gris from Alsace, Pinot Grigio, Riesling, young Bordeaux from the Pomerol district, New World Merlot.
Muenster (Germany)	Cow's Yellow-tan surface and cream-white interior	Mild to mellow, semisoft texture. May become more pungent with age.	Gewürztraminer, a variety of full-bodied reds, Beaujolais, Zinfandel, beer.
Port du Salut (France)	Cow's Creamy yellow with an orange rind	Ranges from mellow to robust and is semisoft, buttery and smooth.	Rosé sparkling wine or Cabernet Franc–based wines such as Bourgueil and Chinon from the Loire Valley in France.
Taleggio (Italy)	Cow's Light yellow	Creamy, semisoft texture that turns runny as it ages.	Vin Santo (Tuscany), young Merlot, dessert wines such as late-harvest Riesling or Sauternes.

As shown in Table 12.2, most of these cheeses can be served with many whites, reds, and dessert wines.

Soft Ripened Cheeses   This category of cheese is ripened from the outside in. This cheese type can be very firm when young and turn soft and runny when mature or ripe. Double- and triple-cream versions can be described as "gooey." The thin skins and creamy centers make these cheeses some of the most popular. The fat content ranges from 50 to 75 percent as a rule, but double-cream cheese has at least 60 percent fat content and triple-cream has at least 75 percent. Soft ripened cheeses ripen quickly and are generally at their peak for just a few days.

Many of the cheeses in this group originate in France. It is difficult to truly appreciate the French passion for cheese. For the French, cheese is more than just a product—it also represents a region's geography, climate, history, culture, and cuisine. In discussing the difficulties of governing France, the late President Charles de Gaulle expressed the regionalism and diversity of the French culture when he stated, "Nobody can simply bring together a country that has 265 cheeses."[9]

The soft ripened cheeses have a texture that is smooth and rich. The flavors can be mild to intense depending on the aging process. Because of their sometimes gooey consis-

Table 12.3   Soft Ripened Cheese Examples

Type	Milk Used and Color	Components, Texture, and Flavor	Wine Suggestions
Boursault (France)	Cow's Off-white	Rich and very creamy. Triple-cream is the consistency of thickened sour cream, slight acidity. Buttery, sweet, and slightly nutty flavor. Takes on the aroma of mushrooms as it ages.	Sparkling wines, Muscat, Riesling, Syrah/Shiraz, spicy Pinot Noir, ice wine.
Brie (France)	Cow's or goat's Pale yellow with white exterior	Soft and smooth. Buttery to pungent.	Blanc de Blancs Champagne, other sparkling wines, unoaked California Chardonnay, sweet Sherry, Merlot.
Brillat-Savarin (France)	Cow's Gray-white exterior and light yellow interior	Triple-cream, rich.	Champagne, other sparking wines, wines of Bordeaux, Fronsac, Saint-Emilion, red Burgundy.
Camembert (France)	Cow's or goat's Pale yellow with white exterior	Soft and creamy, slightly tangy. A slightly more robust flavor than Brie.	Rich aged Chardonnay, sparkling wines, Chenin Blanc, Cabernet Sauvignon.
Limburger (German)	Cow's Brown exterior with light yellow interior	Soft, smooth, and waxy. A very strong aroma, sharp, salty, and pungent.	Beer.
Pavé Affinois (France)	Cow's Pale yellow interior, white-gray exterior	Smooth with runny texture, double-cream; slightly grassy finish.	Sauvignon Blanc, Sancerre.
Pont l'Evêque (France)	Cow's Pale yellow color with a white-orange rind	Rich and soft cheese with full-bodied flavor and intensity; slightly piquant.	Merlot with deep and dark fruit flavors, Pinot Noir, reds from Pomerol or Saint-Emilion, late-harvest Riesling, Sauternes.
Saint-André (France)	Cow's White exterior with pale yellow interior	Triple-cream, rich, smooth, and buttery.	Champagne, other sparkling wines.

tency, the cheeses in this group have a tendency to coat the mouth. The classic match for these cheeses is Champagne. The high acidity and bubbles in Champagne refresh the palate and cut through the fat of these cheeses. In addition to Champagne and other sparklers, these cheeses can be successfully matched with regional red wines and some dessert wines.

Firm Cheeses This category of cheese is probably the most wine-friendly. Similar to classic wine styles, these cheeses generally have subtlety, a refined texture, and a pleasant, lingering finish (persistence). They vary in their degree of mildness or sharpness depending

Table 12.4 Firm Cheese Examples

Type	Milk Used and Color	Components, Texture, and Flavor	Wine Suggestions
Cantal (France)	Cow's Light yellow	Mild to sharp with a slight nutty flavor. Hard texture.	Red French Burgundy, Oregon Pinot Noir.
Cheddar (England)	Cow's White to medium yellow /orange	Hard texture, mild to sharp.	Mild: Champagne, other sparkling wines, Chardonnay. Sharp: dark beer, Cabernet Sauvignon, Cabernet/ Shiraz blend, Rioja, Ruby, Tawny, or Vintage Port, Sauvignon Blanc.
Cheshire (England)	Cow's Light to medium yellow, sometimes with blue marbling	Hard texture and mellow to piquant. Tangy with a crumbly texture.	Riesling, ale, Cabernet Sauvignon.
Double Gloucester (England)	Cow's Yellow/orange	Firm texture. Smooth, creamy, and full-flavored.	Ice wines, other syrupy dessert wines.
Emmenthal (Switzerland)	Cow's Pale yellow	Hard texture, mild flavor, smooth, slightly sweet and nutty.	Beaujolais, Châteauneuf-du-Pape.
Gjetost (Norway)	Cow's or goat's Pale brown	Hard texture, slightly tangy, sweetish, buttery, and caramelly.	Lightly oaked Chardonnay.
Gouda	Cow's Pale yellow	Firm texture, smooth, mild, creamy, and slightly nutty.	Riesling ice wine, late-harvest dessert wines, older Cabernet Sauvignon and Zinfandel.
Gruyère (Switzerland)	Cow's Pale yellow or tan	Hard texture, full-flavored, with sweet nuttiness.	Côtes du Rhône, Syrah, Champagne, Fino Sherry, Chardonnay, Sauvignon Blanc.
Jarlsberg	Cow's Pale yellow	Hard texture, sharp and nutty flavor.	Light reds such as Lemberger, a variety of whites.
Manchego (Spain)	Sheep's Light yellow	Elastic to hard texture. Mellow but persistent.	Older Spanish Ribera del Duero, Amontillado Sherry, Rioja, Merlot.
Provolone (Italy)	Cow's Pale yellow or brown	Elastic to hard, salty, mild to sharp flavor. May be smoked.	Chianti, Chianti Riserva, Syrah, Barolo, Chardonnay.
Zamarano (Spain)	Sheep's Yellow interior	Firm to hard texture, nutty and flavorful.	Aged Sherry, Rioja, Sangria.

on the aging process. The flavor of these cheeses can range from nutty in cheeses such as Cantal or Jarlsberg to buttery and caramel in cheeses such as Gjetost.

Cheddars are very adaptable with wines. Much of the match will be based on level of sharpness—mild cheddars with light wines and sharp cheddars with full-bodied wines. Gruyère, Jarlsberg, and Gouda are also very wine-friendly in this group.

Hard Cheeses   This group is sometimes referred to as the "grating cheeses," and they owe their flavor to extended periods of aging. The moisture content in these cheeses is around 30 percent. The most famous hard cheeses are from Italy (Parmigiano Reggiano, Asiago, Romano, etc.) and can be served as a part of a cheese board, with a salad, or grated and used as an ingredient to finish pasta and other dishes. The texture of these cheeses is hard and many times granular and crumbly. Flavors vary but are usually sharp, nutty, pungent, and piquant. The wine suggestions are a mix of regional white and red wines from Italy. The hard cheeses are very wine-friendly and versatile.

Blue-Veined Cheeses   This group, with its distinctive appearance, smell, and taste, has a tendency to be quite pungent and salty compared to other cheese categories. This has a strong impact on wine pairing decisions.

The molds of *Penicillium roqueforti* or *Penicillium glaucum* create the variegated blue-green appearance in blue, Roquefort, Gorgonzola, and Stilton cheeses. During the curing process, the cheese curds are inoculated with pure cultures of these molds, which penetrate the interior of the cheese, creating a unique appearance, flavor, and aroma.[10]

Classic matches pair many blue-veined cheeses with fortified and dessert wines. Sauternes and Roquefort is a classic marriage, as is vintage Port and Stilton. These full-bodied and sweet wines complement the full-bodied cheeses and contrast the salty and peppery elements in the cheese with the sweet elements in the wine. Gorgonzola is sharp and peppery and matches well with a classic Amarone. Danish Blue Castello has a softer texture and goes surprisingly well with lighter white wines such as Chenin Blanc and even an off-dry Riesling. Maytag Blue is a famous Wisconsin cheese that can be successfully paired with light and simple white wines such as Austrian Grüner-Veltliner as well as full-bodied dessert wines such as Madeira.

Table 12.5   Hard Cheese Examples

Type	Milk Used and Color	Components, Texture, and Flavor	Wine Suggestions
Asiago (Italy)	Cow's Pale yellow	Semisoft to hard texture, mild to sharp flavor.	Pinot Grigio, Tocai Friulano, dry rosé.
Parmigiano-Reggiano (Italy)	Cow's Pale yellow	Hard and granular texture. Sharp and nutty flavor.	Nebbiolo, Barolo, Barbaresco, Barbera.
Pecorino (Italy)	Sheep's Pale yellow	Hard, dry, and crumbly texture. Very sharp flavor.	Vino Nobile di Montepulciano, a variety of whites and medium-bodied reds such as Barbera.
Ricotta Salata (Italy)	Sheep's Cream-white	Hard texture and pungent.	Medium-bodied crisp and dry whites, Frascati.
Romano (Italy)	Cow's, sheep's, or goat's Creamy white	Hard granular texture and a sharp piquant flavor.	Chianti, Chianti Riserva.

Table 12.6 Blue-Veined Cheese Examples

Type	Milk Used and Color	Components, Texture, and Flavor	Wine Suggestions
Blue (Bleu) (France)	Cow's White interior with blue streaks	Semisoft texture, sometimes crumbly, tangy and peppery.	Tawny Port, Madeira, Sherry.
Cambrazzola (German)	Cow's Light yellow interior with blue marbling	Semisoft and fairly smooth texture. Buttery, tangy, and peppery. A cross of Camembert and Gorgonzola.	New World Merlot, Italian Sangiovese, Chardonnay.
Blue Castello (Danish)	Cow's Creamy white with blue marbling	Semisoft texture. Strong, sharp, rich, buttery and mushroomy flavors.	Chenin Blanc, Sauvignon Blanc, Riesling.
Gorgonzola (Italy)	Cow's Creamy white interior with blue-green veins	Semisoft texture, pasty, tangy, sharp and peppery.	Amarone, any big Italian red.
Maytag Blue (U.S.)	Cow's Yellow with blue streaks	Hard and crumbly texture. Strong flavor and salty.	Allegrini Recioto, Austrian Grüner-Veltliner, Madeira.
Oregonzola (U.S.)	Cow's Creamy white with blue-green veins	Semisoft texture, creamy and buttery. Sharp and tangy with fruity characteristics.	Syrah, Pinot Noir, buttery Chardonnay, full-bodied Champagne or sparkling wine.
Roquefort (France)	Sheep's Creamy white interior, blue marbling	Semisoft and crumbly texture. Sharp, pungent, and slightly peppery.	Sauternes.
Stilton (England)	Cow's Creamy white with blue-green streaks	Semisoft texture and more flaky than blue. Piquant and milder than either Gorgonzola or Roquefort.	Vintage Port.

SUMMARY

This chapter provides a detailed description of the categories within the exciting world of cheeses and wines that match them. As you might imagine, an entire book could easily be written on the variety of cheeses around the world. This chapter focused on the most prominent cheese types and the wine and food pairing principles that tie them together. This format provides you with tools that can be used in making pairing decisions in the future.

Wine and cheese have two main things in common that help to create a natural match: both are created by a fermentation process, and both are living things that change substantially during the process of aging. As with other foods, there are no hard-and-fast rules to pairing wine with cheese; much is based on personal preferences. Cheeses can be categorized by a number of characteristics that impact its elements, such as country of origin, type of milk used, aging or ripening procedure used, fat content, and texture. Cheeses are classified here into six main categories: fresh, semisoft, soft ripened, firm, hard, or blue-veined. This classification scheme is consistent with the various components (saltiness, sweetness, acidity, and

bitterness), texture (fattiness and body/power), and flavor (intensity, persistence, and types), and provides guidelines for satisfying food-and-wine pairing decisions.

The adage that red wines go with hard cheeses and white wines with soft cheeses has a number of exceptions. Some additional guidelines for wine and cheese pairing include pairing light white wines with light cheeses, pairing high-acid white wines with high-acid cheeses, pairing low-acid wines with lower-acid cheeses, pairing strong wines with strong cheeses, pairing dessert wines with strong salty cheeses, and pairing wines and cheeses from the same region. However, constant changes in cheeses and wines due to aging, vintage, and processing techniques will affect the quality of each match. Therefore, these rules provide a good starting point for determining good matches, but your own judgment should also help guide you. Basically, the common thread in all of these guidelines is to create balance and harmony between the cheese and the wine: similar intensity levels, matching using interesting contrasts, and similarity relationships such as simple-to-simple or complex-to-complex.

DISCUSSION QUESTIONS

1. What are the six categories of cheese?

2. Describe the typical wine styles that are appropriate for each cheese category.

3. What types of cheeses are easiest to pair with wine?

4. What cheese elements limit wine choices?

EXERCISE 12.1

WINE AND CHEESE MATCHING

For this exercise, you may select cheeses or wines from the list in Table 12.8 or you can make additional selections to suit your interests if you wish to expand the exercise. Use the Food Sensory Anchor Scale (Figure B.1) and Wine Sensory Anchor Scale (Figure B.2) to create basic reference points for the components, texture, and flavor when using the Wine and Food Pairing Instrument.

OBJECTIVES

To distinguish and rank differing levels of elements in each cheese and wine sample; to compare wine and cheese profiles to predict match level, and then do a mixed tasting to determine the perceived level of match.

Mise en Place: Things to Do Before the Exercise Review Figures 11.2a-c and Figure 11.4. Ensure that the cheese and wines are served at the optimal tasting temperatures.

**The exercises in this chapter
test the assumption that all
wines go with all cheeses. Do
you agree with this belief?**

MATERIALS NEEDED

Table 12.7   Materials Needed for Exercise 12.1

1 white paper placemat per student, with numbered or labeled circles to place wineglasses (Figure 7.1)	1 spit cup per student Corkscrew Drinking water for each student
1 copy of the Aroma Wheel per student	Napkins
3 copies of Figures 11.2a, 11.2b, and 11.2c for each student	5 wineglasses per student
1 copy Food and Wine Sensory Anchor Scales per student	Cutting board
1 copy of Figure 12.1 (Food and Wine Perceived Match Level) per student	Bread or crackers to cleanse palate
Plates for tasting samples of cheese	Plastic (or other) forks and knives

Table 12.8   Cheese and Wines Needed for Exercise 12.1

Cheeses

Fresh/soft: Chèvre, Montrachet, or regional equivalent

Semisoft: Bel Paese, Doux de Montagne, Havarti, Livarot

Soft ripened: Boursault, Brie, Brillat-Savarin, Camembert, Saint-André

Firm: Cantal, aged Cheddar, Double Gloucester, Emmenthal, Manchego

Hard: Asiago, Grana Padano, Parmigiano Reggiano, Pecorino

Blue-veined: Maytag, Gorgonzola, Roquefort, Stilton

Wines

Dry white: Chenin Blanc, Gavi, Pinot Grigio, Pinot Gris, Sauvignon Blanc

Medium red: Barbera, Lemberger, Beaujolais, Dolcetto

Full-bodied: Nebbiolo, Syrah, Rioja, Chianti Riserva

Other possibilities: Brut sparkling wine, Moscato d'Asti, off-dry whites, Amarone

Fortified: Ruby or Tawny Port, Madeira, Marsala, Sherry

STEPS

1. Divide the cheeses into 1–1½ oz tasting samples per person and arrange on a small plate. Cheeses should be served at room temperature.

2. Evaluate each cheese, keeping all of the food elements in mind (using Figure 11.2b and/or Figure 11.2c).

3. Pour a sample of each wine for each student, enough to evaluate and to try with each cheese sample.

4. Taste the wine samples and assess all wine elements. Record in Figure 11.2a and/or Figure 11.2c.

5. Taste the cheeses with each wine in ascending order (starting with lightest wines through the most powerful) and record your perceived level of match on Figure 12.1 and/or at the bottom of Figure 11.2c. Once tasted, you can then go back and forth between them to ensure consistent measures, if desired.

6. Discuss and record any sensory observations based on the relationship between wines and cheese. Which wine and cheese had the best match? Was it predicted? Which wine and cheese had the lowest level of match? Were any of the matches truly synergistic? Are there other wines that you feel would create a better match? Any surprises?

7. Rank the match level of each cheese with each wine, from lowest to highest level of match.

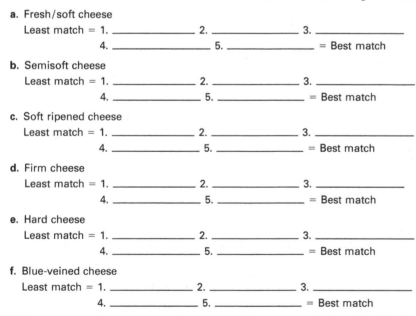

   a. Fresh/soft cheese

      Least match = 1. _____ 2. _____ 3. _____
                       4. _____ 5. _____ = Best match

   b. Semisoft cheese

      Least match = 1. _____ 2. _____ 3. _____
                       4. _____ 5. _____ = Best match

   c. Soft ripened cheese

      Least match = 1. _____ 2. _____ 3. _____
                       4. _____ 5. _____ = Best match

   d. Firm cheese

      Least match = 1. _____ 2. _____ 3. _____
                       4. _____ 5. _____ = Best match

   e. Hard cheese

      Least match = 1. _____ 2. _____ 3. _____
                       4. _____ 5. _____ = Best match

   f. Blue-veined cheese

      Least match = 1. _____ 2. _____ 3. _____
                       4. _____ 5. _____ = Best match

8. Write down any other comments, thoughts, and observations that you identified during this evaluation process. Did the predicted match coincide with your perceived level of match when the cheese and wine were tasted together? Was there a predominant category of elements that impacted the level of match across all of the cheese and wine combinations? If so, was it the components, texture, or flavors?

Date: _____

Overall feeling of food and wine match (circle the level of match below):

Cheese #1: _____ **Type:** _____

Dry White Wine: _____

0-----1-----2-----3-----4-----5-----6-----7-----8-----9-----10
No Match   Average Match   Synergistic Match

Medium Red Wine: _____

0-----1-----2-----3-----4-----5-----6-----7-----8-----9-----10
No Match   Average Match   Synergistic Match

Full-Bodied Red Wine: _____

0-----1-----2-----3-----4-----5-----6-----7-----8-----9-----10
No Match   Average Match   Synergistic Match

Other Wine: _____

0-----1-----2-----3-----4-----5-----6-----7-----8-----9-----10
No Match   Average Match   Synergistic Match

Fortified Wine: _____

0-----1-----2-----3-----4-----5-----6-----7-----8-----9-----10
No Match   Average Match   Synergistic Match

Cheese #2: _____ **Type:** _____

Dry White Wine: _____

0-----1-----2-----3-----4-----5-----6-----7-----8-----9-----10
No Match   Average Match   Synergistic Match

Medium Red Wine: _____

0-----1-----2-----3-----4-----5-----6-----7-----8-----9-----10
No Match   Average Match   Synergistic Match

Full-Bodied Red Wine: _____

0-----1-----2-----3-----4-----5-----6-----7-----8-----9-----10
No Match   Average Match   Synergistic Match

Other Wine: _____

0-----1-----2-----3-----4-----5-----6-----7-----8-----9-----10
No Match   Average Match   Synergistic Match

Fortified Wine: _____

0-----1-----2-----3-----4-----5-----6-----7-----8-----9-----10
No Match   Average Match   Synergistic Match

Figure 12.1

Level of Match Between Cheese and Wine

Cheese #3: _____ **Type:** _____

Dry White Wine: _____

0-----1-----2-----3-----4-----5-----6-----7-----8-----9-----10
No Match   Average Match   Synergistic Match

Medium Red Wine: _____

0-----1-----2-----3-----4-----5-----6-----7-----8-----9-----10
No Match   Average Match   Synergistic Match

Full-Bodied Red Wine: _____

0-----1-----2-----3-----4-----5-----6-----7-----8-----9-----10
No Match   Average Match   Synergistic Match

Other Wine: _____

0-----1-----2-----3-----4-----5-----6-----7-----8-----9-----10
No Match   Average Match   Synergistic Match

Fortified Wine: _____

0-----1-----2-----3-----4-----5-----6-----7-----8-----9-----10
No Match   Average Match   Synergistic Match

Cheese #4: _____ **Type:** _____

Dry White Wine: _____

0-----1-----2-----3-----4-----5-----6-----7-----8-----9-----10
No Match   Average Match   Synergistic Match

Medium Red Wine: _____

0-----1-----2-----3-----4-----5-----6-----7-----8-----9-----10
No Match   Average Match   Synergistic Match

Full-Bodied Red Wine: _____

0-----1-----2-----3-----4-----5-----6-----7-----8-----9-----10
No Match   Average Match   Synergistic Match

Other Wine: _____

0-----1-----2-----3-----4-----5-----6-----7-----8-----9-----10
No Match   Average Match   Synergistic Match

Fortified Wine: _____

0-----1-----2-----3-----4-----5-----6-----7-----8-----9-----10
No Match   Average Match   Synergistic Match

Figure 12.1

(*Continued*)

Cheese #5: _____ **Type:** _____

Dry White Wine: _____

0-----1-----2-----3-----4-----5-----6-----7-----8-----9-----10
No Match   Average Match   Synergistic Match

Medium Red Wine: _____

0-----1-----2-----3-----4-----5-----6-----7-----8-----9-----10
No Match   Average Match   Synergistic Match

Full-Bodied Red Wine: _____

0-----1-----2-----3-----4-----5-----6-----7-----8-----9-----10
No Match   Average Match   Synergistic Match

Other Wine: _____

0-----1-----2-----3-----4-----5-----6-----7-----8-----9-----10
No Match   Average Match   Synergistic Match

Fortified Wine: _____

0-----1-----2-----3-----4-----5-----6-----7-----8-----9-----10
No Match   Average Match   Synergistic Match

Cheese #6: _____ **Type:** _____

Dry White Wine: _____

0-----1-----2-----3-----4-----5-----6-----7-----8-----9-----10
No Match   Average Match   Synergistic Match

Medium Red Wine: _____

0-----1-----2-----3-----4-----5-----6-----7-----8-----9-----10
No Match   Average Match   Synergistic Match

Full-Bodied Red Wine: _____

0-----1-----2-----3-----4-----5-----6-----7-----8-----9-----10
No Match   Average Match   Synergistic Match

Other Wine: _____

0-----1-----2-----3-----4-----5-----6-----7-----8-----9-----10
No Match   Average Match   Synergistic Match

Fortified Wine: _____

0-----1-----2-----3-----4-----5-----6-----7-----8-----9-----10
No Match   Average Match   Synergistic Match

Figure 12.1

(**Continued**)

NOTES

1. Laura Werlin, *The New American Cheese* (New York: Stewart, Tabori, and Chang, 2000).

2. M. King and M. Cliff, "Evaluation of Ideal Wine and Cheese Pairs Using a Deviation-from-Ideal Scale with Food and Wine Experts," *Journal of Food Quality* 28 (2005): 245–56.

3. R. J. Harrington and R. Hammond, "Direct Effects of Wine and Food Elements on Perceived Level of Match," *Journal of Foodservice Business Research* (2006), in press.

4. P. Lambert, "Pairing Cheese and Wine," http://www.mozzco.com/winey.html (accessed February 16, 2006).

5. Werlin, *The New American Cheese.*

6. Andrea Immer, *Great Tastes Made Simple: Extraordinary Food and Wine Pairing for Every Palate* (New York: Broadway Books, 2002).

7. M. Bennion and B. Scheule, *Introductory Foods*, 12th ed. (Upper Saddle River, NJ: Pearson–Prentice Hall, 2004); J. W. Chesser. *The Art and Science of Culinary Preparation* (St. Augustine, FL: Educational Institute of the American Culinary Federation, 1992); Immer, *Great Tastes Made Simple*; S. R. Labensky and A. M. Hause, *On Cooking*, 3rd ed. (Upper Saddle River, NJ: Prentice Hall, 2003); Culinary Institute of America, *The Professional Chef*, 7th ed. (New York: John Wiley and Sons, 2002).

8. Labensky and Hause, *On Cooking.*

9. J.-B. Nadeau and J. Barlow, *What Makes the French So French: Sixty Million Frenchmen Can't Be Wrong* (London: Robson Books, 2005).

10. Bennion and Scheule, *Introductory Foods.*

CHAPTER 13

THE GRAND FINALE: DESSERT AND DESSERT WINES

CHAPTER OUTLINE:

Introduction

Aperitif: Niagara's Wine Region

Dessert Wine Categories

Dessert Selection and Wine Pairing

Dessert Categories

Summary

Exercises

KEY CONCEPTS:

• Ice wines

• VQA

• Botrytized wines

• Noble rot

• Ports

• Sherries

• Marsala, Madeira, and Muscats

• Balance and harmony between wine and cheese

• Beware of excessive levels of sweetness, richness, bitterness, or acidity in desserts

• The impact of fruit type: berries, orchard, citrus, tropical, and dried

INTRODUCTION

This chapter focuses on desserts, dessert wines, and the associated pairing principles. Extravagant desserts and opulent dessert wines can provide some of the most memorable dining experiences.

The opening Aperitif highlights the Niagara wine region in Ontario, Canada. This region features a unique mesoclimate and has a reputation for the variety of quality wines and foods it has to offer. Jeff Stewart, professor and coordinator of the tourism programs at Niagara College, shares his thoughts on changes that have taken place in the region and ideas on how food and wine can be integrated not only across a particular program but also across an entire college.

Aperitif | Niagara's Wine Region

The Niagara wine region has seen vast change and growth in the last twenty years. With over a hundred wineries, it is still growing, and the region's humble beginnings bear little resemblance to its current reputation for wines of high quality. Longtime residents of the region will remember famous brand names such as Baby Duck, Brights' President, and even Jordan Sherry, made mostly from *Vitis labrusca* grapes such as the Concord and the regional namesake grape, the Niagara. The Niagara wine industry's reputation for providing "foxy" wines has been replaced with a reputation for producing quality vinifera wines, and the famous brand names of the past have been replaced by names such as Inniskillin, Cave Spring, Stratus, Hillebrand, and Malivoire.

Vineyards at Niagara College Teaching Winery, Niagara, Ontario (courtesy of Niagara College).

Several factors caused the shift from quantity to quality production in the Niagara wine region. In the early 1980s, European *Vitis vinifera* grape plantings, pioneered by the Inniskillin Winery and Donald Ziraldo, were viewed with skepticism because of the Canadian climate. The introduction of the Vintner's Quality Alliance (VQA) system, which is similar to other European quality control systems such as the AOC and DOCG, also assisted in this transition, albeit much later. Ontario was acknowledged for its wine quality for the first time at the 1991 Vinexpo in Bordeaux, France, when a 1989 Inniskillin ice wine stole the show and helped to put Canadian and Niagara wines on the map. The acknowledgement of Inniskillin ice wine gave Canadian wines, and more specifically Niagara wines, the clout they needed to be recognized throughout the world.

Ice wine is not unique to Canada. To make ice wine (or, as the Germans call it, Eiswein), grapes are left long after harvest to freeze on the vines. Once frozen solid to a temperature of at least −10°C (about 14°F), the grapes are picked and crushed while still hard as marbles. The tiny bit of juice rendered from the delicately preserved extra-late-harvest fruits is so concentrated and so sweet that it is more like syrup than juice. In Canada, the minimum sweetness at the time of harvest must be 40° Brix to be officially called ice wine. The original ice wines in Niagara were made from German grapes such as Riesling and hybrids such as Vidal, but as techniques evolved, new varietals came to be used, including Gewürztraminer and even red grapes such as Cabernet Franc, which has a distinctly strawberry aroma. These ultra-premium, elixir-like wines accordingly carry high prices.

One advantage of planting vinifera in Canada versus other vinifera growing regions is that without exception, Canada is guaranteed to have winter temperatures cold enough to allow for a successful harvest of ice wine grapes. As a result, Niagara ice wines are available to consumers on a consistent basis. In more temperate regions, if the temperature is too warm, the grapes will not freeze completely or, even worse, they will rot on the vine, falling prey to molds, mildews, and volatile acidity that make the grapes unusable.

Aside from its production of ice wine, the Niagara wine region has also become famous for its other wine products and unique wineries. Canada's first and only college with its own self-contained vineyard and winery is Niagara College, which includes the Niagara College Teaching Winery (NCTW) (see www.niagarac.on.ca). The first NCTW vintage in 2000 was released with much fanfare and was the first of many vintages that helped to build their reputation for producing quality wines. With their 2000 barrel-fermented and aged Chardonnay, described by critics with compelling adjectives such as *complex*, *vanilla*, *creamy*, *toasty*, and *tropical*, it is no wonder Niagara College is making a name for itself.

Beyond the winery at Niagara College, the philosophy of this institution is one of integration, much like the nature of the wine and hospitality business. The college boasts a fifty-acre vineyard, a complete winery, greenhouses, gardens, culinary labs, a fine-dining restaurant, and technologically advanced class-rooms.

"The idea is simple synergy," says Jeff Stewart, professor and coordinator of the tourism programs at Niagara College. "The sum of the parts is almost always greater than those parts taken individually, so what has been created here is not just a mini-business or series of businesses but a mini-economy. Under-standing the interconnectedness of these businesses is only one part of what we do here that makes us unique.

"A world-class food-and-wine pairing is not as simple as just having two flavors that work well together. To be truly world-class, it involves the coordination of many entities that may appear to be only slightly related, but which when brought together create something that is truly unique, pleasing to all the senses. . . . The vision at Niagara College is learning through the complete supply chain, or 'farm gate to consumer plate.' This unique learning opportunity is being conceptualized, experienced, and managed by both the students and faculty," says Stewart.

The synergistic concept he describes is evident in the integrated approach on Niagara College's campus. Horticulture students are working in the college greenhouses and landscaping the campus grounds and gardens. Their herbs, lettuces, and flowers from their brand-new Chef Gardens are used in the college's fine-dining restaurant at the School of Hospitality and Tourism. Winery and viticulture students study, experiment, and work in the college vineyard and produce up to five thousand cases of wine annually in the winery, as well as running the retail store and tasting bar. Their wines are also the cornerstone of the wine list in the fine-dining restaurant. The School of Hospitality and Tourism has a newly created four-year bachelor's degree in hospitality operations, two-year management diplomas in culinary arts, hotel and restaurant management, and tourism, and one-year certificate programs in chef training, special events, and hospitality and tourism. Niagara College truly brings something unique to education that demonstrates the complex nature of the business world.

Jeff suggests you try a true Niagara Classic, the Ice Wine Sparkler, for your next special occasion. "Combine your favorite glass of dry (brut) sparkling wine, preferably from Niagara, with a ½ oz dosage of Niagara ice wine added at the end. Pairing ice wine with food can be a challenge, as ice wine with its sweetness and wonderful aromas can be difficult to pair with anything other than rich dishes such as foie gras or opulently sweet desserts. The ice wine sparkler still allows you to enjoy the smells and tastes of ice wine but with a nice amount of crisp acidity from the bubbly. The added effervescence allows for more interesting texture and feel on the palate. All by itself, an ice wine sparkler is a world-class combination, but think of the options for food-and-wine pairing. What would you match with it?"

DESSERT WINE CATEGORIES

The dessert wine category is an area that contains some of the most opulent wines made. This category of wines can be divided into several different types. One type is sparkling

---

Jeff Stewart is a professor in the School of Hospitality and Tourism at Niagara College, where he is also coordinator of the tourism programs. A Canadian native, he is a well-respected chef and wine educator.

wine that can be served with desserts. Sparkling wines were discussed in depth in Chapter 6 and therefore will not be covered in any great detail in the dessert wine section of this chapter. They are included where appropriate in the sections on desserts and wine pairing.

There is a wide range of dessert wines produced in regions all over the globe. The discussion here only scratches the surface of this wine category, but it provides a good framework for categorizing dessert wines regardless of where they are produced. General categories include frozen-grape wines, late-harvest wines, dried-grape wines, and fortified wines.[1] However, you will notice that dessert wines are also created by combining two or more of these techniques.

Frozen-Grape Wines

As discussed in the Aperitif, the traditional frozen-grape wine is created by leaving the grapes on the vine until they are frozen, then picking and pressing them while still frozen. Because the grapes have been left on the vine for a longer period (reducing the water content and increasing the sugar content) and a lot of the water is left behind as ice when they are pressed, the remaining juice is exceptionally sweet, with concentrated flavors.

Classic examples of wines made using this frozen process are German Eiswein and Canadian ice wine. Ice wine and other frozen wines are also produced in the United States (mainly in northern areas such as Washington, Idaho, Ohio, and New York) and in the colder locations of New Zealand. In Germany, Canada and Austria, the grapes are required to be frozen naturally;[2] Some ice wine producers in other regions, such as Oregon, California, and warmer areas of New Zealand, create ice wines by placing grapes in the freezer prior to pressing. This process, referred to as cryoextraction (mechanical freezing), is more reliable and less expensive, but it is considered "cheating" by ice wine purists and generally results in wines of a lower quality. Frozen wines produced in this manner cannot be labeled as ice wine; rather, they are labeled using a variety of terms such as *iced wine*, *vino gelato*, *cryo-cluster*, *frostbite*, and *vin de glacière*.

Table 13.1 provides a list of typical regions that produce frozen-grape wines. The standard grape typically used for frozen-grape wines varies by region. The classic grape is

Table 13.1   Frozen Grape Examples

Primary Regions	Primary Grapes	Typical Producers
Canada—Niagara (over 90% of Canada's ice wine is produced in Ontario) and Okanagan	Vidal Blanc, Riesling, Gewürztraminer, Cabernet Franc	*Ontario:* Château des Charmes, Henry of Pelham, Kittling Ridge, Pillitteri, Reif Estates *Okanagan:* Gehringer Brothers Estate *Both Ontario and Okanagan:* Inniskillin, Jackson-Triggs
Pacific Northwest—Washington, Oregon, and Idaho	Chenin Blanc, Gewürztraminer, Riesling, Sémillon, Sauvignon Blanc, Pinot Noir	*Oregon:* Argyle, King Estate, Ponzi Vineyards *Washington:* Chateau Ste. Michelle, Covey Run, Kiona, L'Ecole No. 41, Preston, Terra Blanca *Idaho:* Sawtooth Winery
Ohio and New York	Vidal Blanc, Riesling	*Ohio:* Chalet Debonne, Ferrante, Firelands, Heineman *New York:* Hunt Country, Wagner.
Germany (mainly from the Rhine and Mosel Valleys)	Riesling, Huxelrebe	Helenenkloster, Selbach-Oster
Austria	Bouvier, Blaufränkisch (also known as Lemberger), Gewürztraminer, Grüner-Veltliner	Heiss Winery, Gsellmann and Gsellmann Winery
New Zealand	Riesling, Chardonnay, Sauvignon Blanc	Brightwater Vineyards, Mission Estate, Nobilo, Selaks

Riesling, which is used predominately in German Eiswein. The majority of grapes used in frozen-grape wines are white, while a much smaller proportion are created from Cabernet Franc, Pinot Noir, and even Merlot and Cabernet Sauvignon. Wines made from white grapes range in color from straw yellow to deep amber. The red varieties range from a pink color (similar to rosé) to a light burgundy.

A quality ice wine retains the character of the grape, with crisp acidity to balance the sweetness and awaken the palate. Without high acidity, ice wines taste cloyingly sweet and dead on the palate. Locally, Canadian ice wine is described as "winter's gift to wine."[3] The temperature must drop well below freezing for the grapes to be picked, a process that is usually done by hand, mainly at night. The nectar that is pressed from these frozen nuggets is then fermented very slowly for several months. The resulting wines are outstandingly rich and of high quality.

The mark of a good frozen-grape wine is that it creates a balance between substantial sweetness and brilliant acidity along with a clean finish. Frozen wine flavors may include tropical fruits, lychee nuts, apricot, peach, mango, melon, or other sweet fruits as well as honey, fig, nuts, and sweet spices, depending on the climate, soil, grape, and process used. Recent research provides evidence that not all ice wines are created equal and that there are substantial sensory differences among German Eiswein, Ontario ice wine, and Okanagan ice wine. In this scientific study, German ice wines had the highest acidity and a nutty/oily character. Ontario ice wines had the highest fruity and floral aromas and a golden copper color. Okanagan ice wines were sweeter and had a stronger body and a more intense after-taste.[4]

Late-Harvest Wines

Late-harvest grapes can be used to produce dessert wines as well. Leaving the grapes on the vine past the normal harvest period creates grapes that are riper, higher in sugar content, and lower in moisture content. These late-harvest grapes may also turn into raisins; get attacked by mold, or both. As grapes shrivel on the vine, they become richer and sweeter. The resulting wine tastes stronger, is sweeter, and may have flavors of dried fruits.

Late-harvest grapes that have been attacked by a mold called *Botrytis cinerea* have a pleasant taste often described as honeyed or mushroomy. Often referred to as "noble rot," it is called *Edelfäule* in Germany and *pourriture noble* in France. The botrytis mold shrivels the grapes into raisins, increasing the sweetness levels and concentrating the flavors and texture. Ultimately, this process alters the grapes' acid balance, creates a syrupy texture, and imparts a honeyed or mushroomy flavor. (It is important to note that mold can be disastrous to a vineyard, destroying part or the entire crop, if it is not achieved under the right conditions.)[5]

Late-harvest wines are most frequently achieved in cool and moderate climates. Growing conditions that provide fair weather, temperate days, and cool nights well after the main harvest period are ideal. For the noble rot to take place, the grapes must remain dry during this period except when they receive moisture from the morning dew. These conditions encourage the growth of the botrytis mold. Most wine-growing regions have a few areas where conditions for growth of the noble rot are favorable, but the most famous locations are in Germany and France. The most notable regions in France include Bordeaux, the Loire Valley, and Alsace. The districts in Bordeaux that excel in sweet wine are prone to these autumnal mists and have soils with high mineral content. Bordeaux subdistricts known for producing these late-harvest wines include Barsac, Cérons, Sauternes, and Ste-Croix-du-Mont. Germany's most notable regions that produce late-harvest wines include Nahe, Mosel, and Rhine. Late-harvest wines are also available from Austria and Hungary as well as New World countries such as the United States, Canada, Australia, and New Zealand. Hungarian Tokaji is an especially famous late-harvest wine that gets its character from noble rot. Tokaji is rated by the amount of botrytis-affected grapes used to make the wine; it can range from 3 to 6 *puttonyos* (the number of 20-liter containers of botrytis grapes used to make the wine).[6] The sweetest and richest is Tokaji Eszencia.

Some grapes are more susceptible to the mold than others due to their thin skins and tight grape clusters that retain more moisture. The most susceptible varietals include Chenin Blanc, Riesling, Zinfandel, Chardonnay, Pinot Noir, and Sauvignon Blanc. Moderately susceptible grapes are French Colombard, Gewürztraminer, and Sémillon. Cabernet Sauvignon and Merlot are some of the least susceptible. It should be noted that while some red grapes are susceptible to the botrytis infection, essentially, all grape varieties used in production of botrytized wines are white varieties. Using white varieties avoids the brown coloration in wine from infected red grapes. When found, the red grapes are either rejected in the field or later in the winery through a process of inspection and sorting.

Late-harvest wines may use grapes with some incidence of botrytis in them, use only affected fruit, or use only affected fruit with some fully raisined. While there is not a nationwide agreement on label terms for late-harvest wines in the United States, winemakers have developed some recommended industry standards. In the United States, wines that use some affected fruit are generally termed "late harvest" and are similar to Spätlese and Auslese wines in Germany (residual sugar content less than 11.5 percent). U.S. wines that use only affected fruit may be termed "select late harvest" and are similar to German Auslese and Beerenauslese wines (residual sugar usually between 11.5 percent and 15 percent). U.S. wines labeled "special select late harvest" use all affected fruit with some of the fruit raisined and are similar to German Beerenauslese and Trockenbeerenauslese (residual sugar usually more than 15 percent).[8]

Dried-Grape Wines   Many wine-growing regions use a planned "raisining" approach to achieve results similar to those that take advantage of noble rot or freezing. In the raisining approach, grapes are harvested, then allowed to dry under controlled conditions. A typical method is to dry the grapes over straw mats or screens. Italy's *passito* wines are prepared this way, as are *Strohwein* in Germany and *vin de paille* in France (the last two names both mean "straw wine"). Other common dried-grape wines include Greece's Muscats, dessert wines of southern France, Tuscany's Vin Santo (for which clusters of grapes are hung to dry), and some Australian dessert wines. Beginning in the 1950s, California winemakers Myron and Alice Nightingale developed a process to induce the botrytis mold in harvested grapes that were spread on drying trays. They inoculated the drying fruit with botrytis spores and simulated an environment required for noble rot to attack successfully.

Not all dried-grape wines are sweet. A classic example is Amarone della Valpolicella (Amarone for short) from the Venetian region of Italy. There are two subgroups in this Italian category: Recioto (a sweet dessert wine) and Amarone (a dry, full-bodied red wine). Both of these wines are made with grapes that have been dried on racks to intensify their flavor. Recioto and Amarone wine are made from the Corvina Veronese, Rondinella, and Molinara grapes. Amarone is one of the most popular wines in Italy, with sales behind only Chianti, Asti, and Soave. The term *amarone* is said to mean "bitter" in Italian, and while some types of Amarone can be bitter, many are very fruity in flavor. Usually, the wine has flavors such as licorice, tobacco, and dried fig. This full-bodied wine goes particularly well with game and ripe cheese.

Table 13.2 provides a few examples and descriptions of some of these dried-grape wines. The examples provided are from the Old World, but New World producers create these wines as well.

Fortified Wines   Fortified wines are strengthened with the addition of wine spirits. Generally, a neutral grape brandy is made by distilling wine to concentrate the level of alcohol. The neutral brandy is added to the wine before the fermentation process is complete. The additional alcohol halts fermentation, and the remaining sugar offers a sweet taste in the finished fortified product. The taste of fortified wines is a vivid sweetness of the ripe grapes along with a full-bodied texture from the added alcohol and tannin if red grapes are used.

The tradition of fortifying wines comes from areas of hot climates, where it originated to preserve the wine while shipping it to England. Countries such as Spain, Italy, and Por-

Table 13.2   Dried Grape Wine Examples

Country	Regions	Wine & Type	Primary Grape(s)	Characteristics
Italy	Veneto	Amarone Red table wine	Corvina, Rondinella, Molinara	Big, full-bodied with high alcohol (15–16 percent), oak aged. Port-like body with bitter chocolate, dried fig, mocha, and earthy flavors.
Italy	Veneto	Recioto di Soave Dessert wine (sparkling and fortified versions are available)	Garganega, Trebiano	Rich and syrupy.
Italy	Sicily and Piedmont	Moscato di Pantelleria Passito and Moscato Passito White dessert wine (available sparkling)	Moscato (Muscat)	Honeyed with grapey fruit flavors balanced by clean acidity and fragrant floral aromas.
Italy	Tuscany, Umbria, Veneto and Friuli-Venezia-Giulia	Vin Santo	Tuscany: Trebbiano Toscano, Malvasia, and Canaiolo are most common, followed by Sangiovese, Cabernet Sauvignon, Cabernet Franc, and Merlot. Veneto: Garganega and Gambellara	Generally sweet but some are off-dry or dry. Viscous texture, high alcohol, smooth, and intensely flavored.
France	Côtes du Jura	Vin de Paille	Jura: Chardonnay and Savagnin	Honeyed flavors, sweet, medium-bodied, dried exotic fruits, and balanced acidity.
Austria	Burgenland	Strohwein	Grüner Veltliner, Muller Thurgau, Blaufränkisch	Full-bodied, sweet and good acidity. Typical examples using Grüner Veltliner, Muller Thurgau grapes have flavors of nectarines, apricots, and sweet spices. Blaufränkisch (Lemberger) is a red grape and provides a cleansing, slightly astringent finish.
Greece	Santorini	Visanto Dessert wine	White and red Mandilaria	This can be aged for up to 20 years before being released and have characteristics similar to a Tawny Port. Or it can be aged 3–4 years and have rich and complex character.
Greece	Samos	Samos Nectar Dessert wine	Muscat	Sweet with balanced acidity and alcohol. Complex with interesting flavors.

tugal have a long tradition of producing fortified wines. Adding wine spirits make fortified wines microbiologically stable, preserving them for transport, and also protecting them from exposure to air. Fortified wines have distinct styles, including Port, Sherry, Madeira, and Marsala. More recently, many New World locations have been making wines modeled after these Old World wines. Australia, South Africa, California, Washington, Oregon, and Florida are known for their versions of these classic fortified wines.

Port originally comes from Portugal and is named for the city of Oporto there. Within the Port category, there are three major styles: Ruby, Tawny, and Vintage. Ruby and Tawny are ready to drink when they are released. Vintage Port is intended to be aged in the bottle for twenty or more years before drinking. Ruby Port is bright red in color, fruity, and young, with a rich, sweet taste. Tawny Port is brick red to brown in color and is less fruity with more oakiness. It comes in several varieties and ages with rich, sweet, and full-bodied tastes and textures. Vintage Port has been aged in neutral oak barrels for two to four years prior to bottling and is deep red and fruity when released. Vintage Port is a classic after-dinner drink that is intended to be savored. Port is also made using white grapes, in which case it is known as White Port. White Port ranges from dry through off-dry to sweet and is usually served chilled as an aperitif or after dinner (if it is the sweet style).

Sherry is traditionally produced in Spain and has the defining characteristic of being deliberately oxidized. There are two basic types: Fino and Oloroso. Yeast is used in the production of Fino Sherry and gives it a distinct bouquet. Manzanilla and Amontillado Sherries are variations of the Fino type. Manzanillas are dry, pale yellow in color, and crisp and apple-like. They are frequently enjoyed with seafood and are great to use as an ingredient in the preparation of seafood dishes. Amontillados are aged longer than other Finos and have a darker color, supply more toasted flavor, and are less pungent. They are light brown in color and range from dry to medium-sweet.

Oloroso Sherry is oxidized without yeast. It is generally sweet, dark brown, elegant, and complex. Currently, Spanish Olorosos provide some of the great fine wine bargains. They are intended to be sipped after dinner with toasted nuts and salty cheeses. A sweet Sherry that falls within the Oloroso group is Pedro Ximénez (PX) Sherry. This dessert Sherry is made from the Pedro Ximénez grape, and it is often sweet, dark, and dense. The grape can also be used to slightly sweeten dry Sherries; it is served dry as an aperitif as well.

A substantial amount of Sherry is produced in California. Most of these Sherries fall somewhere between the flavor and color extremes of Spanish Fino and Oloroso Sherries. They range from light-colored and nutty to richer, darker, and toasted. California Sherries have three general sweetness levels: dry (1–2.5 percent residual sugar), medium (2.5–3.5 percent residual sugar), and cream (7.5–10 percent residual sugar). Inexpensive wines generically labeled as Sherry, Marsala, and Madeira have little resemblance to those produced using traditional techniques and are made using a baking process to mimic the natural oxidation effects.[9]

Madeira is named after the island where it is made, which is located in the mid-Atlantic off the coast of Morocco. Similar to the development of Port and Sherry, Madeira owes much of its success to the primitive shipping conditions of the seventeenth century. Pipes (barrels) of Madeira were put in the hold of ships as ballast as they voyaged to all parts of the world. Early Madeira was exposed to constant rocking and extreme heat as the ships passed through the tropics, turning an otherwise light and acidic wine into a wine with softness, depth, and a pleasant burnt flavor.

Marsala is the best-known fortified wine of Italy and is named for the town in Sicily that produces it. It is used similarly to Sherry and Madeira. Marsalas are graded according to their sweetness, color, and age. The driest Marsalas are called *secco*, medium-dry ones are called *demisecco*, and the sweetest are called *dolce*. It comes in three colors: *oro* (golden), *ambra* (amber), and *rubino* (ruby). And there are five types based on aging: *fine* (aged a minimum of one year), *superiore* (aged in wood two years), *superiore riserva* (aged in wood four years), *vergine* (aged in wood for five years), and *vergine stravecchio* (aged in wood for at least ten years).

Some other important fortified wines include Vermouth, Orange Muscat, Muscat Hamburg, and Floc de Gascogne. Vermouth is a fortified wine that has been flavored with sugar, herbs, roots, flowers, and spices. It is best known as an ingredient in several cocktails, including Manhattans and martinis. There are two main types: dry vermouth and sweet vermouth. It can be served as an aperitif and is also used in sauces that accompany seafood. Orange Muscat and Muscat Hamburg (sometimes known as Black Muscat) are made from a mutant of the Muscat grape. Fortified Muscats are very special dessert wines. Orange Muscat has aromas of orange, orange blossom, and apricot. Muscat Hamburg has aromas reminiscent of roses with a lychee nut character to its flavor. These wines are sweet, rich, and concentrated, with crisp acidity. California and Australia are good producers of these two fortified wines. Floc de Gascogne is a popular fortified wine served in southern France as an aperitif. During a recent visit to Toulouse, I found Floc de Gascogne to be sweet, sensual, and captivating. Floc is produced using a combination of fresh grape juice and strong young Armagnac. It can be made with red or white grapes and has appealing young and fruity flavors.

The family of fortified wines can either be very expensive or provide some of the best values in the wine market. They range widely in color, intensity, flavor, and sweetness levels. Fortified dessert wines that are sweet, strongly flavored, and high in alcohol are intended to be served in smaller portions than table wines for sipping after the meal or with cheeses and desserts. Many higher-alcohol fortified wines such as Ruby Port, Tawny Port, Floc, and Oloroso and Cream Sherries can be kept for several days or even weeks without deterioration. Fino Sherries, Vintage Ports, and Muscats are more delicate and should be consumed shortly after opening to minimize any loss in quality.

Floc, Olorosos, Cream Sherries, Marsala, Madeira, and Ports are generally served at a cool room temperature. Fino Sherries and fortified Muscats are served chilled. Fortified wines are often served in small cordial glasses, but during the ceremony of contemplative sipping, they are best served in small wine or regular wineglasses so their aromas can be appreciated.

DESSERT SELECTION AND WINE PAIRING

Individual preferences for sweets vary from person to person and among cultures. For example, I have a sweet tooth and don't see a problem serving sweet desserts and sweet dessert wines together. However, in planning a dessert course, you must use care to ensure that the majority of your guests enjoy the combination you have selected.

Many sweet foods can be as high as one-fourth sugar, whereas dessert wines rarely have more than 10–15 percent sugar content. This situation requires that care be taken to avoid a mismatch in sugar content—remember the rule of thumb that foods are better matched with wines when food sweetness level is less than or equal to wine sweetness level. I vividly remember a case where I did not follow this rule and paid the price. I had a bottle of Muscat Cannelli (a moderately sweet wine) and served it with ice cream and a chocolate dessert. It was a disaster—the dessert was way too sweet and rich for the wine and ended up making the wine taste thin, bitter, and acidic.

Fruit-based and moderately sweet desserts are the best matches for the spectrum of dessert wines. The following sections classify desserts into five categories and provide suggestions for dessert wines to try within each category. Of course, many other options are possible, and you are encouraged to experiment with your favorite desserts and wines.

DESSERT CATEGORIES

Just as categorizing dessert wines and cheeses is not a straightforward task, categorizing desserts is not totally straightforward either. As you are aware, desserts are frequently a combination of items—fruits, custard, chocolate, and nuts could easily be part of one dessert. The point of separating them into categories is to determine likely matches with individual elements. When multiple dessert elements (fruit, custard, chocolate, etc.) are combined, layers of components, texture, and flavors are created for a wide variety of similar and contrasting elements. This process provides some basic rules to follow in the dessert and dessert wine pairing process, which can be expanded to multiple dessert element situations.

As with the other pairings throughout this text, there are a few tools at your disposal. First is the general rule that the wine should be as sweet as or sweeter than the dessert. Second, excessive food elements such as bitterness, sweetness, acidity, and richness may present pairing problems. Desserts that are only moderately sweet and have fruit or acidic elements are the easiest to use in creating good or great matches. Finally, as with other menu pairing decisions, you will need to determine which is the star, the dessert or the wine. Fine, complex, and mature dessert wines need to be paired with simple desserts that will flatter the wine. Sweet and rich desserts should generally be paired with more moderately priced dessert wines.

The following sections break desserts into five general categories: custards, chocolate, fruit, nuts, and baked desserts. Each of the following sections presents issues relating to each category, suggestions for combinations, and specific wine suggestions.

Custards

Custards A wide array of classic desserts are based on a custard: crème brulée, bread pudding, ice cream, mousse, pastry cream, and pumpkin pie, to name a few. A standard vanilla custard dessert is fairly easy to match with dessert wines as long as the dessert is not too sweet. Desserts such as panna cotta and crème brulée seem to flatter many dessert wines. Any fruit, berry, nutty, or caramel-flavored dessert wine will complement this type of dessert. When pairing dessert wines with custard desserts that include fruit ingredients, a safe bet is to select dessert wines with fruit flavors that match the actual fruits in the dessert. Also, custard and fruit desserts pair up with dessert wines high in acidity. For example, lemon custard or lemon soufflé pairs well with Canadian ice wines or cool-climate botrytis-affected wines. More intense and dried fruits in a custard dessert pair well with wines of similar character, such as date pudding and PX Sherry. Figure 13.1 provides a framework for decisions involving custard-based desserts and dessert wines.

Custard desserts that include chocolate call for dessert wines with attributes that go well with chocolate: orange, caramel, nuts, and so on. Dark chocolate calls for more powerful

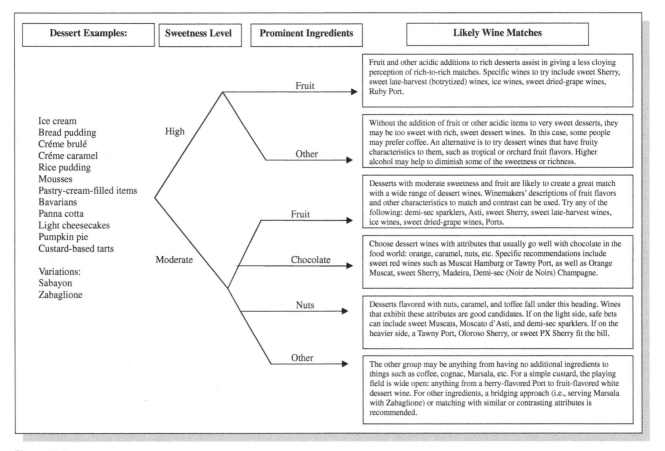

Figure 13.1

Custard-Based Dessert Pairing Decision Process

dessert wines. Specific recommendations include sweet red wines (such as Muscat Hamburg or Tawny Port) as well as Orange Muscat, sweet Sherry, Madeira, and demi-sec (Noir de Noirs) Champagne. A white chocolate bread pudding would be more likely to pair well with sweet dessert wines such as Sauternes, ice wine, or sweet white Port. If the custard/chocolate dessert is light and airy (mousses and soufflés), sweet (or demi-sec) sparkling wine, Champagne, or Vouvray provide a good texture match.

Many other custard desserts integrate items such as nuts, caramel, and toffee. Wines that exhibit similar attributes are good candidates for pairing with these desserts. If the dessert is on the lighter side, a good choice would include sweet Muscats, Moscato d'Asti, or demi-sec sparklers. If the dessert is on the heavier side, you should select fuller-bodied and stronger-flavored dessert wines such as Tawny Port, Oloroso Sherry, or sweet PX Sherry.

There are many custard desserts that don't quite fit directly into any of these categories, including desserts containing coffee, spice, and alcohol-based ingredients (Cognac, Marsala, Cointreau, etc.). Custard desserts infused with coffee flavors, such as Tiramisu, work with sweet white dessert wines (late-harvest wines, botrytis-affected wines, and Muscats). Pumpkin pie is an example of a heavily spiced custard dessert. It pairs well with ice wine, botrytis-affected Sémillon, and (particularly if made using brown sugar) Tawny Port. Variations on the custard dessert category are desserts such as sabayon and zabaglione, which are prepared using fortified wines. Basically, the bridging technique works here—sabayon made with Sauternes is paired with Sauternes, zabaglione made with Marsala is paired with Marsala.

Chocolate and Chocolate Desserts

Many believe that there are no safe choices when pairing with chocolate. It is particularly problematic if you have a chocolate dessert of the rich, gooey, and molten kind. At the other end of the spectrum, others believe that chocolate is good with just about everything. Of course, there are some limiting factors inherent in chocolate, such as its mouth-coating and palate-deadening effects due to richness (cocoa butter) and sweetness. But chocolate can be successfully paired with wine when several basic guidelines are followed. First, you should always avoid serving complex or aged wines with chocolate. Wines of this nature deserve a food partner that allows them to shine. Second, wines with higher alcohol content, such as Port or Sherry, are more compatible with chocolate than lower-alcohol wines. Finally, only moderately sweet chocolate desserts are truly compatible with dessert wines. Therefore, it is assumed during this discussion that the chocolate dessert is only moderately sweet rather than highly sweet and rich. If a chocolate dessert is at the extreme levels of sweetness, a better match might be coffee or a flavored liqueur to cut through the richness.

Another factor to consider is the type of chocolate used. Dark chocolate is less sweet and more bitter, while milk chocolate is sweeter and more mouth-coating as a rule, and white chocolate is sweet and buttery. For all chocolate items, fruit and other acidic additions assist in diminishing some of the richness. Sweet wines are generally best with chocolate desserts. Specific wines to try with chocolate and fruit desserts include sweet Sherry, sweet late-harvest (botrytized) wines, ice wines, sweet dried-grape wines, and Ruby Port.

If there is no addition of fruit or other acidic items to chocolate desserts, an alternative is to try dessert wines that have fruit, berry, orange, caramel, and nutty characteristics to them. These items work with chocolate in the food world and should also provide a match in the chocolate-to-wine world. Specific recommendations include sweet red wines such as Muscat Hamburg, Tawny Port, or Zinfandel Port as well as Orange Muscat, sweet Sherry, Madeira, and demi-sec (Noir de Noirs) Champagne. If you are simply having pure dark chocolate alone, I find Cabernet Sauvignon or Amarone enjoyable with it (or, from the beer world, even a bottle of stout), but this combination is not appreciated by everyone.

Desserts made with milk chocolate seem to work better with higher alcohol and/or higher acidity in dessert wines. Winemakers' descriptions of fruit flavors and other characteristics to match and contrast with milk chocolate desserts can provide strong clues to likely matches. Try any of the following: sweet red wines, Orange Muscat, sweet dried-grape wines, or Ports.

As mentioned above, white chocolate desserts can be sweet and rich but with more of a buttery flavor than dark or milk chocolate. If the white chocolate dessert is on the lighter side, some safe bets include sweet Muscats, Moscato d'Asti, and demi-sec sparklers. If a white chocolate dessert is on the heavier side, try sweet white Port, sweet late-harvest (botrytized) wines, ice wines, or sweet dried-grape wines.

Figure 13.2 outlines the pairing decision process for chocolate-based desserts. The other group within this framework may include chocolate desserts having no additional ingredients or items such as custard, other chocolates, cookies, and nuts. In most cases, such a dessert will be sweet and rich. Possible matches include berry-flavored Ports, fruit-flavored white dessert wines, and sweet sparkling wines. Here again, the match should be based on similar or contrasting attributes, and the likelihood of a successful match will be increased by following the guidelines presented above.

Fruit and Fruit-Based Desserts
Fruit desserts can take on a wide range of forms: fresh plain berries, poached pairs, fruit compotes, fresh fruit tarts, fruit pies, and classical fruit deserts such as Bananas Foster, Peach Melba, and Crêpes Suzette. All of these dessert types require slight differences in the type of wine selected.

A simple solution to matching wines with fruit is the old bridging concept. Wine included as an ingredient of the fruit dessert can then be served with the dessert with an assurance of success. Classics such as ripe peaches in Champagne, strawberries in a fruity red such as Beaujolais, or poaching fruit in wine (pears or plums poached in red wine) are good examples of this technique. Additionally, ripe fruits in a salad can be paired with light,

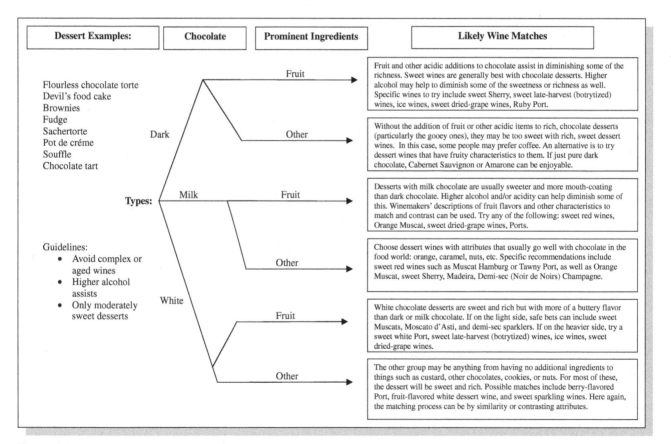

Figure 13.2

Chocolate-Based Dessert Pairing Decision Process

fruity, and fresh wines such as Moscato d'Asti or Asti Spumati. This pairing brings together the fresh fruit with the fruit flavors inherent in these Moscato grape sparklers.

Figure 13.3 provides a framework for pairing decisions based on prominent fruit type. Fruits vary in both ripeness and type. Ripe orchard fruits and berries are moderately sweet. Tropical and dried fruits are sweeter and more care must be taken when pairing these items with the proper wines.

Fruit desserts provide a refreshing sensation due to the acidity/sweetness balance, and this refreshing sensation is particularly evident in citrus desserts. Dessert wines that match this acidity level provide a lighter ending to a meal. Cool-climate dessert wines with higher acidity are likely candidates. The addition of custard, cream, or meringue to citrus desserts levels out the tanginess. Specific wines to try with citrus desserts include sweet late-harvest (botrytized) wines, ice wines, sweet dried-grape wines, and Orange Muscat. For lemon-flavored desserts, late-harvest Riesling or sweet Vouvray can generally cope with the tanginess of this dessert type. Orange-flavored desserts are not as tangy as a rule and can be paired with a variety of dessert and fortified Muscats.

Fresh berries can be a light dessert on their own and become even more wine-friendly with the addition of cream. Strawberries served au naturel are great with Moscato d'Asti. If served with cream and sugar (or shortcake), late-harvest Sémillon or Sauternes is a good selection. Dark berries such as blackberries, loganberries, and blueberries can have a substantial amount of sharpness to them. Late-harvest Riesling or Riesling ice wine should stand up to the challenge; adding cream or custard to the dessert opens up additional pairing possibilities. If berries are used as a base for a dessert, a variety of sweeter wines can be utilized, such as sweet late-harvest (botrytized) wines, ice wines, Muscat Hamburg, and demi-sec sparkling wine.

Desserts of moderate sweetness that include orchard fruits are likely to create a great match with a wide range of dessert wines. Winemakers' descriptions of fruit flavors and other characteristics can be used to match and contrast with tree fruit desserts. As with other

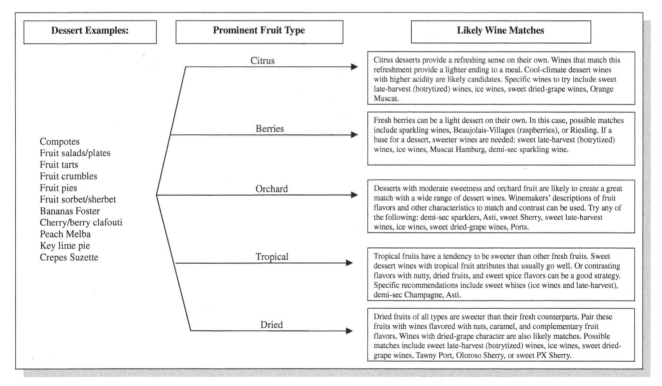

Figure 13.3

Fruit-Based Dessert Pairing Decision Process

foods, it is useful to remember other items that are paired with these fruits in the food world, namely, honey, cream, caramel, and nuts. Selecting dessert wines with these characteristics is a great starting point for pairing decisions. Try any of the following dessert wines with orchard fruit desserts: demi-sec sparklers, Asti, sweet Sherry, sweet late-harvest wines, ice wines, sweet dried-grape wines, and Ports. Here are some specific recommended matches: blackberry and apple crumble with late-harvest (botrytized) Riesling, plum tart with Muscat Hamburg, poached pears in Muscat de Beaumes with Muscat de Beaumes, and apple tart (flavored with butter, rum, and cinnamon) with demi-sec Champagne.

Tropical fruits have a tendency to be sweeter than other fresh fruits. Sweet dessert wines with tropical fruit attributes usually go well with tropical fruit desserts. An alternative pairing selection is to combine contrasting flavors of nuts, dried fruits, and sweet spice flavors in the dessert wine with the tropical fruit dessert. General recommendations include many sweet whites (ice wines, late-harvest wines, and dried-grape wines) and sweet sparklers (demi-sec and doux Champagne, Asti, sparkling ice wine, etc.). A specific recommendation is the combination of lychee and coconut milk sorbet with late-harvest Gewürztraminer.

Dried fruits of all types are sweeter than their fresh counterparts. Dried fruits have an affinity for wines flavored with nuts, caramel, and complementary fruit flavors. Wines with dried-grape character are also likely matches with dried fruits and dried fruit desserts. Some possible matches include sweet late-harvest (botrytized) wines, ice wines, sweet dried-grape wines, Tawny Port, Oloroso Sherry, or sweet PX Sherry. Dried fruits such as raisins, figs, and dates work particularly well with many of the fortified wines, including Tawny Port, sweet Oloroso Sherry, and sweet Madeira. A simple combination that works in this category is dried prunes paired with Tawny Port.

Nuts and Nut-Based Desserts
Nuts provide a range of pairing opportunities. Figure 13.4 provides a framework for decisions in this category of desserts.

Almonds, hazelnuts, and walnuts eaten with wine can create a good combination. Walnuts with a fine and mature fortified wine is a simple combination that allows the fine

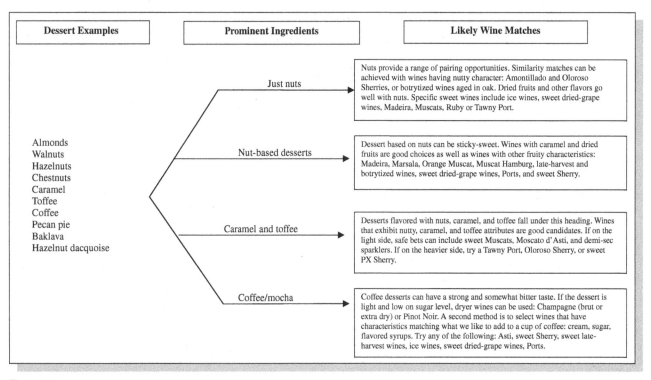

Figure 13.4

Nut-Based Dessert Pairing Decision Process

wine to shine. Similarity matches can be achieved with wines having nutty character: Amontillado and Oloroso Sherries, or botrytized wines aged in oak take on slightly nutty character. Dried fruits and other flavors go well with nuts. Specific sweet wines include ice wines, sweet dried-grape wines, Madeira, Muscats, and Ruby and Tawny Port.

Desserts based on nuts can be sticky-sweet (e.g., baklava and pecan pie). Fortified wines with caramel and dried fruit characteristics are good choices, as are those with other fruity characteristics: Madeira, Marsala, Orange Muscat, Muscat Hamburg, Ports, and sweet Sherry. Pecan pie with a little whipped cream and a glass of Canadian Vidal ice wine is a decadent treat indeed.

Many of these desserts are flavored with nuts, caramel, or toffee (or various combinations). If these desserts are on the lighter side, safe bets can include sweet Muscats, Moscato d'Asti, and demi-sec sparklers. If they are heavier, a Tawny Port, Oloroso Sherry, or sweet PX Sherry should fit the bill.

Coffee-based desserts can have a strong or a bitter taste. If the coffee-based dessert is light and low in sugar level, dryer wines can be used. Brut or extra-dry Champagne or even a Pinot Noir can be a pleasant partner. A second approach to pairing wines with coffee-based desserts is to select wines that have characteristics matching what we like to add to a cup of coffee: cream, sugar, flavored syrups. Try any of the following based on the dessert's characteristics (power and flavor intensity): Asti, sweet Sherry, sweet late-harvest wines, ice wines, sweet dried-grape wines, and Ports.

Baked Goods: Cakes, Cookies, Pastries, and Dessert Breads

Baked goods is a diverse category of desserts and can be combined with a range of ingredients. The decision framework for this group of dessert items is shown in Figure 13.5. Simple cakes such as sponge, pound cake, and angel food allow sweet wines to bask in their glory. Cakes filled or topped with vanilla, butter, or citrus flavors can be paired with cooler-climate late-harvest wines, ice wines, and sweet sparkling wines such as Moscato d'Asti.

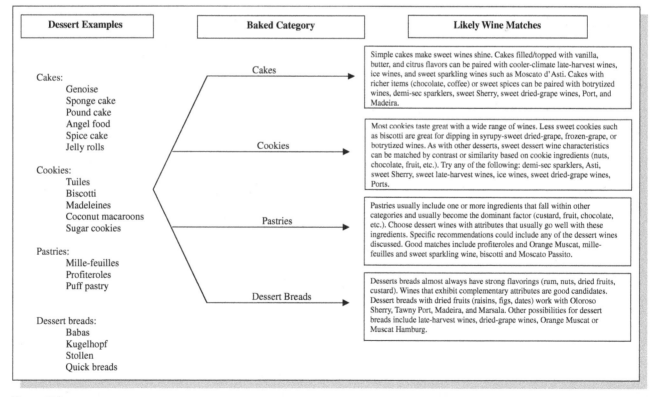

Figure 13.5

Baked Good Pairing Decision Process

Cassati alla Siciliana (sponge cake frosted with ricotta and filled with candied fruits) pairs up well with a dessert Moscato such as Moscato di Pantelleria Passito. Cakes with richer items (chocolate, almonds paste, coffee) or sweet spices can be paired with botrytized wines, demi-sec sparklers, sweet Sherry, sweet dried-grape wines, Port, and Madeira.

Most cookies taste great with a wide range of wines. Cookies come in a variety of forms, from a range of North American types (peanut butter, chocolate chip, sugar) to biscotti, tuiles, and madeleines. Less sweet cookies such as biscotti are great for dipping in syrupy-sweet dried-grape, frozen-grape, or botrytized wines. As with other desserts, sweet dessert wine characteristics can be matched by contrast or similarity with cookie ingredients (nuts, chocolate, fruit, etc.). Try any of the following dessert wines with your favorite cookies: demi-sec sparklers, Asti, sweet Sherry, sweet late-harvest wines, ice wines, sweet dried-grape wines, and Ports. Higher-alcohol dessert wines usually work better with cookies that are loaded with rich ingredients such as butter, chocolate chips, and nuts. The higher alcohol content seems to assist in diminishing the overly rich character of rich cookies.

Pastries are usually prepared with additional prominent ingredients that will factor into the pairing decision. Choose dessert wines with attributes that usually go well with the ingredients found in pastries. Specific recommendations might include any of the dessert wines discussed. Good matches include profiteroles and Orange Muscat, mille-feuilles and sweet sparkling wine, or biscotti and Moscato Passito.

Dessert breads are a much smaller subgroup. Dessert breads with dried fruits (raisins, figs, dates) work well with Oloroso Sherry, Tawny Port, Madeira, and Marsala. These dessert wines are a good match with Christmas fruitcake as well (to my mind, this dessert is more of a bread than a cake). Other possibilities for dessert wines to pair with dessert breads include late-harvest wines, dried-grape wines, Orange Muscat, or Muscat Hamburg. Hungarian Tokaji, Greek Muscat, and Moscato di Pantelleria Passito would be good matches with dessert breads.

SUMMARY

This chapter provides a detailed description of the categories within the exciting world of dessert wines and desserts. This chapter focused on categories most prominent within dessert wines and desserts to provide a framework for making pairing decisions in the future.

The Aperitif at the beginning of the chapter provides an account of how Niagara's wine region has evolved over time and established a strong global reputation for its opulent dessert wines. The evolution of the wine industry has also had an impact in the education arena as more and more institutions embrace the growing demand for wine and food professionals with no end in sight. Niagara College, with its Niagara College Teaching Winery (NCTW), is one of a growing number of schools embracing a synergistic approach to experiential learning across the campus.

There is a wide range of dessert wines produced in regions all over the globe. The discussion in this chapter only scratches the surface of this wine category but clearly describes the main dessert wine categories: frozen-grape wines, late-harvest wines, dried-grape wines, and fortified wines.

The final section of this chapter tackles pairing various categories of desserts with dessert wines. The general rule that the wine should be sweeter than the dessert holds in this case, as it has throughout the other pairings you have explored. Desserts with excessive bitterness, sweetness, acidity, and richness can create pairing problems. Desserts that are only moderately sweet and have fruit or acidic elements the easiest to pair with dessert wines and typically yield good to great matches.

DISCUSSION QUESTIONS

1. What are the five dessert wine categories?

2. Describe the similar and contrasting characteristics of each dessert wine category.

3. What types of desserts are easiest to pair with dessert wines?

4. What dessert elements limit dessert wine choices?

5. Define typical dessert wine styles that are appropriate for each dessert category.

EXERCISE 13.1

DESSERT WINE AND DESSERT MATCHING

For this exercise, you may select desserts from the lists in Figures 13.1–13.5 or choose other examples for each dessert category. Pick a range of desserts from simple and straightforward to those that are more complex in order to provide a full panoply of tasting experiences during the evaluation process. Use the Food Sensory Anchor Scale (Figure B.1) and Wine Sensory Anchor Scale (Figure B.2) to create basic reference points for match based on components, texture, and flavor as you use the Wine and Food Pairing Instrument.

OBJECTIVES

To distinguish and rank differing levels of elements in each dessert and dessert wine; to compare the profiles of each dessert with each dessert wine to predict a match level for each pair, and then conduct a mixed tasting to determine perceived level of match.

Mise en Place: Things to Do Before the Exercise Prepare and portion the desserts to ensure they are served at the optimal tasting temperature. Chill the dessert wines to the appropriate temperatures.

MATERIALS NEEDED

Table 13.3   Materials Needed for Exercise 13.1

1 white paper placemat per student with numbered or labeled circles to place wineglasses (Figure 9.4a)	1 spit cup per student Corkscrew Drinking water for each student
1 copy of the Aroma Wheel per student	Napkins
Tasting sheets for each student (4 copies of Figures 11.2A, 11.2B and 11.2C)	4 wineglasses per student
1 copy Food and Wine Sensory Anchor Scales per student	Cutting board
1 copy of Figure 13.6 (Food and Wine Perceived Match Level) per student	Bread or crackers to cleanse palate
Plates for tasting samples of desserts	Plastic forks and knives

Table 13.4   Desserts and Wines Needed for Exercise 13.1

Desserts

Custard-Based Dessert: Examples in Figure 13.1

Fruit-Based Dessert: Examples in Figure 13.3

Nut-Based Dessert: Examples in Figure 13.4

Baked Goods Dessert: :Examples in Figure 13.5

Wines

Dried-Grape Wine: Examples in Table 13.2

Late-Harvest Wine: Examples in section discussing late-harvest wine

Frozen-Grape Wine: Examples in Table 13.1

Fortified Wine: Examples in section discussing fortified wine

STEPS

1. Divide the desserts into 2-oz tasting samples and arrange on small plates or in bowls.

2. Evaluate each dessert considering all of the food elements (Figure 11.2B and/or 11.2C).

3. Pour a sample of each wine for each student—enough to evaluate and to try with each dessert sample.

4. Taste the wine samples and assess all wine elements. Record your findings in Figure 11.2A and/or 11.2C.

5. Taste the desserts with each wine in ascending order and record the perceived level of match in Figure 12.10 and/or at the bottom of Figure 11.2C. Once you taste everything, you can then go back and forth between them to ensure consistent measures, if desired.

6. Discuss and record any sensory observations based on the relationship between the various wines and desserts you've sampled. Which wine and dessert had the best match? Was it predicted? Which wine and dessert had the lowest match? Were any of the matches truly synergistic? Are there other wines that you feel would create a better match? Any surprises?

7. Rank each dessert with each dessert wine from lowest to highest level of match.

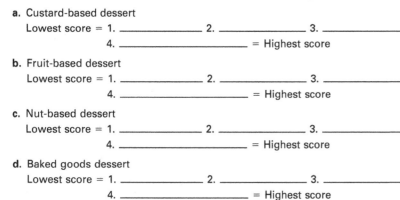

   a. Custard-based dessert
      Lowest score = 1. _____ 2. _____ 3. _____
                       4. _____ = Highest score

   b. Fruit-based dessert
      Lowest score = 1. _____ 2. _____ 3. _____
                       4. _____ = Highest score

   c. Nut-based dessert
      Lowest score = 1. _____ 2. _____ 3. _____
                       4. _____ = Highest score

   d. Baked goods dessert
      Lowest score = 1. _____ 2. _____ 3. _____
                       4. _____ = Highest score

8. Write down any other comments, thoughts, and observations that you identified during this evaluation process. Did the predicted wine type/dessert type match coincide with your perceived level of match when the desserts and wines were tasted together? Was there any predominant category of element(s) that impacted the level of match across all of the dessert and wine combinations? If so, was it a component, texture, or flavor category?

Date: _____

Overall feeling of food and wine match (circle the level of match below):

Custard-Based Dessert: _____

Dried-Grape Wine	0-----1-----2-----3-----4-----5-----6-----7-----8-----9-----10		
	No Match	Average Match	Synergistic Match
Late-Harvest Wine	0-----1-----2-----3-----4-----5-----6-----7-----8-----9-----10		
	No Match	Average Match	Synergistic Match
Frozen-Grape Wine	0-----1-----2-----3-----4-----5-----6-----7-----8-----9-----10		
	No Match	Average Match	Synergistic Match
Fortified Wine	0-----1-----2-----3-----4-----5-----6-----7-----8-----9-----10		
	No Match	Average Match	Synergistic Match

Fruit-based Dessert: _____

Dried-Grape Wine	0-----1-----2-----3-----4-----5-----6-----7-----8-----9-----10		
	No Match	Average Match	Synergistic Match
Late-Harvest Wine	0-----1-----2-----3-----4-----5-----6-----7-----8-----9-----10		
	No Match	Average Match	Synergistic Match
Frozen-Grape Wine	0-----1-----2-----3-----4-----5-----6-----7-----8-----9-----10		
	No Match	Average Match	Synergistic Match
Fortified Wine	0-----1-----2-----3-----4-----5-----6-----7-----8-----9-----10		
	No Match	Average Match	Synergistic Match

Nut-Based Dessert: _____

Dried-Grape Wine	0-----1-----2-----3-----4-----5-----6-----7-----8-----9-----10		
	No Match	Average Match	Synergistic Match
Late-Harvest Wine	0-----1-----2-----3-----4-----5-----6-----7-----8-----9-----10		
	No Match	Average Match	Synergistic Match
Frozen-Grape Wine	0-----1-----2-----3-----4-----5-----6-----7-----8-----9-----10		
	No Match	Average Match	Synergistic Match
Fortified Wine	0-----1-----2-----3-----4-----5-----6-----7-----8-----9-----10		
	No Match	Average Match	Synergistic Match

Simple Cookie/Cake: _____

Dried-Grape Wine	0-----1-----2-----3-----4-----5-----6-----7-----8-----9-----10		
	No Match	Average Match	Synergistic Match
Late-Harvest Wine	0-----1-----2-----3-----4-----5-----6-----7-----8-----9-----10		
	No Match	Average Match	Synergistic Match
Frozen-Grape Wine	0-----1-----2-----3-----4-----5-----6-----7-----8-----9-----10		
	No Match	Average Match	Synergistic Match
Fortified Wine	0-----1-----2-----3-----4-----5-----6-----7-----8-----9-----10		
	No Match	Average Match	Synergistic Match

Figure 13.6

Dessert and Dessert Wine Level of Match

NOTES

1. Andrea Immer, *Great Tastes Made Simple: Extraordinary Food and Wine Pairing for Every Palate* (New York: Broadway Books, 2002).

2. K. MacNeil, *The Wine Bible* (New York: Workman Publishing Company, 2001).

3. J. Arkell, *New World Wines: The Complete Guide* (New York: Sterling, 1999), 140.

4. M. Cliff, D. Yuksel, B. Girard, and M. King, "Characterization of Canadian Ice Wines by Sensory and Compositional Analyses," *American Journal of Enology and Viticulture* 53, 1 (2002): 46–53.

5. M. W. Baldy, *The University Wine Course*, 3rd ed. (San Francisco: Wine Appreciation Guild, 2003).

6. Immer, *Great Tastes Made Simple*; A. Lichine, *Alexis Lichine's New Encyclopedia of Wines and Spirits* (New York: Alfred A. Knopf, 1987).

7. Baldy, *The University Wine Course*.

8. Ibid.

CHAPTER 14

THE CUSTOMER EXPERIENCE: PRODUCT, SERVICE, AND TRAINING ISSUES

CHAPTER OUTLINE:

Introduction

Aperitif: Product-Service Considerations for a Food and Wine Program

The Total Experience: Creating Distinctive Food and Wine Capabilities

Food and Wine Training Process

Summary

Exercises

KEY CONCEPTS:

- Competitive advantage
- Differentiation
- Unique bundle of activities
- Product and service considerations for a food and wine program
- Menus and wine lists
- Service elements

INTRODUCTION

Up to this point, the discussions and exercises in this text have armed you with (1) depth of experience in tasting and evaluating food and wine combinations, (2) the basics of wine evaluation and differences between varietals characteristics, (3) an understanding of gastronomic identity and its relationship with wine and food marriages, and (4) knowledge of how food and wine elements interact and transform each other. These methods provide you with a tool kit of ideas, concepts, and knowledge for quickly identifying key wine and food elements that impact the effectiveness of food and wine pairings. This process combines techniques and ideas from both the art and science of sensory evaluation. The heart of this process relies heavily upon the senses of sight, smell, taste, touch, and hearing.

As pointed out throughout the text, it is important to consider the impact of a region's gastronomic identity on food, wine, and the pairing of the two when considering various matches. A variety of environmental and cultural elements impact preferences and prevailing components, textures, and flavors in wine and food. The Aperitifs in each chapter demonstrate that many business and educational endeavors have found taking the gastronomic identity perspective to food and wine pairing to be rewarding and profitable. This perspective helps to provide unique experiences for locals and visitors alike while preserving (and in many cases exposing) a part of history.

The previous three chapters have focused on the use of the Wine and Food Pairing Instrument and explained how the profile it creates can be used to predict levels of match. The decision tree and scoring sheet help to create a structure to evaluate the impact of various elements on the potential match.

The concept of food and wine pairing is an exciting, challenging, and rapidly evolving topic area and industry. Many issues impact the experience your guests will have in your establishment, including the quality and extent of your food menu and accompanying wine list. Many questions have not been fully explored up to this point: How, specifically, can the food and wine pairing process be used to create a positive experience for my guests or customers? Will these food and wine pairing skills be useful in allowing my business to be more successful and competitive in the marketplace? Will this process ultimately provide greater gastronomic satisfaction for my guests and positively impact the bottom line of my business? The answers to these questions depend on how you implement your particular food and wine program. Successful implementation has to do with your customers' perception of service quality. The key criteria customers use to evaluate service quality include the reliability, responsiveness, competence, courtesy, and communication demonstrated by those providing the service as well as their understanding of the consumer.[1]

Aperitif I Product-Service Considerations for a Food and Wine Program

How large should the portion be in our wine-by-the-glass program? Or, what are the correct food and wine portion sizes in a multi-course tasting menu? Before these and many other questions can be answered, you will need to consider customer needs, seating capacity, the number of meals served, equipment needs, staff skills, and training capabilities.

Product presentation refers to every aspect associated with how the product is presented to the final customer. For food items, the concept of presentation includes the layout and combination of food items on the plate as well as the china, glass, silver, and other non-traditional service pieces that may be used. For wine, the presentation may include the storage unit (a visible cellar), wine buckets (Sterling silver? Or, plastic?), and the glassware.

The table setting plays a large part in the presentation factor of a food and wine product. How formal or informal should the setting be? What is the correct set-up for a multi-course tasting menu? If I am invited to a multi-course, formal dinner will I use the proper etiquette? These and other questions point out some of the issues of creating the right experience for guests attending a multi-course food and wine event. For many of us, serving a multi-course tasting menu in a restaurant or executing a dinner party in our home can be a daunting task. Good planning and organization on the front end will make the evening go smoother and eliminate some of the pre-event nervousness. Basically, a properly set table is designed to make service go smoothly for both the guest(s) and the host. There are many great books available on the topic of table setting and table service as well as many good Web sites. Below, are a few basics to remember that will serve you well whether you are working in a restaurant, you're a host or a guest:

- Dinnerware and flatware should be set about a thumb's width from the edge of the table.

- The standard rule is that you eat to your left and drink to your right. By remembering this guideline, you can easily figure out which bread plate, coffee cup, or water glass goes to which guest. Of course, if a guest drinks from the wrong glass or uses the wrong fork, it should not cause any embarrassment and should be swiftly replaced without any further attention.

- Both flatware and glassware should be placed in the order that guests will be consuming the courses. For instance, the fork for the first course will be in the outside left position and the wine glass for the first course will be in the outside right position. If you are serving a soup or other course that uses a spoon, the spoon will be placed on the right of the dinner knife.

- A water glass should be placed just above the dinner knife. Wine glasses are placed to the right of the water glass. If serving 2 wines, the glasses can be placed in a triangle with the 2 wine glasses to the right of the water glass. The wine glass that is to the front, right hand side is for the first wine, the one behind it for the second, and the water glass is the third glass on the left above the dinner knife. If serving 3 wines, the glasses can be placed in a square surrounding the water glass. The wine glass that is farthest to the right is for the first wine, the one behind it for the second, and the wine glass behind the water glass is for the third wine (basically, starting with the wine glass on the lower right position and moving in a counter clockwise direction. If serving 4 or more wines (and have room on the table to place them), a straight line across the top of the place setting or slightly at an angle going outward from the place setting (in a diagonal formation) is your best bet. If in a straight line, the water glass is the last one to the left and wine service begins to the right and moves to the left.

Properly preparing for service is an important part of the total experience of your guests. The following sections provide an overview of general considerations for food and wine capabilities and the impact on this experience.

THE TOTAL EXPERIENCE: CREATING DISTINCTIVE FOOD AND WINE CAPABILITIES

Each food service experience can be thought of as a unique bundle of tangible and intangible products and services provided to the consumer. This is certainly true of any food and wine service experience. The actual food and wine are tangible, but much of the broader experience is tied to more intangible variables such as atmosphere, service, and image. These are intimately tied in with etiquette, customs, traditions, and fashion.

By creating food and wine matches that are either good or great, you can create value for the customer, which is the ultimate goal of any business. Value is a complex perception that involves many things, including food ingredients and preparation, wine price and value, menu and wine list presentation, a well-trained staff, and professional, unpretentious service. The food and wine pairing capabilities you have developed as you read through this text provide you with a potential distinctive capability that could create a competitive advantage for your business. Food service firms that are able to differentiate themselves by providing unique services can improve their competitive position in the marketplace. This differentiation is an effective strategy to help build customer loyalty and reduce competition based solely on price.[2]

There are a number of tactics that are useful to round out a food and wine pairing capability. Some of these issues include product and service considerations for a food and wine program, menus and wine lists, service elements, and wine selection considerations. Many of these issues are based on tradition and ritual, while others have more to do with innovation and fashion.

FOOD AND WINE TRAINING PROCESS

A key promotional tool of any successful food and wine program is the implementation of an ongoing training process within the food and beverage unit. Prior to its implementation, each food service firm needs to determine an ideal food-and-wine program based on the needs of its customers.

The wine steward—a traditional symbol of knowledge and service.

What constitutes the ideal restaurant experience for the typical food-and-wine customer? Of course, service quality is in the eye of the beholder, and the process has many intangible elements, including reliability, responsiveness, competence, courtesy, and communication, as well as understanding the consumer. One aspect of quality relates to how the organization conceives of its business objectives, how food and wine fit into that perspective, and how it all meshes with the expectations of the customer.

To provide a good wine and food program, several items need to be in place. First, the wine list (in whatever form) needs to be readily available to the guest. Automatically presenting a wine list to each table is one method. A second method is to ensure that all of the members of the team are knowledgeable and excited about wine and food. An ideal situation is an establishment that values the role of wine and how it can enhance the cuisine as well as the guests' enjoyment. In other words, you should strive to create a culture of wine and food.

One simple method to reinforce this culture is to encourage your associates to discuss only wine and food while at work rather than sports, movies, or other unrelated topics. When staffers constantly communicate with each other, interactive and continuous learning will take place and will help the entire staff be more comfortable discussing wine and food with guests and more likely to take the initiative in doing so.

The ideal restaurant will also have a wine-by-the-glass program to encourage individuals and small groups to have wine with their food. This includes offering things such as a single glass of Champagne as an aperitif, a single glass of white wine with an appetizer course, and a glass of dessert or fortified wine to finish the meal.

The ideal restaurant will have a wine list of appropriate length featuring wines that enhance the style of cooking on the menu. The list should provide an ample number of choices in a variety of price ranges; the service should provide enough time to consider wine choices with food selections; the server should be ready when signaled to make recommendations and complete the transaction; and all of the wines on the list should be in stock and be the vintages listed on the wine list.

Having staff that can effectively, confidently, and enthusiastically recommend wine and food pairings is at the heart of an ideal situation. A big part of achieving this objective is tied to the pairing instrument, decision tree, and scoring method presented in this text. All three of these tools become valuable pieces for continuous training for a successful wine and food program. The vision behind the Wine and Food Pairing Instrument (Figures 11.2A, 11.2B, and 11.2C) is to allow it to be utilized as a visual profile for each wine on the wine list and food item on the menu. For example, in addition to the names of wines on a wine list, a book can be created using completed Figures 11.2A, one for each wine on the wine list. The profiles on these lists can then be compared with profiles of menu items (Figures 11.2B) to determine groups of wines that are likely to create a good to synergistic match. An understanding of this process by all of the staff members can assist those in the front of the house in suggesting wines that will be a great match with the dishes guests have chosen. It can also empower those in the back of the house to create recipes that are more wine-friendly.

In order for the food-and-wine training process to be successful and help reinforce employee understanding of and appreciation for good and synergistic food-and-wine matches, it should be continuous and ongoing. One way to achieve this is to get the staff involved in wine selection. A particular wine should not be chosen for the wine list unless you and the staff have an understanding of its characteristics. For instance, before deciding on wine selections for a wine-by-the-glass program, provide price and other criteria to your supplier and have the supplier furnish a bottle of each candidate for a tasting so you can make selections with your staff. It is a good idea to do this in a blind tasting format so that evaluators will not be biased by the label or producer.

Finally, a successful food-and-wine program is based on serving the needs of the guest and creating a pleasurable experience beyond their expectations. Therefore, a successful training program will address issues relating to attitude, and will incorporate training strategies that will move your employees and peers forward. Attitude is an important intangible element that impacts the relationship with the customer. Attitude is communicated through our body language, what we say, and our tone of voice. Positive and negative attitudes can spread like wildfire and can be critical in the success or failure of a food-and-wine program.

Beyond the training ideas discussed above, general training strategies include providing a continuous message emphasizing the importance of creating pleasurable experiences for the guest. This message can be communicated by constantly talking about pleasurable experiences for customers, having it as a topic at meetings, and making a point of searching out those around us who are providing these experiences and holding them up as exemplars. To ensure a successful training strategy, all members of the team need to have a strong knowledge base, training needs to address a variety of intangible elements (service elements, communication issues, and nonverbal communication issues), and role-playing situations should be included in training in order to work though potential customer service break-downs before they happen.

SUMMARY

We have come a long way in a short period! The food-and-wine learning process is a fun but never-ending one—but then again, why would you want it to end? An understanding of food and wine separately and combined demands a truly interdisciplinary approach integrating the arts, science, and the social sciences.

At this point, you may choose to continue to utilize the methods presented throughout this text (measurement tools, sensory anchors, and the like), using a blend of the art and science of sensory analysis. Or you may decide that you have a good fundamental grounding in the process and now want to pursue your future wine-and-food pairing with a strictly artisanal approach. Neither approach is right or wrong as long as you are able to create pleasure for yourself and your guests.

The final end-of-chapter exercises will allow you to use all of your newly developed knowledge and skills, whether the outcome of these exercises is for a course grade or as a treat for your friends and family. As always, what a pleasurable journey it is!

DISCUSSION QUESTIONS

1. How do the concepts of differentiation and competitive advantage apply to a food-and-wine program?

2. What is meant by the idea of a "unique bundle of activities"?

3. What are some key product and service considerations for a food-and-wine program?

EXERCISE 14.1

LOCAL FESTIVALS: THE IMPACT OF FOOD AND WINE (OR OTHER BEVERAGES)

Each group will research a local or regional festival and analyze the role of regional cuisine and the gastronomic identity concepts. Describe the region and the history of the festival. Describe the types of food and drinks produced/served there. Are there any unique treatments of these products? How is the festival marketed? What are the competing festivals? Is the festival successful? Why or why not?

EXERCISE 14.2

TEAM DEGUSTATION MENU AND FINAL FOOD AND WINE PAIRING

Have the class break out into teams that will design a five-course degustation menu that utilizes food-and-wine pairing knowledge/reasoning for menu item and wine selection. The preliminary criteria are as follows:

1. Prepare five courses, matching menu items with wine selections.

2. Assume a $75 price per person for the degustation menu.

3. Assume a 33 percent desired product cost (food and wine)—no more than $25 total or an average of $5 per course.

4. Therefore, no wines should be priced at more than $20 per bottle, and the average food cost should not exceed $3 per course (of course, the main course will be higher than a soup or dessert course).

5. Teams should submit the degustation menu outlines.

6. Teams should prepare one course of their menu and describe the following: Why they have selected the particular foods and wines? Do they create a synergistic match? What decisions did they make due to the vertical series of food and wine courses? Who are the likely customer groups that would appreciate this menu? How large is this target market? How does this menu differentiate your event (or catering business or restaurant) from your competitors?

Your instructor will provide further details for writing an evaluation of the project assignment.

NOTES

1. G. Johns and A. M. Saks, *Organizational Behaviour*, 6th ed. (Toronto: Pearson–Prentice Hall, 2005), 458.

2. M. E. Porter, *Competitive Advantage: Creating and Sustaining Superior Performance* (New York: Free Press, 1985).

GLOSSARY

A

Acidity. The level of acid present in wine and food that creates a sour sensation on your tongue.

Affective testing. A sensory evaluation process that requires a large number of tasters (75 or more) who are representative of the target population but requires little or no preliminary training by the individuals involved.

Amarone. An Italian dry, full-bodied red wine made with grapes that have been dried on racks to intensify their flavor.

American Viticultural Areas. An expanding number of appellation designations in the United States.

Analytical testing. A sensory testing approach used to discover detectable differences between or among samples; requires a small group of trained panelists.

Appellations. The location where grapes and other agricultural products are grown. Many appellations are sanctioned by a government or trade association that has authority to define and regulate procedures in order to guarantee quality and genuineness.

Aroma. The smell present in a young wine and/or a term used generically when discussing the smell of wine.

Astringency. A tactile sensation of dryness and roughness throughout the mouth created by the presence of tannin.

B

Bitterness. A primary taste component generally detected on the back of the tongue.

Blue-veined cheeses. During the curing process, the cheese curds are inoculated with pure cultures of molds that penetrate the interior of the cheese, creating a variegated blue-green appearance and distinctive flavor and aroma.

Body. Mouthfeel characteristics in food and wine that provide a feeling of weight, texture, or power. In wine, it refers to the consistency or viscosity as detected through the tactile sensations in the mouth.

Botrytis cinerea. The Latin name for a mold that affects wine grapes. Under the proper moisture and temperature conditions, botrytis-affected grapes can have a beneficial effect on a finished wine. Famous wines include Tokaji (Hungary), Sauternes (France), and Noble One (Australia).

Bouquet. The smell that develops in wine during bottle aging.

Brix. A measurement system used to determine the sugar content of grapes and wine. It is frequently used to indicate the degree of the fruits' ripeness at harvest.

C

Clarity. The level of transparency in a wine, ranging from cloudy to brilliant; assessed during a visual inspection of wine. Provides an indication of quality and proper handling.

Climate zones. A concept, based on heat summation units, used to define basic characteristics in wine styles such as ripeness, acidity levels, and flavors.

Cloying. Describes wine that is overly sweet; the sensation derives from a lack of balance between sweetness and acidity levels.

Competition survey. A survey used to evaluate a foodservice operation's closest competitors. The survey assesses competitors' hours of operation, restaurant size, menu and wine offerings, décor, location, pricing, level of service, and other relevant characteristics.

Components. Basic food and wine elements that correspond to basic sensations on the tongue such as sweet, sour, salty, and bitter.

Consistency. Refers to the viscosity in a food or drink.

Crisp. Describes a wine with a substantial level of acidity, resulting in a refreshing and mouth-cleansing impact when tasted.

Cryoextraction. A technique where mechanical freezing is used to create frozen dessert wines.

D

Demiglace. A mixture of equal amounts of brown stock and brown sauce that is reduced by half.

Dessert wines. The legal definition is a fortified wine (sweet or dry) that has an alcohol level greater than 15 percent by volume.

Differentiation. A business strategy that refers to creating a perception that a firm's products or services are unique.

Dosage. A small amount of wine (usually sweet) added back to the sparkling wine bottle once the yeast sediment that collects in the neck of the bottle is removed.

Dried-grape wines. Grapes are harvested, then allowed to dry under controlled conditions. A typical method is to dry the grapes on straw mats or screens.

Dry. Dry wines are wines with little or no residual sugar remaining after fermentation.

E

Effervescence. The level of carbonation present in a wine. Most table wines have no effervescence present.

Eiswein. German ice wine. *See* Ice wine.

Extract. Particles of fruit that remains in a finished wine; can create a more intense mouthfeel.

F

Fino Sherry. Yeast is used in the production of Fino Sherry and gives it a distinct bouquet. Manzanilla and Amontillados Sherries are variations of the Fino type.

Firm cheeses. This category of cheese is probably the most wine-friendly. These cheeses generally have subtlety, a refined texture, and a pleasant, lingering finish. They vary in their degree of mildness or sharpness depending on the aging process. Examples include cheddar, Cantal, and Jarlsberg.

Flavor. Sensations detected during a retronasal process as aromas are picked up through the back of the mouth and then flow into the nasal cavity.

Flavor intensity. The relative level of force of the characteristic flavor(s) in the wine or food.

Flavor persistence. A continuance of pleasant or negative effect after a wine or food has been swallowed. Persistence can be a pleasant and important indicator of wine and food quality or it can create a negative aftertaste. In wine terminology, persistency is also described as length or finish.

Flight. A group of wines evaluated side by side in a tasting.

Floc de Gascogne. A popular fortified wine served in southern France as an aperitif. Floc is produced using a combination of fresh grape juices and strong young Armagnac. It can be made with red or white grapes and has appealing young and fruity flavors.

Fortified wines. Fortified wines are strengthened with the addition of wine spirits. A neutral brandy is added to the wine before the fermentation process is complete. The remaining sugar that has not been changed into alcohol creates a sweet taste in the finished fortified wine.

Foxy. Describes an aroma or taste in wine that resembles Concord grape juice. Common in many American species (i.e., *Vitis lambrusca*).

Fresh cheeses. Fresh cheeses are relatively mild and creamy and are neither cooked nor ripened. Examples include chèvre, cottage cheese, cream cheese, fromage blanc, mascarpone, Neufchâtel, and ricotta.

Fructooligosaccharide (FOS). A non-additive sweet carbohydrate where one sucrose molecule combines with two or three fructose units to form a more complex carbohydrate that increases sweetness without adding calories.

G

Gastronomic identity. The concept of identifying the influences of the environment (geography and climate) and culture (history and ethnic influences) on prevailing taste components, textures, and flavors in food and drink.

Gastronomic satisfaction. Pleasure in a dining experience, increased through synergistic matches of food and drink.

Geoduck clam. A large clam from the Northwest; also called elephant trunk clam by the Chinese. Each clam usually weighs between 3 and 5 lbs.

Good match. A wine and food pair that match in terms of the food item's basic components (sweet, sour, bitter, salty) and in terms of the overall body of both.

H

Hard cheeses. Often referred to as "grating cheeses," these cheeses owe their flavor to extended periods of aging. The moisture content in these cheeses is around 30 percent. Examples include Parmigiano Reggiano, Asiago, and Romano.

Heat summation units. A method of classifying vineyard regions, calculated on the basis of the total number of days when the average temperature is greater than 50°F (10°C).

Horizontal pairing. The simplest type of wine and food pairing, involving pairing one wine with a particular food dish.

I

Ice wine. A wine in which grapes are left long after harvest to freeze on the vines. Once frozen solid, the grapes are picked and crushed while still hard as marbles. The tiny bit of juice extracted from the fruits is so concentrated and so sweet that it is more like syrup than juice.

Indigenous ingredients. All types of food products that are native to a particular region or locale.

L

Late-harvest wines. Grapes are left on the vine past the normal harvest period, resulting in grapes that are riper, higher in sugar content, and lower in moisture content. These late-harvest grapes may also turn into raisins; get attacked by mold, or both. As grapes shrivel on the vine, they become richer and sweeter. The resulting wine tastes stronger and sweeter and may have flavors of dried fruits.

Lingcod. Lingcod (*Ophiodon elongatus*) are unique to the West Coast of North America, with most harvested off the coast of Washington State and British Columbia. It is not a true cod but has similar preparation and eating characteristics.

M

Macroclimate. The climate of an overall region.

Madeira. Named after the island where it is made, located in the mid-Atlantic off the coast of Morocco, Madeira is a sweet fortified wine with characteristics of softness, depth, and a pleasant burnt flavor.

Marsala. Marsala is the best-known fortified wine of Italy and is named for the town that produces it in Sicily. Marsalas are graded according to their sweetness (secco, demi-secco, and dolce), color, and age.

Mesoclimate. The local climate of a specific vineyard.

Microclimate. The climate specific to an individual plot within a vineyard.

Mirepoix. A mixture of chopped vegetables made up of 2 parts onion, 1 part carrot, and 1 part celery.

Mixed tasting. A tasting in which the wine and food items are placed in the mouth simultaneously. This type of tasting allows the taster to assess the interacting effects of the wine and food elements.

Mouthfeel. A variety of sensations throughout the mouth that may include moistness and dryness, fluidity and solidity, thinness and thickness, fineness and coarseness, softness and hardness, smoothness and roughness, tenderness and toughness, and porosity and compactness.

Muscat Hamburg. Sometimes known as Black Muscat, this fortified dessert wine has aromas reminiscent of roses with a lychee nut character to its flavor.

N

Nappé. The viscosity of a sauce or other liquid when it coats the back of a spoon.

Neutral match. Pairing situations that are average and pleasant but are missing an element of individuality and a superior gastronomic experience.

Noble rot. *See* Botrytis cinerea.

No match. The interaction of wine and food when tasted together has a negative impact on the senses.

Nosing. The olfactory examination process used in evaluating the smell of wine.

O

Oloroso Sherry. Oloroso Sherry is oxidized without yeast. It is generally sweet, dark brown, elegant, and complex.

Orange Muscat. A fortified dessert wine with aromas of orange, orange blossom, and apricot.

P

Port. A fortified wine originally from Portugal and named for the city of Oporto. There are three major styles: Ruby, Tawny, and Vintage.

R

Recioto. An Italian sweet dessert wine made with grapes that have been dried on racks to intensify their flavor.

Refreshment match. Wine that plays a supporting role in the food and wine relationship, serving as a pleasant, refreshing beverage that accompanies the food choice.

S

Sashimi. Thin slices of fish or seafood, usually raw but sometimes marinated, and usually served with condiments such as shredded daikon or ginger root, wasabi, and soy sauce.

Semisoft cheeses. These cheeses include a variety of mild, buttery types that have a sliceable texture. Examples include Bel Paese, brick, Edam, and fontina.

Sensory evaluation. A scientific discipline that is used to induce, quantify, analyze, and assess the responses to products based on what is perceived through the senses of sight, smell, taste, touch, and hearing.

Sequential tasting. In this tasting process, a wine and food is assessed separately on its own merits.

Servietten knödel. A German bread dumpling made by combing bread, milk, eggs, onions, and seasoning; rolling it and poaching it in a cloth napkin, then slicing into disks and browning in melted butter.

Sherry. Traditionally produced in Spain, Sherry has the defining characteristic of being deliberately oxidized. There are two basic types: Fino and Oloroso.

Soft ripened cheeses. This category of cheese is ripened from the outside in. The fat content ranges from 50 to 75 percent as a rule, but double-cream cheese has at least 60 percent fat content and triple-cream has at least 75 percent. Examples include Brie, Camembert, and Limburger.

Strohwein. German term meaning "straw wine"; a dried-grape wine, typically made by drying grapes over straw mats or screens.

Synergistic match. A combination of wine and food that creates a totally new and superior gastronomic effect.

T

Tannin. An organic compound that is found in the seeds, skins, and stems of grapes. Tannins create an astringent sensation in the mouth and serve as a preservative, allowing wines to be aged.

Terroir. The idea of terroir is French in origin and generally reflects the unique interaction of natural factors (climate, soil, water, wind, etc.) and human skills that create definable characteristics in a specific wine-growing location.

Texture. Encompasses a number of terms used to describe touch (tactile) or mouthfeel sensations.

Touristic terroir. The unique bundle of activities in a location that provides it with a distinctive appeal to tourists.

U

Umami. A proposed fifth taste element that creates a sense of savoriness or deliciousness in some foods, such as soy sauce, tomatoes, edamame, and MSG.

V

Varietal. A specific grape variety.

Vermouth. A fortified wine that has been flavored with sugar, herbs, roots, flowers, and spices.

Vertical pairings. A more complicated pairing process referring to matching several food courses with several wines in a multicourse, progressive dinner.

Vin de paille. French term meaning "straw wine"; typically made by drying grapes over straw mats or screens.

Vinifera. A family of grapes used in production of quality wines, including Riesling, Chardonnay, Pinot Noir, Syrah, Merlot, Cabernet, and others.

Vin mousseux. Sparkling wine made outside of the Champagne region in France.

Vinosity. A common definition is the distinctive color, body, and taste of wine. Others relate it to the level of alcohol present.

Vintners Quality Assurance (VQA). VQA establishes, monitors and enforces a system of quality standards and verification of product origin in Canada's Niagara and Okanagan regions. Participation in the VQA appellation system is voluntary, but only those wines approved by the VQA are allowed to bear the VQA symbol.

Viscosity. The level of fluidness in a wine or food item.

Volatile acidity (VA). The result of growth of acetic-acid-producing bacteria. Bacteria causing VA are found on the surfaces of grapes, winery equipment, and used oak barrels. When left unchecked, these enzymes work to oxidize alcohol into the vinegary-smelling acetic acid.

A

Acid (in wine and food) 107–111
  acetic 107
  citric 107, 109
  in food 110
  in wine 108
  lactic 107
  levels 109, 119, 121, 123, 125
  malic 107
  tartaric 107
  types
Acidity 32, 33, 102, 103, 107, 134, 170
Adaptation (to sensations) 26
Affective testing 22
Aftertaste 216
Aging (wine) 159, 272
Agri-food systems 46
Alcohol level 104, 156, 270
Aligoté (wine) 136
Alois Lageder, Pinot Bianco 16
Alsace 291
Alto Adige 15
Amarone 278, 292, 297
American Culinary Federation (ACF) 68
American Viticultural Area (AVA) 55
Amerine 52
Amontillado 213, 294
Analytical testing 22
Anti-Saloon League 57
Aperitif(s)
  Bayou La Seine: An American
    Restaurant in paris 190–193
  Canoe Restaurant and Bar 168–169
  Chef John Folse & Company 67–69
  Elements of Wine Service 20–22
  Food and Wine of the Pacific
    Northwest 234–237
  How Should Menus and Wine Lists
    Be Organized 46–48
  Peller Estates Winery 130–131
  Release Weekend Wine and Food
    Menu from On the Twenty 210–
    211

The Exemplary Nature of a Symbiosis
  between Food Dishes and
  Cognacs 150–153
The Italian Wine and Food
  Perspective 5–8
Which to Choose First, Wine or
  Food? 102
Appellation 55
Appellation d'Origine Contrôlée (AOC)
  30, 55, 59, 79
Arbois (wine) 191
Archestratus 6
Archetypal ingredients 78
Armagnac 295
Aroma 24, 28
  wheel 24
  quality 24
Aromatic compounds 24
Artichokes 224
Asiago 278
Asparagus 224
Asti Spumate 299
Astringency 32, 154, 155
Attitude 311
Auslese 170, 292
Autochthonous vines 6

B

Baby Duck (wine) 288
Badia di Coltibuono 14
Baked goods 301
Baking 171
Balance
  between wine and cheese 272, 280
  between wine and food elements 9–11,
    253–263
  in wine 107–108
Barbaresco 104, 105
Barbera 158, 160, 174, 278
Barding 244
Barolo 104, 112, 160, 277, 278

Barrier to imitation 46
Barsac (wine) 291
Basics of wine evaluation 23–26
Basque 235
Baton Rouge 68
Bayou La Seine 190
Bazzoni, Enrico 5, 8
Beamsville Bench 208
Beaujolais 29, 84, 109, 158, 192, 260,
  298
Beerenauslese wines 292
Bentwood box cookery 235
Beurre blanc 224
Bianco di Custoza 195
Bias 26
Biscotti 302
Bitterness 32, 33, 138
  in cheese 272
  in food 133
  in food and wine pairing
  in wine 132
  how to identify 32
Bittersweet Plantation 49, 67
Black Muscat 294
Blackening 171
Blanc de Blancs 133
Blanc de Noirs 133
Blaufränkisch 242
Blind tasting 26
Blue Nun 31
Blue-veined cheeses 279
Bluysen, Frederic 190
Bluysen, Judith 190
Body 158, 170, 182
  as texture 154, 168, 171
  in wine 133
  in wine and food pairing 172
Boise 235, 236
Boissy, Etienne 270, 271
Bone dry 104
Bordeaux 83, 291

Botrytis cinerea 291–292
  affected wines 291
Bottle opening 20–21
Bouquet 24, 25, 28
Braising 171
Bread pudding 296
Brie 276
Brights' President (wine) 288
Brillat Savarin 276
British Columbia 235, 236
Brock University Cool Climate
    Oenology and Viticulture Institute
    (CCOVI) 131
Brodi, Tom 168
Broiling 171
Brut 135
  nature 134
Bubbles 24
Buhler, Lawrence 130
Buttery (flavors) 108, 214

C

Cabernet Franc 158, 174, 275
Cabernet Sauvignon 29, 30, 158, 39,
    174, 194, 277, 297
Cahors (region) 89
Cajun and Creole cuisine 67, 190
Cajun Trinity 191
Cakes 301
California 294
Canada
  Green Building Council 50
Canadian 50
  ice wine 288, 290
Canopy climate 52
Cantal 277, 278
Capabilities 56, 82
Cap Classique 133
Capsicum peppers 80, 190
Carbon dioxide 133
Carbonation 24
Carneros (AVA) 52
Cassati alla Siciliana (dessert) 302
Castling, Catherine 50
Cava 100, 133, 135
Cave Spring Cellars 208
Caviar 9, 132
Cedar planks 243
Cérons 291
Cévennes 79
Champagne 58, 134, 297, 298, 301
Chardonnay 30, 38, 60, 75, 133, 158,
    256, 265, 277, 279
Chateau St. Michelle 240
  Eroica Riesling 240
Cheese(s)
  blue 278
  blue-veined 278, 279
  chèvre 273
  cottage 273
  Cougar Gold cheddar 246
  cream 273
  fresh and soft 273, 274
  firm 277

grating 278
Gjetost 278
hard 278
semi-soft 273, 275
soft ripened 275, 276
Cheese-friendly 272
Chef John Folse & Company 67
Chef John Folse Culinary Institute at
    Nicholls State University 67
Chianti 29, 84, 158, 277, 278
  Classico 14, 277, 278
Chiles 80
Chocolate 297
  dark 297
  desserts 297
  milk 297
  white 297
Chocolate-based dessert pairing decision
    process 298
Church, Philip 236
Citrus desserts 299
Clarity 23
Classic wine and food marriages 84
Classic wine grapes 30
Clearwater River Valley 236
Climate 51, 79
  map 52
  zones 53
Cognac 150
Collagen structure 171
Color 23
Columbia River 235
Columbia Valley 55, 236, 241
Commander's Palace 49
Competitive advantage 309
Components 11
Concord grapes 288
Consistency 24
Contribution margins 47
Cookies 301
Cooking method 170
Cool climate (zone) 51, 53, 60
Corked (wine) 21
Corks 21
Corkscrew 21
Cortés, Hernando 56
Corvina (grapes) 292
Cost percentage method 47, 48
Coste, Pierre 29
Costigliole d'Asti 6, 7
Côte d'Or 52
Côte de Beaune 60
Côte du Rhône 245, 277
Côte Rôtie 245
Court of Two Sisters restaurant 68
Cream 274
Cream Sherry 294
Crème brulee 296
Crepes Suzette 298
Crisp 107
Cryo-Cluster 290
Cryoextraction 290
Culinary
  etiquette 49
  identity 49

rhetoric 78
tourism 78
Custard 296
  desserts 296

D

Danhi 49
Danish Blue Castello 278
Dante's Inferno 6
David Hill Vineyard 247
de Gaulle, Charles 276
Decision tree 231, 253, 254
Deep-frying 171
Degustation menu 312
Degree days 51
Demi-sec 135
  Champagne 296, 298
  sparkling wine 135, 298, 300, 302
Demisecco 294
Denominação de origem controlada 55
Denominación de origen 55
Denominación de origen calificada 55
Denominazione di origine controllata 6,
    55
Denominazione di origine controllata e
    garantita 55
Dentzer, Yvelise 150, 153, 271
Dessert(s)
  based on nuts 300–301
  breads 301
  categories 295
  wines 289–295
Diacetyl 108
DiDio, Tony 17
Differentiation 310
Dîner Symbiose 152
Distinctive capability 309
Distinguished Restaurants of North
    America (DIRōNA) 68
Dolce 294
Dolcetto 155, 160
Dom Pérignon 31, 58
Domaine de Clovallon (winery) 50
Donaldsonville 66
Dosage 130, 289
Double and triple cream cheeses 275
Doux sparkling wines 135, 300
Dried
  fruits 292, 299
  grape(s) 292, 293
  grape and late harvest processes 291,
      292
  grape wines 292, 301, 302
Dry 294
  heat cooking method 171
  movement 57
  sherry 294
  White Port 294
  Vermouth 294
Duxelles 93

E

Earthy (flavor) 59, 212
Eberspaecher, Alex 188

Edelfäule 291
Effervescence 24, 131, 135, 136, 138
Eiswein 288, 290
Elmer, Ruben 168
Entrepreneurs 68
Epernay yeast 130
Escoffier 78
Ethnic
    diversity 57
    flavors and influences 49
Evaluation sheets 29
Extract 25, 154, 157
Extra dry 135

F

Fabric sample reference anchors 155
False fine wine 29
Fanet 59
Fat(s) 169
    animal and dairy 172, 256
    plant-based 110
Fendant 24, 135
Fermentation 271
Finish 26, 216
    final de boca 216
    fin de bouche 216
Fino Sherry 171, 213, 294
Flabby 32
Flavor(s) 12, 208
    categories 210
    contrasting 210
    dominant 208
    intensity 25, 214, 215
    layering 190
    perception 210
    persistency 26, 216
    profiles 217
    similar 210
    types 211
Floc de Gascogne 294
Foie gras 169
Folse, John 67
Food and Wine of the Pacific Northwest
        238
Food and Wine Taste Pyramid 11, 98
Food
    and-wine evaluation 249
    evaluation 249
    fattiness 176, 177
    habits 56
    intensity and persistency level 208
    Sensory Anchor Scale 98, 99
    Sensory Pyramid 13
    spice level 197–198
Food Item(s)
    Asian chowder of coconut, smoked
            lingcod, and geoduck clam
            sashimi 241
    baklava 301
    bananas Foster 298
    bistecca alla fiorentina 83
    black truffle potatoes 94
    braised beef in red wine sauce 185
    Cajun Boudin Blanc 191

Cajun Matriochka 191
Cajun pralines 76
Caesar salad 266
cedar-planked Idaho Rainbow trout
        served with citrus-dusted
        asparagus tips and micro-greens
        244
chicken & sausage gumbo 70
chicken en papillote 183
classic hollandaise sauce 227
coq au vin 83
crab cakes Rex 73
dark chocolate truffle tart, roasted pine
        nuts and crème fraiche 169
duxelles 93
egg pappardelle alla lepre 15
fiesta macque choux salad 71
"fire and ice" Northwest oysters 240
French onion soup 93
geoduck sashimi 241
Grand River venison loin, oka poutine,
        kumquats and mulled red cabbage
        169
gratin of sea urchin and scallops with
        Cognac 151
grilled beef sirloin 267
grilled fish 227
grilled pork loin with mustard and
        molasses 184
grilled portobello mushrooms 94
Mardi Gras king cake 77
marinated asparagus with prosciutto di
        Langhirano 16
onion rings 92
oysters Marie Laveau 70
panang curry 10
pasta al pesto 226
pasta mixtures 124
pecan pie 301
peach Melba 298
peaches in Champagne 298
plums poached in red wine 298
poached pears 298
pumpkin pie 296
roasted Columbia Basin pheasant
        marinated in grappa with German
        bread dumplings 243
roasted garlic 92
roasted loin of venison with smoked
        trio of beets and Syrah demi-glace
        246
Rouge Creamery Oregonzola and
        Washington State Cougar Gold
        cheddar served with thyme-
        infused honey, apricot-orange
        conserve and dried cherry-
        hazelnut compote 247
salade Lyonnaise 109
salad of beef, arugula, with roast garlic
        vinaigrette and Beaujolais 259,
        262
shrimp and melon with mint-curry
        cream 266
simmered La Ferme foie gras, Beluga
        lentils, celery root and cocoa nibs
        169

smoked corn and chicken pasta and
        Sauvignon Blanc 258
soul pork roast 75
spice-cured salmon with spring radish,
        melon, yogurt, and Abiti caviar
        169
strawberries served "au naturel" 299
sweet and spicy chicken etouffee 74
tiramisu 297
voodoo greens 72
walnut lacey cookie cup filled with
        homemade vanilla ice cream and
        strawberry-rhubarb sauce 248
white truffle risotto 94
Fortified Muscats 294
Fortified wines 292–295
French
    national drink 29
    nouvelle cuisine 78
    oak barrels
    Onion Soup 93
    Sancerre 9
    Quarter 69
Frizzante 135
Frog's Leap 50
Fromage blanc 273, 274
Frostbite 290
Frozen grape wines 290
Fructooligosaccharides (FOS) 104
Fructose 104
Fruit
    desserts 298, 299
    flavors in dessert wines 291, 299
    flavors in fortified wines 292–295
    flavor in wine 51
    type 299
Fruit-forward wines 59, 199
Fumé Blanc 119
Fusion 81

G

Gastronomic identity 46, 47, 48, 50, 66,
        82, 85, 234, 308
    in Italy 82
Gastronomy 46, 67, 150
Gavi 195
General Menu Planning 237
Geoduck clams 241
Geography 46, 79
German
    Beerenauslese 290
    dumpling (servietten knödel) 241
    Eiswein 288, 290
    Kabinett 10, 171
    Rieslings 10
    Spatlese 290
Gewürztraminer 104, 190, 241, 300
Gjetost 278
Globalization 81
Glycerin 24, 31
Gorbachev, Mikhail 67
Gorgonzola 278, 279
Gouda 277, 278
Grappa 56, 241

Grassiness 38 213
Graves (region) 60
Greek Muscat 302
Grilling 171
Grüner-Veltliner 224, 278
Gruyère 277, 278

H

Hammond 272
Hänig, D. 150
Harazathy, Agoston 57
Harmonization 160
Harrington 272
Heat summation
    units 51, 53
    method 51
Hennessy 150
Herbaceous 38, 213
Herbal 194
Herbs 192
Hill, David 247
Hilling 51
Hollandaise Sauce 224
Horizontal and Vertical Pairing
    Decisions 237
Horse Heaven Hills 55
Hot
    peppers 194
    spices 193, 195
How persistency is measured 217
How spice is assessed 195–198
Hue 7

I

Ice cream 296
Ice Wine 288, 297
    Sparkler 289
Idaho 235, 236
Identity movement 78
Indicazione geografica (IGT) 55
INAO (Institut National des Appellation
    d'Origine) 27
Indigenous
    ingredients 234
    products 50
Individual differences 210
In-mouth 212
    flavor evaluation 212
    smells 212
Inn On The Twenty 208
Inniskillin 136, 288
Intensity 195, 210
Interaction
    between wine and food sweetness 106–
        107
    of food spice types and wine varietals
        198–200
    wine and food flavor intensity 215–216
    wine and food flavor persistency 217
Innovations 57, 81
Intimidation 48
Italian Culinary Institute for Foreign
    Professionals 5, 7, 26

J

Jarlsberg 277, 278
Jean Lafitte's Blacksmith Shop 69
Jean Moulin Lyon III University 153
Jura region 190

K

Kekfrankos 242
Key food pairing elements 251
Key wine pairing elements 250
Kiona (wines) 242
Kirrage, Paul James 153
Kir 136

L

Label drinkers 29
Lafitte's Landing Restaurant 67
Lag time 217
Lake, David 245
Lambrusco 6
Late harvest wines 103, 291, 292, 298,
    299, 300
Le concours du Meilleur Ouvrier de
    France 270
Le Diner Symbiose 152
Leadership in Energy and Environmental
    Design (LEED) 50
Legs (tears) 24
Lemberger 194, 242
Length 26, 216
Length of soak 155
Lercara, Gianfranco 6
Level
    of alcohol 156
    of match 177, 283
    of sweetness 99, 100, 105
Lewiston 236
Light-to-light and rich-to-rich matching
    146
Lighting (during wine evaluation) 27
Loire Valley 107, 291
Longitude (length) 216
Longueur (length) 216
Louisiana cuisine 190
Lugana 195
Lyon (France) 153, 271

M

Macque Choux 71
Macro-climate 52
Madeira 278, 294, 297, 300, 301, 302
Madeleines 302
Malbec 199
Malolactic fermentation 108, 160, 213
Maniaci, Kevin 208
Manzanilla sherry 171, 294
Mapping of the tongue 33–35
Marché aux Truffe 89
Mardi Gras 69
Mark-up method 47, 49
Marsala 294, 297, 301, 302
    colors 294

sweetness levels 294
Mascarpone 273, 274
Mateus (wine) 31
Matriochka 191
Maturation process 270
Maytag Blue Cheese 278, 279
McCrea Cellars 245
McCrea, Doug 245
Mêdoc (wine) 60
Meilleur Ouvrier de France de Fromage
    270
Menu(s) 49
    and wine list pricing 48
    aesthetic factors 49
    organization 47
    pattern 47
    presentation 47
    planning 47
Merlot 30, 38, 158, 160, 194
Meso-climates 52
Méthode Champenoise 130, 133
Meunier 133
Micro-climates 52
Micro-oxygenation 160
Milan 82
Mission San Diego 57
Mixed tasting 230
Moist cooking methods 171
Molinara grapes 292
Mondavi, Robert 119
Moscato 24
    d'Asti 31, 136, 213, 297, 298, 301
    di Pantelleria Passito 302
    Passito 302
Mosel 134, 291
Moses Lake, Washington 241
Mousse 296
Mouth-coating 297
Mouth-feel 12, 153, 155, 168
    wheel 155
Muscat(s) 294, 301
    de Beaumes 300
    Hamburg 294, 297, 300, 301

N

Nahe 291
Napa Valley 52, 55, 61
Naples 82
Nasal cavity 212, 217
Nebbiolo 31
Neufchâtel 273, 274
Neutral brandy 292
New World 46, 59, 61
Niagara
    College Teaching Winery 289, 302
    Escarpment 52, 210
    grape 288
    Ice Wine 288–291
Niagara-on-the-Lake 130
Nightinggale, Alice and Myron 292
Noble, Ann C. 24
Noble rot 103, 291
Nosing steps 24

Nouvelle cuisine 78
Nut-based dessert 300
Nuts 300
Nutty 213

O

Oak 25
    aging 157
    Alley Plantation 68
    barrels 157
Oakville Bench 55
Odor blindness 27
Odors, foreign 28
Okanagan
    Ice Wine 291
    Valley 52, 236
Old World 46, 59, 61
Olfactory examination 24
Oliver Bonacini Restaurants 168
Oloroso Sherry 294, 297, 300, 302
Olympia oysters 240
On the Twenty Restaurant 210
Ontario
    ice wine 288–291
    wine producers 291
Oporto 293
Opus One 31
Oral cavity 212, 217
Orange Muscat 294, 297, 301, 302
Orchard fruit desserts 299
Ordering wine in a restaurant 102
Oregon 235, 236
Oxidation 58

P

Pacific Northwest 234, 236
    menu 238
    recipes 240–248
Pacific Rim 234
Palate
    cleansing 131
    fatigue 26
    mapping 33–35
Palouse Hills 235
Panang curry 10
Pandozy, Father Charles 236
Pan-frying 171
Pannacotta 296
Parmigiano-Reggiano 278
Passio 103
Passito 292
Pastry cream 296
Paul Bocuse Institute 150, 153, 270, 271
Pavan, Angelo 210
Pectin 24
Peller, Andrew 130
Peller Estates 130
    Ice Cuvee VQA 130
    Winery 130
Penicillium
    glaucum 278
    roqueforti 278
Pennachetti, Leonard 210

Pepper 194
Perceived level of match 9, 10, 253–254
Persistence 216, 217
Persistency 210
Pétillant 135
Peynaud 156
Phalernum 6
pH scale 108
Physiological factors (during tasting) 26, 208
Pinot
    Bianco 15, 17
    Menuriur 133
    Noir 9, 38, 133, 301
Pipes (barrels) 294
Plateau time 217
Polymerization 160
Popeyes Chicken and Biscuits 49
Port 293, 297, 302
Portland 236
Portobellos 90
Potassium chloride 131
Pourriture noble 291
Power 146, 154, 169
Pricing psychology 47
Primary components 98
Prime cost 47
Prince Edward Island 57
Profiles (food and wine) 253
Progressive wine list 48
Prohibition 57
Prosciutto di San Daniele 6
Protein 170
Psychological factors (during tasting) 26, 208
Psycho-sociology of taste 151
Puckery 32, 33
Pungent 38
Puttonyos (botrytis amount) 291
PX Sherry 297, 300

Q

Qualitätswein bestimmter Anbaugebiete 55
Qualitätswein mit Prädikat 55
Quebec 57

R

Raisin wines 292
Raisined 103, 292
Rattlesnake Hills (AVA) 245
Recioto 292
Recipes (see Food Items)
Reagan, Ronald 66
Red Mountain appellation 242
Red Willow Vineyard 245
Research Chefs Association (RCA) 67
Residual sugar 104
Retronasal 25, 208, 212
Reverse marinade 157
Rhine 291
Rhubarb 247
Ricotta 273, 274, 278

Riesling 37, 104
    ice wine 299
Rio Negro 52
Ripening procedure 272
Risotto alla Milanese 82
Rispal, Philippe 150, 153
Roasting 171
Rogue Valley (AVA) 236
Roseburg, Oregon 236
Romano (cheese) 278
Rome 82
Rondinella (grapes) 292
Roquefort 278, 279
Ruby Port 293, 297, 301
Rutherford (AVA) 55

S

"Ss" of wine evaluation 23
Sabayon 297
Sainte Chapelle Winery 236
Sake 195
Salmon 235
Salt 131
Saltiness 32, 33, 138
Sancerre 83, 104, 109
Sangiovese 8, 14
Sauer, Mike 245
Saumur Champigny (region) 192
Sauternes 24, 291, 297, 299
Sauvignon Blanc 9, 29, 30, 38, 85, 158, 256
Savor 25
Savory spices 195, 198
Seasoning 194
Sec 135
Secco 294
Sekt (German sparkling) 133
Sémillon 297, 299
Semi-soft cheeses 273, 275
Semi-sparkling wine 135
Sensory 22–28
    anchor scales 98–100
    evaluation 22, 32
    fatigue 239, 270
    symbioses 150
Sequential tasting 230, 249
Serra, Junípero 57
Serving temperature (wine) 29
Setting up a tasting session 27
Sherry 294, 297
Shiraz 30, 75, 193, 199
Sipping 25
Slightly sparkling wine 135
Slow Food 79
Smoky 213
Soave (wine) 195
Sodium chloride 131
Sodium glutamate 131
Sofitel Royal hotel-school 150
Soft-ripened cheeses 275, 276
Sparkling wine 133–136
Spätlese (wine) 10, 170, 292
Special select late harvest 292

Spice(s) 190, 192, 194, 195
  level 195
  sweet 195
Spicy 193
Spitting 25
Spittoon 27
Spumante 133
Stags Leap District 55
Standard tasting glass 27
Steaming 171
Ste-Croix-du-Mont (region) 291
Stewart, Anita 235
Stewart, Jeff 288
Stilton 83, 278, 279
Stir-frying 171
Stirring It Up 67
Stratus 50
Strohwein 292
Structure 47, 146, 154
Sub-appellations 55
Sugar 105
Sulfur 104
  dioxide 110
Summers, Rob 131
Superiore 294
  Riserva 294
Sur lies 51, 130
Sustainable farming 50
Swallow 25
Sweetness 33, 102, 103, 105, 112, 113,
  114, 134, 295
Swirl 23
Synergistic 208, 272, 310
Synergy 6, 10, 289
Syrah 30, 84, 158, 193, 194, 245

T

Table setting 309
Tactile sensation 32, 169
Tannin 102, 155, 175, 177
Taste 25
  components 31
  examination 25
  modifiers 27
  thresholds 27
Taste of Louisiana, A 67
Tasting 25–26
  session 27
  temperatures 29
Tawny Port 293, 297, 300, 301, 302
Taxation structures 56
Tchelistcheff, André 236
Tears (legs) 24
Temperature 27, 28, 29
Tempranillo 194, 214
Terrroir 55, 59, 79
Texture 12, 146, 163, 169
Thai cuisine 195
Thanksgiving American Grocery Store
  190
The Encyclopedia of Cajun & Creole Cuisine
  67

The New American Cheese 272
Time-intensity curve 217
Tiramisu 297
Tocai del Collio 6
Tokaji
  Eszencia 291
  wine 291, 302
Tomato & Herb Fest 69
Torino 79
Tourism 46, 85
Touristic terroir 86
Tourists 78
Trade 81
Training issues 310
Traminer (grape) 193
  Aromatico 193
Trial and error 57, 82
Trius Brut VQA 130
Trockenbeerenauslese 292
Tropical fruit desserts 299
Tuiles 302
Turducken 191
Tuscany 82

U

Umami 31, 46, 212
Umqua Valley 236
United States
  Alcohol and Tobacco Tax and Trade
    Bureau 55
  Green Building Council 50
  law 50

V

Valpolicella 292
Varietals 9, 23, 193, 194
Vegetal 213
Venice 82
Venison 244
Verdicchio (wine) 224
Vergine (sherry) 294
  Stravecchio 294
Vermentino (wine) 224
Vermouth 294
Vertical pairings 239
Vidal Icewine 288, 301
Vigonier 30
Vin de Glaciere 290
Vin de paille 292
Vinosity 156
Vin Santo 292
Vinexpo 288
Vinifera 288
Vino Gelato 290
Vino Veritas 188
Vins Mousseux 133
Vintage 56
Vintage Port 293
Vintner's Quality Alliance (VQA) 210,
  288
Viscosity 154, 157

Visual examination 23
Viticulture practices 58
Vitis Labrusca grapes 288
Vivaldi, Antonio 5
Volatile acidity 110
Vouvray 104, 297

W

Walla Walla Valley 236
Walsh, Anthony 168
Warm zones 51, 54, 60
Washington
  State 55, 234, 236
  State University 236
  State University Creamery 246
Weight 146, 169
Werlin, Laura 272
White Oak Plantation 68
White Port 297, 298
White Zinfandel 100, 104
Willamette Valley 235
Williams, John 50
Wine
  anchor references sheet 100
  and cheese pairing 283
  and food pairing instrument 234, 252
  big six 30
  brand-name 31
  cellar 48
  cellaring 159
  descriptions 30
  evaluation process 249
  flavor categories 213
  faults 28
  intensity and persistency level 211
  list 48, 310
  pouring 21
  sensory anchor scale 98, 100
  sensory pyramid 13
  spice level 196
  tasting 22
Wine-by-the-glass program 50
Winemaker's marinade 25
Wines with spice, herbal and taming
  characteristics 194
Winkler (degree days) 52
Woman's Christian Temperance Union
  57

X

Ximénez, Pedro 294
X.O. Cognac 152

Y

Yakima Valley 236

Z

Zabaglione 297
Zampone 6
Zinfandel 107, 199, 297
Ziraldo, Donald 288
Zraly 29